Extravagant Abjection

Extravagant Abjection

*Blackness, Power, and Sexuality in the
African American Literary Imagination*

Darieck Scott

NEW YORK UNIVERSITY PRESS
New York and London

NEW YORK UNIVERSITY PRESS
New York and London
www.nyupress.org

Library of Congress Cataloging-in-Publication Data

Scott, Darieck.
Extravagant abjection : blackness, power, and sexuality in the African American literary
imagination / Darieck Scott.
p. cm. — (Sexual cultures)
Includes bibliographical references and index.
ISBN-13: 978-0-8147-4094-1 (cl : alk. paper)
ISBN-10: 0-8147-4094-4 (cl : alk. paper)
ISBN-13: 978-0-8147-4095-8 (pb : alk. paper)
ISBN-10: 0-8147-4095-2 (pb : alk. paper)
[etc.]
1. American fiction—African American authors—History and criticism. 2. African American
men in literature. 3. Power (Social sciences) in literature. 4. Race relations in literature.
5. Rape in literature. 6. Homosexuality in literature. 7. Pornography in literature. 8. Abjection
in literature. I. Title.
PS374.N4S36   2010
813'5409896073—dc22   2010002954

New York University Press books are printed on acid-free paper,
and their binding materials are chosen for strength and durability.
We strive to use environmentally responsible suppliers and materials
to the greatest extent possible in publishing our books.

Manufactured in the United States of America

c 10 9 8 7 6 5 4 3 2 1
p 10 9 8 7 6 5 4 3 2 1

A book in the American Literatures Initiative (ALI), a collaborative
publishing project of NYU Press, Fordham University Press, Rutgers
University Press, Temple University Press, and the University of Virginia
Press. The Initiative is supported by The Andrew W. Mellon Foundation.
For more information, please visit www.americanliteratures.org.

Contents

Acknowledgments

I CANNOT THANK enough Julie Carlson and Lisa Moore, who contributed hours and ergs of intellectual and editorial support—as well as calming professional advice—through several stages of the development of *Extravagant Abjection*: true dear friends and super-colleagues both. Many other colleagues and friends in the English departments of UC–Santa Barbara and UT–Austin were chapter readers, and sources of advice, encouragement, and inspiration: At UCSB I am especially grateful to Rita Raley, Guy Mark Foster, Chris Newfield, Shirley Geok-Lin Lim, Stephanie LeMenager, and Aranye Fradenburg, as well as to all the excellent students (from various departments) in my graduate seminars on Fanon, neo-slave narratives, and black masculinity and abjection. My department chairs during my time at UCSB, Carl Gutiérrez-Jones and William Warner, were generous in ensuring I had as much time as possible to work on this monograph, and in providing guidance and feedback during the process of writing. At UT–Austin I enjoyed an abundance of riches in terms of dynamic, inspirational, and fun colleagues, whose intellectual stimulation and companionship I continue to miss—I would particularly like to thank Ann Cvetkovich, Joanna Brooks, Barbara Harlow, Helena Woodard, Mia Carter, my chair Jim Garrison, and the ebullient students of my very first graduate seminar on Fanon.

My Ph.D. studies at Stanford in Modern Thought and Literature of course were the foundation for this first academic book project. I am grateful to my wise and generous dissertation adviser and mentor Ramón Saldívar, and to Mary Pratt, Renato Rosaldo, Sharon Holland, Yvonne Yarbro-Bejarano, and Horace Porter. As Hazel Carby—whose graduate seminar on race, gender, and the culture industry at Yale is largely responsible for my decision to pursue a Ph.D., and who, along with my M.A. thesis adviser Vera Kutzkinski, I also would like to thank—once advised me, fellow graduate students are as much your teachers as professors are, and this proved to be very true for me: I and this project have been hugely influenced by, and I am especially grateful to, Danny Contreras, Lisa Thompson, and Diana Paulin, and also to the whole host of my fabulous fellows in MTL.

Thoughtful observations and encouragement along the way from the late Barbara Christian, Lauren Berlant, Ken Warren, E. Patrick Johnson, Dwight McBride, Jennifer DeVere Brody, Phillip Brian Harper, Howard Winant, Elizabeth Abel, Abdul JanMohamed, Ian Duncan, and Geoff Mann were of invaluable assistance.

Of crucial importance was institutional support in the form of fellowships and faculty education from the Ford Foundation, the UC President's Postdoctoral Fellowship program, UCSB's Faculty Career Development Award, and the 2004 UC Humanities Research Institute's faculty seminar on psychoanalysis.

Many thanks also for the attentive and ever-helpful shepherding of this project by my editor, Eric Zinner, and his assistant, Ciara McLaughlin, and Sexual Cultures series editors, José Muñoz and Ann Pellegrini, at New York University Press. Michael Cobb and Robert Reid-Pharr disclosed to me their roles as manuscript reviewers for NYU; I am deeply grateful for their criticism and enthusiasm.

In every writing project I have had the luxury of vital emotional and spiritual support—and no small amount of editorial assistance—from my partner, Stephen Liacouras, and this has never been more true than during the long, long process of bringing *Extravagant Abjection* to fruition; I am profusely grateful for his presence, generosity, and tireless cheerleading.

Introduction

Blackness, Abjection, and Sexuality

> "Yeah. It didn't work, did it? Did it work?" he asked.
> "It worked," she said.
> "How? Your boys gone you don't know where. One girl dead, the other won't leave the yard. How did it work?"
> "They ain't at Sweet Home. Schoolteacher ain't got em."
> "Maybe there's worse."
> "It ain't my job to know what's worse. It's my job to know what is and to keep them away from what I know is terrible. I did that."
>
> —Toni Morrison, *Beloved*[1]

LET US TAKE this dialogue, from a novel which is in many ways the ur-text and bible of my project, as an instructive fable, a fragment to expound upon for a sermon. Sethe's decision to murder her toddler daughter—a decision we should be careful not to name as a *choice*, at least not without troubling assumptions about individual agency that are commonplace in a liberal democratic society—is of such a final and extreme nature that it begs readers to differ as Paul D does. But the logic by which she reaches the decision, and the declared limits of her survivalist epistemology, are difficult to gainsay. The murder itself to one side, Sethe's seems a compelling strategy for responding to the demands of the moment, and to the tremendous pressures on her existence and on her very embodiment. As such, the structure of her logic is of a piece with the harsh structures of her social world, where sociality is governed by strict racial hierarchy and property law.

We are not Sethe and we do not live her exigencies, and thus we cannot judge her actions. Her creator, Toni Morrison, does not call us to do so. Sethe of course is not really a slave or ex-slave, even though she is inspired by a historical personage: she is a speculation on history (as well as on psychology and politics) of Morrison's, and a shifting point of identification for her readers. Sethe figures us in the guise of our ancestral past. "Us" here is all who are connected by dint of ancestry or culture to the practices of chattel slavery in the Americas, all who bear any relation at all to the concept of blackness—the connection obviously being stronger the more invested, consciously or unconsciously or both, one is in that concept, which, from my point of view, ought to mean that a conscious white supremacist of the Aryan Nation variety is roughly equally the "descendant" of this experience as a person who takes on a highly politicized conscious African American or black identity. We are not Sethe, but we are her inheritors.

The salient matter in this exchange Sethe has with Paul D and with us pretends to be about moral judgment, but this path quickly peters out in either impasse or fanaticism. The productive road Morrison opens for us has to do less with what should be judged than with what it is our "job" to "know." Certainly we are being called, from that pulpit Morrison shares with James Baldwin and many before him, where willful ignorance of the injustices of one's society earns thunderous condemnation for the carnage that such ignorance enables, to know more than Sethe dares: to know what is worse and what is better, and to what degree, and how, and why, and to track the ripples from the range of ancient Sethe-like decisions as they eddy to our own doorsteps, as they flow in the memory of our own cells. What Morrison of course is saying to us in *Beloved* is that the all-too-easy accord between the decision to murder a child and the epistemes of a racially organized economic and social system of the United States in the mid-19th century, though it may remain unexamined, unmapped, unknown, persists in our world as a latency sporadically but inexorably reactivated, and that if the particular logic of the deed and the world that made it possible has through the passage of time faded like an ancient painting to near invisibility, its frame, capacious and insidiously flexible, still sets the boundaries of our own world.

Of course to acquire this knowledge, and to be positioned to make use of it, is by comparison to Sethe's historical moment a luxury, earned precisely by the canniness and suffering of forebears of whom she is a literary avatar. It is only from a position of relative privilege that we can will ourselves to "know" what Sethe refuses to take cognizance of, but which haunts her in the hideous form of mystifying, counterintellectual traumatic memory. At the same time, because we are her inheritors, we *need* to know what she knows but refuses to know, in order not to be haunted just as she is. Thus the luxury bought by the (bloody) successes and (bloodier) ancestral failures that Sethe figures is also, paradoxically, a necessity for us: our freedom is relative and measured by rods others than hers, but we, too, are imprisoned.

(I am going to try to establish in this book that these paradoxes—luxury that is necessity, freedom that is imprisonment, and, perhaps surprisingly, their correspondent vice-versa formulations—speak to the very core of what blackness is in our culture and how we embody it.)

In some ways the range of strategies perceived as available to those of us doing the work of African Americanist cultural criticism in particular, and of African American politics and Afro-Diasporic antiracist politics in general, often does not seem a great deal broader than Sethe's. It is easy enough to see how the emergency continues, to still hear the sirens of warning, to feel the body readying itself yet again to receive a lash or a blow—and thus the demand for strategies that remove us from harm's way or counterattack the source of harm, are, or seem, of paramount importance. This readiness to flinch—bodily, psychically, intellectually, a multidimensional response I will take up further in my discussion of Fanon's references to the flinching and "tensed muscles" that characterize blackness—seems especially evident to me at the moment of this writing, shortly after the inauguration of the first black president of the United States. In the view of many of us steeped in the lessons of our history, the antiracist triumphalism or eager anticipation of a transformation in "race relations" that Obama's electoral victory might inspire in some quarters (the house, perhaps, not the fields) seem to belong to the realm of glib immaturity and delusion. The "change" that was a watchword of Obama's campaign we judge to be only "symbolic" rather than being a credible foundation on which to build plans or policy. This is a dismissal-in-the-form-of-description that would seem ill suited to those of us in the academy whose daily bread consists of the claim that what occurs on the symbolic level and in discourse is highly relevant to, and often indistinguishable from, the material and the lived—except that what we are able or willing to "know" is, still, in close alignment with what Sethe knows. Sethe's inheritors, we are confronted with our own exigencies, which are simply the progeny of those she confronted. To think of these events this way is a habit, not unlike the physiological process that arranges and renders sensible the vast array of visual stimuli bombarding us which we experience simply as "seeing" when it is in fact also editing; it is a product of battle-tested strategies and hard-won epistemologies honed into tools for carving out a space and habitation of survival. Morrison—and of course

she is not alone in this call—would have us retrain our habituated perceptions. She implies that just as Sethe's healing ultimately depends on seeking to know consciously what strategies of survival habitually hold at bay,
for us to explore the "worse" that every demand for safety and for righ-
teous vengeance would compel us to flee may prove fecund for the formulation of tools and strategies that take us further, and give us more freedom, than ways of knowing and decisions that track Sethe's fight, flight, or
both at once all too closely.

The genesis of this project for me lies in encountering a resistance that
runs through the core of two intertwined political currents which, despite
the sometimes sclerotic ways of seeing of which they are justly accused,
continue to seem vital to me (I'll say why in chapter 1), and which are
major contributions (if not foundations) for the field of African American
studies: the Black Power/Black Arts Movement and Frantz Fanon's work.
This resistance—the same, essentially, that Morrison figures in Sethe's response to Paul D—is to what Fanon and Black Power thinkers perceived
to be a pervasive abjection in the historical experiences of people in the
African diaspora. I am using the term *abjection* somewhat loosely here—it
is not a term used by Fanon or Black Power thinkers, particularly—and
I will discuss further later what I mean by it. In this context, the abject
describes a kind of lowering historical cloud, a judgment animating arguments and rhetoric in both currents in which the history of peoples in the
African diaspora—having been conquered and enslaved and then, post-
Emancipation, being dominated by colonial powers or by homegrown
white supremacists—is a history of humiliating defeat, a useless history
which must be in some way overturned or overcome. To this way of seeing, the past is an obstacle to imagining and building an empowered political position capable of effective liberation politics.

We see an example of this attribution of abjection and its avoidance as
we follow the trajectory from Fanon's essential point in *Black Skin, White
Masks* that blackness functions in Western cultures as a repository for
fears about sexuality and death—fears, in other words, about the difficulty
of maintaining the boundaries of the (white male) ego, and fears about
acknowledging the repressions and renunciations on which Western civilization depends. As such, blackness is an invention that accomplishes the
domination of those who bear it as an identity; and for that reason, blackness (like the more dominant term in Fanon's corpus, "the native"), while
it is something that, because it has been degraded under white supremacy, must be embraced and lionized as a first step, eventually needs to be

surpassed in favor of a conception of nation (which is also a conception of self) that does not depend on racial definition. Hence, Negritude—and Black Power—is insufficient and ultimately misleading for Fanon, and it partly is so because blackness is constituted by a history of abjection, and *is* itself a form of abjection.

This posture toward the black past has been widely identified in nearly half a century of criticism, from various quarters, of the political, ideological, sexist, and homophobic shortcomings of Black Power, black nationalism, and black cultural nationalism, and the now seemingly near-exhausted identity politics to which they gave rise. Certainly Fanon comes in for a lot of criticism as having an unsound relation to real history in his work (about which more later). As a literary scholar I have tended in my thinking about this issue to follow the line of critiques in the work of novelists such as Morrison, Gayl Jones, Ishmael Reed, Octavia Butler, and others who wrote the neo-slave-narrative novels of the late 20th century. Collectively, their fictive interventions sought to interpret the historical record in a more complicated way than it appears in Black Arts dismissals, emphasizing in their representations the wily political and personal resistance of slaves and freedmen, and demonstrating the complexities involved in coming to terms with the myriad traumas of physical and psychological violation.[2]

Revisiting and reframing Morrison et al.'s conversation with the Black Power/Arts Movements and Fanon about how blackness is constituted and lived, I am interested in examining the abjection that makes the black past appear to be so useless (and terrifying), and which always has to be surpassed, or that, even from the overall perspective of the neo-slave-narrative writers (and this of course distorts their individual nuanced representations), has to be shown not to be solely abjection, but also to be heroism in disguise. In this reframing I am not averring that blackness is produced *only* as a result of traumatizing violent domination and historical defeats, but my interest is in trying to grapple further with that apparently inescapable *aspect* of blackness—lying coiled at its historical heart, repeated, echoed, in part through the collusion of historically produced circumstances and the practices of our collective habituated perceptions—which can be described by terms such as defeat, violation, and humiliation. Thus, insofar as Fanon's and the Black Power thinkers' misreading of history, their essential lack of historicist rigor, nevertheless touches on something that is true—that the history and experience of enslaved Africans being racialized as black and their descendants assuming a black subjectivity does entail (and perhaps fails to *contain*) abjection—my questions are as follows:

If we are racialized (in part) through domination and abjection and humiliation, is there anything of value or to be learned from the experience of being defeated, humiliated, abjected? Or is this question ultimately best focused on identifying those elements of that experience, that history, which tend toward the overcoming and surpassing of domination and defeat? What can the historical, inherited experience of that enslavement and what it might have taught, conscious and unconscious, provide for us by way of useful lessons or templates?

And particularly, I want to search for the answers to these questions not from a historicist perspective—a project which would have to be governed by foundational questions such as, what was it really like for slaves or for those in the very worst grips of Jim Crow? and the like, which I do not endeavor to answer—but rather to ask, what is the potential for useful political, personal, psychological resource in racialization-through-abjection as historical legacy, as ancestral experience? How do we work with that legacy now, how do we *use* it to fit our own exigencies? For the inheritor of blackness who confronts it as a historical artifact marking the defeat of his ancestors and defining the obstacles to his present possibilities, can blackness-as-abjection be understood or experienced as an aspect of historical experience—a resource for the political present—that broadens and even enriches the expanse of what is human being rather than setting its limit or marking its terror-bound underside?

.   .   .

I seek one set of answers to these questions in what would seem to be an unpromising place: black sexuality. In a fundamental way this is a book about black sexuality as much as it is about abjection—but not, alas, in a fun way, because, as we well know, to confront the notion of a "black" "sexuality" is to run, at top speed, into the puckered but nonetheless sturdy walls of an often deforming articulation between blackness and the production of sexual expression and repression in Western societies. As Frantz Fanon elegantly dissects the matter, Negrophobia is essentially a sexual phobia, because blackness is primarily associated in Western (and Western-influenced) cultures with perverse, nonnormative sexuality. Amid such pressures, for which overdetermination seems too wan a description, those who are ushered into or assume black social positions continually must enunciate those positions while contending with the articulation of blackness to sexuality—including, understandably, contending with it via denying its significance. To speak, then, of black sexuality is to do so unaccompanied by the pleasurable illusion of choice or self-mastery, but again to find ourselves instead with Sethe-like choices, dodging a hail of the most powerful bullets—our Kryptonite—in the arsenal that makes being black a "problem" rather than the easily assumed mantle of yet another ethnic heritage.

This often seems to be a kind of conceptual prison, which constrains liberatory and even reformatory imagination and strategizing, and certainly makes intellectually challenging, and highly fraught, any approach to the subject of black sexuality. There is of course no necessary connection between black people and sexual ex/repression, just as there is no definite centrality of sexuality to subjectivity or to personhood or to the "truth." But these connections are rife, and thickly imbricated, in the stew of our cultures. As a consequence I am drawn *to* them rather than to the laudable attempt to surmount them. I am drawn *to* the lie, to find something there that might be beautiful and progressively productive for a political project of cultural reform, or a cultural project of political reform. It is entirely possible that my search for something useful in the ever-problematic construction of black sexuality risks reproducing that familiar set of false equivalencies that make, say, Isiah Thomas's sexual harassment case, Kobe Bryant's rape trial, Michael Jackson's trial for child molestation, Mike Tyson's conviction for rape, R. Kelly's child pornography trial, O. J. Simpson's murder trial, and so on, the obscuring spectacles—and the consolidations of whiteness and its social and political privileges—that they are. But at the same time it seems to me that a contribution to the analysis of this articulation, and a determination to work *with* its obvious power to incite, as well as aiming to deconstruct and, perhaps, alter or even destroy it, is useful, and perhaps necessary.

The twinning of blackness and the sexual—the relentless, repetitive sexualization of black bodies, the blackening of sexualized bodies—also fails always fully to contain the forces that articulation works to control: eruptions occur or can be provoked. In this sense this is a book about black sexuality, but not in a direct way: as I consider black sexuality I feel, like Herbert Marcuse (to whom I look for guidance frequently in these pages), that I must consider how it is or can be a vehicle for, or the realization of, black freedom and power—however vexed, attenuated, and provisional those concepts must be—even though, and *especially* though, deployments of notions of black sexuality are frequently the very means by which that freedom and that power are curtailed.

This is one way among several in which the concept of queerness comes to our aid—though at first only to complicate any movement toward a goal of black freedom and power. Its usefulness and its complications both stem from the way that the representation of queerness in an African American or Black Atlantic context, by drawing attention to nonnormative sexuality and sexual practices—again, an arena already obsessively linked in Western cultures with the figures of blackness and the imago of the black body—might be said to create a vertiginous doubly queer register that matches, reflects, and helps constitute the well-known double-consciousness of blackness. Examining queer blackness provides opportunities to consider how the history that produces blackness is a sexual history, that is, a history of state-sanctioned, population-level manipulation of sex's reproductive and pleasure-producing capacities. Whereas the initial political impulse animating reclamations of the term *queer* emphasizes a liberatory dissolution of fixed boundaries between genders, sexualities, and races, the queerness of blackness entails a confrontation with the likelihood that a historical context that provided for the defiance of conventions of sexual propriety and for the relatively unpoliced expression of sexual variation—racialized slavery in the Americas—was a practice of physical and psychic domination, meant to enslave rather than liberate, to fix the human beings whose racialized bodies made the enjoyment of a certain kind of queer freedom possible in a particularly bound identity rather than release the fluid potentialities of that identity formation. As Sharon Holland remarks, the *first* sexual revolution occurred under the auspices of American slavery.[3] In considering the relation between the queerness of blackness and of the conception of queer freedom's possible dependence on productions of blackness—which is in part to say, in considering the spectacularity which is blackness in American culture—we come back, then, to the scene of historical conquest and its effect, which is the defeat and subordination of the being who will be called by his conquerors and come to know himself as black.

One approach to this problematic is to identify its operation and its deleterious effects—to historicize the categories of blackness and black sexuality—and put forward that historicization as a means either of dissuading the powers-that-be that exploit it from continuing to do so or of prodding those who are its victims to organize politically (and psychologically) to combat it: this is a strategy aimed at diminishing, at overcoming, the operation of this spectacularity. The pursuit of such a strategy in those realms where sexualizing black bodies and violence against black bodies go hand in hand has been in operation since at least the time of our forebear Ida B. Wells-Barnett, and the need to continue this pursuit is clear. This is, we might propose, a central strategy of the neo-slave-narrative line of critique that I noted earlier has been an initial guide to me in considering the questions of this study.

There is another strategy, too, that is less often pursued and very possibly less likely to be effective but that nonetheless may offer helpful information in carrying forward the project of resistance that informs African Americanist inquiry: to examine those deleterious effects not only for the purpose of demonstrating their injurious outcomes but to see how the effects, indeed the injuries themselves, may themselves be tools that can be used either to model or to serve as a means of political transformation (at least as we see "politics" becoming manifest in the domain of "culture"). This is *another* strategy we can find sometimes employed in those same neo-slave narratives, though it is subordinate, on the whole, to the former.

In this sense the frame that I am proposing here and attempting to work out avers that though sexuality is used against us, and sexual(ized) domination is in part what makes us black, though sexuality is a mode of conquest and often cannot avoid being deployed in a field of representation without functioning as an introjection of historical defeat, it is in and through that very domination and defeat also a mapping of political potential, an access to freedom.

As I try to answer these questions, I argue that the abjection in/of blackness endows its inheritors with a form of counterintuitive *power*— indeed, what we can begin to think of as *black* power. This power (which is also a way of speaking of freedom) is found at the point of the apparent erasure of ego-protections, at the point at which the constellation of tropes that we call *identity, body, race, nation* seem to reveal themselves as utterly penetrated and compromised, without defensible boundary. "Power" in this context thus assumes a form that seems repugnant or even nonsensical, for its conditions of appearance are defeat and violation, and thus it seems to be antithetical to the robust self-endorsement that the definition of Black Power in American political history emphasizes. Yet in the texts I read to answer this study's set of questions, capabilities emerge *through* the unflinching investigation, depiction, and manipulation of an originary history of violation.

Again I want to emphasize that mine is not a historical or even a historicist project. In this book the tool of historicizing will be less important than the tools of theorizing and imagining—inventing by use of the stage set by history without attending too scrupulously to the particulars of historical incident. My aim here is not to seek the revelations of history but to emphasize that key component of the work of historical excavation that involves the construction of the past: that is, to work imaginatively *with*— and rework, and work over, and maybe, if we are lucky, work through— the material that history provides.

I approach the questions in my project from a couple different postures: one a literary reading of a recurring metaphor in Fanon's work that, I argue, represents in his theory blackness in its relation to the abject; the other a derivation of theoretics about the relation between blackness, abjection, and sexuality from close reading of literary texts.

Thinking Black Abjection

Extravagant Abjection investigates the relation of blackness and abjection; and it examines one of the ways that blackness is rendered by the various cultural, social, and economic processes of white supremacist domination as the exemplar of nonnormative genders and sexualities. I therefore follow and expand on Fanon's essential point in *Black Skin, White Masks* that blackness functions in Western cultures as a repository for fears about sexuality. As a particularly revelatory set of representations through which we can theorize the relation between blackness, abjection, sexuality, and power, I focus for most of the book on scenes of the sexual exploitation or humiliation of black men—some violent and explicit, some largely metaphorical—in novels and essays written by canonical African American authors in the 20th century. With such a focus, *Extravagant Abjection* proposes a queer reading of various literary assays of the existential condition of blackness, ways of thinking about how blackness *is* queer.

Metaphorical references to or depictions of sexual exploitation in texts by the writers James Weldon Johnson, Toni Morrison, Amiri Baraka, and Samuel R. Delany seem generally to present themselves for shock value, hyperbolically representing the outrage of racist practices as an assault on what in Western culture stands as the paradigmatic trope of citizenship and of the achievement of willed autonomy: the inviolable masculine body. The shock of these depictions of course draws on the longstanding conflation between the identity of the race and manhood that black feminist scholars have criticized, and it also draws from the well of homophobic disgust at sexual contact between men. I treat the figure of male rape in African American literature as a symptom of this conflation and homophobia, but also as a device that helps us understand the ways that gender informs blackness—especially where blackness becomes a mode of or figure for abjection. I also posit the figure as a representational strategy for productively working through or with the history of abjection that underpins and in part constitutes blackness.

If representing black male characters being sexually humiliated or violated is effective on a visceral level only because the measure of autonomous or free selfhood is really masculinity, and the Other of the masculine is feminine, such a set of basic assumptions generally tends toward either a defense of masculinity through the disavowal of the feminine (as exemplified by a writer such as Baraka, but even, more equivocally, by Morrison) or some kind of avowal of the feminine as the model of an abject consciousness, of powerlessness. In contrast to both those trajectories, my reading of these scenes contends that despite being hedged about or even permeated by such repressive and regressive political strategies, these fictional representations attempt to bring into history (albeit fictionalized history) rape of men by other men as a means of racial domination. They name rape as a sexual trauma that produces racial identity, but they also move beyond this recognition to suggest that this historical subjugation endows its inheritors with a form of counterintuitive black power.

Extravagant Abjection thus attempts to delineate some of the capabilities of blackness in its abjection by using the figure of male rape to disarticulate blackness from its quest for successful masculinity. I argue first that these capabilities center around the figure's usefulness for dramatizing or actualizing alternatives to linear temporality: such alternative temporalities arise largely in the temporal paradox that characterizes trauma (in which the trauma patient may recall the traumatizing event in literal detail but, failing to have understood it or to have been conscious of it at the time of its occurrence, loses access to it in the mode of narrative memory). I argue that this paradox, typically understood as one of the indicia of psychic dis-ease and debility, in the context of black abjection provides a resource for representing—and to some extent, achieving, if only by expansions of a reader's consciousness—a *liberating* escape from linear time. I base this part of my analysis on Marcuse's argument that the perception of time as linear is an important element of internalized self-defeat, which authority regularly exploits. The male rape figure as a way to represent an alternative relationship to linear time also arises in a simpler and perhaps more familiar way, through acts of literary imagination that actively attempt to rewrite the past. The twist here—and the bridge to what I am identifying as the second arena of capabilities inhering in black abjection—is that the text I take to do this work of imaginative revision of the past in the most useful fashion, Delany's *The Mad Man*, is an explicitly pornographic literary novel that aims to arouse readers sexually (i.e., at once bodily and psychically) precisely through its evocation of the history of blackness constituted through abjection.

The second arena of capabilities of blackness in its abject aspect, then, centers on the male rape figure as a mode for African American writers to represent and/or produce *pleasure* from fantasized identification with violated ancestors. This is an idea of pleasure I will want us to understand in the manner of paradox: both in its commonsense meaning, in the meaning attached to it through its association with sensuality and sexuality, and at the same time in a way analogous to Sethe's not-choice—that is, framed by the history of violation and humiliation that underpins blackness and crafted from the very material of that inherited trauma. Pleasure found in narrative manipulations of the male rape figure also owes a great deal to that aspect of abject experience that psychoanalytic critics such as Julia Kristeva have described, in which normative gender and sexuality are (however momentarily) not yet defined, and therefore in abjection gender and sexuality appear as a range of limited though significant possibility. In sum, representations of the sexual exploitation of men as part of the historical trauma that in part produces blackness operate in the texts as almost therapeutic enactment, allowing reconceptions of a racial identity paradoxically enriched, even empowered, by the suffering that constitutes it and that it psychically repeats.

In making this argument I will also be pushing it further, though I am not choosing to make these implications the central point or the teleological end of this inquiry: blackness in abjection, blackness *as* one of the go-to figures for referencing the abject, grants us a vantage point for viewing the movement, direction, and inchoate shapes that characterize or arise from the fluid potentialities of subjectivity formation itself—despite, and *because* of, the various cultural, economic, and political operations aimed at producing blackness as fixed and objective. The possibilities or capabilities I find in blackness-in-and-as-abjection emerge out of the subjugation (at once past and present, material and discursive) that makes a black subjectivity possible. But these possibilities and capabilities are not only related to blackness and not only inherent to the subjects to whom the category of black is applied: they are powers of human consciousness which can operate on both the individual and the collective level: existential powers in a sense. What makes them *black* is partly the vantage point from which I choose to view these powers—but in larger part because the choice of perspective from which to view them is really a Sethe-like choice, determined by my—by our, retaining that definition of "us" with which I opened—inescapable relation to the history of racialized slavery and racial segregation in the Americas. That history and the relation to it of those of us who hold (or are forced to hold) it as a legacy, and those of us who live in and as black bodies, allows us to perceive somewhat more clearly the properties of embodied alienation than those who are unconscious of that legacy and/or living in racially unmarked or "white" bodies. But the alienation of an embodied consciousness is common to all humans. Blackness is nonetheless in the Americas *one* (but only one, among the brethren of racially marked bodies) of the primary means to access that alienation and its (perhaps surprising) powers.

· · ·

That the unpromising—black abjection, black sexuality—should be the pathway along which to quest for the promise of power and freedom is, admittedly, something of a backward approach. The governing notion of this inquiry is to explore the *counterintuitive*, to sidestep the compelling *sense* of Sethe's reasoning—and thus, perhaps, to step sideways around the limits of her impossible decision and around the habituated perception of narrow, dire options that what she represents bequeaths us.

Thus, my method of analysis is often to read vigorously against the grain. This is because the body-psyche nexus wherein I find the relation between blackness and abjection to be experientially lived, as well as the various qualities the relation of blackness and abjection might be said to possess, enter representation vexed by particular challenges: they do not so much defy or resist narrative as simply pose a problem for narrative machinery, because the marvelous fictions of I, self, linear temporality, or coherent perspective on which narrative usually depends are in the state of abjection awash in those fictions' opposites, their negations and what is in excess of them. *Extravagant Abjection* proposes that we can see this nexus, and gain access both to it and its powers, as they are represented textually in the metaphor of muscle tension (in Fanon), in a lynching scene (in Johnson), and in narrative scenes of the sexual violation of black men (in Morrison, Baraka, and Delany). Nevertheless, the toolbox of the literary and theoretical that I employ often will seem, both for characters within the given fictional domain and for readers, to represent blackness-in/as-abjection through frustratingly elusive strategies of indirection. These strategies—paradox rather than straightforwardness, suggestion rather than direction—call attention to and even seem to wallow flamboyantly in the essential indirection which is symbolic activity itself: what the characters either cannot or do not say in the case of Johnson's and Morrison's novels, what readers refuse to read in Morrison's novel or what Black Arts/Black Power readers of Fanon skip over, what appears in Fanon's text as only peripheral, metaphorical, or seemingly throwaway rhetorical figures, and what is condemned or disavowed but appears as parenthetical pleasures or inarticulate screams in Baraka. These indirections are, however, necessary aspects of an investigation conducted along counterintuitive lines, and I believe they are the best devices by which power and freedom that inhere in the abjection of blackness can be described.

Sex, Masculinity, Psychoanalysis, and Black Abjection

I would like to discuss further here what I mean when I use the term *abjection*. As I noted earlier, initially in this book the abject has a somewhat flexible definition, because I am deriving its content from its peripheral evocation, the echo of its denied, transcended, or overcome presence, in the texts, while at the same time I assert that its appearance is highly salient. At first as I work with the concept, abjection largely denotes what my first theorist, Fanon, attributes to the defeat suffered by African peoples in a distant past, a past from which we as their descendants are at once thoroughly cut off and yet bound to, in the persistence of the economic and political systems and their cultural concomitants that resulted from ancestral failure. As I move forward in my analysis the abject takes on a more distinct profile and begins to depend for illumination on Julia Kristeva, the theorist who has made the term applicable to what Fanon is peripherally describing. Kristeva's psychoanalytic (and thus all-too-typically deracinated) account of abjection has many facets; one that I take up is that abjection is a universal experience in the developmental trajectory of the subject, which can be observed in phobic and borderline patients.

Abjection establishes itself in the development of subject-object relations: the subject is produced by relation with objects, as the two mutually bring one another into being. Abjection is experienced in the realm where the development of object relations is belayed or strays—thus preventing, even if only transiently, the subject from making its "normal" appearance. Abjection is part of the process of becoming a subject—which is to say it is part of the process of encountering language (the Name of the Father).

But almost precisely due to the usefulness of Kristeva's definition, the object of my analysis remains necessarily shadowy. For to enunciate the properties of abjection from the standpoint of critical knowledge—even critical knowledge that maintains in the forefront its orientation toward *discovery* rather than argumentation, as I wish to do here—is to alter the object that is defined and constituted by the fact that it slips over the fictive ramparts of ego and "I" and, thus, of knowing and asserting. Often this abject is understood by the writers I work with as an affront to personhood, an experience of terrible suffering. But while this affront and this suffering cannot be avoided, what my reading suggests is that within the black abject—within human abjection as represented and lived in the experience of being-black, of blackness—we may find that the zone of self or personhood extends into realms where we would not ordinarily perceive its presence; and that suffering seems, at some level or at some far-flung contact point, to merge into something like ability, like power (and certainly, like pleasure) without losing or denying what it is to suffer. As I explore this latter account of abjection, the concept is particularly well described as an aspect of sexuality and sexual pleasure.[4] Abjection as it finally takes shape in *Extravagant Abjection* is a term that speaks to various states of apparent and real disempowerment—which is in a sense to brush off and look again at a somewhat hoary concept, popular in the 1980s and sucked up into the vacuum bags of corporate workforce-management diversity seminars, but which, with its origins precisely in the power-seizing politics of 1960s movements, is what I am groping for here.

My use of the term *abjection* clearly owes a great deal to iterations of the concept in queer theory. As I have said, *Extravagant Abjection* performs queer readings of various literary assays of blackness and in this way is an example of ways of thinking about how blackness *is* queer. It thus broadly engages with works in the emerging field of black queer studies such as Siobhan Somerville's *Queering the Color Line* (2000), Robert Reid-Pharr's *Black Gay Man* (2001), Roderick Ferguson's *Aberrations in Black* (2004), and E. Patrick Johnson's collection *Black Queer Studies* (2005), and more broadly still, with such classics in queer theorizations as Judith Butler's *Bodies That Matter* (1993) and Leo Bersani's *Homos* (1995) and his essay "Is the Rectum a Grave?" (1987). The mutually defining relation between blackness and queerness is, however, an effect, or a secondary step, in the development of my argument, which is principally aimed at theorizing blackness-in/as-abjection and discovers queer sexuality as an element of that abject state and as a strategy and capability for working with that abjection. These studies provide important direction for my project, but they generally do not focus on the way blackness is founded and maintained in a historical and psychic defeat as a primary matter, nor do they explore in depth representations of black men's sexual humiliation and humiliation as the source of racialization. My project actually links these studies of black queerness to defining texts in African American literary-informed theory, such as Hortense J. Spillers's "Mama's Baby/Papa's Maybe: An American Grammar Book" (1987) and Abdul JanMohamed's *The Death-Bound-Subject* (2005), which examine disempowered modes associated with black history such as loss of gendering under slavery or the immanent threat of death in lynching and illuminate the political possibilities those devastations enable. Spillers's essay in particular proposes a series of key formulations regarding the nonnormative operation of gender in African American contexts that informs this book. Still, whereas these latter texts do not fully elaborate on queerness as an element of and response to such disempowerment, *Extravagant Abjection* does so.

A recent work, Kathryn Bond Stockton's *Beautiful Bottom, Beautiful Shame* (2006), like my project bridges the investigations of black queerness and disempowered modalities; it posits the embrace of shame as central to the confluence of black and gay identities and their politically radical potential. Stockton's investigation of shame considers the relation between blackness, abjection, and queer sexuality as *Extravagant Abjection* does, though she tends to take up the term *abjection* in a way consistent with its deployment in much other work in the field (in Butler, for example, and in Reid-Pharr). There the use of *abjection* follows another of Kristeva's accounts of it, this one emphasizing the processes of exclusion and boundary setting that are components of subject formation: as in Kristeva's mapping of the development of subjectivity, this use of the term *abjection* describes how the (always incomplete and at-risk) achievement of an identity depends on certain objects-to-be (such as phobogenic elements or the feminine body or excrement) becoming reviled and cast off in order to consolidate the subject, which thereby becomes not only itself or *a* self according to its idealized definitions but "clean" and defended—while retaining an attraction and repulsion relationship to what is abjected. This process reflects and is reflected by social boundaries between races, genders, and sexualities. In queer usages of *abjection,* generally we begin with the inescapable slippage across necessarily porous but desperately defended boundaries: the boundary between the ego and what it excludes in order to constitute itself (the female excluded—ab-jected—to make the male, the homosexual to make the heterosexual). This formulation of abjection (boundaries and exclusion, the abject as what is abjected) underlies my own uses of it.

Stockton's *Beautiful Bottom* considers some of these same questions I do, though using different terms—and, as it happens, reaching a set of answers that, though hers and mine are, I think, complementary, differ in particular content and overall emphasis.[5] The shame she emphasizes is related to what I am calling abjection in the way that Stockton says debasement relates to the ultimate aim of her book: for her, debasement is an "informant" concerning the links between black and queer signs (and black and queer communities).[6] For me, affective states, and even processes of identification, are "informants" concerning black abjection and its powers. I am not seeking here the links between "black" and "queer"—I am largely *assuming* those links by piggybacking on the work (like Stockton's) that has come before mine.

For my project abjection is a way of describing an experience, an inherited (psychically introjected) historical legacy, and a social condition defined and underlined by a defeat. *Extravagant Abjection* utilizes but does not focus on mapping the crucial process of the back and forth between the binary poles that make meaning, or on making visible the essential fluidity of, and connection between, politicized identities. The proposal here is that black people have had to be inside, as it were, abjection, have had to embody it and to *be* it in the lack of command of their embodiment that becoming black decrees; they have had to do this, be this, and survived, after a fashion, giving rise to the questions: What then is that fashion of survival? What are the elements of that survival *in* abjection, or *as* abjection? Though I therefore necessarily utilize terms and ideas from psychoanalytic theory and from the history of black politics—both of which concern themselves with formulations of identity—my argument does not so much aim to delineate aspects of black/queer identities or to trace the operation of negative affects or emotions in the production of political performance or personae. Rather, my hope here is to reform and revivify an element of what has been called—and, with transformed meanings, I would call again—black nationalist thought, in which my final object is to suggest not a set of identity-positions or identity-performances but a set of capabilities and potential strategies for experiencing or seizing—and above all, for redefining—*power* that the social construction of blackness makes possible.

.   .   .

As a related matter, I want to flag another conversation into which *Extravagant Abjection* enters: though this is a general study of the powers in abjection where it is the historical legacy and lived present of blackness, I focus on readings of fictions involving *male* characters and on an abstract human proposed by the likes of Fanon and Maurice Merleau-Ponty that, like its counterparts in the vast majority of Western philosophy, is by and large imagined as male. The maleness of these literary and theoretical figures for blackness is of course not incidental: Fanon's black everyman ensnared in epidermal schemas and James Weldon Johnson's Ex-Coloured Man both become representations of a certain persuasive power because of the longstanding phallocentric conflation between the identity of the race and manhood—a conflation that black feminist criticism has exposed and worked hard to disestablish.[7] My purpose in this selection of figures is not to repeat that conflation uncritically but rather to work with a cognizance of the ways that gender always informs blackness in its relation to abjection. I aim to employ the tools that arise from black feminist criticism as the means to show how the powers in abjection become revealed precisely as the disarticulation of masculine privileges and postures from blackness.

The accomplishment of this purpose is especially tricky where this disarticulation is effected in the particular example of writers elucidating as (black) power the pleasure produced by representations that invite identification with (sexually) humiliated or violated ancestors, or with sexual violation as the legacy of racialization. Focusing on such scenes, one potential complication is that my argument will buttress the assumption, often enough shared by black feminist work as well as by more traditionally masculinist African Americanist criticism, that for black people in general, but black men in particular, the abject is *like* the feminine, or is definitively feminine—that is, to abject is to be feminized. Again, to represent black male characters being sexually humiliated or violated is arguably effective on a visceral level only because the measure of autonomous or free self-hood is really masculinity, and the Other of the masculine is feminine.

Regarding these complications, then, *Extravagant Abjection* necessarily draws on work in African American feminist and gay criticism that exposes the contradictions and instability of the black masculine figure (and black male subjectivity). In this body of work, the de rigueur application of the concept of double-consciousness to objects of knowledge assigned to the category of "black," "male," and "African American" generally finds the "black male" to be a self-contradicting and self-reinforcing position at once hypermasculine and feminine, exemplifying an erection/castration paradox. In this black male figure gender appears both in its idealized form (if extremely so) and in gender's undoing, and therefore in the revelation of gender's basic plasticity; correspondingly in this figure gender cannot have meaning without a clarified racial marker, and in this figure sexuality exists almost purely—but never truly so—as the excess, the feared, indicator of and movement toward that state of undifferentiation in which linguistic categories of knowing and communication (and thus, of course, of identity) are momentarily without ballast, in crisis. My project engages especially with the latter dimension which scholarship has shown to be a constituent of the black male cultural figure, and thus it follows publications such as Philip Brian Harper's *Are We Not Men?* (1996), Maurice O. Wallace's *Constructing the Black Masculine* (2002), and especially Lee Edelman's *Homographesis* (1994), which demonstrates how literary representations of blackness frequently attempt to manage the challenging fact that racialization is accomplished through subjugation by containing or marginalizing threats of *penetration* to black male figures in the texts.

In reading representations of violations and humiliations in various scenes, I refer to the abject as accessing gender in a state of relative undifferentiation, gender as (however momentarily) not-yet-defined. This positioning of gender possibility—possibilities which are *im*possible within the epistemes structured by the perceptual requisites and mechanisms that underpin the ego—needs to show itself as *not*-masculine. But this does not mean that it is necessarily feminine, or only feminine, merely that it cannot be narrated except as the negation of what it exceeds or overruns—all of which is to say that it participates in the prevailing paradoxical logic in operation throughout this book. The delineation of vexed masculinity, then, is, like queer uses of abjection and the various linkages between blackness and queerness, not my focus; rather, vexed masculinity is one of this study's privileged modes for the expression of the power of abject blackness.

The abject as a mode of working with blackness need *not* necessarily privilege masculinity, vexed or otherwise, nor need it center male actors, subjects, or characters—though this study does both. It does both because it originates in a conversation with work in the fields of gay male and black queer studies, and with the study of black masculinity having its origins in black feminist critiques of masculinism, and also because of the usual essentially arbitrary limitations on project conceptualization (an arbitrariness that cannot but betray a masculinist tilt on my part, at least with regard to this project).

It bears noting, however, that we do not *have* to focus on vexed masculinity in addressing this subject because, again, the abject and the feminine as the penetrated or violable are cotravelers and overlap. From that vantage point the masculine as the site of black abjection thus might only be the "hard" case in terms of gender norms, and the "easy" case in terms of finding power in the context of black abjection. Women or female characters, in other words, may be too easily shown to have a relation to the abject—this risks simply underlining the structure resulting from the production of normative gender—and thus may be harder to affirm as evincing some form of power in abjection. Where the abject is always something to be resisted and overcome for nationalist politics, and where feminist politics labors to establish a human dignity for women that does not *enforce* the definition of the feminine as the abject—*there* it is possible that male privilege, the effect of male domination that permits men to invest in the fantasy that they have no essential relation to the abject, makes abjection something that can be consciously entered into, "played" with, manipulated: which is not to say that women cannot manipulate or play with abjection but that where women do so the political ramifications may more easily appear to be a confirmation of the defeat with which abjection works rather than a complication of it. Of course such a proposition risks distorting matters in the very ways that this study is meant to challenge, for both the "hard case" and "easy case" formulations presume the definitions of masculinity on which a masculinist ideology insists (i.e., precisely that to be or act masculine is to be or act with a kind of performative "strength" which does not permit or admit defeat and violation). Even if we can avoid this trap by insisting at every step that the abject is not definitively feminine, and that there is an abjection that men or male characters can experience or be represented in relation to that is only characterized as "feminized" from a male supremacist or misogynist point of view, it is nonetheless just possible that the working with abjection I describe in this book *is*, in some way, more easily recognized in its political implications where men are concerned, precisely because such working does not confirm a prevailing cultural definition of masculinity or femininity. This is a question I can flag but only answer suggestively, not definitively, due to the limitations—self-imposed, admittedly—of this study.

I engage this matter throughout the main text.

.   .   .

Extravagant Abjection's conceptual foundation follows Fanon's essential point in *Black Skin, White Masks* (1952) that blackness is rendered by the various cultural, social, and economic processes of white supremacist domination as the exemplar of nonnormative genders and sexualities. My deep investment in utilizing aspects of Fanon's theorizations of blackness puts this project into conversation with various contemporary interlocutors of Fanon, especially Ato Sekyi-Otu (*Fanon's Dialectic of Experience*, 1996), as well as with essays by Lewis R. Gordon, T. Denean Sharpley-Whiting, Ronald A. T. Judy, and Lou Turner (many, though not all of the essays with which I engage, are collected in *Fanon: A Critical Reader*, published in 1996 and edited by Gordon). This group of scholars has been identified with a development in the study of Fanon that aims to plumb the entirety of Fanon's published work, in order to, as Gordon, Sharpley-Whiting, and Renee T. White put it, "work *with* and *through* Fanon," taking him as a guide for the development of original theoretical projects "across the entire sphere of human studies."[8] These scholars' work to some extent counters—or at least positions as inadequate—analyses associated with *literary* critics such as Homi Bhabha that were primarily focused on *Black Skin, White Masks* and were animated by the need to theorize the complexities of postcolonial subjection and subjectivities, and to find a signal theoretical text—deemed to be sorely lacking elsewhere—that rigorously assumes and proves the mutually constitutive relation between race, gender, and sexuality. My own project is positioned between these two groupings of Fanon study, in that I am beginning with *Black Skin, White Masks*'s conclusions regarding the relationships between race, gender, and sexuality as my assumptions and engaging with the broad palette of Fanon's publications in order to find guidance concerning blackness and abjection. The bulk of my engagement with Fanon's texts is with *The Wretched of the Earth* (1961) and essays collected in *A Dying Colonialism* (1959) and *Toward the African Revolution* (1964)[9]—yet, further illustrating the confluence of the two sometimes disparate schools of Fanon study in this project, I use the instrument provided by my training, literary analysis, in order to derive theoretics for the relation between blackness and abjection, because in these particular texts Fanon discusses both blackness and abjection largely by implication, or through the deployment of metaphorical figures. The attempt to derive these theoretics also puts me into conversation with those who have read Fanon as black feminist and black queer critics, such as Spillers, bell hooks, Francoise Verges, and Kobena Mercer. Their engagements with Fanon (some of which are collected in another 1996 anthology, *The Fact of Blackness*) inform my working with and through Fanon, as well.

Hortense Spillers's name in the foregoing list is an important pivot turning us toward the consideration of another of the fields with which this project engages: the field studying psychoanalysis or psychoanalytically informed concepts in African American and Afro-Diasporic contexts. Spillers's essay "All the Things You Could Be by Now, If Sigmund Freud's Wife Was Your Mother': Psychoanalysis and Race" (1996), along with others collected in Elizabeth Abel, Barbara Christian, and Helene Moglen's *Female Subjects in Black and White: Race, Psychoanalysis, Feminism* (1997), are texts that have done the crucial work of clearing the ground for the use of psychoanalysis in African Americanist criticism—a critical application that has been for various, and variously persuasive, reasons assailed as inappropriate to its object. I do not wish here to rehearse this controversy or to engage directly with doubts about this usage, but rather firmly to locate myself in the clearing provided by these feminist elders, as I work my way primarily through Fanon and thus to some extent, by necessity, through Freud and Lacan, and then by choice through psychoanalytic critics such as Julia Kristeva and Herbert Marcuse. In this respect my project's engagement with the field of psychoanalysis in African American contexts also participates in the field of the study of psychoanalytics and racial formation. Works such as David Eng's *Racial Castration* (2001) and Anne Anlin Cheng's *The Melancholy of Race* (2001) argue that a kind of "racial melancholia" and its attendant processes are core elements in the identifications that produce Asian American subjects—and, by extension, of racialized American and hyphenated-American subjects generally (the latter is especially true of Cheng's work, since she balances portions of her arguments on accounts of racial formation drawn from African American texts). These descriptions of how racial formation occurs through or along with ostensibly debilitating psychological processes, and the authors' determination to demonstrate the ways these apparent debilitations also open up politically useful ways of seeing and/or performing and living as racialized subjects—lines of argument that also can be said to take up psychoanalytically informed inquiries into the operation of identification processes along the axes of gender, race, and sexuality that are explored in Butler's analysis of Nella Larsen in *Bodies That Matter* and in Diana Fuss's *Identification Papers* (1995)—are, to my mind, important models and sister texts for my own inquiry, in which humiliation and those processes attendant on the psychoanalytic abject are central to my understanding of blackness.

. . .

As I have said, the ultimate trajectory of the individual experiences and cultural associations and meanings I hope to illuminate by use of the term *abjection* is toward something I can call *power*. *Power* is of course an even more complex—and more contested—term than *abjection*. Per Lewis Gordon,

> Power is a term that is not often clarified these days in the academy. . . . Most often . . . it is Foucault's use of the term that is presumed, as if his formulations were the be-all and end-all of discourses on power. We should, however, remember that power emerges in the thought of such thinkers as Hegel as a function of dialectic opposition of consciousness and recognition; Marx, as ownership over the means of production; Gramsci as hegemony; Hannah Arendt, as uncoerced exchange in a public sphere the emergence of which are deeds of glory; Thomas Hobbes and Carl Schmitt, as legitimate force, which is issued only by the sovereign or the state; and Elias Canetti, as the godlike range of actions that transcend those locked under its grips as mere mortals.[10]

I am not certain that *Extravagant Abjection*'s contribution will prove to be any clearer than the vagueness that Gordon indicts, but as a general matter I seek here to trouble the notion of power: I want to theorize that which is *not*-power according to the ego-dependent, ego-centric (and masculine and white) "I" definitions we have of power, but which is *some kind* of power if by power we mean only ability, the capacity for action and creation in one or several spheres, be they internal or external to the empowered.

Power in my usage will sometimes slip over into *freedom,* and both will be bound up a great deal with indeterminacy—at which the reader may raise reasonable objections. Mere indeterminacy is not freedom or power, it may justly be said; but the effort in these pages will be to show that in a context where overdetermination is the hallmark of the figure of blackness, the presentation of or the access to the *in*determinate bears a potency worth reckoning. Drawing on Fanon's discussions (as well as on Sartre's and Merleau-Ponty's and thus on existential philosophy and psychology), indeterminacy appears as an essential descriptive element of the operation of human consciousness and thus perhaps the foundation—if not, to push it further, the breadth and the limit—of what power and freedom for humans (as opposed to for systems or for imagined divines) *can* be—and, I argue, blackness can get us there.

From this point of view, greater attention ought to be accorded to the "mere" that describes indeterminacy; it is indeed a gossamer mere when measured against the near absolutes of historical events and extant institutions, but a mere that we ought to see as having recognizable strength when measured against our existential conditions. While the achievement of something we can see as a "real" material, wide-ranging freedom or power—because it looks enough like the operation of institutions in the present and the past—is certainly a good goal for progressive and radical politics, do we only recognize freedom or power when they approach the direction of infinity on the asymptotic curve? I say not. Thus, power here appears against the grain, provisional and to some degree slippery and suggestive—*literary,* a form of knowledge making contiguous and simultaneous apparently disparate, temporally separate constituent elements— exactly because our definitions of power (again, bound to gender position, bound to racial position) obscure even the possibility of its existence. I am wagering that *it*—this set of abilities, powers—does exist, however.

Black Abjects

In chapter 1, "Fanon's Muscles: (Black) Power Revisited," I interpret the argument Frantz Fanon makes throughout his corpus that blackness (as well as nativity) is an invented racial category created by the enslavers of Africans. The implication of Fanon's argument is that a clear-sighted examination of the "fact of blackness" yields larger truths about the human psyche and about how liberation from Western oppression can be achieved. Fanon rejects the notion of ontogeny for sociogeny, arguing that all the elements of the human being are created in the social world, essentially without fundamental attributes. This is demonstrated by the fact that each black person can, through a *traumatic* encounter with the blackness that his societal indoctrination has taught him to hold in contempt, become conscious of the *imposition of blackness* upon him. The black person can identify the source of his self-division, his internalized self-defeat. That which is fully internal to the nonblack or nonnative, especially those persons securely identified with a given dominant culture, and which remains obscure without the revelation of analysis or art, becomes external in the conscious black person. Thus, one can see through the invented prism of blackness both the deprivation on which the person in Western civilization is created and the possibilities for the transformation of that person—and the first step in the process of coming to this consciousness involves working through an experience of trauma (a forced recognition of his blackness).

The chapter unfolds the ramifications of Fanon's sociogenic understanding of blackness in order to uncover what, in the process of being made black, of being blackened, can be seen to evince the power, pleasures, and freedom that blackness was created to deny its bearers. Glimpses of that power begin from Fanon's "mirage of muscle power," which appears in several of his texts as a recurring metaphor, "tensed muscles." Fanon repeatedly employs "tensed muscles" to represent an unconscious recognition of the colonizer's manifold injustices, a way in which the colonized knows and resists his historical subjugation; and the state of muscle tension or contraction simultaneously is the transitional precursor state to revolutionary action. This tension is represented as physical, but its full dimensions are psychic; and its form of knowledge is not fully intellectual because it inheres in a nexus between bodily sensation and perception, and in the structure of consciousness itself. Thus, "tensed muscles" represent a form of bodily (un)knowing that recognizes its existence in a history of defeat while instancing its unconscious preparation to meet and resist that defeat. Chapter 1 then considers the possibilities latent in this stance by referencing the existentialist (Jean-Paul Sartre), phenomenological (Maurice Merleau-Ponty), and psychoanalytic (Jacques Lacan, Julia Kristeva) tenets that inform or parallel it: temporal dispersal, anonymous existence, double-bodiedness, vertigo, trauma, abjection. What each of these (anti) concepts share is a nonconscious, nonunified, and dispersed relation to selfhood, action, or change in which the ego is not defended. Thus, in

reading the metaphor of tensed muscles of the black/native, I make a set
of conceptual moves, a number of which I enunciate in the terms of the
existential philosophy and existential psychology with which Fanon is in
conversation. I find gestural and postural possibilities, which loop (rather
than align or stick on a pyramid) the past, present, and future, an approach
to time that I call interarticulated temporality; a state of death-in-life and
life-in-death characteristic of the paradox of a being that experiences utter
defeat yet that is not fully defeated; a "lack" that is nonetheless not a void
and that refers the native/black back to anonymous existence, to indeterminacy and a kind of freedom in the form of anguish and vertigo, as Sartre
and Merleau-Ponty defines these terms: a vertigo appropriate to the (non)
subject—that is, object in the world—both imprisoned in this highly attenuated freedom and yet free in imprisonment.

   In chapter 2, "'A Race That Could Be So Dealt With': Terror, Time, and
(Black) Power," I link the terms I derive from what is essentially a literary reading of Fanon's mid-20th-century theoretical and activist texts to
an attempt to derive theory from a literary scene of lynching in a novel of
the early 20th century. James Weldon Johnson's *The Autobiography of an
Ex-Coloured Man* (1912) is the only text I examine that was not written in
the latter part of the century, but its temporal position pre-Fanon demonstrates the usefulness of reading African American texts through psychoanalytically informed theories of liberatory processes. The biracial narrator
of the novel confirms Fanon's observations when he decides to reject the
possibility of adopting a black identity. For most of the novel the narrator struggles, mostly unconsciously, with both a racial and (as other critics
have pointed out) a sexual ambiguity that in some ways makes him a paradigmatic American subject, both tortured and invigorated by the opportunity of creating an identity of his own choosing. But when he witnesses
a terrible lynching of a black man he decides to become "ex-colored"—in
essence, white. This lynching bears the connotations of a kind of rape, not
only because of the savage interest the lynchers display in dismembering
the black man's body but because of the narrator's own subtly sexualized
regard for the white male lynchers. The narrator's experience identifies a
specific aspect of racialized trauma. The trauma that he experiences is entirely bound up in his perception of the lynching as a collective injury—
indeed, a collective annihilation. His trauma lies in his intense imagination
of connection to "a race that could be so dealt with."[11] The lynching thus
becomes a kind of primal scene for the narrator in which the violent, and
sexually violent, elements of the relation between whiteness and blackness

are revealed; he looks directly at the construction of blackness but can only read it as humiliation and defeat, so he abandons it—and in so doing abandons an opportunity of self-making, of taking the reins of Fanon's sociogenic power, that an acceptance of abject blackness would enable.

The chapter focuses on how the representation of the Ex-Coloured Man's traumatic response to the lynching he witnesses enacts one of the chief symptoms, and puissant forms, of the black power explicated in chapter 1: temporal dispersal, hostility toward, as Fanon describes it, "conformity to the categories of time."[12] Though the novel is designed as a narrative of failure in many senses, peripheral suggestions of actions alternative to those the narrator chooses emerge in the miscegenation with which the novel concludes—this miscegenation is at once denied (the Ex-Coloured Man passes as white) and affirmed (not only because he is a once-colored man but also through his desire for his white wife's desire for his black boyhood friend, Shiny)—possibilities that, if consciously embraced, would position the Ex-Coloured Man as a kind of race- and family-terrorist.

Chapter 3, "Slavery, Rape, and the Black Male Abject," concludes the set of readings in which I am attempting to derive a theoretics of the relation between blackness and abjection and provides the bridge into considerations of male rape thematics as a specific representation of that relation. Toni Morrison's Paul D, a secondary character in *Beloved* (1987), like all the members of the household in the novel, has to confront the active, living past in the person of the corporeal ghost Beloved. Paul D's sexual relationship with the ghost and the consequences of this liaison for his relationship with Sethe hinge on his working through the mostly repressed memory of his sexual violation while laboring on a chain gang. Chapter 3 thus intensifies the *sexual* nature of the paradigmatic scene of conquest and defeat and portrays a less-failed, though similarly riven, male survivor than the Ex-Coloured Man. Foregrounding Paul D's traumatized re-membering of the experience of "breakfast" (forced fellatio) on the chain gang, I explore alternate possibilities for the figure of black manhood that eventuate from the scene and its highly elliptical rendering. The scene troubles the dominant trope of black masculinity, "emasculation" (the parallel to "rape of black women") by attributing emasculation *to* the rape of men by other men. Its mode of rendering figures at once the sexual exploitation of men and silence about it—a silence enforced by the anger and disbelief that black audiences manifest toward this scene and that suggests that the horror the scene seems to provoke also signals a repressed memory of homoerotic domination. Paul D's road to healing, then, in embracing abjection in his quest to define "manhood," opens other, less-defended modes of being male in the world.

The homophobia implicit in Sethe's and Paul D's refusal to explore the homosexual implications of his sexual humiliation on the chain gang is both addressed and redressed in this book's final two chapters, where *Extravagant Abjection* transitions from a meditation on the abject in Fanon's "tensed muscles" metaphor to use another, not unrelated metaphor: the bottom. I use *bottom* to signify the nadir of a hierarchy (a political position possibly abject) and as a sexual position: the one involving coercion and historical and present realities of conquest, enslavement, domination, cruelty, torture, and so on, the other involving sexualized or erotic consent/play which references the elements of the former. The connection between the two meanings of *bottom* (1) shows the correlation between scenes of blackening and of rape and homosexuality, (2) investigates the nature of the black power inherent in such (ostensible) forms of pain and abjection, and (3) ventures the question of the kinds of *pleasure* that might inhere even in such experiences. I mark the transition between these two metaphors—the first, broadly speaking, abstract and theoretical, the second, exemplary and unfolded in narrative—with a discussion of the various questions and troubled terms that emerge in the encounter between the concepts of blackness-in/as-abjection and queerness.

In particular I gloss the possibilities and problems of using the term *pleasure* in the context of racialized abjection. I discuss how *pleasure* here must be understood in a manner analogous to the way Spillers suggests the term could be productively applied to the experience of our enslaved ancestors, which is to say, in a way requiring us continually to turn our attention to a markedly *different* set of referents and meanings—different though, here and there, overlapping—from those to which our ordinary (and perhaps even our psychoanalytically informed) notions of pleasure direct us. This is a pleasure that at once depends on an at least amoral and perhaps immoral *use* of the history, and memory, of ancestral suffering, and that simultaneously attempts to maintain that use as an empathetic form of identification and as an ethics derived from such identification: pleasure that emerges through both a voyeuristic, even prurient appropriation of ancestral scenes of suffering and a potentially transformative refusal to obtain protective distance from such scenes.

In these introductory notes prior to the final chapters, I also show that though such familiar (if nevertheless endlessly fascinating and near limitless) terms as *masochism* and *castration* overlay, overlap, and even partly describe the relation between blackness and abjection, and the powers that inhere in that relation, these do not fully encompass that relation and those powers, adequately name them, or exhaust them.

Chapter 4, "The Occupied Territory: Homosexuality and History in Amiri Baraka's Black Arts," focuses primarily on Black Arts Movement intellectual LeRoi Jones/Amiri Baraka and his semiautobiographical novel *The System of Dante's Hell* (1965) and essays that appear in the collection *Home* (1966). It also engages with Eldridge Cleaver's *Soul on Ice* (1968). Jones/Baraka and Cleaver enthusiastically endorse Norman Mailer's valorization of black men as the authentic avatars of the socially and politically radical "moral bottom" in his notorious essay "The White Negro" (1959). Extending Mailer's reversal of the traditional white-over-black hierarchy, Jones and Cleaver cathect the moral-bottom superiority of blackness in the despised figure of the black male rapist. Jones and Cleaver frequently use rape (and analogized acts of sexual or sexualized domination), especially interracial rape, as an arguably "queer" political trope—queer insofar as the black male rapist figure is relished precisely for its nonnormativity (in the form of its violence and perversity), its putative defiance of the ruling powers' designated boundaries. For them, rape gestures explicitly or implicitly toward the experience of slavery and viscerally represents the historical injustice of white supremacist practices. Rape is their metaphor of choice both for the historical crime committed against black people and for the fantasy of racial revenge. Thus, rape—and the perverse, violent, queer sexuality that rape is drafted to represent—is presented as historically constitutive of the political and existential condition of blackness.

But Jones's and Cleaver's macho attempt to incite rage and to rally against the external enemy—to erect the protections of the masculine ego—forces them to discard the most radical and humanist elements of blackness that Fanon identifies: the characters (and/or the narrative authority) often accede to an ostensibly liberated black wholeness by dismissing the nonmasculine, queer implications of a history characterized by the complex psychic devastations and compromises that result from institutionalized sexual domination. Yet it is the very queerness of this past, the threatened dissolution of fixed boundaries between genders, races, sexualities, and even subjectivities experienced perforce in such a history of sexual domination, that endows blackness with the protean qualities that make it a powerful vehicle for imagining freedom in these texts. At times and usually against the authors' intentions, *bottoming* and/or a vulnerability to penetration is portrayed in their texts as a willed enactment of powerlessness that encodes a power of its own—a kind of skill set that includes pleasure in introjecting and assimilating the alien (perhaps, alienation itself), a sense of intimacy acquired even in situations of coerced pain, a transformation, through harm, of the foreign into one's own.

In the final chapter, "Porn and the N-Word: Lust, Samuel R. Delany's *The Mad Man* and a Derangement of Body and Sense(s)," I attempt to traverse the difficulties that narrative machinery encounters in blackness-in/as-abjection by visiting a kind of text that generically aims to work with (and to work) psychic/body responses: pornographic writing. In *The Mad Man* (1994), a literary pornographic work, arousal and climax are achieved for John Marr, *The Mad Man's* protagonist, through his inheritance of specifically racialized (i.e., black) abjection. John Marr is a black gay male character who feverishly seeks out the pleasure of sexual acts that involve some form of apparent humiliation or degradation. These acts are frequently explicitly racialized—John's partners call him "nigger" repeatedly. John uses his activities and fantasies and their historical resonance of racial subjugation, and the intense pleasure these acts give him largely *because* of that resonance, to open the way to a sense that he operates within a greater sphere of freedom and power than he did before engaging in his sexual practices. His experiences represent the possibility of overcoming the internalized defeat demanded by the legacies of history.

The novel attempts to achieve for readers what it represents for John Marr through a sexual or erotic practice—in this case, primarily, an erotic and sexual *reading* practice—of Marcusian exuberance. In *The Mad Man* the combination between the evocation of the history of racialization through humiliation and the pornographic form itself doubly represent the apparent paradox of power in abject blackness. Delany's text addresses the messy imbrication of blackness with a queerness that is simultaneously subjugating and yet psychically freeing, and it does so by making central what from an antiracist point of view must appear to be a political paradox: the historically charged erotic fantasy of white male sexual domination of black men. In this chapter we find what Morrison and Baraka et al. suggest is most recalcitrant to the politics of black empowerment—black men sexually violated or degraded, homosexuality, masochism—in the realm of what common hierarchies of discourse assign as one of the sites most unlikely to demonstrate anything "redeeming"—porn.

The smudged and traversable line between representation and fantasy on the one side and practice on the other—the projection and reflection (or refraction) of the mind and the body's relation—permits me to argue that what is represented in *The Mad Man* is something in the nature of a rough model of working with the legacies of a history of conquest and enslavement (which is to say, with blackness, with having-been-blackened) through the transformation provided by erotic/sexual fantasies. Delany thus imagines a position that takes on board race without having at the same time to take up its fellow traveler, so often mistaken for the thing itself, ego. Is it possible to have race without ego, without defensive postures, without boundaries to police and ramparts on which to stand watch? The character of John Marr tries to model for us this position. Delany imagines him living his black body in its collective, sociogenic dimension, in which the demand to self-protection of that seductive individual *I* is refused in favor of one's becoming immersed in, lost in what it is to *be* the race, precisely as to be black means to have-been-blackened, to have been rendered abject.

1

Fanon's Muscles

(Black) Power Revisited

I WANT TO begin my exploration of blackness in its relation to abjection and sexuality where this relation is at once seen to be foundational, and strenuously denied, by following the flow of two currents I identified earlier, Fanon and Black Power/Black Arts. In doing so I want to explore as thoroughly as I can the key theoretical questions and terms of this project that I flagged in the introduction—mainly, abjection and power. This exploration will merge into a close consideration of one of the figures for black abjection that the book examines, the recurring metaphor in Fanon of "tensed muscles."

Not Your Daddy's Fanon

Frantz Fanon, a son of the French Caribbean island of Martinique, psychiatrist of Lyons, France, and Blida, Algeria, activist, propagandist, and politician in the war for Algerian independence, theorist of decolonization in Africa, was also, of course, a kind of Abrahamic father for intellectuals and artists associated with the Black Power Movement in the United States. The "of course" here flows smoothly on the tongue in the context of a project of African American literary and cultural analysis because the notion of a "Black Atlantic," in which the forced expatriation of millions of Africans to European colonies in the Americas gave rise to a cross-oceanic transferal not only of bodies, goods, and capital but also of discourses, ideas, memes, and cultural practices, is now well established as an almost required foundation for African Americanist inquiry.[1] That the activists of the Black Power Movement were enthusiastic participants in this theater of exchange long before the term *Black Atlantic* came into use in the various fields of cultural studies is evident in the almost insouciant facility with which they invoked Fanon's name and work. Fanon's *The Wretched of the*

Earth was published in English in 1965, having been translated from the original French *Les damnes de la terre* (1961). In the preface of the 1967 call to action *Black Power*, Kwame Ture (formerly Stokely Carmichael) and Charles V. Hamilton evoked Albert Camus and Jean-Paul Sartre, but directly quoted only two figures, Frederick Douglass and Frantz Fanon; Fanon's *The Wretched of the Earth* claims precedence, a lengthy quotation from it given the last word of the preface and positioned as the summation of Ture and Hamilton's project, which is the elucidation of a Black Power analysis and politics.[2] The Black Panther Party, the official dogma of which often departed from the more cultural nationalist stance of many Black Power thinkers, but the appeal and image of which was solidly associated in public representations with the Movement, anointed Fanon as one of the leading theorists of its revolutionary struggle: Huey P. Newton cited Fanon first and foremost along with Mao Tse-tung and Che Guevara as the most influential figures he and Bobby Seale read when they conceived the party. In Newton's 1967 party newspaper column, "The Correct Handling of a Revolution," the Algerian Revolution as depicted in *Wretched* provides a primary example of how to pitch battle against the powers-that-be by embodying the wisdom of the masses rather than relying on the elite secrecy of a self-styled vanguard. Eldridge Cleaver proclaimed *Wretched* the "Bible" of black liberation, as did Newton.[3] LeRoi Jones, on the cusp of his transformation into Amiri Baraka, in an essay signaling his abandonment of Greenwich Village Beat bohemianism for Harlem Black Arts Movement nationalism, called on Fanon without first name, as if to a body of work with so solidly established a presence that its syllables alone are its credentials: "If we take the teachings of Garvey, Elijah Muhammad and Malcolm X (as well as Frazier, DuBois and Fanon), we know for certain that the solution of the Black Man's problems will come only through Black National Consciousness."[4]

This last invocation is most interesting to me, not only because of the bent of my academic training but because it seems to me to encapsulate the way Fanon in the minds of Black Power thinkers became a name with which one conjured broadly vague but puissant political effects. Fanon is in Baraka's mention a rhetorical device: a metaphor that moves beyond the simple metonymy of "Fanon" for "the works of Fanon" to "Fanon" for the revolutionary struggle in Algeria in which he participated, for the engaged intellectual analysis of that struggle, for engaged intellectual work as such in revolutionary struggle against colonialism and white supremacy in general, and as a kind of imprimatur endorsing Baraka's personal struggle to attain influence and effect the kind of successful social and political change that his invocation imputes to Fanon.

Fanon's power as a name to conjure with was a quickly achieved effect. Baraka's essay appeared in 1965, the same year of the first appearance of the English translation of *Wretched*, which Jones must have read speedily, and been powerfully affected by, as by the world-altering shock of revelation. Baraka, looking back in his autobiography, writes that his arrival in Harlem could "only be summed up by the feelings jumping out of Cesaire's *Return to My Native Land* or Fanon's *The Wretched of the Earth*." Interestingly in this account of the period just prior to his move to Harlem in 1965, Baraka notes that "Frantz Fanon's books were popular, Grove Press had brought out *The Wretched of the Earth*."[5] Baraka's recollection partially condenses the passage of time and the ordering of events. Only half of Fanon's books were available to the non-French-reading audience during the years about which Baraka writes in his autobiography: *Wretched* was published by Grove in 1965; the same year, Monthly Review Press published the English translation of Fanon's collection of essays about the Algerian Revolution, *L'an V de la revolution africaine* (1959), under the title *Studies in a Dying Colonialism*, which was subsequently republished by Grove in 1970, along with *Toward the African Revolution* (*Pour la revolution africaine*). *Black Skin, White Masks* (formerly *Peau noire, masques blancs*) did not appear until 1967. Newton's similar statement that "[w]e read the work of Frantz Fanon, particularly *The Wretched of the Earth*" in his account of the founding of the Black Panther Party probably also refers to he and Bobby Seale having only read *Wretched*, and possibly *Studies in a Dying Colonialism*, by the time that the party began operating in 1965–66.[6] The enthusiasm of their first falling-in-love encounter with Fanon through *Wretched* and the telescoped memory that fuses their later readings of subsequent translations of Fanon's work with that encounter together illustrate my point about the way that Fanon's adoption by Black Power intellectuals had something akin to the quality of references to, in Cleaver's and Newton's ecstatic words, the biblical, or to any set of works agreed to be foundational:[7] the ease of reference to what Jesus or Shakespeare or Marx or Freud said or would say—the popularity of these figures, at least as, or most precisely as, names—is also a fairly clear indication of how difficult it can be to square what the names are evoked to suggest with anything the thinkers themselves have actually argued.

Certainly Baraka's summons of Fanon to the altar of "Black National Consciousness" in his essay, particularly in a paragraph that Baraka begins with the assertion, "Nations are races," would indicate that he misread Fanon just as he later misremembers the timing of his encounter with Fanon's work.[8] Especially in Wretched, Fanon is at pains to repudiate the equation between the nation and race.[9] In "Spontaneity: Its Strengths and Weaknesses," Fanon discourses at length about how the failure to articulate a sufficiently thought-through political program during revolutionary action against the colonizers in Africa too easily leaves the revolution's accomplishments vulnerable to racist dogma—"foreigners out"—that merely masks the native bourgeoisie's attempts to assume the social and economic position of the ousted colonials, and leads eventually to the reassertion of tribal conflicts, and sometimes to the identification of the government with one tribe. In Fanon's estimation, to believe that nations are races is to defeat the truly liberatory nation before it can be achieved, and enthusiasms such as Baraka's, taken too far, are a triumph of counterrevolutionary stupidity, a relapse into the "primitive Manichaeism" of white supremacists and colonialists.[10] It is not without reason, then, that Baraka scholar Jerry Gafio Watts wonders "whether Baraka had actually read Fanon."[11]

Black Power and Black Arts intellectuals ignored or deemphasized Fanon's tendency to treat blackness as a strategic instrument in a contest for political supremacy: for Black Power writers and activists, blackness describes a social and economic condition, a vibrant culture to be endorsed on its own terms, an essence and a kind of telos. As Baraka writes in 1965, despite—and because of?—being enthralled by Fanon, "blackness . . . is the final radical quality in social America."[12] But my interest here is not in needling Baraka or his contemporaries for failing to report accurately Fanon's complex and rather capacious arguments—particularly since Newton's misreadings, if they can be called such, were different from Baraka's because he did not espouse cultural nationalism; and Baraka, in one of his many about-faces, later came to similar conclusions as Fanon about the mistake of equating nation and race.[13] Their positions and Fanon's on blackness are deeply intertwined despite their divergence, in that blackness cannot be a successful instrument either of domination or resistance without its also being lived as a set of conditions that are endowed with truth-value, without its becoming, in practice, a social "essence."

In any case, Black Power intellectuals were not unaware of how Fanon's theorizing of the Algerian, African, and Caribbean situations complicated their attempts to transplant him to a U.S. context, despite the lucidity with which they felt Fanon's prose could describe their own battles. Fanon himself of course had freely made reference in *Black Skin, White Masks* to the works of Richard Wright as fictionalizations and examples of the racial dynamics viciously operating on both sides of the Atlantic and had thus indicated a methodological sympathy for analyses relying on a kind of black universalism. But in *Wretched*, in a discussion of the question of culture in its relation to nationalist revolution—a moment he chooses, as he does at moments in *Black Skin*, to lay bare the insufficiency of Negritude (and thus black cultural nationalism) as a foundation for his notion of nationalist revolution—Fanon asserts the essential heterogeneity of struggles against white supremacy and struggles against colonialism. "The Negroes of Chicago only resemble the Nigerians or the Tanganyikans in so far as they were all defined in relation to the whites, . . . and . . . the problems which kept Richard Wright or Langston Hughes on the alert were fundamentally different from those which might confront Leopold Senghor or Jomo Kenyatta."[14]

Such admonitions undoubtedly played a part in shaping the apparent self-consciousness with which Newton, Ture, and Hamilton, at least, tried to make use of Fanon's writing. They could quote him at length, and selectively, as we all do when we quote those whom we revere, but the looseness of these appropriations was also balanced by—was also linked to, as the necessary and constitutive obverse of those sloppy appropriations— an explicit effort at *translation*, the result of which was the sometimes awkward model of internal colonialism, spelled out at some length in *Black Power*. The "analogy" between Fanon's struggles against colonialism on the African continent "[o]bviously . . . is not perfect," Ture and Hamilton admit; still, pace the revered Fanon, they ask, "But is the differentiation more than a technicality?"[15] In the late 1960s, in a context in which the FBI would soon identify the Black Panther Party as a premier threat to the nation's internal security and unleash COINTELPRO to destroy the black nationalist movement, it understandably seemed direly urgent for Ture, Hamilton, Newton, and others to judge the difference between Algeria and the United States as that between different techniques applied to a fundamentally similar situation—white domination and exploitation of black or colored folk. For these writers, the appropriations and translations we might now group under the heading of "Afro-Diasporic Black Atlantic transnational intellectual flow" asserted the political ideal of a Pan-Africanism that was a straw to be grasped against the hurricane winds of white supremacist anti–Civil Rights Movement backlash, and it was an act of solidarity with "Third World" anticolonial struggles generally.

What Fanon said to them is naturally not what Fanon might say to us, today. I invoke their invocations of Fanon precisely for their enthusiastic imprecision, exactly because of this forty-year pedigree of creative, even sloppy interpretations of his texts in a U.S. context, in order to stake a claim to Fanon as a theorist on whom I can rely to read the politics of African American literature. In the middle and late 1960s, in the formation of the Black Power Movement and black nationalism from which flow, at the very least, the predicates of contemporary academic study of African American literature and culture, in that crucible which still informs the political terms and cultural forms by which those of us asserting a black identity or participating in a tradition of black creativity operate—for, despite my (or our) reservations about, distaste for, and conscious opposition to nationalisms, is our project not still the same, the valorization of blackness under the conditions of, and against, a persistent white supremacist domination?—for that project, there was a perceived *need* for Fanon. This need established a place for him in the African American, as well as the Afro-Diasporic, intellectual tradition. If it is arguably true that Fanon was often wrong, as recent biographer David Macey quotes one of Fanon's Algerian comrades as regretfully acknowledging, and if it is true that his American interpreters were sometimes wrong even concerning those things about which Fanon might have been right, and if it is the case that Americanizing Fanon dangerously ensnares his work in the misleading labyrinths of "seriously flawed translation," I say that it is also true that this need for Fanon—for what he assayed but might not have been able to complete or achieve, for what could not or did not translate of his thought from Martinique to France to Algeria and from French to English—strongly persists.[16] I reach for Fanon, with the eagerness and hunger of Jones becoming Baraka, in Fanon's invented and admittedly spurious capacity as the sketch artist of a hazy black universalism, the Einstein of an inchoate Unified Theory of Blackness, the very kind of theory which, arguably, he both attempted and disavowed. I take Fanon up in the manner that Newton et al. did, in much the same partly reverential, yet nevertheless ruthlessly appropriative spirit, with an attitude of willful—though, I hope, scrupulous—misreading that one brings to bodies of work occupying biblical status.

For me, Fanon is still needed to provide guidance for interpreting the meanings and operation of blackness in fields of representation. Fanon is a useful guide for analysis of the black literary—and his work is equally an object of such analysis—because in *Black Skin, White Masks* he proposes that to "be" black is to have been black*ened*. Viewed with the assistance of his psychiatric training and Sartrean existential phenomenology, blackness is revealed to Fanon as a figure, a clever and pernicious invention serving the particular cultural and psychological functions set for it by its inventors, the enslavers and conquerors of various African peoples: Fanon's is a psychoanalytic and phenomenological rendering of the cultural construction of blackness—a constructive process he calls "sociogeny." Fanon elucidates the qualities of the black figure, and how the identities that refer to that figure as if to an image stenciled into a mirror are rendered "abnormal" and pathological, so that a "true" *black* identity (even if, according to Lacanian psychoanalytic orthodoxy at least, a misrecognized one), a black integrated consciousness, even a black ontology, become all but impossible to attain. Fanon's purpose is to free his readers from the tyranny of a blackness that by its nature is subjugating: one becomes black in order to be subjugated by a conqueror who in creating you as black becomes white; blackness is both the mark and the means of subjugation. He means to disarticulate the cultural figure of blackness and its assigned properties from the persons who by dint of skin color are called on to introject it, or failing that, to have them seize control of the cultural figure en route to achieving a radical reconfiguration of what it is to be human, independent of, and in contradistinction to, racialized categories of being invented to facilitate conquest and domination.

Fanon's revisions of psychoanalysis and existential psychology describe how blackness comes to be and functions in and because of an ongoing history of social, political, and economic subjugation. It is for this reason that the most convincing part of Fanon's argument in *Black Skin* is not the aspect that concerns itself with the inner workings of the black subject— or perhaps, it is for this reason that insofar as Fanon does concern himself with these inner workings, he is often thought to be wrong.[17] Certainly Fanon's discussions of black subjectivity or the subject under conditions of colonialism open the way for theorizing race, gender and sexuality together with a thoroughness Fanon does not attempt to accomplish, and it is precisely his intriguing false starts in this arena that were the source for the wave of "critical Fanonism" that we generally attribute to Homi Bhabha and those following in his wake, with all the attendant strengths and weaknesses of that particular appropriation of Fanon.[18] But for my purposes the enduring strength of Fanon's argument lies in its theorizing of the sociogenic creation—and therefore the implicitly somewhat malleable quality, the capacity to be of use—of the *figure* of blackness, in a

Western culture that renders itself psychopathological (or proves its fundamental, constitutive psychopathology) by the invention and incorporation of the figure.

I am interested in using Fanon as he implies that blackness itself can be used: in some ways despite itself. Fanon is my guide in considering the cultural figure of blackness—but my purpose is not so much to help free us from the power of that figure as Fanon dared imagine, but the more modest but nevertheless daunting purpose of understanding better and more flexible uses of the figure than tend to prevail, and to examine whether it is also possible that even within Fanon's own account of a blackness-as-subjugation that must be abjured or surpassed, even within the lived experience of subjugation perceived to be at its worst, there are potential powers in blackness, uses that undermine or act against racist domination. These latter uses—the uses of blackness against the project of domination that constitutes it—Fanon mostly does not explicitly recognize, and when he does so, his endorsement of them is tepid. But I hope to show that these powers make a more powerful appearance than Fanon himself acknowledges, in the margins of his thought, in the rhetoric and metaphors with which he chooses to communicate, and that they operate as a kind of undertow within his theorizing.

In using Fanon in this fashion I am trying to learn something from Fanon about how to work *with*—that is, not dismissing, overcoming, transcending, or only struggling against—defeat. It is reasonable to say Fanon is about nothing so much as resistance to defeat, and about a refusal to give defeat any final acceptance, a refusal to acquiesce to it even while acknowledging the many wily ways that it can be effected—in fact, an insistence, as in *Wretched*, on anticipating the manifold and insidious forms of defeat so as to prevent it. Fanon will not *allow* defeat; he must be actively defeated, he will not collude in the process. But in so doing Fanon tells us what defeat is: he illuminates what he explicitly works to transcend or to deemphasize, and I am as drawn to these dismissals and obscurities as to his ringing avowals. And in fact I think that the most ringing avowals, those flights of rhetoric especially evident in *Black Skin* that stray both from hard-headed analysis of the facts and from practical planning for the real struggle on the ground to faintly glimpse a utopian emancipated future of the "new human," are mirrored and linked as we imagine mirror images are linked to the objects they reflect, to the very things he transcends, dismisses, obscures. As Fanon reads it, the resistance to defeat is the resistance to history, for history is defeat.

New Times: Culture and History in Fanon

> The body of history does not determine a single one of my ac-
> tions. . . . And it is by going beyond the historical, instrumental hy-
> pothesis that I will initiate the cycle of my freedom.
> —Frantz Fanon, *Black Skin, White Masks*[19]

To be black is to *have been* blackened: this is how I am describing a central
thesis of Fanon's.[20] This thesis is in large part argued in *Black Skin, White
Masks*, though it is also the case that in *The Wretched of the Earth*, Fanon's
discussion of the category of the "native" and that figure's late-kindled absolute opposition to the ruling powers of colonial Africa seeks to banish
from the reader's thought any notion that blackness is an a priori truth,
natural or eternal in its all-too-transparent meanings; in both texts Fanon
wishes to restore blackness/nativity to what he calls "the current of history."[21] I take this phrase to mean both that blackness must be revealed
in its historical character, with the origin of it laid precisely at the foot of
historical (not divine or natural) events, and that people who have been
rendered black, having been thus removed *from* history—petrified in the
fixed forms of European enslavers' projected fears and desires—must re-
enter a kind of Marxist-informed (or Hegelian) notion of historical becoming, as they remake themselves and bring about the disappearance of
both colonialism and the colonized man himself.[22]

Thus, Fanon endorses a strategy of historicizing, but only for the purpose of surpassing a condition defined as itself the arrest of historical
progress: only in order to restart, as it were, a progressive history always
latent in the very ontology of human being. Fanon expresses his view of
the limited uses of historicism in the battle against racist and colonial
domination thus: "The problem considered here is one of time. Those
Negroes and white men will be disalienated who refuse to let themselves
be sealed away in the materialized Tower of the Past. For many other
Negroes, in other ways, disalienation will come into being through their
refusal to accept the present as definitive."[23] It is to statements such as
these that Ato Sekyi-Otu refers when he observes that in Fanon there is
a demand to *restore* time. "What the figure of time loses in the 'colonial
context' is its status as a regulative principle in the narrative of social
being and the critique of domination; [in Fanon] it . . . functions . . . as
an 'ought,' an eviscerated organ of the social body that demands to be
resurrected."[24]

The temporal and historical are for Fanon *lived* partly as the cultural, and the challenge presented by the former is addressed by the remaking of the latter in the elongated struggle of throwing off the yoke of colonialism and establishing the nation. Culture is collective practices, beliefs, material creations that are in some sense adaptations to environmental—which is to say historically produced—conditions; culture is the sediment of and the response to, as well as the source for, historical legacies. Culture offers both constraint and possibility, in its being at once constituted by routinized past practices and naturalized (for Fanon, petrified) ideological positions, and by its capacity to be altered by different practices and new ideas. Fanon's decided preference in his elucidations of culture is for culture's malleability rather than for, say, the transmission of "values" or prejudices from ancestors. For him, true culture is opposed to custom, "for custom is always the deterioration of culture." This is so despite the fact that these deteriorations of culture nevertheless can provide a basis for spontaneous rebellion. Ultimately though, Fanonian culture is not worthy culture unless it is being daily remade by the demands of liberation struggle, a process in which "everything . . . [is] called in question" and the "former values and shapes" ascribed to tradition disappear, soon or late, because these former values have become the guarantors of colonized existence. "After the conflict there is not only the disappearance of colonialism but also the disappearance of the colonized man." Culture is made and remade in and through the continual making of the nation. The nation is a "necessity" for any true culture, and the forging of national consciousness (which is distinct from nationalism) is "the most elaborate form of culture."[25]

In a way, of course, Fanon's insistence that culture only truly comes to life as the very stuff on which revolution works and only exists as the practices that the development of national consciousness materialize is a sleight of hand: a way of playing with definitions, saying culture is not truly culture unless and until it is a culture bound up with national consciousness. The effect of this rhetorical redefinition is, at its strongest, to dismiss—and at its weakest, to deemphasize—the value of any prestruggle (which is to say, any postconquest or postenslavement) cultural practice: the past is where conquest and enslavement occurred, culture is the product of this past, and the overcoming or transcendence of the legacies of conquest and enslavement involves the transcendence of the culture which is their living—or rather, petrified, "mummified," undead—remainder and guarantor.[26]

The way that Fanon defines the cultural in *Wretched* is at one with the focus in *Black Skin* on the various psychopathological manifestations of introjected blackness; both inquiries point toward the psychic interiority of political defeat. That is, the challenge of achieving liberatory social and political goals is a challenge of how to remake unjust and oppressive social conditions, which is in large part a problem of confronting the psychological and psychic effects of historical events (themselves manifest as, or continually reestablished in the form of, cultural practices), since it is the past that bequeaths the boundaries of the conceptions of self and community—conquest/enslavement provides the ground for racialization and thus is constitutive of blackness—with which we have to labor (and against which we have to fight) in the present. The problem of history—the problem of being the inheritor of a past of conquest and the imposition of blackness or the category of the native, and of having introjected the lessons of that past in the form of culture and blackness in the form of an identity—can make a person consciously black or native feel he is "the living haunt of contradictions which run the risk of becoming insurmountable."[27]

Thus, when Fanon says, "In no way should I derive my basic purpose from the past of the peoples of color," he means that he cannot see how it would be possible to derive an emancipatory purpose from a past that established the conditions of enslavement and that repeats that enslavement in the repetitive forms of custom, tradition, and false culture.[28] The links between such a past and the present and potential future must be determinedly broken. "Like it or not, the past can in no way guide me in the present moment," he declares. "I will not make myself the man of any past. I do not want to exalt the past at the expense of my present and of my future." And "I am not the slave of the Slavery that dehumanized my ancestors"; "I am not a prisoner of history. I should not seek there for the meaning of my destiny. I should constantly remind myself that the real *leap* consists in introducing invention into existence."[29]

The profusion of Fanon's rhetorical attempts to cordon off the effects of the history of enslavement which establishes blackness (I have quoted only a few and will consider others more closely later) acquires a density in the text that calls attention to it as a supremely effortful, and therefore arguably abortive, move in his argument. Not surprisingly, given how the orientation of progressive analyses and politics in academia has become insistently, perhaps even dogmatically, historicist, Fanon's leap beyond historical constraint has not been convincing to contemporary interlocutors.

Hortense Spillers remarks that Fanon's "flat out" claim that history does not determine his actions is "too loud to be plausible." "While it is likely true that one can, on occasion, choose the narratives that he will call his own, it is also undeniable that certain other narratives will choose him, whether he will or not."[30] Paul Gilroy, invoking Fanon's pronouncements on history as an inspiring frame for his own appeal for a postrace future, nevertheless notes that Fanon's words bespeak a "youthful enthusiasm for existentialism" that by implication more mature reflection could only dampen; and though Gilroy aligns himself with Fanon's project and intent, he recognizes that Fanon is "struggling" without ultimate success to turn away from a past that insistently tugs him back into its decidedly racialized and imprisoning maw.[31] Similarly endorsing Fanon's commitment to futurity, Abdul JanMohamed notes that Fanon is sometimes "hyperbolic" in his dismissal of the past, though Fanon also addresses this matter with "better-modulated formulations."[32] For Sonia Kruks, Fanon's is an unfortunate partial reading of the existentialism he adopts and revises: Fanon "interprets the Sartrean claim that in authentic freedom 'I am my own foundation,' to mean that one can . . . through sheer commitment, leap beyond the bounds of historical situation."[33] Francoise Verges has been among the most forceful in her criticisms of Fanon's antihistoricist tilt, arguing that Fanon's failure to engage adequately the history of the Creole society of Martinique that he analyzes in *Black Skin* avoids theorizing "the *defeat* that slavery had been" and leads him to construct "a fantasmatic original innocence," thus cutting short a potentially productive elucidation of the psychological dimensions of racialized experience.[34]

My own view of this matter was once like Verges's, but I have come now to a position that is better reflected by Sekyi-Otu, who argues that Fanon's texts are haunted by "a repressed discourse of temporality," a repression that arises from Fanon's simultaneous incorporation and pointed revision of the temporality that is central to Marxist and Hegelian dialectics and conceptions of ontology.[35] That *temporality* is repressed in Fanon shapes his representations of *history* and its effects in profound ways. It may be the case not that Fanon ignores or merely wishes history away but that his theory of the historical, his way of thinking of its presence in the ongoing emergency of the now, involves an attempt to organize the information of history along nonlinear axes and in ways that frame its effects as not fully determinative: a reorganization and reframing that the all-questioning revolution which accompanies and grounds the formation of national (as opposed to racial) consciousness permits us to envision. It is true that such a formulation of the historical emerges in Fanon's texts rather as the symptom of the repression of temporality than as a worked-through philosophical view, but then the nature of temporality was not Fanon's primary concern in his writing, and the final shape of such a discourse, insofar as it swims somewhere below the upper fathoms of his prose, would undoubtedly for him make itself known in response to the needs of the people as they participate in forging the new nation and the new human. Which is to say, for Fanon, when a new conception of time and history are required to achieve a further degree of freedom, they will be invented.

In this sense what Fanon presents suggestively, even in the repression of an explicit engagement with the implacable ways that historical narratives "will choose him" against his will to be free of them, is not so far from what Spillers calls for in correcting him: "The question, then," Spillers says as she criticizes Fanon's evident misapprehension of historical necessities, "is how best to *interarticulate* the varied temporalities that arrive on the space of the 'now.'"[36] I would argue that Fanon's temporalities are in fact interarticulated; it is just that he does not map for us the thick webstrands that bind and colocate his often dismissed past, his catastrophic present, and his preferred future.

Spillers recruits Lacan to fill in Fanon's gaps; and though it is arguable that Lacan is the psychoanalyst Fanon least engages in his flirtations with the psychoanalytic,[37] it is useful to follow Spillers's lead for a moment to some of Lacan's remarks on time and history, to illuminate better the discourse of temporality that Fanon represses, since Lacan, like Fanon, is engaged with the operation of Hegelian dialectics in understanding the temporal. Spillers refers to Lacan's four temporalities: the physical past; the epic past of memory; the historic past in which man finds the guarantor of his future; the past that is the emergence of the Truth into the Real, which reveals itself in repetition.[38] In attempting to expand the seemingly narrow and ruthlessly instrumental vision of temporality and the effects of history critics find so unconvincing in Fanon, Spillers notes, "it is not a matter . . . of relocating, or 'remembering' something prior so much as it is *inventing* and *bringing to stand* the intersubjective formation."[39]

The centrality of the intersubjective in constituting history, historical events, and their persistence in—their apparent determination of—the present is for Lacan a way he describes how events, even those of an unconscious or "instinctual" nature, take place in subjectivity, on the stage, as it were, of an already subjectified (in and by language) consciousness; "in so far as they have been recognized in one particular sense or censored in a certain order," they are therefore always already historicized.[40] Like the past, what is being experienced now is historical and intersubjective, that is, penetrated and saturated by an omnipresent human discourse. "In order to be recognized by the other, I utter what was only in view of what will be. . . . What is realized in my history is not the past definite of what was, since it is no more, or even the present perfect of what has been in what I am, but the future anterior of what I shall have been for what I am in the process of becoming."[41]

Lacan's is in some ways a very Sartrean statement, and it is Sartre who provides the most convincing guide for reading Fanon's attempts to wrestle with the problem of history—with the problem of how encountering blackness and nativity is to encounter past defeats and traumas. I will return to Sartre later. For the moment, the *future anterior* as the nominative of the past corresponds to Fanon's way of working with temporality and history's effects as he represses or dismisses them. The past as future anterior is for Fanon constituted as that which prepares the way for what is to come—the realization of national consciousness, liberation, the new human—even though what is to come has not arrived (and never will arrive in the absolute, since the present recedes into the past and always flees toward its future, according to Sartre); and what the past has been cannot actually become clear except as a function of what it is becoming in the present oriented toward a chosen future. "If the question of practical solidarity with a given past ever arose for me," Fanon declares, "it did so only to the extent to which I was committed to myself and to my neighbor to fight for all my life and with all my strength so that never again would a people on the earth be subjugated."[42] The past only assumes a practical meaning in light of the liberated future (and the struggling present) that perhaps provides the necessary seed for it and that it could also correct— that is, rewrite, reconstitute, and even, for Fanon, erase.[43]

Thus, it is not so much a fantasy original innocence that Fanon points us toward—even if this is what he actually sometimes refers to—but a *future* innocence to be discovered in the clearing away of the viciously antihuman customs and cultural ways passed forward from the past, or, put another way, an "innocence" defined by its capacity to be constructed and that exists in the *now* of revolutionary struggle, and that is no less real for being menaced and fragile, because the process of true decolonization involves above all a willingness to participate in the process of remaking human being. This remaking is a fundamental aspect of Fanon's conception, because that process of making and remaking is what he calls sociogeny. Sociogeny as a concept refers both to the past—it is how black-ness comes to be in *Black Skin*; it is the mechanism of the invention of the native in *Wretched*—and to a malleable now, a plottable future. Sociogen-esis opposes the false universality of Western ontology, in which the par-ticulars that arise from historical and cultural forces are transposed into a realm of transcultural and transhistorical (or acultural and ahistorical) ideal.[44] Thus, the concept of sociogeny historicizes the lived experience of humans; but I would argue that Fanon's ultimate emphasis is not on the determinative qualities of the historical particularity that sociogeny unveils but on the very limitedness and political *partiality* of that history, and thus on what we might think of as the existential partiality that his-tory produces—which is to say, sociogenesis reveals the degree to which blackness, since it is not eternal or natural, is also not in any sense final or complete: blackness is instead a particular and partial molding of human possibility—an "amputation," as Fanon refers to it;[45] history does not take the place of God.

To my reading of Fanon, and others', it is reasonable to object that there is still in Fanon's texts an unwillingness to grapple with the often in-tractable and at the very least exceedingly tricky persistence of past nar-ratives in their constitution of the subject itself, as well as "race," "nation," and the like. But it seems to me Fanon's bifurcated focus on the sociogenic process that produces blackness (from a pessimistic perspective), on the one hand, and on sociogeny's *power* to make a "new human" in the present and future, on the other, are most usefully viewed as indissolubly linked. In this sense what has been done in the past—a sociogenic process—is a demonstration of what can be done better, in a prohuman, rather than antihuman, way, in the present that builds toward its utopian future. The terrible past proves the possibility of the liberated future rather than re-lentlessly constraining its possibilities (which is what Fanon fears a doctri-naire historicist argument might tend toward, by ascribing overdetermina-tive qualities to the history it carefully excavates). If man was not made by God but by man, then that he *has been* made in the past proves he *can be* (and for Fanon, is being) made again. The very process of becoming "fixed" as an embodiment defined and determined by its skin color, which renders Fanon's black "I" in "The Fact [or Lived-Experience] of Blackness" the repository of a subjugating historicity (tom-toms, cannibalism, etc.), is an example of the tangible possibility of the new human that Fanon's liberatory practice hails from afar; they are spoken of in the same lan-guage, for the "new man" of the future appears in his antihumanist guise as "a new kind of man, a new genus . . . a Negro!" when white supremacy operates successfully.[46] In this sense the past is not necessarily fully transcended, but the past is not a prison, either; it is rather the record and example of its own revision—however difficult that revision might be, and however clearly beset by the forces of reaction, which *Wretched* spends the bulk of its pages warning against, that ceaselessly work to bear us back into a present and past defined by white supremacy and colonialism. Thus, my earlier reference to the directionality that constitutes the past in Fanon's conception as a "seed" for the present is somewhat misleading: it is a seed without a teleology of certain growth, a gene without determinate expression—it is more properly an *analogy* for present and future sociogenic processes; it is a model or a metaphor.

Hence, Fanon, in the midst of arguing against what was a widely held assumption in the community of European psychologists that colonized peoples possessed an innate (culturally prescribed) "dependency complex," asserts that whatever psychological postures are associated with such a complex ought properly to be ascribed to a sociogenic process.

> A Malagasy is a Malagasy; or, rather, no, not he *is* a Malagasy, but rather . . . if he is a Malagasy, it is because the white man has come and if at a certain stage he has been led to ask himself whether he is indeed a man, it is because his reality has been challenged. . . . I begin to suffer from not being a white man to the degree that the white man imposes discrimination on me, makes me a colonized native.[47]

In this context Fanon boldly states that the effect of colonial conquest (and thus of enslavement) is to extirpate wholly the preconquest psychology of the conquered and enslaved.

> The reactions and the behavior patterns to which the arrival of the European in Madagascar gave rise were not tacked on to a pre-existing set. There was no addition to the earlier psychic whole. . . . The arrival of the white men in Madagascar shattered not only its horizons but its psychological mechanisms. . . . [The black man's] customs and the sources on which they were based, were wiped out.[48]

In *The Wretched of the Earth* this assessment of the effect of colonial conquest takes a slightly different form, though substantially the same, as Fanon shifts focus from psychology to culture; there the pattern illuminated is one of perpetual arrest, of a preconquest culture which has been exsanguinated and exists only as a shell of its former being. "By the time a century or two has passed there comes about a veritable emaciation of . . . national culture. . . . [T]here is no real creativity and no overflowing life. . . . [Under] colonial domination we find a culture that is rigid in the extreme, . . . the dregs of culture. . . ." And, "In the colonial situation, culture . . . falls away and dies."[49]

Such narratives of total rupture, of one psychology, one culture, effectively erasing another, are less statements of the lived process of conquest and enslavement (i.e., they are not accurate or reliable historicist renderings of those events) than reflections and conscious repetitions on Fanon's part of the very epistemic and hermeneutic work of effective conjury that informs the colonizer's and enslaver's narratives. The colonialist, as we know, imposes a concept of history on those he conquers and enslaves, as a mode of conquest and enslavement: "The settler *makes* history. . . . He is the absolute beginning," Fanon writes. "Colonialism . . . turns to the past of the oppressed people, and distorts, disfigures, and destroys it." The settler's ability to assume this position is due to his building the world on the foundation of his invention, which is "primary Manicheism."[50] Fanon's identification of the imposition of the historiographic as a mode of domination thus tries to take a view on what counts as history without necessarily conceding to what the colonizer and enslaver defines as a historical process; if historicism is one of the enslaver's tools, then not only is it useful to take a stance with respect to history that does not respect orthodox historicist strictures,[51] but it is even more useful to take note of and use the power to *invent* a mode of history in much the same way that Fanon perceives the colonizer to do under the guise of historicism. Such a powerful *creative* (sociogenic) capacity also lies within the ambit of those struggling to achieve decolonization; the break between what has existed before and what will exist in the future is analytically (or rhetorically) similar to the break that was effected between preconquest and the instantiation of the colonial period. Again, "After the conflict there is not only the disappearance of colonialism but also the disappearance of the colonized man."[52]

Fanon's absolutes with regard to history, then, are rhetorical incitements. When Fanon closely considers the question of how culture and tradition are lived in relation to conquest, he is more nuanced: "Colonialism obviously throws all elements of native society into confusion. . . . [C]olonial domination distorts the very relations that the colonized maintains with his own culture. . . . [T]he practice of tradition is a disturbed practice."[53] This description of labilities, of distortions and disturbances rather than ruptures and erasures, is the view of how history affects current practice on the ground and how change actually occurs. But if one is thinking about the immense power of sociogeny, then such a view is too cramped; it is insufficient: what is then required is an acknowledgment of, and a willingness to move toward, the radical otherness envisioned by an idea of life different from those ideas which have controlled the past and condition the present. The possibility of radical difference, which is after all a *proven* possibility because colonialism was established and reorganized the world in precisely the manner of the introduction of a radical difference—the possibility range that is inherent to sociogenic process—is what Fanon's rejection or diminution of historicism and his nascent alternative temporality attempt to capture.

"[T]here must be an idea of man and of the future of humanity," Fanon writes, if real freedom is to be achieved. That the radical difference colonization makes is not just a matter of an idea, of course, shows itself also in Fanon's thinking about how the future can be made different. Colonialism becomes colonialism as such through the coordination and confluence of countless acts of bloody violence, countless iterations of evolving justificatory ideologies, and countless bodies, minds, and material and financial resources committing the acts and iterating the set of beliefs that justify them. Thus, a change of mindset, a revision of culture, is not effective without the forms of action Fanon labels—more complexly than is sometimes imagined—as violence. "Violence alone, violence committed by the people, violence organized and educated by its leaders, makes it possible for the masses to understand social truths and give the key to them."[54] At this point in Fanon's argument he is no longer mapping out the various ways in which the violence of colonization is reflected back on the colonizer by those who have been blackened and made natives; the violence he speaks of here is not that of primary or primitive Manicheism but that of the deeply transformative action that reorients social and political relations as and through shaping the epistemes of reality anew.[55]

Demarcations between the past, present, and future, while not susceptible to a thorough demolition, can in the crucible of sociogenic power lose their apparent certainty. Hence, Fanon writes in *The Wretched of the Earth*, as he concludes his discussion of the case studies of mental disorders he encountered during the Algerian revolutionary war,

There must be no waiting until the nation has produced new men;
there must be no waiting until men are imperceptibly transformed by
revolutionary processes in perpetual renewal. It is quite true that these
two processes are essential, but consciousness must be helped. The
application of revolutionary theory, if it is to be completely liberating
and particularly fruitful, exacts that nothing unusual should exist. One
feels with particular force the necessity to totalize the event, to draw
everything after one, to settle everything, to be responsible for everything. Now conscience no longer boggles at going back into the past,
or at marking time if it is necessary. This is why in the progress made
by a fighting unit over a piece of ground the end of an ambush does
not mean rest, but rather is the signal for consciousness to take another step forward, for everything ought to keep pace together.[56]

The language here suppressing the "unusual" and assuming responsibility for everything speaks to how central consciousness and theorizing are
to sociogenic processes, matters that I will explore more fully later. Note,
however, how the historical is subject in this vision to what a progressively
developing consciousness renders it to be, and how the temporal is pli-
able, an instrument rather than a parameter. The "draw[ing] of everything
after one" is a cultural change, in the now, that also changes what has gone
before it—the past—as each piece has to be reassessed and rearranged according to current exigencies. Sociogenic process implies the active revision of history. Such temporal facility is in marked contrast both to the
"cultural mummification" suffered at the societal level because of colonization and to the individual mummification that the colonized native experiences when he continually crashes without sufficient resistance against
the wall of colonial and racist power: "The past for him is a burning past,"
Fanon says of the black/native. "What he hopes is that he will . . . never
again be face to face with that past."[57]

Note also that the "particular force" impelling such sociogenic revisions
of history is represented by the metaphor of bodily movement (i.e., not
resting, steps forward, keeping pace). This is a common enough rhetorical
choice, to be sure, but one which holds a particular significance for Fanon,
because, as we shall see, the body and its movements are frequently a central metaphor for him, in addition to being—and perhaps it is the metaphor of choice precisely because of this fact—a literal site in which the
struggle for freedom is fought.

Declarations of the absolute decimation of the preexisting psyche of the colonized in the event of conquest thus can be read as versions of the past—historically inaccurate versions, to be sure, invocations of Verges's "original innocence"—that stand in rhetorically for the blank slate of the future. The future's slate is not really blank, of course, but it can be written; the words already on it are not vouchsafed by anything transhistoric like God or nature. If Fanon's rhetoric proposes at times a truly blank slate, then his considered examinations of the process of cultural and subjective transformation (or, more modestly, reformation) suggest rather that he employs the absolute of "total" cultural loss and the like only to mark a place for the successful achievement of a future utopia; neither the absolute past as defeat nor the absolute future as liberation and victory are the areas of anything other than directional emphasis—it is instead the fact that there *can be* movement toward one or another that is truly to be grasped and that demonstrates for us what the *power* of sociogeny is.

The interarticulation of temporal frames that underwrites Fanon's approach to the problem of history is nicely demonstrated in a curious form of logical proof he offers for the transformative psychological effects of colonialism: when arguing that the European's arrival in Madagascar utterly eviscerated the pre-Malagasy "earlier psychic whole," Fanon says, "If . . . Martians undertook to colonize the earth men—not to initiate them into Martian culture but to *colonize* them—we should be doubtful of the persistence of any earth personality."[58] This bit of speculative futurism, the conflation of historical Europeans with space-trekking Martians, partaking as it does of anxieties and fantasies running rife in the 1950s because of the competition between the United States and the Soviet Union to put men into space, represents the way that Fanon sees the past (European arrival on the shores of what they will call Madagascar) as a mirror of the future. We might say that Fanon gestures both backward and forward when he tries to wrestle with history—backward to the loss that occasioned the originary act of self-fashioning or cultural reinscription (and this for him has to do with the notion that the precolonial world is utterly obliterated) and forward toward the new productivity that has its foundation in the example of the old rupture.

Thus, when Fanon asks, "Have I no other purpose on earth, then, but to avenge the Negro of the seventeenth century?" and when he remonstrates with the historicist reader, "Moral anguish in the face of the massiveness of the Past? I am a Negro, and tons of chains, storms of blows, rivers of expectoration flow down my shoulders. . . . But I do not have the right to allow myself to bog down. . . . I do not have the right to allow myself to be mired in what the past has determined," we need not read these statements as mere rallying cries to turn one's back on history in order to meet a present emergency, or as an entirely wishful leaping over the persistent effects of the 17th century—effects which, after all, Fanon elucidates as the psychopathologizing properties of blackness itself.[59] We can rather see such rhetoric as suggesting that the determinative powers of the past do not lie solely in the dominion of past events; for Fanon, the present is *like* the past in its capacity to determine the future. In this sense, there is not only one past, forever lost to us but nevertheless enslaving present and future, but also the past being made (and ever receding) in the now, which, as future anterior, has the capacity retroactively to refigure even the more remote, traumatic past that we have no access to. Fanon's rhetoric identifies a *leap* in the construction of the human world in the past and uses this as a basis for proposing another such leap in the present, oriented toward a more humanist future.

This alternative temporality is not linear. Nor is it exactly nonlinear, since Fanon's temporality preserves linearity of a kind in the desired teleology of a humanist future, which he never abandons. The alternative temporality that Fanon gestures toward as a riposte to the colonizer's use of historicism as the prop of its domination, then, it is perhaps more properly described as *counter*linear, insofar as the linear as a key component of temporality too often helps buttress the overly determinative powers of a miserable "burning past" of conquest and enslavement.

If, as I have noted earlier, culture is the sediment of and the response to, as well as the source for, historical legacies, then for Fanon, despite its tendency under colonial domination to ossify, culture can share the qualities of counterlinear temporality with which sociogenic processes endow the historical (as that concept is tentatively and incompletely revised by Fanon). Culture as the mediation of the historical—especially the "true" culture wrought in the necessary inventiveness of revolutionary (and violent, in its physical and epistemic sense) struggle—is how the interarticulation of temporalities is lived.

We begin to see, then, glimpses of ways to work with the problem of history: through culture, which is the product of history. We begin to see how the burning past—the terrible past of being rendered native, of blackening—lived in the now as blackness, does hold within it certain resources for resistance: blackness as that which has been made proves, and provides a template for, the process of *making human* that is sociogeny. The presence of this resource—a resource of blackness, a resource available in defeat: black power, as I am working with it here—is generally passed over or diminished by Fanon, consigned to the realm of necessary-but-surpassed in the main thrust of his theorizing. It appears as an under-theorized portion of his argument, in the crevices of Fanon's thought, almost purely as metaphor: as the metaphor of muscular tension.

.   .   .

I consider the metaphor of muscle tension later in this chapter. But in bringing this segment of the argument to a close, briefly I would like to note the resonance between Fanon's approach to history and the Black Power thinkers who frequently misread him, a resonance that might well be the result of the fact that, despite the avowed dissimilarities between the situations of Jomo Kenyatta and Richard Wright, there was not such a clear dissimilarity between Wright and Fanon himself, since both were natives of the Americas.[60] Culture as the shackle left behind by a history of enslavement might, again, make Fanon's texts a poor bible for the Black Power/Black Arts Movement insofar as cultural nationalism is its central tenet—as it is, say, for Baraka. But a similar stance toward the temporal and historical animates aspects of Black Power's confrontation with white supremacy. What Fanon shares with Newton, Cleaver, and Baraka is a distinctly New World ancestral history that converges and parallels: African capture, enforced dispersal across the docking points of the Middle Passage, enslavement, racialization. Though Fanon is keen to elucidate the mechanisms of the most lasting of these historical developments, indeed in the act of analyzing racialization to historicize it, at least insofar as he removes it from the realm of eternal truth and renders it a particular creation of a set of political, military, and economic events, Fanon is not historicist, and neither were most Black Power intellectuals. Both have a tendency, arguably shared by many people working feverishly to effect political change against the inertia of established and jealous hegemonic powers, sometimes to play loosely with history.

The attempt to reclaim the history of black folks from the deliberately disempowering caricatures of Africans and African Americans in the accounts endorsed by the U.S. educational system and accepted as more or less common knowledge was of course a popular strategy among Black Arts writers, particularly for inciting people to revolutionary action. In the

1960s period of racial re-formation, when culture was a primary terrain of battle, the push was to illuminate the achievements of heroic black male figures such as Nat Turner, as against figures associated with minstrelsy which had so saturated American popular representation.[61] This project of reclamation underlay the ardent revisions of notions of the acquiescent American slave that informed the new historiography of slavery in the 1970s and the advent of fictional treatments of the slave period—both of which owe their directions of inquiry and representation to the Black Power/Black Arts Movements. At the same time, this historicizing strategy sometimes led black cultural nationalists to disparage what they perceived as the docility and failure of previous generations of African Americans—hence the transformation of Harriet Beecher Stowe's character into the quickly proliferating insult of calling someone "an Uncle Tom," a rhetorical assignment that starkly differentiated the virile (and definitively masculine) revolutionary of the present from his meek and accommodating ancestors.

This recurring drift toward the notion of the black past as irredeemable (rather than complex, and a resource, i.e., "usable" for the present) and the liberated future as that past's repudiation Fanon and Black Power intellectuals to some extent shared. Baraka's and Ture's decisions to discard their "slave names," a practice popularized by the example of Malcolm X, might be said to parallel Fanon's approach to history; the slave name rejected is the slave history erased, with all its Uncle Tomming and Stepin Fetchit legacies trampled under the feet of the vanguard's march of progress. Moreover, it is a strategy which interarticulates temporal frames, reaching backward and forward: backward to the unstained preslavery semimythological past of Mother Africa, forward to a pan-African liberated future where "Imamu Amiri Baraka," a concoction of Bantu and Muslim naming not tied to a specific cultural location in the African homeland, acquires resonant meaning in the context of an international Black World.

Perhaps, then, there is a distinctly American optimism that underlies both Fanon's and Black Power thinkers' partial readings of history and the antihistoricist turn (or the counterlinear interpretation of temporality) they sometimes take—or rather, there is an adoption, even an unconscious acceptance, of accreted representations and ideological formulations of American exceptionalism itself. As Toni Morrison succinctly puts it, "that well-fondled phrase, 'the American Dream,'" for European immigrants usually entailed a "rushing from" conditions of "constraint and limitation" supposedly left behind on a continent that earned the sobriquet "the *Old* World" because its realities and exigencies had, by the apparent magic of geographical relocation, become transcended history.[62] In this sense nowhere is what we might perceive to be Fanon's perhaps overly optimistic conviction concerning the malleability of historical legacy better justified—or at least, more strongly affirmed by habitual modes of thinking—than in the context of the Americas, where the rhetoric of new Edens, new slates, New Worlds has long constructed the historical as a narrative abruptly ended and then begun anew.

A conceptual mapping of the relation between Old and New Worlds— between the sociogenic reconstitution of reality that colonizing and enslaving enacts—underlies Fanon's argument in *The Wretched of the Earth*, when he dismisses the Western-educated native intellectual's thirst for cultural traditions preexisting the colonial period. "Colonial domination, because it is total . . . very soon manages to disrupt in spectacular fashion the cultural life of a conquered people. . . . Within the framework of colonial domination there is not and there *will never be* such phenomena as new cultural departures." Colonial conquest effects "cultural obliteration"—eternally, until revolutionary struggle, which is movement in and along with the teleological current of history, dispatches the old in a manner both imperceptible (since "mummified fragments" and "outworn contrivances" remain visible) and total, writing history in a way that charts epochal transformation in the same space and time as gradual evolutionary or dialectical growth occurs.[63]

Fanon's assessment of the variegated ancient cultures of Africa north and south as they change under colonial domination would sometimes appear to underestimate a richness of creative adaptation that it seems reasonable to state is always the province of what we call culture: culture is never wholly static or utterly bereft of the foxy persistence of the people that practice and make it in their claim to live—a fact which Fanon asserts to be true during revolutionary struggle but does not perceive operating in the absence of it. Moreover, it would be difficult to adduce a reasonable account of any human culture that has not been powerfully shaped, somewhere in its history, by an encounter with "the foreign" under conditions of unequal exchange (in fact, some form of inequality in these encounters would be more likely the norm than the exception): human culture *becomes* culture precisely by borrowing and by imposition, under domination and in the process of dominating, rather than by mythical autochthonous development. Fanon denies or overlooks the complexities of cultural adaptation under conditions of political and cultural domination in order to illuminate rhetorically—and thus to make it possible to seize culturally and politically—the power of remaking reality for revolutionary purposes; and in these arguments it seems to me that Fanon, as a native of the Americas, has transferred the model of history that has come to him through the legacy of Europeans' stories about their journeys from Old to New Worlds, to Africa and the rest of the Third World. It is thus in the temporal dimension and approaches to historical legacy that I make a plea for the Americanist Fanon, the Fanon who is "getting it wrong" even as those Americans who appropriate him misread him—and it is all the more appropriate that the temporal should provide this avenue of appropriating Fanon, because time in Fanon is the forgotten, the undertheorized, just as in the whole of Fanon's corpus the (black) Americas are a backwater, a repressed and peripheral presence.

Of Muscles and Mirages

For Fanon, blackness is largely either a fetter of colonialist domination or a means, though not an end, of incipient revolutionary resistance, to be eventually superseded by categories of the national (for example, the Algerian) or even the international (the African). Yet it is precisely at this to-be-surpassed early point in the progression of an emancipated consciousness in Fanon's discussion in *Wretched*—largely detailed in his chapter "Spontaneity: Its Strengths and Weaknesses" but referred to at other points throughout *Wretched* (and in the writings collected in *A Dying Colonialism* and *Toward the African Revolution* as well)—that I see the opportunity to translate between the worlds of white supremacist domination in Fanon's Africa and his Caribbean/Americas, and that, I would argue, might better have served as a point of entry for Black Power intellectuals' adoption of Fanon than the more famous "Concerning Violence" to which they and so many of his interpreters turned.

The "spontaneous" rebellion of Fanon's Africans against colonial regimes erupts from the boiling cauldron of "racial feeling" inculcated by the colonialists themselves and, for the peasantry, from the fact that they "never stopped clutching at a way of life which was in practice anti-colonial."[64] Fanon cautions that such resources are substantial, even indispensable, but ineffectual in the long term. They "cannot sustain a war of liberation"; "the leader realizes, day in and day out, that hatred alone cannot draw up a program." In the absence of this program (a lack, as we know, retrospectively identified in many movements and revolutions throughout the world in the mid- to late 20th century) the colonized people, blackened like their cross-oceanic American cousins by the ingenious discursive domination of the colonizers, rely, with initial joy but to their eventual detriment, on "the mirage of [their] . . . muscles' own immediacy."[65]

Mirages and muscles are Fanon's metaphors for ways of life that become significant anticolonial resources because they are rendered distinct from the ways of life of the colonizers, by laws and daily social practices that create races in order to segregate them. Together the metaphors speak both to ephemerality, the "error" of what is in truth only an imagined fundamental difference, and to materialization, the apparent embodiment of this difference as lived experience. In back of the metaphor of muscles is of course the metaphor of the body. Fanon's rhetoric, or his turn to arguably literary device, touches on what we currently take to be a truism, that the body is both material and discursive (or, to put it differently, that we only know the body as the material trace of discourse), that it is both a social construction and a concrete reality—because concrete reality is socially constructed and, arguably, because the social construction of reality finds its template in the construction of what might be called the physical or the flesh as *body*.[66] The immediate perception of a real difference, of an absolute alterity, in the colonial scene is a hallucination, a mirage; nonetheless that mirage is lived, experienced, materialized *as* the (blackened) body, or rather *on* black skin.

My point here is to highlight Fanon's use of mirages and muscles as profoundly limited (i.e., erroneous, hallucinatory, illusory) but nevertheless active (or material, embodied) resources of resistance and rebellion. They have a potency that can be used, which seems particularly important for the translation of Fanon's theorizing of decolonization to the context of the Americas, since Fanon's description of the colonized African's reliance on "racial feeling" and the "legitimate desire for revenge" most closely accords with the social and political situation of the Black Power intellectuals who adopted his work and, I would argue, accounts in great part for the enthusiasm with which they read him—or felt moved to claim to have done so.[67] My interest is in looking to these muscles not as providing *the* answer to the riddle of decolonization or antiracist triumph, not as a substitute for what must become the rationality of a program aimed at creating or abetting national consciousness which Fanon advocates, but as a space properly to be viewed in its own right: in the depths of subjugation, where what appears to be available is only violent resistance (motion), still other (but not decisive with respect to decolonization) forms of possibility present themselves—and by *possibility* I mean attributes or instances of the possible as such, the potential of transformation in however limited, constrained, or attenuated a configuration, perhaps even forms of freedom (and pleasure?). To be clear: as I go forward I do not wish to unduly valorize these possibilities, as better than, or substitutions for what are, in Fanon's view and mine, the ideal, material (and politically hard-sought) freedoms they fail to sustain successfully. Nevertheless my interest is in these meager resources and the failed and even abortive strategies that flow from them, because they have been useful and because even in meagerness and failure they are rich, and not without effective capability; and there may yet be something to gain from the recognition of them as we try (as Fanon did) to meet the challenge of the defeat already imposed on us (the defeat that *makes* us) by the problem of history.

.   .   .

The alliterative alignment of *mirage* and *muscles* (in French and English) performs for the eye reading the page what Fanon's argument asserts: spontaneity, that is, race-consciousness, incipient race-nationalism, metaphorically represented as the muscles of the body, is an insufficient resource for achieving decolonization; rather, action (muscularity) in accordance with an ever-developing and all-questioning national *consciousness* is required. What muscles provide—immediacy, and immediate satisfaction—is illusory, without ultimate substance, a mirage, in much the same way that Negritude is "the great black mirage."[68] That the body would be Fanon's metaphorical site for revolution's beginning and its threatened failure is not surprising, since one of the most consistent arguments in *Black Skin, White Masks* is that the very category of blackness in the European cultural imaginary is a kind of offal-bin for fears and desires that coalesce around the body, where the body is a site cleaved from the supposedly higher and more rational mind; *Black Skin* asserts that such fears and desires are themselves pathological, symptoms of cultural as well as individual dis-ease. Thus, to rely, as the colonized in the initial stages of revolutionary process do, on Western culture's misapprehension of reality as defined by the black/white binary is to rely also on a misrecognition of the body as a low and fearful entity. Alongside blackness, linear temporality, historicity, and the cultural and historical presence of the Americas, then, we might also place the metaphor of body and muscles on the list of the surpassed, the repressed, the undertheorized and largely suggestive in Fanon's thought. These concepts and figures are connected to one another; and all of them, in their appearance in Fanon's theory as minor terms, present us with a sketch of the psychic and political dimensions of living with—and indeed, having or exercising a form of power within— the condition of defeat (of having been blackened).

The term that haunts "the mirage of his muscles' own immediacy" of course is the mind, which would represent national consciousness. Fanon does not wish to take a Cartesian stance and elevate the mind over the body with this rhetoric: he exhorts us, "Let us decide not to imitate Europe; let us combine our muscles and our brains in a new direction. Let us try to create the whole man."[69] Muscles (body; blackness) and mind (national consciousness) are to work in tandem. Again, the choice of this particular metaphor-bundle is in some ways common, if anything overdetermined, though the relationship of blackness to the body in the Western cultural imaginary as Fanon maps it gives a definite (and indeed, historicized) shape to that overdetermination.

Nevertheless, the language collapsing muscles with mirages and reinvigorating them with the intervention of a mind suffused with its revolutionary engagements is not entirely figurative: Fanon was a psychiatric practitioner, and the concluding section of *The Wretched of the Earth*, "Colonial War and Mental Disorders," concerns itself precisely with the body-mind nexus as Fanon encountered it in patients whose psychological and physical afflictions bore a direct relation to the traumas they experienced in events related to the Algerian War. "Today, we know very well that it is not necessary to be wounded by a bullet in order to suffer from the fact of war in body as well as in mind," Fanon announces. Similarly, one of Fanon's earliest published essays, "The 'North African Syndrome,'" concerns itself with North African immigrants to France and discusses the "pain without lesion, illness distributed in and over the whole body" that immigrants suffer as a symptom of colonial depersonalization.[70]

Arguably the most famous passage from *Black Skin, White Masks*, published in the same year as "The 'North African Syndrome,'" from the chapter "The Fact [or Lived-Experience] of Blackness," centrally concerns itself with the impact of racism on the black person's perceived bodily integrity. In that passage, Fanon's black everyman, an anonymous "I," is traveling on a train in France, and a white child sees him and screams, "Look, a Negro!" From an initial amused reaction—the child's cry is "an external stimulus that flicked over me," the narrative says—Fanon's black "I" descends quickly to a point where his "corporeal schema" crumbles, and he experiences the nausea of having been made an object.[71]

The point I wish to draw attention to in this much-discussed scene of racial interpellation is the disintegration of Fanon's figure's corporeal schema; because the black everyman has been made aware of a constellation of culturally shared ideas about his body, he no longer has an organic—or perhaps even ontological—access to his body: he loses his touchstone to reality. This state of being at a distance from the body one inhabits and that one is, is the condition of blackness, an ever-present state of which Fanon's Negro becomes most intensely aware at moments of traumatic contact. As a consequence of such traumatic encounters, the Negro does not properly develop his bodily schema. To be forced to be conscious of the body is to Fanon a "negating activity"; it creates a "third-person consciousness." The healthy self-consciousness, by contrast, has an "implicit knowledge" of its body.[72] A healthy man slowly becomes aware of his-body-as-himself by experiential fashioning of a physiological self, through a dialectic engaged with the spatiotemporal world; knowledge of the body and bodily experience occur in one fell swoop and are indeed more or less the same: "I do not bring together one by one the parts of my body; this translation and this unification are performed once and for all within me: they are my body, itself."[73] Explicit knowledge of oneself or one's body in relation to the world, on the other hand, is self-consciousness in its conversational sense, as in, "I was nervous, and so I became self-conscious." This is the constant experience into which the Negro is interpellated, because he has to work with two frames of reference, not only to be black but to be black in relation to the white man, to become "responsible" for his own body, for his race, and for his ancestors.[74] Neither we nor Fanon need make the claim that this kind of self-consciousness (in the conversational sense) is something that only people of color experience, merely that it is a core constituent of blackness in a way that such self-consciousness is not a core constituent of whiteness. Moreover, the fact that this cultural and psychological mechanism is manifested in a host of economic, social, and political tangibles that impress themselves powerfully on the daily lives of the black/native would tend to distinguish it from types of self-consciousness whose origins lie in more local and circumscribed individual or family dynamics (and this fact would also distinguish black third-person consciousness from those forms of self-consciousness which we might deem universal).[75]

The experience in this disassembled corporeal state is of "nonexistence," at least insofar as the "mental oneness" of "I"-experience devolves into a curious twoness: "straddling Nothingness and Infinity," as Fanon describes it.[76] Of course, the assertion of *mental oneness* as the mark of nontraumatized subjectivity, especially appearing as it does in Fanon's long footnote—and primary extended reference—to Lacan, must strike us as ironic, or misguided, since for Lacan such mental oneness is always, precisely, a mirage made up of *imago* and language, and subjectivity itself is constitutively traumatized. But Fanon is revising Lacan: for him, the constitutive trauma has a specific historical location in colonial conquest, enslavement, and racialization. Moreover, Fanon posits an authentic state untouched by that trauma, toward which his participation in revolutionary activity enables him to aspire.

This authenticity is not, as Verges contends, merely the fantasy of an impervious masculinist ideal, in which all "ambivalence, weakness, and ambiguity" are banished in favor an "autonomous self, uninhibited by ties of desire and love."[77] It is instead an authenticity only provisionally secured by the ceaseless development of national consciousness, but which can be experienced in and as an ideal—but a materialist ideal—of bodily integrity. Verges is correct, however, that Fanon's vision of the "new man" is masculinist at the core of its conception, and even his concern to reintegrate the black body as a form of healing—which, for him, is ultimately to transcend and transform its historically prescribed blackness—arguably references a male rather than a female body, in that bodily integrity has a metonymic relation to ideals of self-containment, defensible separateness, and inviolability, which the Western paradigm of the female body, as vessel of children and as entered by the penis in reproductive sexuality, does not support; even where Fanon is most visionary, a masculinist bias shapes his otherwise conscientiously radical thinking.

The twoness of black experience, its always straddling putatively opposing categories of being, is of course not new in Fanon, especially from an Americanist perspective. But for Fanon, Du Bois's double-consciousness is slightly recast as double-*bodiedness*. Speaking as a psychiatrist confronted with the too easily dismissed physical problems of his North African patients (such as muscle contraction), Fanon encapsulates his encounter with these symptoms in the following terms: "this body which is no longer altogether a body or rather which is doubly a body since it is beside itself with terror."[78] Double-bodiedness is the price of being constructed in the Western cultural imaginary as *the* body—"the unidentifiable, the unassimilable" body, the hypersexual, hypertrophic body, the body that is *bad*. It is "with the Negro that the cycle of the *biological* begins," Fanon states.[79]

The moment of contact removes Fanon's Negro from a presumably au-thentic, integrated embodied experience and snares him in the meshes of in-authentic racial-epidermal schematics, inscribes on his skin overlapping chi-merical and hallucinatory grids that mask social, political, and psychological truths—which is to say, these schematics and grids are the concealed record of a sociogenic process.

Fanon locates the deforming effects of racialization and the ideal against which such deformations should be measured in the body partly because that is the most fundamental foundation of human freedom that his read-ing of French phenomenological theory leads him toward. We should see Fanon's repeated use of the metaphor of muscles as always in some way referring to his diagnoses of mind/body disease and to the theoretics of the body in French existential phenomenology. Fanon explains the im-proper development of the Negro's corporeal schema by quoting from Mau-rice Merleau-Ponty's *The Phenomenology of Perception*; and of course, Sartre informs Merleau-Ponty, as Sartre informs Fanon. It is from Merleau-Ponty that Fanon takes the concept of the corporeal schema. The notion of the bodily schema, and its fundamental place in the universe of human being, is described by Merleau-Ponty thus: "My body is the seat or rather the very actuality of the phenomenon of expression . . . , and there the visual and auditory experiences, for example, are pregnant one with the other, and their expressive value is the ground of the antepredicative unity of the perceived world, and, through it, of verbal expression . . . and intellectual significance." Further, "My body is the fabric into which all objects are wo-ven, and it is, at least in relation to the perceived world, the general instru-ment of my 'comprehension.' . . . It is my body which gives significance not only to the natural object, but also to cultural objects like words."[80]

This sort of statement is arguably an elaboration on statements such as the following by Sartre, which assert that the body and the for-itself (consciousness) are constitutively linked: "the body is a necessary charac-teristic of the for-itself. . . . The very nature of the for-itself demands that it be body"; "The body is not a screen between things and ourselves; it manifests only the individuality and the contingency of our original rela-tion to instrumental-things."[81] It is for this reason that Sartre, as well as Merleau-Ponty, frequently speaks of consciousness, that fundamental unit of human existence, as *existing* the body.[82] In this ruthlessly antispiritual conception of reality, consciousness has no meaning without the physi-cal body that it can only metaphorically be said to "inhabit"; conscious-ness *is* the body, of necessity, presumably both in its physical location of the brain and also in the brain's connection to all aspects of the corporeal entity. Existence itself is at once psychic or psychological (consciousness) and corporeal, and in some sense the idea that there is a duality is merely a creation—and a mistake—of thought. This understanding of *existence*, which Sartre et al. posit as being constituted by a body/consciousness nexus rather than a distinction between body and mind, is one I want to carry forward in discussing Fanon's use of the muscles metaphor. Merleau-Ponty and Sartre offer useful illumination of Fanon's assessments of those "times when the black man is locked into his body," and in the next section I will consider their work on the subject of corporeality in the context of Fanon's declarations, after we have examined more closely the recurrence of references to the muscles as the synecdoche of the body in Fanon's texts.[83]

For the moment, it is important to understand that, as Sekyi-Otu observes, Fanon replaces the trope of time and rhetoric of temporality that is central to Hegelian and Marxist dialectics and conceptions of ontology with a trope of *space*, a rhetoric of spatiality. Spatiality, according to Merleau-Ponty and others such as Eugene Minkowski working out existentialist thought, privileges the body as the site of the production of self. Human spatiality and human embodiment are intimately linked in existential thought, as Sekyi-Otu points out.[84] Fanon adopts this concept in order to revise it, since for Fanon any conclusion reached by European philosophical inquiry must, like Marxism, always be "slightly stretched" when applied to the colonial situation and to the condition of blackness.[85] Thus, where Sartre would see the "hodological space" of each for-itself consciousness (the fundamental phenomenological unit) as basically free, with a wide range of possibilities, Fanon sees the space created by the colonial situation to be one that is divided, in which the colonized is physically, psychically, existentially confined. The narrow space of the colonial world split along Manichean lines (however illusory, however much a mirage such apparently absolute demarcations may be) is the concomitant, and also the result and reflection, of that nonintegrated double-body in which the native/black is entombed and which he *exists* as the foundation for his life.

Of course, Fanon in his theorizing is by no means content to rest in that narrow space and that divided double-body: even the violence that must be employed for that double-body to break free of its boundaries ultimately fails to assure human freedom (or, more modestly, true postcoloniality) unless it rallies its ambition to do more than simply replace the colonizer in his bed or settle on sham independence as a political solution.

And, as Sekyi-Otu convincingly shows, the *movement* that an identification of narrow spatiality implies as a solution is, like the crude Procrustean physic of somehow forcing the doubled body into a single whole, actually insufficient.[86]

Nevertheless, what Fanon does propose as sufficient (which is to say, what he models in the very form of his writing and activities: an all-questioning engagement in a process of *becoming* free) is not my subject here. I am interested rather in the capaciousness, however paradoxically diminutive, extant in the narrow space itself, in the constrained capabilities of the constitutively split blackened double-body, and I am interested in how to read the double-body's flinches at the moment that the external stimulus which cleaves it in two flicks across its boundaries. I am interested, in other words, in how to read and interpret the metaphor of Fanon's black body's muscular tensions. Though the whole of *Black Skin, White Masks* is concerned to delineate the pitfalls of racial consciousness, which *The Wretched of the Earth* and Fanon's writing associated with the Algerian Revolution then resolves (or leaps beyond), the metaphor of the black body's muscular tension and what it represents in the latter texts encompasses the conditions of racialized identity the former text describes, while also suggesting other dimensions: powers in the midst of debility.

"The native's muscles are always tensed," Fanon observes. "You can't say that he is terrorized, or even apprehensive. He is in fact ready at a moment's notice to exchange the role of the quarry for that of the hunter."[87] This is the first of several moments when Fanon summons the trope of muscle tension to describe a state which might be defined as arrested activity, as a trembling, held back by a restraint, on the edge of a new consciousness—and which might also be defined as a form of consciousness (an inchoate theoretics) that readies itself to direct the body in activity (i.e., revolutionary action). Fanon references the state of muscular tension only as a nodal point, a kind of knot in the long string of teleological progress toward fully realized revolutionary projects. He does not investigate its properties, but I think it possible to delineate aspects of this state that can be called powerful. While the particular meaning of muscular tension gets tweaked in each of Fanon's references, tense muscles in general in the texts represents the state of unconscious or undeveloped reaction to colonial domination—which is that resistance to oppressive colonial or racist power that lacks the benefit of national consciousness and perhaps even of its to-be-surpassed antecedent, Negritude or race-based nationalism. The muscles, in contraction or tension, are a metaphor referring to some reservoir of resistance to the colonizer's acts of subjugation and enslavement.

Despite the appearance of cool calculation in the native figure Fanon first describes, terror is one of the constituent elements of the state of muscle tension to which Fanon refers. If we read his references to muscle tension as also referencing Fanon's diagnoses of psychosomatic muscular disorders suffered by his North African patients, as I think we must, then the blackened body he describes as "beside itself with terror," and the always-tensed muscles he describes the native having, are metaphorical descriptions of different aspects of a single state. What is common to both is the lived experience of blackness or, more precisely, of *existing* a body culturally constructed (i.e., sociogenically created) as black or native by conquest, enslavement, and colonial domination. In this experience, this existence, blackness and nativity are not only the product of colonial domination but also the substance of that domination, being-dominated lived in and as body. The native is ready to take over the space of the settler, and this is manifested as muscular tension; the North African is terrified by the disorienting—and indeed disordering at the level of bodily experience—fact of living under conditions of colonial domination, where he must despise his own skin and abjure his own body: these are the same bodies, living out similar moments in the constitution of their double-bodiedness, their perpetual tension.

Sartre in his preface to *The Wretched of the Earth* illuminates the relation between terror and resistance, and their cohabitation in the same body, when he describes the revolutionary native as a "child of violence" whose humanity is found in and wrested from the depths of the "torture and death" to which he has been subjected. "Hardly has the second generation [of natives] opened their eyes than from then on they've seen their fathers flogged," Sartre writes. "In psychiatric terms, they are 'traumatized' for life. But these constantly renewed aggressions, far from bringing them to submission, thrust them into an *unbearable contradiction*"—and here Sartre takes up Fanon's trope of muscle tension—"Make no mistake about it; by this mad fury, by this bitterness and spleen, by their ever-present desire to kill us, by the permanent tensing of powerful muscles which are afraid to relax, they [the natives] have become men."[88]

This state of muscle tension, resistant *and* terrified, tensely quivering at the juncture of the split by which the black/native subject is constituted, is a state which is constantly renewed. Muscle tension is repetitive; and its repetition effects the historical conquest and enslavement that is at the same time its foundation. Muscular tension, as literal physical condition that is also a psychic state, is worked out and released in ritual performances that fail to address the root cause of the tension, and the tension perpetually recurs because of that failure. The native's psychic disturbance can be observed, Fanon says, "exhausting itself" in ecstatic dances. "The native's *relaxation* takes precisely the form of a *muscular orgy* in which the most acute aggressivity and the most impelling violence are canalized, transformed, and conjured away. . . . [S]hakes of the head, bending of the spinal column, throwing of the whole body backward—may be deciphered as in an open book the huge effort of the community to exorcise itself, to liberate itself, to explain itself." Relaxation is achieved through a muscular acting out, by means of enacting tension; choreographing tensions in the active body dispel psychic disturbance and yet also prepare the ground for that disturbance's reassertion as renewed tension. The dance "relaxes their painfully contracted muscles," Sartre repeats. "[T]he dance mimes secretly, often without their knowing, the refusal they cannot utter and the murders they dare not commit." Sartre's identification of the dance as mime follows Fanon, who says that the dance is "a seemingly unorganized *pantomime*, which is in reality extremely systematic."[89]

The repetitive character of the state of muscle tension, and the mimetic quality of its activity—action that does not act in a political sense but nevertheless acts out, a physical mapping of psychic tumult and desires that are repressed, consciousness held back from conscious recognition, trembling with the force of what it corrals but does not contain—gives us Fanon's description of what it is to *live with and in* defeat, to be fully immured in the historically produced consequences of conquest, colonization, and enslavement: to be black (or native), in other words, before acquiring national consciousness. It is indeed the state of continually reliving that defeat, since for Fanon the culture of the colonized—their lived reality—lists like a docked boat in a state of arrest. The (black) body is the material reality of sociogenic construction as well as the metaphor in Fanon's text for the socius of the black/native. Similarly, muscle tension is the state of flexure that has the appearance of movement but is in substance barely moving and static, in a state of attenuated atrophy.

Though the existential psychology on which Fanon partly relies posits because of its phenomenological stance (and its cultural arrogance) a universality unconditioned by specific histories (and which therefore can be

told in representative fables of primordial encounters between consciousnesses), Fanon's body, its muscular tensions and flinches, is only to be understood as created—sociogenically—by the fecund process of conquest
and domination: this body's flinches have a presumably universal existential dimension, but this is a body that becomes—or *exists*—a *black* consciousness only by dint of an originary conquest which was the destruction of its old and now irretrievable corporeal schema. Its resistance to
its domination may take many forms, but those forms have no necessary
reliance on preexisting unconquered structures, since these have been extirpated or rewritten or have become inert; the forms of resistance emerge
as a consequence of—or, more precisely, they are only intelligible *through*
the inherited toolbox provided by—the defeat itself. Thus, these bodily
tensions express for Fanon a particularly black/native *abjection*.

It may be useful here to recall Julia Kristeva's psychoanalytic account of
abjection: Kristeva's abjection is a universal experience in the developmental trajectory of the subject. By this account, abjection establishes itself in
the development of subject-object relations: the subject is produced by relation with object, as the two are mutually constituting. Where the development of object relations "strays," the "normal" subject fails to appear, is
unable to demarcate from its putative objects. This straying or (normally)
transient failure is part of the process of encountering language (the Name
of the Father). The transient foreclosure of the Name of the Father—non-
achievement of the introjection or assimilation of language (which is the
prohibiting and desire-producing Other that stands as obstacle to a separated mother's body or mother's breast)—occasions a sense of language
as alien, thus creating a "challenge to symbolization." This phenomenon
can be observed in the cases of borderline patients, where the challenge
appears as *affect*: "The affect is first enunciated as a coenesthetic image of
painful fixation: the borderline patient speaks of a numbed body, of hands
that hurt, of paralyzed legs. But also, as a motion metaphor binding significance: rotation, vertigo, or infinite quest."[90]

These symptoms or expressions, described in terms of numbness, pa-
ralysis, pain, along with seemingly contradictory motion, correspond with
Fanon's observations of the blackened body's muscular tension. For Fanon
of course their origin does not lie in an ontological or psychological history; they are precisely an expression of racialization. When he proclaims
that "[t]he body of history does not determine a single one of my actions"
in *Black Skin*, it is with the determination to move beyond the muscular

tensions as expressions of a particular history of conquest, enslavement, and racialization that are the subject of my inquiry.[91]

That the particular form of muscular tension exemplified by the dance traces its provenance to compensations and redressing responses to conquest and enslavement seems to be buttressed—at least in a context where I am claiming an Americanist Fanon—by the correspondence of Fanon's and Sartre's observations with those of Frederick Douglass. As Fanon sees the native's dance as a sublimation of aggression which would otherwise be directed against the colonialist authorities and therefore also as an unconscious preparation for such action, Douglass remarks that the festivities permitted in the slave quarters between the Christmas and New Year's holidays—chiefly "wild and low sports peculiar to semi-civilized people" such as dancing and drinking whiskey—functioned as clever methods of pacification: "I believe those holidays were the most effective means in the hands of the slaveholders for keeping down the spirit of insurrection among the slaves." Douglass lists along with dancing a number of sports that were encouraged by the masters during the holidays, especially if they were performed under the influence of alcohol: "ball-playing, wrestling, boxing, running foot-races."[92] Thus, the flexing of muscles, the body engaged in activity that enacts, releases, and yet also contains the tensions generated by an at once thwarted and incipient resistance, appears as a practice and as a figure of political significance across oceans and historical epochs. The common observation illustrates how the repetition of cultural practice (which is cultural production itself) loops past and present in a knot: to dance in the present of Fanon's observation is to invoke the past of conquest and enslavement and to make it present, to reenact its defeat and the possibility of its overthrow, to interarticulate the temporalities of subjugation and domination.

"In the colonial world," Fanon writes, "the emotional sensitivity of the native is kept on the surface of his skin like an open sore which *flinches* from the caustic agent; and the psyche shrinks back, obliterates itself and finds outlet in *muscular demonstrations* which have caused certain very wise men to say that the native is a hysterical type."[93] The psychic retreat that characterizes it suggests that Fanon's muscular demonstration is distinct from the forms of cognition that would be grouped under the rubric of the conscious. Muscular demonstration would seem to be located on the side of that which is unconscious or that which does not rely on the "I" narratives of an intact ego, especially since for Fanon conquest has obliterated the psyche of the native even as it has obliterated his culture—which, again, is really to say that it has arrested and disoriented both psyche and culture at the point of contact between colonized and colonizer, and, in so doing, rewritten or rearranged psychic and cultural content: it has provided the model of epistemically violent sociogenic creation.

"Muscular demonstrations" here is a partly metaphorical usage; it is an umbrella term encompassing all those reactions that are "like" the flinches of an open wound when it is touched and that are truly manifestations of affect, or "emotional sensitivity." Yet this muscular activity clearly is also a literal description. In "Colonial War and Mental Disorders," Fanon observes what he deems to be the physical manifestations of obliterated egos: "These are disorders which persist for months on end, *making a mass attack against the ego*, and practically always leaving as their sequel a weakness which is almost visible to the naked eye." Group G, the Algerian patients suffering from a psychosomatic affliction that Fanon says is "specific to the colonial war in Algeria," demonstrate a "generalized contraction with muscular stiffness." This malady, found solely in male patients, severely curtails their mobility; it prevents them from climbing stairs, walking quickly, and running. "No relaxation can be achieved. The patient seems to be made all of a piece, subjected as he is to a sudden contraction and incapable of the slightest voluntary relaxation. The face is rigid but expresses a marked degree of bewilderment," Fanon notes.[94]

Fanon refers caustically to a rogues' gallery of European psychologists who have opined about the congenital underdevelopment of the Algerian's psyche (and physical brain) when he mentions the "very wise men" who have misdiagnosed the condition underlying such symptoms as hysteria. It probably strikes the contemporary reader as suspect that Fanon dismisses hysteria, since, after all, standard psychoanalytic definitions of conversion hysteria involve the expression of psychic conflict in the symbolism of somatic symptoms. But we may suppose that Fanon ridicules the attribution of hysteria to his patients because of the political uses—colonial domination—to which such diagnoses, affixed to something called the North African or Algerian or black "type," were put; and moreover, given that Fanon in *Black Skin, White Masks* denied that the Oedipus complex had any purchase whatever on the psyches of those in Caribbean societies, he was opposed to explaining his patients' muscular rigidity by recourse to repression of Oedipal conflicts.[95] In Fanon's view such a diagnosis too easily works on the one hand to pathologize a race and on the other hand to misplace root causation within an individual narrative without reference to the political and social reality.

"This contracture is in fact simply the postural accompaniment to the native's reticence, the *expression in muscular form* of his rigidity and his refusal with regard to colonial authority," Fanon declares.[96] In other words, when Fanon notes that the native's muscles are always tensed in the colonial world, it is equally a psychiatric diagnosis and a political observation; tense muscles are a metaphor but also a reference to physical and psychological symptoms. Muscular rigidity is not only—or even properly—a *mental* illness, since it expresses *political* "refusal."

This refusal in the form of muscular expression originates in a mode of cognition or knowing that may not appear as intellectual or reasoned from the viewpoint of Western rationality, to which it will seem simply "primitive," ignorant, and childishly recalcitrant. The refusal signally appears in the form of an apparent lack of "comprehension" of linear time ("conformity to the categories of time is something to which the North African seems to be hostile")[97]—or it appears that the native is lazy: "The native's laziness is the conscious sabotage of the colonial machine; *on the biological plane* it is a remarkable system of auto-protection," Fanon says. This suggests the ways in which the body in its apparent laziness and the perceptual and mental mechanisms that count the passage of time work in tandem. Fanon here describes ways the black consciousness, which is also the (blackened) body, "knows" how to defend itself even when the tools of organized politics and revolutionary theory—what Fanon deems national consciousness—are not available, or as yet unformed.[98]

And this apparently reactive and seemingly nonconscious or preconscious political refusal, operating on the biological plane and manifesting itself as laziness, as bewilderment that announces itself in the musculature of the face, as a focus on the present to avoid both the "burning past" and the future of servitude in the linear chronology that the colonizer wishes the conquered to adopt, and appearing overall as muscular tension and rigidity, finds its correlate in the culture of the colonized itself. Using language similar to that he uses to describe his patients' symptoms of muscular rigidity, Fanon remarks that the native's attachment to the traditions of his "clandestine culture" under colonial domination is an expression of "faithfulness to the spirit of the nation and . . . a refusal to submit."[99] Such refusal—such resistance, within the lived experience of nativity and blackness—must be surpassed if any truly liberated state, psychologically and politically, is to be achieved; but though Fanon does not value this form of resistance except as the sketchy lineaments of a figure yet to be fully realized, it possesses an intriguing quality: defeated, working within and saturated by the defeat that constitutes its foundation and the limits of its effectiveness, yet not defeated, in such a way that it exceeds the defeat and takes on a powerfulness that the defeat does not quash or necessarily succeed in assimilating.

Fanon notes, "This persistence in following forms of culture which are *already* condemned to extinction is *already* a demonstration of nationality; but *it is a demonstration which is a throwback to the laws of inertia.*"[100] The "demonstration" here of cultural tradition recalls the demonstration of muscular rigidity and is another instance of the twinning of the native/ black body and his culture. More interesting is the way that Fanon coins a paradox wherein inertia coexists with demonstration or movement; and this counterintuitive pairing is itself framed by a paradox of temporality, in which "already" extinct cultural forms are an expression of their own surpassing: that the native/black clings to these forms as gestures of refusal expresses a nascent nationality—a nationality that does not yet exist but is being made in and by those forms that, by dint of their being followed at all, prove they are "already" dead, because the nation, and the all-questioning revolutionary praxis that daily rebuilds it, does not need them. And all these developments are a "throwback" to the event of conquest and enslavement that instantiates them but which they contest.

The past as future anterior looms large here as the operative concept. The Chinese-box nesting of temporal frames is expressed in Fanon's texts in metaphor and, simultaneously, represented as *lived*, as (and in) the muscular tension of the black/native body.

Fanon's play here with the simultaneity of and delicate relation between a nation that is and that is not yet (and that also was, since the expression of it flows through "faithfulness" to the past) echoes Sartrean formulations of temporality, as we will see; and in this way we detect the temporality that is repressed in Fanon returning under the guise of cultural folkways and, more to the purpose of this discussion, in the expressively damaged blackened native body. Thus, the power of the blackened body—the colonized's body in its defeat—seems to lie in its *mimes*, its gestural and postural possibilities, which loop, rather than align or stack on a pyramid, the past, present, and future.

Life-in-Death, Temporality, and the Black Body

Fanon's blackened body, in addition to expressing, living, or *existing*, a counterlinear temporality—and because it exists such a temporality—is both dead and alive.[101] Just as the culture of the colonized is "sclerosed, dying," in which "the only existing life is dissimulated," so is the muscularly tense black/native body, which is inert and yet moves by means of miming, acting out in gesture and posture, the resistance it does not yet fully or authentically embody.[102] Of the North African in France, who like his French Antillean brethren is "[s]ealed in . . . crushing objecthood,"[103] Fanon writes, "he will feel himself emptied, without life, in *a bodily struggle with death, a death on this side of death, a death in life*—and what is more pathetic than this man with *robust muscles* who tells us in his truly broken voice, 'Doctor, I'm going to die?'"[104] Robust muscularity as the ironic counterpoint to death then goes on to become almost death's exemplar in Fanon's summary of the Algerian bodies suffering from muscular rigidity in Group G: "The patient . . . is constantly tense, waiting between life and death. Thus one of these patients said to us: 'You see, I'm already stiff like a dead man.'"[105] Muscle tension in Fanon is a state of death-in-life and life-in-death; it describes the paradox of a being who experiences utter defeat but who is nonetheless not fully defeated.[106]

This death-in-life and life-in-death are, not at all surprisingly, modes whereby the colonized subject wrestles in the temporal field with his political and cultural subjection. In Fanon's essay "Medicine and Colonialism," summarizing his experiences of practicing in Algeria, he observes again the "rigid" bodies of his patients. "The muscles were contracted. There was no relaxing," he says, and theorizes the relation of this muscular rigidity to the temporal:

> [T]he colonized person . . . is like the men in underdeveloped countries or the disinherited in all parts of the world, [in that he] perceives life not as a flowering or a development of essential productiveness, but as a permanent struggle against an omnipresent death. This ever-menacing death is experienced as endemic famine, unemployment, a high death rate, an inferiority complex and the absence of any hope for the future.
>
> All this gnawing at the existence of the colonized tends to make of life something resembling an incomplete death. Acts of refusal or rejection of medical treatment are not a refusal of life, but a greater passivity before that close and contagious death.[107]

The colonized subject lives an incomplete death, and his refusals or rejections of medical attention offered by doctors whom he rightly identifies with the dominating praxis of colonialism itself, equally describe muscular and political posture.

The language here portrays how, in the psychic life of the colonized subject (and thus in the cultural life of the colonized not-yet-nation), the capacity for historical progress is lost due to a "permanent struggle" against "omnipresent death." The apparent timelessness of the struggle, its eternity, is a deliberate effect produced by the colonizer: European time imposed like a sealing lid over both past and future. This is given concrete form—literally concretized, in some instances—by the French colonialists' policy and mania for building: "The structures built, the port facilities, the airdromes . . . often gave the impression that the enemy committed himself, compromised himself, half lost himself in his prey, precisely in order to make any future break, any separation, impossible. *Every manifestation of the French presence expressed a continuous rooting in time and in the Algerian future*, and could always be read as a token of an indefinite oppression." This "continuous rooting," which must remind us of the "homogeneous, empty time" Benjamin describes as the fascist's and ruling class's production of history, is in Fanon (as in Benjamin) reinforced by historicism: "To the history of the colonization the Algerian people today oppose the history of the national liberation," Fanon says, announcing the birth of a new accounting of time, a different temporality.[108] "Instead of integrating colonialism, conceived as the birth of a new world, in Algerian history," he says, "we have made of it an unhappy, execrable accident, the only meaning of which was to have inexcusably retarded the coherent evolution of the Algerian society and nation."[109]

The arrest of any true progress in the production of colonial temporality—the suspension and slow strangling death of anything like a Hegelian or Marxist dialectical progression that might forecast or enable revolutionary change—is for Fanon countered by that interarticulated temporality that he suggests without charting. (And we might note that, writing from within Algeria's revolutionary struggle and the broader movement for independence throughout Africa, he suggests this achievement without charting its dimensions precisely because what he tentatively describes is always a work *in progress*, wherein the terms of the past and present are being reconfigured in the forging of the future.) The colonizer's continuous rooting has as its Janus-face the day-to-day sociogenic creation whereby the revolutionaries, masses and their leaders, become "responsible"—that is, act and theorize their actions in a continuously dialectical process—for "everything." The appearance and even the reality of stasis—the effect of the colonizer's continuous rooting in time that renders the native culture "sclerosed, dying"—is coexistent with, and bears a mutually constitutive relation to, the furious activity that achieves it, as well as to the seething inchoate resistance that shapes spontaneous rebellion and (if guided and abetted by appropriate theorizing activity) its development from nationalism to national consciousness. Both continuous rooting effected through a mania of building and the colonized people's sociogenic acts of creation are characterized by movement, restlessness: "The colonial society is in perpetual movement. Every settler invents a new society, sets up or sketches new structures"—just as, of course, the revolutionary creates the new man and woman.[110]

This simultaneous movement and stasis as a description of culture in the colony finds its metaphoric representation in Fanon's text in his clinical observation of the colonized person's body as it absorbs, succumbs to, and yet also resists the daily, obdurate and pervasive machinations of colonialism: muscular rigidity and death-in-life, life-in-death.

The expression of the differing emphases on life and death in the same state, and the fundamental linkage between them, can be discerned in the following two passages, in which Fanon uses the trope of muscle tension. In the first of these, Fanon employs muscular tension to represent the breakdown of the corporeal schema of the native intellectual—a figure of whom Fanon is relentlessly critical, and whom he identifies as a counterrevolutionary element in any decolonization war. The native intellectual, Fanon notes, quests uselessly after some better past in which a Negro civilization matched the achievements of Europe's supposedly formative Greece and Rome. "[I]f he fails to find the substance of culture of the same grandeur and scope as displayed by the ruling power, the native intellectual will very often fall back upon emotional attitudes and will develop a psychology which is dominated by exceptional sensitivity and susceptibility. This withdrawal, which is due in the first instance to a begging of the question of his internal behavior mechanism and his own character, brings out, above all, a reflex and contradiction which is muscular."[111] Here the colonizer's discourses, its self-glorifying stories of its civilizing mission and its insistence on the reality of racial alterity fully occupy the psychic, psychological, intellectual, and emotional territory of the native intellectual's self; these discourses overtake his consciousness, dismember the schema of his body, and expose the split, the "contradiction" that exists as the foundation of his being (and that he exists)—that is, the rupture of conquest and enslavement. The native intellectual's "exceptional sensitivity," however much Fanon subtly ridicules it, is just another expression of that "emotional sensitivity" that causes the nonintellectual native in the colonial world to flinch. It is death-in-life.

In the second passage muscle tension has a somewhat different emphasis. Speaking of the process of the development of national cultures during the revolutionary struggle, Fanon says that after the long years of cultural obliteration and mummification, "[t]he contact of the people with the new movement gives rise to a new rhythm of life and to *forgotten muscular tensions*, and develops the imagination."[112] Here the exposure of constitutive contradiction that occurs in beginning revolutionary struggle, the rummaging back to the "burning past" of conquest, tips toward resistive action rather than rigidity; it is life-in-death.

In both these passages, as in others, muscle tension suggests a state of interarticulated temporality insofar as the past fully determines and occupies the present: a particular past, that is, the arrival of the colonizer and the world he has wrought in his guise of negative Promethean, bestowing and burning at once. Again, "conformity to the categories of time is something to which the North African seems to be hostile. It is not lack of comprehension," Fanon declares. "It is as though it is an effort for him to go back to where he no longer is. The past for him is a burning past. What he hopes is that he will never suffer again, never again be face to face with that past. This present pain, which visibly *mobilizes the muscles of his face*, suffices him."[113] The burning past extinguished the world it conquered, and the calamity of it is itself extinguished by a protective focus on the present; and yet even if it escapes conscious recollection, it lives on as a memory of the body, in the contracted muscles of the face. In this interarticulated temporality the future dimension is in part that future accorded to the shades of an underworld, who struggle on perpetually in gray half-life without hope or succor—until the resurrection provided by dawning national consciousness. The future by its nature only appears as an ideal, as a product of consciousness; and, applying this schema to the development of the nation, before the introduction of the ideal of the nation its future does not have substance, and thus little or no reference in the state metaphorically (and also physically) represented by muscle tension. If we can read through the aporias left by Fanon's repression of temporality, it is possible to discern that, in existentialist fashion, he emphasizes the contingency of futurity: in the colonial/black context, the future is, of course, unwritten, but the important question is not what or when but *whether* it will be written, whether the consciousness tending toward national liberation makes a future possible rather than the endless past/present of colonial domination and its state of arrest, its underworld shade quality. The future is a mirror held up to the present and to the past, which has no solidity except as a reflection of what is done to make it, what is done in the service of its realization.

For Sartre, the future is almost a modality of the present, since the present itself is completely elusive, existing only as consciousness's flight toward the future. "It is impossible to grasp the Present in the form of an instant, for the instant would be the moment when the present *is*," Sartre describes. "But the present is not; it makes itself present in the form of flight. . . . For-itself [the ontological unit of consciousness] has its being outside of it, before and behind. Behind, it *was* its past; and before, it *will be* its future. It is flight outside of co-present being and from the being which it was toward the being which it will be. At present it is not what it is (past) and it is what it is not (future)."[114] If in Fanon the past is future anterior, in Lacan's terms, then the future is past posterior: the future is *not*—in the sense that the future is a product of the nihilating withdrawal from the present which characterizes consciousness itself—and at the same time the future is always, because it slips away as it becomes present, what has already been—in the sense that the future is the repository for the (political, social, sociogenic) changes we mean to make in the present which also revise the past.

Thus, the state of muscle tension, in its inchoate resistance, its mime of unconscious turmoil poised at the lip of consciousness, also trembles at the edge of a future that does not yet, for it, exist even in the manner of futures, since it lacks an ideal shape. Still, that *lack* is only comparative; it does not describe a void. As my readings of Sartre and Merleau-Ponty suggest, tense muscles refer the native/black back to *anonymous existence*: they refer him to an indeterminacy which is "freedom" in the form of anguish and (as a physical manifestation) vertigo, as these terms are given substance in Sartrean phenomenological thought. The anonymous existence marked in Fanon's texts by muscle tension is reached because "torture and death" strips away ego-protections in such a way as to reveal an irreducible *something*; to break in on this existence is therefore a product of having-been-black*ened*: one, or the most signal, of its black powers.

But anonymous existence as it appears in existentialist thought purports to be an ontological, and therefore universal, quality. Fanon suggests his agreement with this notion. For Fanon, this particular anonymous existence, experienced under colonial and racist domination, is the aspect of blackness and nativity that, even without all the necessities of revolutionary action and the development of national consciousness, *asks us to listen to it.* Fanon writes of the double-body, the body beside itself with terror, that constitutes the so-called North African Syndrome, that it is the "body that asks me to listen to it without, however, paying too much heed to it."[115] The "North African Syndrome" is a concoction of racist psychiatry and thus an instrument of colonial domination; its truly salient manifestation is the sufferer's claim on Fanon's listening, and this claim, this demand for recognition, issues as a cry from a portion of being that either is universal human authenticity or that becomes constituted as such through a cry of this kind. *See me in my double-body,* the cry seems to say, *the one that hurts*—in which "each organ has *its* pathology," Fanon notes—*and also the other one,* which is the echo, perhaps, of that "implicit knowledge" that informs the integrated body and which is strangled in the imposition of blackness.[116] This muscle tension—which I will shortly be describing under the existentialist term, anonymous existence—is what is not void, even in the seemingly fallow fields where the terrible mirage of blackness so obscures reality that a humanist future is vanishingly fragile, and yet somehow a claim is staked to some kind of freedom that is, or can become, humanity. To inhabit this state, to plumb the experience of this terror-struck and terror-constituted double-body which is inert and moves, rigid with death and with active resistance—all, Fanon would say, to no ultimate avail—is I would argue a "practice of 'disalienation,'" however partial, "within the resources of black culture," which is to say, a practice of disalienation within and underwritten by alienation.[117]

Vertigo, Anonymous Existence, and the Black Abject

But can we escape becoming dizzy? And who can affirm that vertigo does not haunt the whole of existence?

—Frantz Fanon, *The Wretched of the Earth*[118]

The state that must be surpassed for which Fanon adopts the trope of muscle tension is in some part also the inescapable reality of living any human life, since everyone must bow down to the limits set by structures one has had little or no hand in choosing—which is to say, that state and the muscle tension that represents it in Fanon's text grapple with the problem of history, or historical necessity. This correspondence seems to give rise to the provocative statement of the epigraph: "we are forever pursued

by our actions," Fanon says—counter, of course, to how he is read by
Verges and others. "Their ordering, their circumstances, and their motiva-
tion may perfectly well come to be profoundly modified *a posteriori*. This
is merely one of the snares that history and its various influences sets for
us. But can we escape becoming dizzy? And who can affirm that vertigo
does not haunt the whole of existence?"[119]

There is an alluring loveliness about this question of Fanon's. It makes
a kind of optimistic art of despair: it bows perforce to seeming inevitability—that is, the constant failure of our efforts to transform the world
along the lines of justice or merely "sense," the strangeness of living in a
world of such pain and suffering and knowing that it is our world and that
therefore the pain and suffering is in some way our doing. And yet, by
means of posing and ending on a question for which there is no reassur-
ing answer, this passage suggests that the terrible things (and the terror)
that structure human life, while possessing the frightening force to haunt
and disorient, are not proof against the willingness to query its conditions,
and it suggests, too, with a hint of Zen-like bemusement, that questioning
and resistance are as inevitable as the defeats that make them necessary.
As Fanon himself once remarked, explaining that he could not sometimes
fully explain passages in his work that seem obscure, but that there is a
productive, indeed almost sensual, pleasure in his difficult and quizzical
formulations, "I find myself incapable of escaping the bite of a word, the
vertigo of a question mark."[120]

I am interested in Fanon's statement about the vertigo that haunts existence because, as much by the tone it strikes as by its content, it allows me
to read Fanon describing what it is to live in defeat when you must (as you
inevitably do, though not constantly or indefinitely). If the statement were
a body it would be one in *potential* movement, "arms . . . raised . . . as if to
sketch an action."[121] It functions in emblematic fashion like the raised fist
as the signature of what I am calling, by way of shorthand and provoca-
tion, Black Power.

Fanon raises this question as he begins his discussion of "Colonial War
and Mental Disorders." He describes the "border-line case" of a man from
an unnamed African country which had already won its independence, as
the paradigm for all those he diagnoses in the section. During the course
of revolutionary conflict, the man had set a bomb at a popular café re-
puted to be frequented by colonial racists, killing ten people. After independence was won the man became friendly with individuals who were
nationals of the former colonial power. "The former militant therefore had

what might be called an attack of vertigo. He wondered with a feeling of anguish whether among the victims of the bomb there had been people like his new acquaintances."[122]

Fanon lists insomnia, anxiety, and suicidal obsession as the symptoms of this "vertigo," but the use of this case as a paradigm of course points to that same body/mind, history-and-politics/individual-psyche nexus that imbues Fanon's references to the black/native's muscular tension: vertigo, as an affliction of disorientation that clearly reaches beyond the sensation of distorted inner-ear balance, might well be another term for what Fanon identifies in Group G as muscular contraction. But the "vertigo" and "anguish" of the paradigmatic patient are terms that also have particular resonance in Sartrean existentialism, to which I think Fanon's question refers—and which provides intriguing ways of interpreting the trope of muscular tension in Fanon's texts.

In Sartre's *Being and Nothingness*, consciousness, the ontological fundament of human being, arises from a kind of Hegelian negation. Consciousness is the nihilation, the withdrawal, of itself from the world around it (which it so constitutes as a world by such withdrawal) and from itself; consciousness surges up to become for-itself, distinguished from the in-itself of unconscious or nonconscious being. Thus, consciousness depends on "nothingness"; that is, it nihilates what is in order to be—it transcends the world and itself in order to know them. This nothingness is for Sartre the basis of human freedom. Sartrean consciousness continually experiences itself as the nihilation of its past and also of its future. "Freedom is the human being . . . secreting his own nothingness," Sartre declares. "In freedom the human being *is* his own past (as also his own future) in the form of nihilation. . . . [T]here ought to exist for the human being . . . a certain mode of standing opposite his past and his future, as being both this past and this future and as not being them." This mode is *anguish*: "it is in anguish that man gets the consciousness of his freedom, or if you prefer, anguish is the mode of being of freedom as consciousness of being."[123]

Sartre's account of "standing opposite" temporal dimensions while not being completely detached from them, of *being* the irrevocable past and the unmade future and not being them, accords well with Fanon's own suggestive play with counterlinear temporality, and with the paradoxes of muscle tension. What seems particularly significant here is that for Sartre this anguished state is the freedom that human beings possess. This is distinct from the freedom toward which human beings can aspire—which we would justifiably say is Fanon's chief concern.

But just as Fanon gestures backward to a sociogenic process that re-placed one world with another in order to figure the possibility of remak-ing the world in the future, the freedom which human beings ontologi-cally possess is not unconnected to the political freedom produced by the best of revolutionary efforts. This is so even though the freedom that an-guish apprehends and *is* clearly is not the halcyon freedom of Edens or Golden Ages. Sartre writes, "The For-itself can never be its Future except problematically, for it is separated from it by a Nothingness which it is. In short the For-itself is free, and its Freedom is to itself its own limit. To be free is to be condemned to be free."[124] The for-itself is a nothingness: it is profoundly limited by the past (which it *has* to be, without being it; i.e., consciousness is produced by its past but does not occupy the past, only the slipping-away present); and its future opens before it in the form of possibilities, which it also is not and cannot be. That the for-itself is nothingness—that it has nihilated the object of its consciousness—is the substance of its freedom, and at the same time of its imprisonment, since it cannot be other than this consciousness, with its particular inescapable past and its future possibilities.

This is a dialectical concept of freedom, to be sure, but I would prefer in the context of this discussion to deemphasize the oscillation and synthe-sis that dialectics imply and rather to focus on the paradoxical dimensions of the dialectic: freedom is imprisonment, imprisonment is freedom, be-cause both are *not* in the sense that they are the nothing that conscious-ness is. These terms speak to the conditions of consciousness as Sartre de-scribes them and as Fanon takes them up; they do not speak to freedom and imprisonment in relation to, say, release from and incarceration in a prison. *But* they *do* relate to these concrete, material forms of "freedom" and "imprisonment," in that, if the Sartrean existential account of human ontology has any reasonable purchase as a description of human reality—and I am going to assume here at least provisionally that it is as persuasive as any other account, because Fanon assumes so—release from and incar-ceration in a prison is, in addition to whatever else it may be, a materializa-tion of constitutive elements of consciousness. (We can put it differently, too: going to prison and getting out of it become possible events because of fundamental experiences of consciousness—constituted by or reflected in discourse, take your pick—wherein *limit* and its opposite are gleaned and become apparent.) Thus, the analogy between Sartre's freedom and imprisonment language, and the operations of a prison system (and, of course, any number of other dominating relations between institution and individual) does not just describe a parallel or a similarity but a structural relation.

The dialectic has a strong paradoxical dimension, since it involves reciprocal constitution of putatively opposite but dialectically related terms—and the extent to which freedom constitutes imprisonment, and imprisonment constitutes freedom, is germane here.

In *Black Skin, White Masks*, at the conclusion of the chapter "The Fact [or Lived-Experience] of Blackness," Fanon encapsulates this state as particular to blackness, describing it in Sartrean terms as "straddling Nothingness and Infinity," a condition which for him parallels the perpetual state of arrest in which the culture of the colonized exists. Again there the metaphors of movement and body are drafted to produce Fanon's meaning: "I refuse to accept . . . amputation. . . . I am a master and I am advised to adopt the humility of a cripple."[125] For Fanon the freedom of anguish is insufficient and at best a beginning point. But this does not vitiate the philosophical genealogy on which this formulation relies, since the two descriptions so closely align: blackness, particular and historically produced, for Fanon aligns with Sartre's supposedly ontological and universal (masked European) "anguish as the apprehension of nothingness," where nothingness is a freedom which one enjoys—which is one's power—and also a freedom to which one is condemned and which is its own limit, since it is, at its core, alienation.[126]

The vertigo of Fanon's paradigmatic case is another form of anguish. "Vertigo is anguish," Sartre says.[127] "Vertigo announces itself through fear; I am on a narrow path—without a guard rail—which goes along a precipice. The precipice presents itself to me as *to be avoided*; it represents a danger of death. At the same time I conceive of a certain number of causes . . . which can transform that threat of death into reality. . . . Through these various anticipations, I am given to myself as a thing; I am passive in relation to these possibilities; they come to me from without; in so far as I am also an object in the world, subject to gravitation, they are *my* possibilities." There is in this moment that Sartre describes passivity and possible activity; there is the recognition of possibility that derives, in fact, from the passivity of being presented to oneself as an object in relation to the world of which one is a part but from which consciousness separates one. "[C]onsciousness of being is the being of consciousness."[128] Death meanwhile is its own form of nothingness, which consciousness reflects and is opposite of, but is subordinate to. The threat of death presents consciousness to itself as subject and object at once. Thus, anguish/vertigo, as the consciousness of "my" possibilities, is the consciousness of myself and the very essence or being of consciousness itself: though linear time separates me from the future self I will be (which could be dead, could be menaced, etc.), though "no actual existent can strictly determine what I will be"— which is the nature of that which constitutes the freedom of (and that is) consciousness—so that I am *not* the foundation of what I will be (which is to say, the foundation of what I will be is a "nothing"), though all of this is true, "*I am the self which I will be, in the mode of not being it.* It is through my horror that I am carried toward the future, and horror nihilates itself in that it constitutes the future as possible. Anguish is precisely my consciousness of being my own future, in the mode of not-being."[129] Further, "The decisive conduct will emanate from a self which I am not yet. Thus the self which I am depends on the self which I am not yet to the exact extent that the self which I am not yet does not depend on the self which I am. *Vertigo appears as the apprehension of this dependence.* I approach the precipice, and my scrutiny is searching for myself in my very depths. In terms of this moment, I play with my possibilities."[130]

This insight, this apprehension, is also an infinitesimal moment when the past (the self which I have to be) in some sense achieves the ephemerality of the future, since the action of the self which I am not yet will profoundly affect—determine—the self that I am. Thus, vertigo, by unbalancing us, seats us in the state of being conscious of being (and its inherent freedom/imprisonment), and thus in the very essence of what is to be a consciousness. Instead of unconscious absorption in our headlong flight toward a seemingly certain future (which militates against and renders past every present, so that the present is something we can never capture, and consciousness *is* its withdrawal into the future that does not exist), we linger, dangle, over the empty space of our possibilities.[131]

These possibilities stretch out in seeming infinity (though in truth they are limited by the ways in which we are made objects by the world we perceive) just as—to the same extent as—they are compressed within the limits of the nothingness (i.e., the withdrawal) that consciousness is. In this sense vertigo describes a (relative) freedom to move in time, or rather, the freedom to decide to move in a way which helps to inaugurate temporality itself.[132]

It is in light of this that we should read Fanon's question about vertigo haunting the whole of existence. Playing with possibilities, as an *object* in the world, *imprisoned in freedom / free in imprisonment*, in and as the state of horror; consciousness of self: these are vertigo. Such a listing of qualities seems a not unreasonable interpretation of what is operating in the description of Fanon's black/native, with his muscles tensed for incipient action that the body mimes but does not yet take, and tensed too in resistant flinching before the external stimulus that defines and dismembers him, locked into a blackened body that exists a "third-person consciousness." Sartre's and Fanon's vertigo have a relation—perhaps synonymous at points, always at least analogous—to Fanon's muscle tension.

And Fanon's formulation of his version of vertigo illuminates the correspondence between the three states. The vertigo that we *cannot affirm* does *not* haunt the whole of existence is surely a vertigo that informs without fully subsuming all existence. Fanon's double-negative language is a way of demonstrating and elaborating on the verb he uses: this condition "haunts," in the manner of that spectral familiar-unfamiliar homely-unhomely we associate with Freud's uncanny; it lies in back of or beside the everyday, as a past that breaks through to remind us of its continuing reality. This vertigo is but the larger manifestation, the common experience, of what is specific to nativity and blackness—what Fanon represents as muscle tension.

Merleau-Ponty helps us further to understand the relation between Sartre's freedom and the muscular tension of Fanon's blackened body. For Merleau-Ponty, the idea of freedom-as-imprisonment and the slipperiness of linear temporality as it is manifested in the state of vertigo is integrally related to the fact that consciousness *exists* a body. Merleau-Ponty finds a version of this anguish, this sense of vertigo, manifest as a minute but inescapable dimension at the heart of sensory perception itself.

Merleau-Ponty restates Sartre's freedom as "a principle of indeterminacy" that pervades human existence and that arises from the fundamental structure of being human—this fundamental structure being the body. The attributes of the body, its senses, its movements, the way that it becomes for consciousness "the fabric into which all objects are woven," and "the general instrument of . . . [our] 'comprehension,'" are not, however, unconditioned possessions: "this human manner of existence is not guaranteed to every human child through some essence acquired at birth, and . . . it must be constantly reforged in him through the hazards encountered by the objective body." The necessity of constantly reforging the powers of the human body finds its chief example in the "acts of consciousness" we think of as sensory perception, which produce our perceived reality as the "spatial and temporal furrow" these acts of consciousness leave in their wake.[133]

Again, as in the description of Sartre's vertigo, the link between linear temporality (and disturbances thereof) and consciousness is key. As Sartre argues that temporality is a function of and produced by consciousness, Merleau-Ponty emphasizes that temporality is a function of the body's perceptual properties; time is ushered in by, secreted by, the body. He analyzes the way that time—or, to put it differently, the human inclination to apprehend the world by means of narrative—is a function of sensory perception:

> [S]ubjectivity, at the level of perception, is nothing but temporality. . . . The act of looking is indivisibly prospective, since the object is the final stage of my process of focusing, and retrospective, since it will present itself as preceding its own appearance, as the "stimulus," the motive or the prime mover of every process since its beginning. . . . In every focusing movement my body unites present, past and future, *it secretes time*, or rather it becomes that location in nature where, for the first time, events, instead of pushing each other into the realm of being, project round the present a double horizon of past and future and acquire a historical orientation. . . . My body takes possession of time; it brings into existence a past and a future for a present; it . . . creates time instead of submitting to it.[134]

The perceptive act, shaped by the limitations and capabilities of the perceptive functionality of the body, brings into being temporality; it inaugurates time—and must keep doing so with fresh acts of perception. The perception-as-act is an inherent of the body; the body, instead of being *in* space and time, belongs to them dialectically, as constitutive and constituted: "my body combines with [space and time] and includes them." "The object remains clearly before me provided that I run my eyes over it," Merleau-Ponty notes. "The hold which it gives us upon a segment of time, the synthesis which it effects are themselves temporal phenomena which pass, and can be recaptured only in a fresh act which is itself temporal." The perception of a continuous present, an ongoing now, which we inhabit is thus less reality than laborious construction of reality. "[E]very synthesis is both exploded and rebuilt by time which, with one and the same process, *calls it into question and confirms it* because it produces a new present which retains the past."[135]

The phenomenon of time being called into question—its becoming labile, just as consciousness (nothingness) is labile and free, because temporality *is* a function of consciousness—and the fact that time exists as a patchwork rather than as a seamless continuity, Merleau-Ponty calls *temporal dispersal*. Temporal dispersal is always threatening to break into the illusion of a continuous present, because fresh acts of perception are required to reforge the present as reality. While of course by Merleau-Ponty's lights it is chiefly phenomenological inquiry that reveals the labile nature of temporality, that lability is a function of the principle of indeterminacy that pervades—haunts—human existence itself. To develop Merleau-Ponty's metaphor, perceptive acts may leave a spatial and temporal furrow that we designate as reality, but there is an act of plowing that must make its mark, and the act of plowing—not so much whether to do it or not, but where and to what end—is an imprisoning, limited freedom that recurs moment by moment in sensory perception.

> The claim to objectivity laid by each perceptual act is remade by its successor, again disappointed and once more made. . . . [T]his perception will in turn pass away, the subject of perception never being an absolute subjectivity, but being destined to become an object for an ulterior *I*. Perception is always in the mode of an impersonal "One." The person who, in sensory exploration, gives a past to the present and directs it toward a future is not myself as an autonomous subject, but myself in so far as I have a body and am able to "look." Rather than being a genuine history, perception ratifies and renews in us a "prehistory."[136]

This prehistory refers to having been endowed with and being a body, a history which has no narrative available in the experience of a given consciousness, and which Merleau-Ponty refers to as *anonymous* or *amorphous existence*.

Merleau-Ponty further describes this concept by an analogous reference to prenatal existence. He distinguishes sensible from intellectual consciousness thus: sensation takes place in an atmosphere of generality, and it is anonymous and incomplete. He likens sensation to birth and death, arguing that you are not any more aware of "being the true subject of . . . sensation" than you are of your birth or death.

> Neither my birth nor my death can appear to me as experiences of my own. . . . I can . . . apprehend myself only as "already born" or "still alive." . . . Each sensation, being, strictly speaking, the first, last and

only one of its kind, is a birth and a death. The subject who experiences it begins and ends with it, and as he can neither precede nor survive himself, sensation necessarily appears to itself in a setting of generality, its origin is anterior to myself, it arises from *sensibility* which has preceded it and which will outlive it, just as my birth and death belong to a natality and mortality which are anonymous.[137]

Here sensation, and the sensible consciousness that it comprises and yet does not exhaust, are continually reforged without being able to apprehend or determine their absolute origin or limit. There is no beginning here and ending there available to consciousness, since "time slips away as fast as it catches up with itself," and thus "nowhere do I enjoy absolute possession of myself by myself, . . . [because] the hollow void of the future is for ever being refilled with a fresh present," and "we can never fill up, in the picture of the world, that gap which we ourselves are."[138] The beginning and end, the coordinate points of a historical narrative, are general conditions in which you are immersed without being able to be aware of them. "[I]n pre-natal existence," he observes, "nothing was perceived, and therefore there is nothing to recall. There was nothing but the raw material and adumbration of a natural self and a natural time. This *anonymous life* is merely the extreme form of that *temporal dispersal* which constantly threatens the historical present. In order to have some inkling of that *amorphous existence* which preceded my own history, . . . I have only to look within me at that time which pursues its own independent course, and which my personal life utilizes but does not entirely overlay."[139]

What Merleau-Ponty refers to as anonymous existence, or prehistory, or by analogy to prenatality, he elsewhere denotes as habit, "that implicit or sedimentary body of knowledge." This is a body of knowledge which is the body, possessed of capacities to acquire and make meaning—if, that is, we observe the operation of the body phenomenologically and find we must endow the concept of "'significance' [with] a value which intellectualism withholds from it"; that is, significance is something achieved and experienced in and as motor effects, in and as sensation or as processes hovering around and about—haunting—perception, sensation, and motility.[140]

This embodied fund of meaning-making should remind us of Fanon's black body whose tension mimes a resistance without knowing that it resists. The correspondence between Fanon and Merleau-Ponty exists despite the fact that Fanon asserts that the Negro lacks the "implicit knowledge" that characterizes the integrated body. Again what we see in Fanon's analysis of blackness is a projection of what Sartre and Merleau-Ponty propose as ontological human characteristics onto the specifics of sociogenically produced blackness: habit, prehistory, the apprehensions of vertigo speak to the schism between "myself and myself," "the gap which we ourselves are" in Sartre and Merleau-Ponty, while double-bodiedness and muscular tension speak to the schism between a politically free and a politically subjugated self in Fanon, even as that tension refers at another level to that schism Sartre and Merleau-Ponty presume to be general, particularizing it, revising it, and also relying on it. Thus, when Fanon writes of the native's emotional sensitivity and muscular demonstrations in *The Wretched of the Earth*, "This sensitive emotionalism, watched by *invisible keepers* who are however in unbroken contact with the core of the personality, will find its fulfillment through eroticism in the driving forces behind the crisis' dissolution," the invisible keepers are to some extent—they are at the very least *like*—what Merleau-Ponty refers to as anonymous existence.[141]

Of course, Fanon claims in *Black Skin, White Masks* that ontological inquiries fail to describe anything concerning black people because "every ontology is made unattainable in a colonized and civilized society," and in colonized people "there is an impurity, a flaw that outlaws any ontological explanation." Fanon's explanation for the insufficiency of ontological explanations is, simply, that the black man has had "two frames of reference" imposed on him.[142] Du Boisian double-consciousness need not obviate entirely the idea of universals, however; the concept rather brings them under a certain suspicion and complicates their enunciation. Fanon's own arguments obviously do not eschew appeals to universals, and he tends to stretch rather than discard the concepts in which he has been educated. Sociogenesis is clearly more important to Fanon than the posture of the ontological, but presumably sociogenesis can underlie experiences or characteristics which take on a universal quality. As Sekyi-Otu notes, Fanon does not really veto every ontology for the black man/colonized person: "Not even in the peculiar world of the colonized are intimations of human universals rendered inexpressible."[143] Just as temporality is repressed and returns in other guises in Fanon's texts, so too do other aspects of the ontological, particularly as the ontological is mapped by Sartre and Merleau-Ponty; and like temporality, these ontological characteristics emerge in the metaphor of muscle tension.

In all these descriptions of Fanon's muscle tension, Sartre's anguish and vertigo, and Merleau-Ponty's anonymous existence, the overriding concept is the opacity of the subject in and as its body. As Sartre says, the body is a given and a structure, a point of view and a point of departure; "the body is the *neglected*, the '*passed by in silence*'"; for consciousness it has an absolute facticity (its only contingency being whether one lives or not), though an elusive reference—"And yet the body is what this consciousness *is*; it is not even anything except body."[144]

For Fanon, however, the black body is a point of view and a point of departure which is sociogenically produced, a historical contingency, and thus not absolute. It is "the body of history." If Merleau-Ponty's consciousness is opaque to itself to the degree that it is or exists a body which structures its point of view, if he can declare "what I understand never quite tallies with my lived experience. . . . I am never quite at one with myself," the opacity of Fanon's blackened body, exemplar of all that is dark in the cultures in which it comes into being, is ironically more susceptible to illumination. The fact that blackness entails an incoherence in bodily schema, that it makes the black/native be black in relation to the white man, enables the black/native, through an analysis such as Fanon's, to perceive—and to experience—the alienated quality of the embodied consciousness.[145] Where this alienation may remain unconscious for the white man—that is, for the supposed universal man of Sartre and Merleau-Ponty—it can become consciously apparent to the black/native: "Since the racial drama is played out in the open, the black man has no time to 'make it unconscious,'" Fanon says.[146] This is an overstatement since Fanon spends a good portion of all his texts unmasking the effects of the racial drama in and on the unconscious—but the point here is that the racial drama, distorting Being by epidermalizing it, nevertheless by the very mechanism of that distortion calls *attention* to dramas racial and otherwise in their relation to the ontological characteristics of human being. The black/native's corporeal incoherence, his double-bodiedness, enables him to ameliorate that alienation since the script that determines his alienation, whether at base universal or particular, has been played out on the level of a military, political, cultural, and economic confrontation (a process of sociogenesis, in other words) that can be identified and contested. Hence, it might be said that blackness propels those whom it marks toward a certain kind of questioning, a certain kind of knowledge, conscious and explicit, rather than implicit. "The body is surrounded by an atmosphere of certain uncertainty," Fanon writes: the healthy, authentic body, he means;

the bearer of the black body is called upon to make the uncertain as certain as he can.[147]

Even without the illumination of an analysis such as Fanon's, the resistance to sociogenically produced alienation we find in the midst of black abjection relies on a fundamental anonymous existence; that is, it relies on that "other self" which in the form of sedimentary bodily perceptive habit "has already sided with the world, . . . is already open to certain of its aspects, and synchronized with them."[148] It is possible to access this anonymous existence and thereby glimpse the "gap which we ourselves are," *through* and because of the psychic pain that blackness forces you to endure.

Sartre discusses the revelatory power of pain and the way in which ontological qualities of existence can be accessed in the matrix of trauma, by using the example of eye pain. (This is a particularly apt illustration, since pain in the eyes, both the chief organs and the master metaphor of perception, suggests the blurred and only vaguely discernible appearance of consciousness to itself.) Sartre remarks that pain in the eyes is really "the-eyes-as-pain or vision-as-pain." Pain does not exist anywhere among the actual objects of the universe but is instead "[s]imply *the translucent matter of consciousness, its being-there.*" And, "The pain exists beyond all attention and all knowledge since it slips into each act of attention and of knowledge, since it *is* this very act. . . . Pain-consciousness is an internal negation of the world; but at the same time it exists its pain—i.e., itself—as a wrenching away from self. Pure pain as the simple 'lived' can not be reached. . . . *But pain-consciousness is a project toward a further consciousness which would be empty of all pain.* . . . [T]his is the unique character of corporal existence—the inexpressible which one wishes to flee is rediscovered at the heart of this wrenching away; . . . it is . . . the being of the flight which wishes to flee it."[149] By this I take Sartre to mean that the consciousness of being pained intrinsically involves one's attempt to wrench attention away from the pain; yet pain is purely an effect of consciousness, and when one is in pain, pain is the very substance of consciousness—so that what you are wrenching yourself away from is your own consciousness, a process that brings you back to the awareness of your *self* as consciousness.

Aligning Fanon's statements with Sartre's, we can see blackness in its abjection in similar terms: as a "translucent matter," crafted by sociogenesis, which, as the negation of freedom and as the means and product of a process of alienation, is or *can be* a project toward the experience of consciousness itself: and the experience of consciousness is an experience of essential indeterminacy, and thus of freedom in all its limited limitlessness (in Fanon's words, "between Nothingness and Infinity"). It is this kind of analytic, I think, that lies in back of Fanon's benediction in *Black Skin, White Masks*, "O my body, make of me always a man who questions!"[150]

To put this differently: the state of muscle tension evoked as symptom and metaphor in Fanon's texts arises as a response to racial and colonial domination, as a kind of bodily knowledge—and by bodily knowledge I am trying to get at what Merleau-Ponty describes, the ways in which the body gives or acquires meaning in a fashion that our commonplace episteme of knowledge as intellectual fails to capture. The state of tension points toward, suggests, is, a space of irrepressible existence even in the absence of ego-protection, at the point of defeat. This state of muscle tension, both psychic in character and physical, draws its vitality, its existence even, from the anonymous life that, while it could never have meaning or know itself without its social production, illustrates a property or quality that is not limited to blackness itself.[151] Insofar as muscle tension is a metaphor for a kind of black *power*, that power is the ability or opportunity to access this condition, state, or facticity that is anonymous existence, which, to paraphrase Merleau-Ponty's words, muscle tension and its incipient resistance utilizes but does not entirely overlay. In blackness or nativity, the fall back onto the body in incipient or preparatory action—tensed muscles—operates to point toward "the gap which we ourselves are."

This return to the gap does not provide the narrative resolution of a homecoming; as Lacan warns, such resolutions are sweet dreams of philosophy. What muscle tension represents as a fall back onto the body and into (and also *as*) the "gap" that is consciousness itself, with all its indeterminate freedoms and limitations, may nevertheless dangle before us the dream of an integrated whole. But while the body can appear to be this—so Lacan's Mirror Stage fable enables us to understand—Merleau-Ponty reveals that the bodily schema which Fanon pronounces lacking when the body is blackened is founded on something that cannot be accessed. "I perceive with my body," Merleau-Ponty declares, "since my body and my senses are precisely that familiarity with the world born of habit, that implicit or sedimentary body of knowledge. . . . In perception we do not think the object and we do not think ourselves thinking it, we are given over to the object and we merge into this body which is better informed than we are about the world." Intellect and reason fail in the full apprehension of what the body knows, since what it knows is of a different order than intellectual process: "there is this latent knowledge which our gaze uses—the possibility of its rational development being a mere matter of presumption on our part—and which remains forever anterior to our perception."[152] That we cannot access this implicit knowledge in the terms that consciousness requires—nihilating withdrawal—means that as conscious beings we are always divided from ourselves: hence, the body is integrated only in the form of a haunting, as a seen-unseen tantalizingly out of reach. Thus, the fall back onto the body and into—as—the gap of *embodied* consciousness gains access to the inescapable ground for the escapades of consciousness that flee this ground and that build social worlds on its partly neglected, partly revered terrain. It is not that no other consciousness other than the one existing a blackened body can or does gain this access, or that blackness/nativity insists on achieving that access; it is that blackness/nativity forces its bearers to become vaulters who linger as if suspended over (or in) that gap, that range of possibilities, which we are.

It is perhaps this access which blackness provides that Fanon gestures toward as he chastises Sartre's too-quick reduction of Negritude to a minor term in the dialectical progression toward the more "universal" struggle of the proletariat. Whereas Sartre views Negritude as the predictable and intrinsically limited negation of white supremacy, Fanon cautions that Sartre "forgot that this negativity draws its worth from an almost substantive absoluteness" which ought to be allowed to operate, even if its activity appears to be "ignorance" of the greater truths (as Sartre sees them—and very likely Fanon, too) of the historical dialectic. This quality from which the negating activity of Negritude flows, its source, which would seem to prefigure or contain the resistance that blackness offers to its creators and conquerors, and also to exceed blackness, is an *absolute* that is *almost substantive*—a paradoxical description of the concrete and the elusive that, I would argue, either is an alternative description of or is in alignment with that anonymous existence that the body, in its tension, is and "knows."[153]

Translating the Lingual Black Body

I conclude here by once again surveying the pitfalls of misreading Fanon's work—but treading as closely as I can to the edge. Diana Fuss expands on a line of Fanon criticism that considers it problematic to read Fanon as a transcultural global theorist (whether of blackness or of anticolonial revolution), given the evident "self-divisions" in a biography that sites him in a series of disparate locations (Fort-de-France, Lyon, Paris, Blida, etc.) and finds him making a succession of claims to belonging in different groups. In this line of thought, as Gates puts it, we must recognize Fanon as the product of a far-flung Western culture in the throes of contradictions brought on by its colonialist and imperialist history, as a "battlefield in himself."[154] These agonisms born of his specific time and his various cultures, it is contended, determine the content of Fanon's theorizations in ways that must always give us pause. Hence, Fuss finds intriguing and ironic the confidence with which he diagnoses the political and cultural dis-ease manifest in his Algerian patients' physical symptoms, given the fact that his lack of fluency in Arabic or any of the Berber languages meant he could not *speak* to them and had to rely on nurses, orderlies, and even other patients as interpreters. For Fuss this language barrier—though, in fact, it was common enough in the hospitals run by the colonial administration in Algeria[155]—meant that the daily scene of colonial domination inscribed within paradigms of supposed healing highlighted for Fanon language as the site wherein "historical struggle and social contestation" was waged, since his lack of mastery of the native languages was itself a mark of the way in which he stood in the guise and place of "master" to them, the colonized, whose language need not be known. And to Fuss this meant, too, that he missed much of what psychiatric training would have illuminated for him as the stuff of his trade: "the analysand's own speech, . . . the slips and reversals, the substitutions and mispronunciations . . . that provide the analyst with his most important interpretive material, the traces and eruptions of the patient's unconscious into language."[156] Thus, Fanon's reliance on interpreters may well have led him to pay particular attention to the body as the expression of the unconscious, to locate in its mute expressiveness—in particular for our purposes, its tensions and torsions—the material to be interpreted and "worked on," as it were, which he himself could glean without necessarily relying on interpreters.

Fuss's observation would seem also to be in accord with Kobena Mercer's identification of the Bahktinian multiaccentuality of Fanon's text, especially in *Black Skin, White Masks*: the difficulty of translation at the scene of Fanon's psychiatric practice might be what accounts for the productive difficulty, the opaqueness of Fanon's text; Fanon's "many-voicedness," his melding and serial adoption of the "autobiographical, clinical, sociological, poetical, philosophical, political"—and I might add, literary-critical—in Mercer's view reflects, refracts, and represents "the presence of the body in language, the intonations, inflections and 'emotive-evaluative' elements of an utterance."[157] Mercer therefore suggests that Fanon's textual style and analytic method (at least on the page) reproduces in language that dimension of his patients' expression which remained opaque or garbled to him, that Fanon makes lingual and textual—by way, of course, of metaphor—the corporeal. This is at the same time as the limitations of Fanon's mastery of his subjugated patients' language may have led him to overestimate or to interpret overzealously bodily symptoms that he had perforce to think of as corporealizations of language. T. Denean Sharpley-Whiting balks at the implicit criticism of Fanon's thinking in such observations, pointing out that Fuss inaccurately assumes that Fanon was working as a psychoanalyst rather than a psychiatrist.[158]

But for my purposes, what Fuss and Gates identify as a problematic lacuna or a warning flag in the development of Fanon's analysis renders his suggestive comments regarding his patients' muscular rigidity all the more useful. While the attenuations of translation may present us with a battery of cautions, perhaps chastening our willingness to read too much into Fanon's recursion to the body as metaphor and as site of dis-eased symptom as well as the promise of authentic (decolonized) existence, these attenuations also actually point precisely to the nexus of, and the cross-pollination between, the discursive and the corporeal—the discursive corporealized, the corporeal as the materialization of discourse—that the lived-experience, the ironic "fact" of blackness insists upon: whether we label it as anonymous existence or vertigo or nausea, it is here, as language struggles to spread its defining web across a corporeal that it also constitutes but which in crucial regards it fails to address fully, as corporeality accrues to itself and as itself a form of knowing or knowledge that it expresses without language but simultaneously as the supplement to a language undergoing repression or failure—in the seesaw of this relation, and in its suspension between the "successes" of either project, in its productive tension—it is here that the power of blackness lies. Fanon, as I have said, wishes to move beyond this position; sometimes it is "the body of history" he would transcend, and at other times it is the body itself.[159] But my intention here is to hold at the point that Fanon's progress would surpass: to hold the tension.

One property that marks the positioning in the gateway toward a form of power in alienation, or, in Merleau-Ponty's terms, in that gap of possibilities which we are, as we have seen, is an hostility toward "conformity to the categories of time"—a debility from the perspective of colonizers promoting their self-serving versions of civilization, a form of unconscious resistance for Fanon, and for my reading of Fanon, just one (though perhaps the most puissant) of the *powers of blackness*, the powers of lingering in the gap of being.[160] These abilities that are also debilities can take the form of political resistance as they do for Fanon, or not. But we will need sweeter or perhaps more fabulous fables of lived experience than those dreamt of in Fanon's, Sartre's, and Merleau-Ponty's philosophies to enumerate those powers and the forms they take, all the more so if we are to find anything as perverse as *pleasure* in this context; we shall need a literary imagination.

2

"A Race That Could Be So Dealt With"

Terror, Time, and (Black) Power

The Black Male Body Abject

The figure of the Negro, Fanon says, is "woven . . . out of a thousand de-tails, anecdotes, stories."[1] Blackness is *lived*, but it is a representation. Even if, as we believe, all identities and subjectivities are falsities of this sort, *imagos* as hollow as old bones that language or father or the forces of eco-nomic production generate, blackness is a representation of rather recent historical vintage, unlike far older and presumably transcultural repre-sentations such as "woman." The historical proximity of its provenance makes tangible to us, visible, the operation of sociogenesis by which all of our human world comes into being. If blackness functions as the dark distorted mirror of the (thus whitened) Western self, reflecting its fears and obsessions concerning the body, sexuality, and mortality, then that blackness exists and that it is possible to historicize it mirrors for us the process by which the terms of self and socius have been constructed. In this way we can read blackness as a patchwork of narratives condensed on the skin of the blackened and referenced in the images ascribed to them, an articulation of meaning to image, the circulation of which occurs in the symbolic, a realm both collective (as all that we might call culture) and id-iosyncratic (as what we deem the individual unconscious). What emerges most forcefully from Fanon's ruminations in *Black Skin, White Masks* is the idea that blackness is an artifact of the symbolic, one of the clever de-ceptions of language as it attempts to give substance to the void that it is and as it vainly attempts to impose order on the riotously excessive world with which it is confronted.

Like all language, then, blackness is code. And as with all language, this encoding can by its proliferating processes of abstraction and asso-ciation virally replicate itself; it generates more encoded language—and thus more knowledge, more of a *something* which it codes—otherwise unavailable. Artistry that makes language its primary medium of cre-ation explores and exploits language's essential coding: it does so through metonymy. Such art generates "insight" (or, strictly speaking, a new or different idea) by combining, collapsing, conflating in some jarring or beautiful or shocking way things, ideas, memes, that were heretofore not in contiguity or not placed in contiguity in that way. Thus, language art— trope work—routinely conducts a thought-experiment in the manner we ascribe generically to speculative fiction, by creating seemingly impossible, or at least difficult to imagine, conjunctions: conjunctions not unlike those troublesome "contradictions" we find lurking in Fanon's corpus, such as the paradoxes of the rigid black(ened) body that is both living and dead and both inert and in movement, the facticity of human freedom as its imprisonment, the decidedly nonlinear temporality that folds a past as future anterior under and over a future as past posterior.

This is why at the conclusion of the preceding chapter I said that a literary imagination is required to enumerate the powers of blackness at the point of its defeat; a literary imagination can locate abilities and "power" at the point of the apparent erasure of ego-protections, the point at which the constellation of tropes that we call identity, body, race, nation seem to reveal themselves as utterly penetrated, without defensible boundary. What Fanon epigrammatically refers to as muscle tension or rigidity, and what he considers significant only insofar as it is inchoate revolutionary action, the literary imagination, sporting the kind of dramatic license with temporality that we allow to opera, can expatiate upon at length and sound to its depths on its own terms. If blackness is metonymic, or is a metonym that demonstrates for us the associative coding and translation that constitutes all our individual and social categories of meaning, then the literary—by one definition, metonymy elaborated and exploited—is a mode that can demonstrate the operation of blackness, both how it is lived and how it might be. The literary is an apt mode of theorizing blackness. In this and the chapters that follow, then, I want to link arms between my appropriative literary reading of the muscle tension metaphor in Fanon's theoretical text and a derivation of theoretics from literary representations of blackness.

The first text I examine predates Fanon by half a century, but in James Weldon Johnson's *The Autobiography of an Ex-Coloured Man*, Fanon's observation that blackness is the repository for Western culture's unconscious fears about the body and sexuality is plumbed, dramatized, and deployed as an instrument of societal critique. As in Fanon's theorizing, Johnson's black male character as victim, as object of the savage violence of human beings and simultaneously as the *imago* of human savagery, is through his experience of trauma the bearer of what for Fanon is universal truth: the sociogenic root of human personality and the power of a conscious sociogeny to reshape politics (and reality). Moreover, Johnson's character comes to experience blackness precisely as defeat, as the abject and undefendable, missing (arguably as Fanon sometimes does) its abilities, which include, in that text, an anguished, vertiginous encounter with what we found described by Merleau-Ponty as anonymous existence, and the possibilities inherent in the temporal dispersal that partly defines that state.

Fanon often relies for evidence (and method) on African American and Afro-Diasporic literary representation in his exegesis of the various facts of blackness in *Black Skin, White Masks*. In that field, the slave narrative is of course the ur-text and the skeleton on which subsequent literary creations drape themselves. The bourgeois (or aspirationally bourgeois) subject constructed and represented in narratives of the 17th, 18th, and 19th centuries is in the slave narrative, in ways more nakedly explicit than in other Western traditions of writing, the exemplar and advocate for a race; the slave narrative thus constructs and represents a race in individual voice. Johnson's is a distinctly modern revision of a form that has become venerable by the time of his writing. His fictional autobiography sutures a private individual story to the public collective history of a race—but, as interpreters of Johnson such as Robert Stepto have noted,[2] unlike Booker T. Washington's *Up from Slavery* or Frederick Douglass's *Narrative of the Life*, *The Autobiography* is a story of failure. Johnson makes this failure clear with a lament that closes the novel, in which the narrator fears that his decision to abandon his affiliation with black people has left him, like Esau, with little more than "a mess of pottage."[3] Essentially the Ex-Coloured Man fails to accede to an empowered black male identity as "race man"; and as Henry Louis Gates, Jr., details in his introduction to the 1989 Vintage edition of the novel, a "race man" is precisely what Johnson, a prolific writer and editor, civil rights activist, and onetime U.S. consul, himself was. Johnson's narrative thus charts a trajectory of identity formation that his own biography did not mirror, a fact which, for us as readers, certainly heightens the cautionary stakes of the novel and limns in bold red the dimensions and reasons for his character's failure.

Of course, the ways in which we find Johnson's narrator *failing* differ according to the historical moment in which we assess them and to our own idiosyncratic attentions: certainly a failure that Johnson would probably have been little cognizant of has to do with the limitations of the novel's implicit definition of success, since the ideal of "race man" looms over the text trailing all the familiar baggage of its masculinism.[4] Masculinism is at stake in the novel in much the same way as it often is in Fanon's texts, in that an assumption is made that black people ought to live up to the challenge of assuming an ideal "manhood" which their conquerors and enslavers have introduced to them as part and parcel of the very notion of race. Thus, an anxiety hovers around the conflation of the achievement of the masculine with the success of racial identity—manifesting itself for Fanon in, as one example, a much-discussed histrionic denial of the incidence of homosexuality in the black French Antilles, and appearing in Johnson's novel in various narrative moments when gender identity and sexuality are in apparent crisis. These crises, as critics such as Phillip Brian Harper and Siobhan Somerville have shown, illuminate how, within the cultural economy of the United States, racial identity has a mutually constitutive relation to constructs of gender and sexuality.[5]

These crises are indications not only of Johnson having put his finger on the complexities of identity formation but also of the extent of the operation of the sociogenic principle in the shaping of human reality: I read Johnson to suggest that, though his character fails to become truly ex-colored (and, concomitantly, ex-masculine and/or ex-heterosexual), nevertheless *through* a certain kind of conscious, willing embrace of the defeat, abjection, and violation that blackness inescapably is, it becomes possible to access the ability to *shape* race, gender, and sexuality and other world-forming ideations—even if only partly or for what seem to be moments of vanishing brevity. Blackness, having been blackened, the blackness that is defeat, gives Johnson's narrator the opportunity to know that one's self, indeed, as we shall see, one's very body and flesh, is shaped by stories, anecdotes, and a thousand discursive details. While it is of course easier as assertion than as praxis, there is power in this recognition: those stories and anecdotes—since they engage in a deadly play in the empty air, as it were, of "a void that is not nothing,"[6] a void that Sartre describes as vertiginous freedom and choice and that Merleau-Ponty describes as anonymous existence—describe or encompass sociogenic possibility, precisely through that relation to the void, which is to say that those stories can be retold, or other details may alter their meaning. And the mark of this power, as well as the means of access to it, lies in temporal dispersal for Johnson's narrator, much as it does for Fanon's black/native.

In *Autobiography of an Ex-Coloured Man*, the unnamed narrator, the son of a black woman and a white man, traces a personal history in which

he not only moves back and forth between playing white and black social roles—"black" and "white" should always be understood as positions
enunciated in quotation marks in the novel—but he also shuttles across
lines of status and class and lifestyle, moving from respectable to bohemian and back again, at different times a classical pianist prodigy, a student
in an all-black college, a cigar factory worker, a gambler, a ragtime pianist,
a bon vivant in Europe, and a real estate businessman. On one level, this
movement across social lines is a kind of freedom that others in the novel,
even his wealthy white patrons, do not enjoy to quite the same extent, for
the narrator draws his mobility from the rigidity of the black/white binary
and the various ways that the binary is manifested: his freedom is facili-
tated and at times almost impelled by his ability to pass as both black and
white. Because he is conscious of the constructed quality of the binary, he
is able to make and remake himself. But only to an extent.

There are two key moments in the novel when the narrator's freedom
is sharply curtailed: one, when his schoolteacher tells him that he is black,
a "fact" of which he had been unaware and which sends him fleeing to his
mirror in anxiety; and the second, when while traveling in the South gathering material for his work as a musician, he witnesses a lynching. This
second experience, which I focus on here,[7] is so searing that he utterly
abandons artistic ambitions: thereafter he vows that he will not choose
between black and white and will let others perceive him in whatever way
they choose, in effect, since his skin is not dark, electing to pass as white
for the rest of his life—and, in effect, putting an end to the movement that
has characterized his life in the past and settling him into a more static,
psychologically isolated existence.

The lynching the Ex-Coloured Man witnesses offers him a lesson in
what he calls "the transformation of human beings into savage beasts."
When he first sees an armed band of Southern white men solemnly gathered at a railroad station, he regards both their physical and moral qualities with great admiration. "[S]tern, comparatively silent" and "orderly,"
"blond, tall, and lean, with ragged moustache and beard, and glittering
grey eyes," they are, he indicates with some emphasis, "fierce, determined
men."[8] His description of them has an almost classical quality: manly vir-
tue and the beauty of the (white) male body fuse.

That masculinity, beauty, and whiteness are overlapping and mutually
defining idealities in the narrator's perception is evident in other moments
in the text, as well: from an early age, before he becomes aware that he is
a person of color, the narrator considers himself to be different from other

boys, because of his refined artistic sensibilities. His innate love for music makes him prone to girlish fits of "sentimental hysteria" and "temperamental excesses": "I should have been out playing ball or in swimming with other boys of my age," he remarks.[9] While such wistful regrets about the foundations of his masculinity never come to the forefront of the novel in the way that concerns about the narrator's place in the black/white schema of the world do, the issue merges with the difficulties surrounding the black/white divide. Twice the narrator develops relationships in which he is protected by white males who seem to occupy traditionally masculine roles with greater ease than he does: as a child he is the favored friend of "Red Head," a boy five years older than all the other boys in his class; and as an adult he receives the patronage of a white man whom he refers to as "my millionaire."[10] The narrator's relations with other black men are by contrast tentative and less embracing. Describing the students at the all-black college Atlanta University, he notes that "among the boys many of the blackest were fine specimens of manhood, tall, straight and muscular." But as this is only the second time he has seen so many black folk gathered together (his first such experience, in the streets of Atlanta, filled him with "a feeling of almost repulsion"), the countenance and bearing of these young men are a mystery to him. It is noteworthy to him that in the crowd, the "more intelligent types . . . predominat[e]" because he does not expect this to be the case, any more than he expects some of the "brown" girls actually to be pretty ("I could not help noticing"). Soon enough he manages to box these intelligent new "types" in ready-made categories he has brought with him to Atlanta: "these were the kind of boys who developed into the patriarchal 'uncles' of the old slave regime." Their "type" has no purchase, then, on the novel's present, and the paradigmatic patriarchal role of father is denied them, its privileges and powers displaced onto the uncle who serves the white master. Of his millionaire, by contrast, he says warmly, "I looked upon him . . . as about all a man could wish to be." This is a prophetic statement, certainly; the millionaire is about all the narrator could wish to be as a *white* man, and this is all the more clear since he will in fact end up passing as one.[11]

It is this admiration for white masculinity, tinged, as Harper and Somerville agree, with the erotic desire that subtends projections of the ideal onto the Other, that informs the narrator's initial interest in men who will prove to be lynchers. When the captive for whom the white men have been waiting is finally brought to the station, these beautiful and virtuous creatures undergo a metamorphosis; in the presence of a black man bound by ropes, the white men, whom the narrator has been gazing upon almost as though they were works of folk art (he rhapsodizes that they are "picturesque"), become frighteningly animate. From stern reserve they erupt into blood-curdling rebel yells; a cry of "Burn him!" is heard that electrifies the assemblage with excitement. The narrator's terror in witnessing this transformation is confirmed in the visage of the black man they chain to a stake in the ground. "There he stood, *a man only in form and stature*, every sign of *degeneracy* stamped upon his countenance."[12]

The black man is a degenerated man, whereas the white men are ideal men. But the narrator swiftly concludes that neither the black man nor his white tormentors in this scene are recognizably human. The black man's figure invigorates the white men because it is the object, the repository, of bloodthirsty desires—"old, underlying animal instincts and passions" that everyone shares, according to the narrator, but that have no place in "this day of enlightened . . . thought." Elsewhere in the novel, Johnson indicates that the institutionalized bigotry of the South is rooted in a refusal to abide by "the ideals of twentieth-century civilization and of modern humanitarianism." Brutal treatment of black people is a hallmark of premodernity; like "the bloody deeds of pirates and the fierce brutality of vikings,"[13] it is as primitive as its victims are supposed to be. It is the white men who stamp on the lynched man's face the signs of degeneracy, of devolution to a premodern, noncivilized state; his body—the other body, the "not-self," as Fanon terms the black male body[14]—bears the mark and the brunt of their savagery.

"Before I could make myself believe that what I saw was really happening, I was looking at a scorched post, a smouldering fire, blackened bones, charred fragments sifting down through coils of chain; and the smell of burnt flesh—human flesh—was in my nostrils."

The lynched man's smell is set aside by a semicolon in this list of the fragments made of his body. It is the narrator's most powerful sensory impression, yet a nonsensory realization is the key piece of it: the recognition that what he smells burning is *human* flesh. The narrator has no prior experience of this odor. He cannot identify it the way he might recognize the smell of coffee roasting, by his sense-memory; on the evidence of his senses alone, he can only tell that what he perceives is a different smell. The moment of his realization, like the listing of the smell itself, is set aside by special punctuation, by a dash. It is here, in the recognition of this new, alien smell, that the humanity of the man who is being lynched is first affirmed; he becomes human—though perhaps not a "man"—in the moment of his body's destruction, in the moment in which he is in the process of losing the sole visible and existential claim to humanity, his body. Prior to his murder and dismemberment, the narrator sees the lynched man purely in the terms of his role as victim, and as the degenerated less-than-man his captors exult to pretend that he is: the lynch victim is merely a husk for projected qualities—"dull and vacant," too stupefied to demonstrate "a single ray of thought"; the narrator up until this moment is not even especially certain that the black man ever evinced the qualities of a civilized person, noting that present circumstances have "robbed him of *whatever* reasoning power he had ever possessed."[15] Thus, in the recognition of the smell of burnt human flesh, the alien affirms the familiar, and the recognition of abjection confirms the presence of the subject: it is a shock of recognition that seals the narrator's identification with the lynched man, an identification that he otherwise might not experience, since until that moment the man only resembles a human being in form.

This identification is deeper than a political or intellectual affiliation or an admiration for the cultures of black folk, feelings the narrator experiences prior to this moment: this is a recognition of kinship, tied to the physical experience of smell, that acts as a kind of psychic synesthesia; it is an experience bound up in the recognition of the fragility of the body, of its violability, the recognition as a kind of bodily knowledge that in human experience lies the possibility of being subjected to treatment worse than that which would be accorded animals and therefore that in human experience lies the capacity of being an instrument, an object. It is, arguably, a bodily knowledge of the fragility, the essential gap or void, the apparent nonselfness or anonymity, of the human self.

The narrator cannot name the recognition of this fact, this assault on the ego, as anything other than shame: "Shame that I belonged to a race that could be so dealt with"—the shame of this intimate, bodily knowledge of suffering, the shame of not being able effectively to separate this suffering from himself, not being able to project it out onto something that is the not-self: the shame of having to harbor in his body the abject, the unassimilable. He does not have available to him the psychic mechanisms of the white spectators, who yell and cheer or are sickened and appalled: whatever their response, their relation is to some thing not themselves; they need not be conscious of their actual kinship to the body that has become less than a body, a mere figure, in front of their eyes. The narrator is denied the safety of such a distant vantage point; he is at once his body, intact, on the sidelines, and the body reduced to a figure for what is despised, the body roasting, like an animal slaughtered to provide a kind of psychic sustenance for the hunters who capture it.

For the narrator this feeling is intolerable. After witnessing the lynching, he says, "I was as weak as a man who had lost blood." It is not only the horror of what he has seen that enervates him: he is exsanguinated by the knowledge he has gained; he is rendered almost bodiless by the shock of this violent contact with the white world. This is the case though his own body is not touched by the violence. In fact, as a passive spectator, indistinguishable from the white onlookers, he might be said to have been a participant in the violence, to have in a sense enacted it himself: he has, in seeing what he has seen, immolated himself.

Fundamentally the narrator's sense-determined identification with the lynched man tells him, "I too could be burned and dismembered and extinguished." It is a confrontation with the fear and the inevitability of death. As I noted in the previous chapter in my discussion of Sartre, the threat of death presents consciousness to itself as both subject and object. Sartrean anguish and vertigo, in forcing a consciousness to confront the empty space of possibilities which in their indeterminacy are as fully "nothing" as death is, and indeed are the echo, the reflection, of death, paradoxically immerses the consciousness in living and in its at once vast and profoundly limited freedoms. To be thus conscious of being alive is potentially thrilling but mostly terrifying—hence Sartre's choice to signify these events as informed by fear (anguish and vertigo). That terror is, Fanon tells us, a key portion of what constitutes blackness, what splits the blackened body in twain. Muscular tension as metaphor and symptom of racialization is manifested as a rigidity that is potentially active but appears to be, mimics, necrotized flesh. The nothingness that is blackness or that identification with blackness threatens, with which the Ex-Coloured Man is confronted, is terror as the very essence of consciousness: his act of witnessing reveals that to be conscious is to be terrified, to be aware of how one is constituted by a void of possibilities of which the most absolute and the most certain is death. Little wonder, then, that he banishes this terror, by repeating the work he has seen so ably performed by the white men he admires: he banishes it under the sign of blackness. What he fails to perceive—and this measures to the full the depth of his failure in the novel—is that to turn from the terror is also to turn away from the full range of possibilities and freedoms given to him as a human, which blackness, precisely in its appearance as abjection, provides a way of accessing.

The narrator banishes the terrors and powers of blackness by deciding he will refuse to belong either to the spectators or to the victim. This refusal of identification with blackness or whiteness projects the experiences of victim and responsible actor outside himself. He will "neither disclaim the black race nor claim the white race," but he will "raise a moustache" and change his name.[16]

The moustache is a telling detail at this moment of decision, because it echoes his observation of the white male Southern type, who wears a ragged moustache as one of his distinguishing characteristics. In deciding to wear one himself, the narrator belies his announced strategy of neutrality and accentuates the fact that he has chosen to identify himself with white men.[17] Moreover, the moustache is of course a bodily sign of masculinity—facial hair distinguishes men from women, and in the course of the 20th century, different groups of men who have felt excluded from the status of manhood in a patriarchal social order, including African American men and gay men, have embraced it as a necessary part of their politicized aesthetics. Since a moustache conjures the image and status of male dominance and privilege—dominance and privilege enjoyed solely by white men in the narrator's society—and since it is and functions as an accouterment of the body, the narrator's cosmetic choice reasserts the integrity of his masculine body and serves to wall off an identification that might suggest his body is not whole or complete. In choosing this path, the Ex-Coloured Man can safely disown the knowledge of abject suffering that identification with blackness threatens to make him confront.

This move underlines the way that, in the Ex-Coloured Man's world, whiteness is associated with embodiment, and blackness hovers spectrally as a kind of ethereal, mysterious quality—counter to the usual alignment of blackness with bodies, whiteness with "the mind" and unmarked privileges. At one point he describes being black as having to wear "a label of inferiority pasted across [one's] . . . forehead"—a description that by synecdoche reduces the full-body sheath of black skin to a forehead sign, thus further diminishing and distancing the "mask" that Fanon designates as an epidermal schema from what, in the narrator's view, counts for fully embodied reality. (The narrator's imagination is enabled by his light complexion, another way that whiteness stands in for his own embodied truth.) Prior to the lynching scene, the narrator discusses "different phases of the Negro question" with a dark-brown male doctor aboard a ship returning from Europe to the United States, and though the narrator is light-skinned and can pass for white, he rather ostentatiously uses the pronoun "we" in the conversation, with apparent satisfaction; he feels himself to be a member of tribe, in large part because here he has decided to embark on an artistic career of melding ragtime with classical music forms. The racialized sensibility he embraces at this point in the novel has primarily to do with *knowing* he is *marked* even though the mark is invisible to others; it is this knowing and being accepted among other black people that puts him *in the know*. It grants him access to that realm of esoteric language and knowledge hidden from the whites among whom he is also accepted: "the freemasonry of the race," in Johnson's elegant phrase. Yet he wonders if he is native enough to play native translator in the realm of music. Listening to gospel music performances in a black Southern "big meeting," he is struck: "As I listened to the songs, the wonder of their production grew upon me more and more. How did the men who originated them manage to do it? The sentiments are easily accounted for; they are mostly taken from the Bible; but the melodies, where did they come from?"[18] Johnson's purpose here is almost certainly to draw attention to the inventive genius of an American art form that his readers, white and black, might be likely to disdain, but the narrator's query reverberates at the core of the character, for it echoes his most vexatious question. How deeply does the mark of blackness penetrate, especially if no one really sees it? He wonders anxiously whether there is not, in fact, some special racial quality that contributes to the genius that he wishes to use in his project, and whether that quality is at work in him. Blackness for him represents something that has little to do with the skin that makes a body black; it represents, as it turns out, a far broader and possibly more powerful set of qualities than the attributes of the body. It represents, as we shall see, Fanonian sociogenesis, because blackness is one of that process's most remarkably fecund products.

Nevertheless the narrator grasps for the body in his confrontation with the terror of blackness. The narrator's reactions and responses to the lynching are all modulations and metaphors of bodily experience: from smell as recognition, and shock and shame as exsanguination, to disclaiming black identity as the decision to grow facial hair. This set of choices is determined by any number of influences, not least the simple urge to save his "skin," but his decided bent toward the (white) body seems to owe a great deal to what for the Ex-Coloured Man is the other insufficiently thought-through measure of self in the novel: masculinity, and his understanding of masculinity as white—and, of course, the designation of this ideal as erotic object.[19]

Again, the narrator's searing recognition of the fragility of the self is twinned with, inaugurated by, an admiring homosocial, homoerotic gazing at white men. The Ex-Coloured Man's desire for the white man—aesthetic, erotic—is linked with a witnessing of the white man's aggression toward the black male body. This linkage between powerful desire and destructive violence has profound effects. In *Black Skin, White Masks* Fanon rather blithely claims that Negrophobic white women who fear being raped by black men harbor a secret desire to be raped; following Freudian notions about the teleology of female engenderment from clitoral to vaginal sexuality, Fanon's assessment is that there is an unclaimed "masculine" aggression a Negrophobic woman has against her femininity—against herself as a woman—that makes her take pleasure in the fantasy of being the victim of sexual aggression.

Johnson's contemporary Freud describes this mechanism more elaborately, and in a manner somewhat less encumbered by the sexist assumptions that Fanon and Freud partly share. In Freud's 1919 essay "A Child Is Being Beaten," he observes in his male and female patients a recurring sexual fantasy in which the patient watches a child being beaten by the patient's father. This fantasy, Freud argues, is created by the patient's childhood desire to be sexually or genitally loved by the father. The patient's guilt about this forbidden desire and repression of it leads to a scene of punishment: the father beats a fantasy child, but this fantasy child is merely a stand-in; it is the patient who is being punished. At the same time the beating is a substitute for the forbidden sexual liaison. In effect, a sadistic fantasy is founded on a masochistic self-loathing because of incestuous (and in the case of male patients, homosexual) desire.[20]

It is not difficult to see how this mechanism might be at play when the soon-to-be Ex-Coloured Man witnesses the lynching: shuttling in his psyche back and forth between spectator and victim, he experiences a just punishment for his desire—*just* because he did admire the white men who show themselves to be savages, and he feels guilty; *just* because he yearns still to receive the approval of the white father figure that he has never received and for which this child-is-being-beaten scene of projected punishment and self-destruction must substitute.

The profundity of the effect of this scene on the narrator and the degree to which it utterly boggles his attempts to settle into a clearly raced identity should be evident in the way that this scene is arguably one of the primal scenes of American race relations under slavery and Jim Crow: the child, taught to see all paternal authority resting in the white male master, witnesses the master beating a black adult. (I think, of course, of Frederick Douglass watching his aunt being beaten.) That there is a relation between this scene of slavery and the fantasy of the beaten child is made clear by Freud: he notes that the beating fantasy is frequently ignited when young people read *Uncle Tom's Cabin*.[21]

The result of all these factors being in play—the confrontation with the fear of death and the abjection which is blackness, the threat of loss of ego defenses, sexualized desire for the white father's love, guilt—is that the narrator cannot successfully work through or work with the experience of witnessing the lynching. He therefore cannot choose a relationship to other men based on anything else but an irreducible sense of difference that always threatens to erupt into violence. "I began to wonder if I was really like the men I associated with; if there was not, after all, an indefinable something which marked a difference," he says (which again speaks to that notion of blackness as an ephemeral, disembodied quality).[22] The men he associates with are white, and, arrested in the memory of the lynching he witnessed, he cannot imagine a relationship to white *men* on any other basis than fear of being different from them; and thus, though he is attempting to avoid conflict by passing as white, he is locked into a psychic adversarial relationship with white men that cannot be resolved. To be locked into this opposition proves to be psychologically near-fatal for him. And he has sacrificed his capacity for relationship with the black men whom he had once fancied brethren in a collective "we," as well.

Materially, however, the narrator's act of disidentification has positive effects. He goes on to make a comfortable living as a real estate investor, to marry and to have children, to live "as an ordinarily successful white man." This would seem to be a reasonable, if morally questionable, decision under the circumstances. Yet the Ex-Coloured Man senses, in a moment of wistful reflection that closes the novel, that there is perhaps some other way of being that lies hidden in what he perceives to be the horror of his experience of the lynching, some possible form of movement in the stasis of the black/white binary, some flip side to the terror of abjection. There is, he realizes, the "glorious" work of "making history" and "making . . . a race."[23] This lost opportunity haunts the Ex-Coloured Man with a kind of possibility and knowledge of existence—that is, that the ego and its defenses do not encompass the breadth of what we call the self or the subject; the self has far broader potentialities, which can become manifest in the collective work of making a race and making a history: in sociogenesis, in other terms.

Robert Stepto examines in persuasive detail the milieu of the Club in New York City where the narrator first imbibes the allure of the urban and samples the joys of life among bohemians. In the Club the narrator meets a class of black people of whom he had largely been ignorant, including minstrel show performers, jockeys, and musicians, who brush shoulders with the gamblers and pool sharks. Stepto surveys the topographical and metaphorical relation between the Club's parlor sitting room, where the walls are adorned by framed photographs "of Frederick Douglass and of Peter Jackson, of all the lesser lights of the prize-fighting ring, . . . all the famous . . . celebrities, down to the newest song and dance team," and a back room where singers and dancers perform in the middle of the floor for patrons gathered at the tables.[24] The photographs and the performers have a relation to one another, Stepto notes, that is figured in the performers' discussions of ways to prevent their work from being exploited by white promoters and performers; the gallery of photographs is a figure for the tradition of black cultural production in the making: the fresh artistic expressions formed in the performance space of the back room take place with "Frederick Douglass . . . staring . . . from the parlor." In Stepto's view, the narrator misreads the cultural significance of this space, ignoring the Club's "deep structure"—ignoring, in Johnson's terms, the possibility of making a history and a race and, in Fanon's terms, ignoring the power of sociogenesis which blackness exemplifies and to which blackness permits access.[25]

It seems to me that this willful ignorance on the narrator's part figures his response to the lynching. That the Ex-Coloured Man is barred from the more pleasurable and "positive" aspects of race-making and the camaraderie of freemasonry, and that he refuses to wend his way through the terrors of identifying with "a race that could be so treated," are dual aspects of the same failure; and the events can be seen as echoes of one another, narrative demonstrations of the same idea: from the novel's outset the narrator works hard to evade the ways in which he enters the world as its *object*, as *blackened*, rendered by history in a social position that compels a confrontation with abjection. He flees blackness, little understanding what Johnson sets as his task to understand: that to become a subject *too* (which is to say, in Sartrean terms, that he would be foolish in any case to imagine he can eschew being the world's object *in part*, because everyone is such an object insofar as we all have a past that exceeds us), he will have to trek through the subterranean environs of that confusion between subject and object that marks abjection.[26] Thus, the Ex-Coloured

Man cannot assume a heroic or communal voice *insofar as* he recognizes but refuses to occupy, to *exist*, the fact that blackness is produced through humiliation and degradation.

In the lynching scene, the process of being made black, illuminating the condition of blackness, and *blackening* the flesh are all the same: the body as it blackens in being burned is rendered as the body in its abject dimensions, as the (barely or only contingently) existing nonexistent, the existential condition that is *not* a subject. In this sense the Ex-Coloured Man's is not only a failure to embrace those aspects of black history, black wisdom, or black arts that are cannily creative in the face of, and even triumphantly resistant to, white domination, but also a failure to understand that the capacity to resist can be marshaled precisely through an embrace of degradation and that canny creative responses might require an unflinching recognition of the very dangers that he experiences so viscerally in witnessing the lynching.

This recognition and its capacity to empower him (even if in ways and with forms of power inconceivable to him) requires, or might best be accessed through, what might crudely be suggested in the text as an acceptance, assimilation, or occupation of the black body, as opposed to the white (which is not in the novel by any means an absolute opposition, of course). This means a reconfigured relation to the body or to bodily existence along the following lines: the dislocation of body-image in its relation to the ideal self, since the confusion between the two, at least as it arises in the Mirror Stage in the Lacanian account, introjects to the core of the ego racialization, through the simultaneous eroticization of whiteness and disavowal of blackness.

The white male body is for the Ex-Coloured Man like the mirror image: an image of control, an image that appears in the eyes of the misapprehending viewer as the exemplar of wholeness. Just as in the Mirror Stage described by Lacan, in response to such an image the narrator attempts to assimilate it to himself, and thus he splits off those aspects of his psyche—those roving desires, those questions, impulses, fears—that fail to match or that threaten the cohesion of that image. The narrator's move to become a white man cosmetically is a move that requires and that enacts repression: a repression of his blackness—which in this context means the knowledge and experience in the body of not being or possessing the coherence of an inviolable identity with clear demarcations between it and the rest of the world—not being recognized as human, not being recognized as a *man*. And it is a repression accomplished through an identification experienced in his desire for and admiration of the image of the white man.

The Ex-Coloured Man's confusion is figured in the novel after the narrator's initial realization that he is black, an event in the novel that has the contrived and incredible character of a staged event. One day in elementary school the principal interrupts class and asks "the white scholars" in the room to stand up. The narrator dutifully rises to join his fellows, only to be reproached by his teacher. "You sit down now, and *rise with the others*," the teacher tells him. The narrator is aghast. "I sat down dazed. I saw and heard nothing," the Ex-Coloured Man recalls. The narrator races up to his room after school to stare at himself in the mirror. "For an instant I was afraid to look," he says, fearing to see the face of the Other staring back at him.[27] The narrator's fear and loss of his senses neatly accords with Fanon's theory; the black(ened) subject, who had thought of himself unconsciously in white terms, who had unconsciously identified with whiteness as the measure of human in his world, suddenly is made to occupy the position of blackness—he is made to become one of *the others*—and as a consequence loses the orientation of his bodily schema. The narrator's self is bound up entirely with his body image.

Judith Butler reads race into Freud's accounts of the ego-ideal which serves as the basis for the super-ego and into Lacan's Mirror Stage, arguing that the ego-ideal against which the self is measured (and always found wanting) is a bodily ego—the child in the Mirror Stage identifies with a specular *body*—and that this bodiliness is the site where racial morphology can be introjected to the concept of self: the ego is thus a racialized ego.[28] Fanon formulates this matter with a clarity that seems almost Olympian in its intervention into Eurocentric psychoanalytic paradigms, when he notes in *Black Skin, White Masks* that for Antillean patients the "mirror hallucination" is "always neutral." Questioning Antillean patients about their encounters with mirrors in dreams, he reports, "I always ask the same question: 'What color were you?' Invariably they reply: 'I had no color.' . . . [Thus] [i]t is not I as a Negro who acts, thinks, and is praised to the skies."[29] This neutrality is on one level false; though it may evince in Fanon's Antillean patients the more or less healthy persistence of a pre-racialization self-concept,[30] it is more likely evidence of what Fanon produces it to show: that the Antillean, the colonized black/native, in his subconscious flees a self-perception of himself as black because of the negative meanings that constitute blackness. Thus, the Antillean's Mirror Stage race-neutrality is a restatement of Johnson's ex-colored figure.

In order for the Ex-Coloured Man not to fail, the relation between white body-image and ego-ideal must give way to that form of bodily knowledge which Fanon's metaphor of muscle tension references, and which Merleau-Ponty refers to as anonymous existence. The narrator has defined the bodily by its whiteness insofar as the body he aspires to exist (his ego-ideal/body-image) is one defined by its masculine inviolability; and this body is a structural reflection of the ego precisely in its essential defensive posture. Concomitantly he has defined blackness by its being violated and abject, as, in fact, the *loss* or threatened loss of bodily integrity, and even as disembodied. Instead he must try to assume a black body that is not the physical reiteration of the ego's defenses but that physicalizes the self *without—or almost/always without*—ego, which we can understand in the terms with which Merleau-Ponty describes that inescapable hauntedness of embodied existence that makes itself hazily known through the sensibility that precedes the ego form of consciousness: the "'already born' or 'still alive'" of amorphous existence.[31] (This physicality would be particularly important for the Ex-Coloured Man in its formulation as "still alive.") He must assume, that is, a black body abject that is the contact point with a void that is not nothing, the kernel of subject and self. One way of putting this is to say that, in a racist and sexist society, the racialized ego is always already white and masculine, which is what the Ex-Coloured Man's erotic compulsion to emulate and incorporate white masculinity demonstrates, and what Fanon means when he grandly provokes us, "For the black man there is only one destiny. And it is white."[32] The anonymous or ephemeral or void (void in the form of empty possibilities) existence that exceeds or subtends the ego is projected and introjected as racial and gender referents—blackness and the feminine—and may be accessed through the occupation, especially insofar as they are abject, of those social and referential positions.

And how would the Ex-Coloured Man know when he has occupied such a position, when and how he has such access? What would such access look like, and what would it afford him? According to Johnson, and to Fanon, Sartre, and Merleau-Ponty, the when, how, and substance of that access lies in part in his loss of *when* itself, which heralds and accomplishes the retreat of the (in any case incomplete) stabilization effects of ego. Here, too, temporal dispersal is a power of blackness.

(Ex-)Colored Temporalities

In several moments in the Ex-Coloured Man's autobiography time gets lost. The narrator's loss of his senses when the teacher cruelly reveals to him that he is black is accompanied by another loss in his desperate encounter with the image of his body at the mirror. There he loses track of time: "How long I stood there gazing at my image I do not know." Later, when he is flirting with a white woman in the Club and her jealous black lover shoots her—their pairing is the first interracial relationship he has observed apart from the glimmerings of his mother's with his white father—the Ex-Coloured Man rushes out into the night. "How long and far I walked I cannot tell," he says. Finally, after the lynching, before he decides to pass, he crumbles to the ground: "How long I sat with bitter thoughts running through my mind I do not know."[33]

In each "how long . . . I do not know" event the narrator's short-term inability to count time is, of course, simply a way for Johnson to dramatize the event's emotional impact. But if we are reading Johnson as theorizing in narrative form aspects of blackness, then the fact that at each of these points the narrator is confronted with the violence of the relation between black and white in his world, or is presented with the mystery of the content of those terms as touchstones for identity, or both, casts the momentary instability of chronology in these moments as possible indications that Johnson is working with those questions concerning the problem of history we discussed in Fanon, and is staging that problem in the form of his character's symptom. As in *Black Skin, White Masks*, then, in *The Autobiography of an Ex-Coloured Man* "the problem considered . . . is one of time."[34] Perhaps lost time in these narrative events marks and/or is an effect of other kinds of losses: psychical, insofar as being presented with a stark choice between black and white necessitates the loss of whatever the rejected choice signifies; historical, insofar as the loss of time is not unlike the muscular rigidity of Fanon's patients, whose bodies are partially arrested in the past conquest and enslavement that has made them the inheritors of the category black/native and has left them scarred by that originary loss of an irrecoverable precontact persona.

Is this lost time then largely a symptom of trauma? Certainly our understanding of trauma provides useful tools for decoding what Johnson is indicating to us: it is true that difficulty in locating the traumatizing event in narrative and disarrayed chronology mark the impact of trauma.[35] Therefore Johnson's placement of these moments when time is lost in an autobiographical narrative, the generic conceit of which is that all that is significant is *accounted* for, holds (and clears) a space for what falls outside such accounting. Johnson's structuring thus mimics how we understand trauma to operate: trauma appears paradoxically in its disappearance, its emptiness, as that holding space bordered by forgetting, latency, delay, which preserves a historical event that it nonetheless cannot render as narrative. The witnessing of the lynching, and the witnessing of the white woman's murder in the Club, and the encounter with his own suddenly blackened image in the mirror, might reasonably enough be called traumas of a sort, but it is not so much a matter of reading these *events* as traumas. In fact, the ways the Ex-Coloured Man responds to these events is not all in line with standard psychiatric descriptions of traumatized behavior: the Ex-Coloured Man does not appear to be plagued by nightmares or flashbacks regarding these events, nor does the usual temporal paradox obtain, in which the trauma patient may *recall* the event in literal detail but, lacking a frame for understanding it at the time of its occurrence, fail to have *access* to it in the mode of narrative memory. The Ex-Coloured Man narrates the events lucidly enough; it is his response to them that is not narrated.

Thus, it is, rather, that the narrative itself, a novel masked as an autobiography (and thus a fabrication disguised as "true") and initially, through clever marketing, received as such by its reading public, is structured and functions as if *it* as a whole is a product of trauma, as if it is the necessarily fragmented expression of a traumatized consciousness—a trauma, moreover, that brings it (the narrative itself and the ex-colored persona who supposedly writes it) into being, since it is the trauma of having been blackened. The novel demonstrates, fictionalizes, that mode of traumatic memory wherein the traumatic scene "is not a possessed knowledge, but itself possesses . . . the one it inhabits."[36] By these lights we can say, particularly as *The Autobiography of an Ex-Coloured Man* is a novel of *failure*, that the "self" (which is in all cases being fictionalized, even in the case of a real autobiography) rendered by the autobiographical form is not fully in the Ex-Coloured Man's possession—that is, he cannot successfully tell the life story he professes to tell; he cannot *access* it—but the Ex-Coloured Man's "self" is rather possessed by the trauma that constitutes it. Johnson marks this constitutive trauma in the text with the empty spaces where counting of time ceases and where the temporal, at least in its linear guise, is dispersed: the Ex-Coloured Man is possessed by blackness as its trauma, or blackness in its being the mode and effect of abjection.

What is key here is to read the temporality of the Ex-Coloured Man's lost time as *dispersed* rather than paradoxical as in strictly traumatic temporality. The "timeless" aspect of trauma as we generally view it focuses us more on fixation and delay as constituent elements of the experience: fixation on the traumatic event (which is nonetheless held as an emptiness, as a gap) and delay in the possession or assimilation of it. These are certainly elements that attend blackness-as-trauma, and arguably the novel stages these elements in the Ex-Coloured Man's continual wrestling with his racial identity and in his final inability to situate himself within the social narrative of racial identity or to participate in making a race. But Merleau-Ponty's term "temporal dispersal," moves us away from delay to permit us to see the way that blackness functions in the novel as endowing the Ex-Coloured Man with an ability that he rejects. Merleau-Ponty's formulation helps us to see the Ex-Coloured Man's traumas as windowing into a non-chronological or *a*chronological space. For these moments of lost time are traumatic symptoms, but they are also experiences of alternative temporality, in which different modes of "access" are available: access, that is, that either is not exhausted by or does not even include the kind of access described by narrative memory, access that opens rather to that bodily knowledge I explored under the rubric of muscle tension in the previous chapter, which gives to "'significance' a value which intellectualism withholds from it," and access also to the limited freedom, the void of possibilities, that helps connects the individual consciousness to sociogenic processes.[37] The Ex-Coloured Man is not only swept backward in the form of a psychical trauma into the historical events of conquest and enslavement that his ancestors experienced but also is momentarily opened to *powers* enabled by an escape from the confines of linear temporality.

The position and operation of blackness with respect to this access need not be seen as unvarying, or as precise. But blackness is effective in providing the access. The "double existence" of trauma patients, characterized by simultaneous existence in two temporal frames (that of the trauma and that of the "bleached present"), arguably finds another face in Du Bois's double-consciousness and in Fanon's double-bodiedness.[38] In this sense being blackened and the split engendered by that process—blackness itself, doubly conscious, doubly bodied—not only is an example of trauma but also illustrates and grants access to what may well be a universal human reality. If, as Lacanian psychoanalysis would have it, all speaking beings are constitutively traumatized and all subjects are split, so that we are all living a "double existence," then potentially for all there are at least two simultaneously lived temporal frames: a timeless traumatic temporality and the everyday. If the ontic produces the ontological, and historical events are a deontologized ontology, then the historical events that give rise to blackness are of sufficiently recent vintage that the historical and the ontological slip neatly over one another to appear as one and the same.[39] Though the historicity of blackness is obfuscated under cloaks of shame and of the many highly seductive forms of forgetting peddled by the hegemonic powers as knowledge and history—and though these forces threaten always to submerge the means of access to it as narrative memory—the encounter with blackness as an identity and a meaning established by historical events of conquest and enslavement renders accessible (both as narrative memory and as the nonnarrative access I have gestured toward) a constitutive split of subjectivity. Either Merleau-Ponty's anonymous existence lies within the ambit of that traumatized other that Lacan calls the Real, or it *is* that Real.[40] It is possible to say that blackness either is another layer of the constitutive split or that it is the constitutive split for those who exist it; but whichever of the two it may be, its attributes are the same, and what it accesses is ultimately of similar significance.

The loss of time ushered in as a traumatic effect becomes as potentially powerful as it is debilitating, because to count time lays the foundation of a linear temporal arrangement of past, present, and future, and its loss connotes a collapse of boundaries and rational structure—perhaps a condition or state, however momentary its realization, "straddling Nothingness and Infinity," as Fanon puts it.[41] "Timelessness is the ideal of pleasure," according to Herbert Marcuse.[42] Marcuse usefully bridges our theorists because his work is an elaboration of Freud's repression thesis and because he is a contemporary of Fanon's and the Black Power thinkers, one whose name had a similar conjuring power for many in the U.S. countercultural movements.[43] In his "Political Preface 1966" to *Eros and Civilization*, Marcuse notes that what characterizes the young radicals of Sixties protest movements, along with "[r]evolt against the false fathers," is "solidarity with the wretched of the earth"—a fairly clear reference to Fanon's book, which, again, had been translated into English in 1965.[44]

Glossing Freud's *Civilization and Its Discontents* (1930) and *Totem and Taboo* (1913), Marcuse argues that the history of humanity's development is founded on harsh repressions of desires (largely erotic, understood in the broadest sense) and multiple renunciations of happiness. These repressions and renunciations were adopted in order to achieve the security of tribal cohesion in primordial times of material scarcity. But, says Marcuse, in the modern world where conditions of scarcity no longer obtain, this legacy of unnecessary constraint, ingrained in the psyche, leads people regularly to refuse or to betray opportunities for freedom. Repression from without in history is supported by repression from within; the two are essentially coterminous and simultaneous processes. For Marcuse, the history of civilization, via Freud, begins with the (ongoing) historical event of loss of freedom: the archetypal primal father's domination and the imposition of the paternal authority, followed by the sons' rebellion, followed by reinforced domination and self-repression of the claims of the pleasure principle. This "history" repeats in Oedipal trauma that functions as the enforcement of the reality principle of scarcity which disrupts all experience and perception of the organic, closed-circle relation between child and mother. The introjection of the father-master into the individual psyche reproduces the primordial historical act of domination, and thus psychoanalytic theory is social psychology and a form of social history. The "disturbing implications of Freud's theory of the personality," Marcuse notes, are that the "autonomous personality appears as the *frozen* manifestation of the general repression of mankind." Thus, the "concrete and complete personality as it exists in its private and public environment" is not a fruitful object of examination: "this existence conceals rather than reveals the essence and nature of the personality. It [the personality] is the end result of long historical processes which are congealed in the network of human and institutional entities making up society"—an argument that of course is thoroughly compatible with Fanon's insistence on looking to sociogeny when diagnosing the apparent psychopathologies of black Antilleans.[45]

Marcuse attempts to show that the psychological tendency to surrender to authority arises from the way that the history of the "struggle for freedom reproduces itself in the psyche of man." The perception of linear time, he argues, is a key element of historically produced psychological self-defeat, and the ground for political and social tyranny is prepared by the tyranny of time—most specifically, the loss always occasioned by time's perceived "passage": "Time has no power over the id," he observes. "But the ego, through which alone pleasure becomes real, is in its entirety subject to time. The mere anticipation of the inevitable end, present in every instant, introduces a repressive element into all libidinal relations and renders pleasure itself painful." Since all pleasure and satisfaction is experienced as fleeting, and human beings constantly experience *loss* in the perceived passage of time itself, a habit of submission to loss, scarcity, and defeat is established in the psyche and in behavior—which the ruling powers of any given social group work methodically to reinforce: "The flux of time is society's most natural ally in maintaining law and order, conformity and the institutions that relegate freedom to a perpetual utopia."[46]

Thus, time—which we must understand as linear time, rationalized time, and, à la Marx, on whom Marcuse is also partly relying, alienated (labor) time—is for Marcuse one, if not the chief, concept that psychologically defeats political attempts at ending suffering or eliminating alienation. Moreover, this defeat is woven into the fabric of any active attempt to overcome the past that has bequeathed its injustices to the present: the past that is continually *transcended* (rebelled against, mastered, conquered) repeats and entrenches the experience of loss and ensures a process of increasing alienation. The concept of history is itself a form of alienated mastery over the past, a subject-object split that further educates us in resignation to loss. "Unless the power of time over life is broken, there can be no freedom," Marcuse declares in a discussion of Hegel and Nietzsche.[47]

Marcuse proposes that the power of time over life is weakened by attempts to model politics on or to utilize the pre-ego and pre-subject/object-split libido (archetypally represented by Narcissus) which, as one prominent example, persist in the form of the sexual perversions. But what is significant for purposes of this discussion is that his prescription for working against the problem presented by history is a kind of radical remembrance that permits the primordial past (which, again, lives in and is repeated in the individual psyche) to live in the present and to set the standard for a liberated future. Thus, "the restoration of remembrance to its rights, as a vehicle of liberation, is one of the noblest tasks of thought."[48] In a sense for Marcuse, the better pre-ego past and the better postcapitalist future are, if not precisely one and the same, at least reflective of one another; this makes sense if *repression* is the hypothesis, and if conquest or defeat is the historical truth: that which preexisted serves as a screen on which to project something that might exist in the future. Yet even without a repression thesis, Fanon gestures toward similar thinking, with his suggestion that the path to decolonization involves a working with history as interarticulated temporality, in which past-as-future-anterior and future-as-past-posterior relate to the present as anticipations and reverberations of one another.

Marcuse's discussion of the inculcation of the habit of defeat is, simply put in Freudian terms, the persistence and pervasiveness of castration anxiety (or object-loss).[49] Marcuse's innovation is to emphasize the degree to which castration anxiety resides in temporal perception itself—at least insofar as temporal perception imposes or presupposes a *sequence* of events: Marcuse notes the way that Western philosophy and art variously deify or wish away time, but he does not suppose the temporal can be escaped in its entirety, merely (though this "mere" sketches a mountainously prodigious task) that its sequential nature can be broken, its subtending simultaneities evoked. This notion corresponds well with the dialectic with which physical perception and linear temporality relate to one another, in which Merleau-Ponty instructs us: as the phenomenologist remarks, the body *secretes* time by becoming "that location in nature where . . . events, instead of pushing each other into the realm of being, project round the present a double horizon of past and future and acquire a historical orientation."[50] The necessarily repetitive and laborious production of a present in relation to history also calls the stability of its product (linear temporality) into question and evokes therefore what Merleau-Ponty refers to as "prehistory" or anonymous existence and what Sartre designates as the very being of consciousness in its nihilating withdrawal that imprisons and frees at once, which state, like the "pre-ego" or the Real, is not readily available to us—except where we are thrown into it, shifted into it, opened to it, through vertigo, through anguish, through trauma.

It is in this way that the Ex-Coloured Man's experiences of "how long . . . I do not know" timelessness become not just traumatic—or rather, *in* their traumatic impact, become also experiences of *freedom*, which potentially form the basis for powerful action. The visual traumas the Ex-Coloured Man suffers before the mirror and witnessing the lynching, these nodal points in which he teeters on the edge of a plunge into identification with an abject blackness that he fears, and in his fear actually thus becomes abject, without clear demarcations between himself as subject and an other as object, are encounters of or with existential vertigo and anguish. The time lost in these encounters is an escape from linear time and, thus, too, from the loss inherent to sequential temporality that, according to Marcuse, helps found habits of political submission. It is also a suspension of those perceptual acts that Merleau-Ponty tells us situate the individual consciousness (albeit provisionally) within the double horizon of past and future. "How long . . . I do not know" bespeaks the lapse not only of counting but of *knowing* in the usual sense; the knowledge that is produced by perceptual acts as narrative is lost. This abeyance of narrative knowing is not a sustainable state within the insistent perceptual mechanisms of the body that the Ex-Coloured Man's consciousness exists or within the equally insistent consensus reality of the socius: both tides will bear him powerfully back to the structured world, where time and a black/white divide reign. But blackness itself, especially in its abjection, remains the aperture through which it becomes possible to suspend linear time and to weaken the various psychological and political limitations for which linear time is the foundation stone. Blackness as the effect and the experience of abjection is also the mark—it holds the place for—the be-ing of consciousness Sartre locates in vertigo and anguish, with the terror of its dangling possibilities, just as blackness is the effect and the experi-ence of sociogenic processes and power.

The Ex-Coloured Man's lost time is thus a literary device that can be read as representing the potential and (apparently paradoxical) freedom that might be realized in the suspension, arrest, or temporary disarrange-ment of linear time, which is also a momentary untying of the Gordian knot of history and its determinations. By showing us the obverse of that potential (the narrator turns *away* and is "frozen" by the terror of abjection and the void that subtends it, that makes itself known in the breakdown of the structure of sequential time), Johnson allows us to imagine how things might be if a different choice were made; the void of timelessness, rather than the hell it is for the narrator, haunts him as a resource.[51]

What is the power that identification with blackness might permit him to use, the possibilities that come into play? Its highest form in the novel is the "glorious" work of "*making* history" and "making . . . a race"—to which the mess of pottage that has become his life as an affluent, essen-tially "white" businessman stands in stark contrast. But it appears in other moments, less grandly than in the concluding gesture of the novel. While in Europe attending the opera with his millionaire, the Ex-Coloured Man unexpectedly is seated near his white father, whom he has rarely seen, and a young woman who captures his attention and, he soon realizes, is his half sister. The inability adequately to narrate what he sees again marks this scene: "I cannot describe her either as to feature, or colour of her hair, or of her eyes. . . . I felt to stare at her would be a violation; yet I was dis-tinctly conscious of her beauty." Along with this breakdown of narrative acuity, we see also the symptoms of bodily extinguishment ("I felt that I was suffocating") and an indication of lost time, here recorded as its con-comitant, lost space and location, as his anguish drives him out wandering into the night: "I walked *aimlessly* for about an hour or so."[52] The narrator, here again somewhat traumatized, slips out of linear time, encounters or brushes up against alternate possibilities, unlived lives, parallel universes: What if he were as accepted as his sister is accepted and attended opera with his father? What if he had fallen in love with a woman who was not only white but his sister?[53] These are possibilities barred to him and also made possible because of his racial status.

He experiences vertigo in the way that Fanon's "border-line" patient in "Colonial War and Mental Disorders" did: as a psychic disorientation brought on by the apprehension of unlived possibilities. Fanon's patient, who had murdered in the cause of his nation's independence, became friendly with nationals of the former colonial power and "wondered with a feeling of anguish whether among the victims of the bomb there had been people like his new acquaintances."[54] The anguish, the vertigo that the Ex-Coloured Man experiences is the dizzying effect of possibilities—other lives or other ways of living—that might have been, that are precisely imaginations of freedom or of forms of freedom that the dominant powers have denied him. This is in accord with Marcuse's notion of how escape from linear time enables a political imagination of liberation—but here such an imagination comes through the back door, as it were, in the experience of abjection, of being barred from these possibilities. These possibilities are less a lack, a complete fantasy, and more a "real" possibility *if* the Ex-Coloured Man would engage in race-making, participate in racial formation—sociogenesis—because he would challenge the prohibitions that prevent his fantasy from being truth: they are an endowment of blackness.

Blackness as the embodied metaphor, the lived representation that grants access to unlived possibilities, is present in the Ex-Coloured Man's relationship to his millionaire as well. Their relationship is partly built on the management of the psychic dimensions of time: of the millionaire he observes, "I was his chief means of disposing of the thing which seemed to sum up all in life that he dreaded—time. As I remember him now, I can see that time was what he was always endeavouring to escape, to bridge over, to blot out."[55] The millionaire intends to exploit in his living black charge qualities for which blackness has become a metaphor, and qualities which the racist social system his privileges partly rest on make unavailable to him on his own; but what Johnson suggests, and what the Ex-Coloured Man misses, is that the blackness that the Ex-Coloured Man continually endeavors to dodge or renegotiate does, by its relation to sociogenic processes and to anonymous existence, bridge—if not truly escape or blot out as the millionaire desires—the limitations of linear time and the foursquare consensus realities that linear time underpins.

Similarly, when the Ex-Coloured Man and the white woman whom he eventually marries have a chance encounter with his old school friend whose nickname was "Shiny," the Ex-Coloured Man is able to glimpse the possibility of occupying a black male body, but only because his white future wife finds "Shiny" desirable: "The polish of his language and the unpedantic manner in which he revealed his culture greatly impressed her; and after we had left the Musee she showed it by questioning me about him. I was surprised at the amount of interest a refined black man could arouse. Even after changes in the conversation she reverted several times to the subject of 'Shiny.' Whether it was more than mere curiosity I could not tell."[56] The narrator had previously reacted to Shiny's arrival on the scene with embarrassment and reserve. Now he is moved to do what he dared not do since the moment of lynching: reveal to another person (his fiancée) that he is black. This revelation stems, of course, from the Ex-Coloured Man's desire for her desire, in order to feel fully secure in what he imagines to be his authentic being; but it is not simply a matter of revealing his hidden authenticity when he asks his fiancée to look at him as she has looked at Shiny. He is imagining other worlds, in a sense; he is trying to assimilate to himself, to claim for himself, the body-image he has never permitted himself to possess fully (but which possesses *him*, or at least his narrative) and that he has twice actively repudiated. For the image of Shiny is the obverse of the image of the lynched, burning black man: Shiny is the image of the visibly dark black male body, glowing because he is illuminated by the fires of more-than-curiosity, the fires of a mysterious desire that does not incinerate but refines as it makes the skin the visible sign of an unseen possibility.

In the case of the Ex-Coloured Man's wife this possibility—as is generally the case when he chooses desire as the mode of his contact with the white semi-Other—is vaguely sexual; and for the Ex-Coloured Man it is a mode of eroticism that windows into the broadest conception of Eros, which has to do with the drive to establish bonds beyond the isolated self with communities ever more variously conceived—those bonds that, among other trajectories, constitute the freemasonry of the race, in other words.[57] His encounter with Shiny, and his wife-to-be's interest in Shiny, arouses in him the unspoken, unrecognized wish to be in the company of and to be like these black men. Arguably, like his white millionaire, the Ex-Coloured Man is now moved to melancholy: he desires for himself what blackness represents—but since he cannot see and has never been able to see what that desirable quality might be, since he has repressed it in himself, he cannot assimilate it; it eludes him.

The erotic dimension of the Ex-Coloured Man's wish to be seen as Shiny is seen, of his chance encounter with his sister, his relationship with the millionaire, and his admiration of the lynchers all point to another set of possibilities, potentials, and powers that Johnson's narrator fails to wield. These relationships all to some degree parallel the miscegenous relations between the narrator's mother and father, and, like the primal scene which his later traumatic encounters repeats, rests in large part, both as dramatic ploys within the narrative and as overarching thematic appeal, on the suggestion of taboo interracial sexuality. Stepto quite credibly reads the transgression of such taboos to be a kind of false revolution, and that Johnson, in constructing a narrative about a narrator who fails, intends as one of his many projects to expose it as such; in this line of argument, defying the taboo against interracial relationships, far from being transgressive, amounts merely to "modulations and exploitation of race rituals along the color line" and has nothing to do with the serious task of, as the narrator would have it, "making a race."[58] Yet if we bring Fanon into the conversation, he would maintain that, in a sense, race ritual *is* race; unlike Stepto and probably Johnson, building the "tradition" of a race is not a teleology for Fanon—in his view, we must shatter the very concept of race (even as we use it). Johnson's text does suggest that there is a source of power, however true or untrue the source and however limited the power, in the race rituals themselves. *The Autobiography* could be read as a Salome-like dance of revelation, whose "naked" face shows the illusory nature of the black/white opposition. The object of seduction in this Salome's dance is a white reading audience's sympathy for black people and a call to white action in support of that sympathy (say, in opposition to lynching. which was most certainly not confined to the page and imagination).[59] On the one hand, the narrator at the novel's end is not threatening because he has become white (he no longer poses the threat of blackness); on the other hand, of course, he is threatening because he *has* become white, revealing the intimacy, the porousness of the two positions. Despite his manifold failures, few narrative choices could be more potentially explosive than the fact that the Ex-Coloured Man recapitulates the image of his parents at the novel's end: he reverses the more acceptable image of his white father, the best blood in the South deigning to give his seed to the poor black woman, or of the white millionaire dressing his servant as an equal. By the novel's end, the narrator is a black man who has married and is sleeping with a white woman. The narrator, the text seems to say to its white readers, is a black man pretending to be a white man who may or may not exist (is it an autobiography, or is it fiction?); the narrator is a black man pretending to be a white man sleeping with your daughter.

Stepto establishes the now generally accepted reading that Johnson's ironic stance with respect to the narrator is that the narrator refuses participation in an African American tradition of artistry and political struggle of which Johnson himself was very much a part.[60] The narrator is thus a failure—but this failure is not wholly passive and capitulating; this failure has bite, in that it moves into the very midst of the wagon-circled domain of the white family and brings to pass one of its greatest fears: black male–white female contact, the suborning, indeed the infection, of its white daughters with blackness. While we need not read it as prefiguring an Eldridge Cleaver–like exhortation of black men to rape white women, this aspect of the story is accomplished with as much aggressiveness as it is with self-effacing tentativeness. The mulatto figure familiar to the audience of *The Autobiography* often has a white father and an ambiguously disturbing relation to relatives white and black, but now, as white (ex-colored) father, the figure comes back to haunt and unsettle the racial-Oedipal schema of that familiar figure: the Ex-Coloured Man is the black white brother married to his white sister; he is the black white father who is patriarch to a white daughter. He poses the nightmare of undifferentiation. Thus, in one respect the narrator's play with race rituals accentuates and brings home, as it were, the bourgeois political we-should-be-treated-equally-because-racial-differences-aren't-real argument to which the text lends itself. In another respect, potentially the Ex-Coloured Man's play with race rituals even radicalizes that argument; for sneakily, underhandedly, the Ex-Coloured Man's final masquerade figures the dissolution of white communities and black communities by, in effect, hinting at the destruction of "black" and "white" families. Indeed, perhaps the "family" itself is threatened. Taboo is founded in prohibitions of desires that we have a strong propensity to satisfy, but the "original" desire is by no means easily identified.[61] The Ex-Coloured Man's evocation of incest and his accomplished race-crossing, his breaking of the taboo against interracial sexual contact in a context of rigid black/white divisions, are potentially sparks in a line of gunpowder that could give rise to a series of fiery explosions—and when the smoke clears, the novel seems to hint, we might all be ex-colored and ex-white, since racial boundaries cannot, of course, be maintained unless the sexual choices of those who are defined as members of a given race, especially the women, are limited to other members of the group. And perhaps we are ex-father, ex-mother, ex-brother/sister, too, at least as the intelligibility of those roles and positions is constituted by the prohibitions (proscribing who is sexually available and who is not, prescribing what one does and how one behaves to fulfill one's designated familial role) that demarcate them. All this remains potential, vaguely threatened, as long as the Ex-Coloured Man permits himself to be taken as a white man and goes no further. But what if the Ex-Coloured Man were to take on the position of race-and-family terrorist that Johnson builds him up to be, and from which his fear withholds him?

These possibilities and the power to bring them to some form of fruition necessarily—since Johnson's is a novel of failure—appear as hauntings, as rhetorical gestures, as peripheral suggestions, much as Fanon's considerations of muscle tension and the powers of the native/black do. It is the remainder of what might have been that makes its appearance: a list of intangibilities that the Ex-Coloured Man, in his headlong flight from abjection, has snuffed out—"a vanished dream, a dead ambition, a sacrificed talent." These dreams and talents cannot become substantial in the rigidly divided world of his place and time unless the Ex-Coloured Man would dare to immerse himself in blackness, unless he would look through its translucent prism. "I cannot repress the thought," he laments, "that, after all, I have chosen the lesser part, that I have sold my birthright for a mess of pottage."[62] The narrator's cheaply sold birthright is his advantaged position to plumb the sociogeny that produces human life, to engage actively in the process of social "making" that makes race. But he "cannot repress" it—despite his refusal of the paradoxically *advantaged* position of blackness (precisely as and in its abjection); the unlived possibilities are insistently present, vaguely known by the effort required to not know them. Johnson's narrator's mistake is not only that he fails to identify with the race that grasps hold of the sociogenic foundation of race itself to shape its identity, its meaning in the world, anew. It is that he fails to perceive that an identification with the state of being violated (like the lynched man) has value. Though the violation seems to undermine the possibilities of survival, this value lies in the sense that, in highlighting the protean qualities of human ways of being, the identification with being violated, the embrace of the abject, accedes to its own form of power—almost precisely by calling into question "race," "gender," and the like: by pushing those categories to the edge of their defining capacities, where they nearly tip over into the death which they are meant to defend against, and which simultaneously, as "black" or "woman," they are meant to represent. This a "truth" that stands apart from, or without the necessity of, the scene of extreme domination that reveals it, though this scene of domination may, unfortunately, be the easiest way to access that truth from the location of frightened egos conceived in the drive and desire to flee pain.

. . .

Fanon would not sell this human birthright that blackness bequeaths him. It is in company with the dramatizations of a writer such as Johnson that I would read those seemingly opaque rhetorical flights that entice and confuse us in the introduction to *Black Skin, White Masks*. Dreaming Hegelian dreams, Fanon writes, "In a savage struggle I am willing to accept convulsions of death, invincible dissolution, but also *the possibility of the impossible.*"[63] What I am drawn by is "the impossible" here. How ought we to read it? Is it Lacan's impossible, the domain of the Real that escapes the attempts of language to describe it?

In part I think this is the impossible of the abject.[64] In Fanon, the proximity of the "impossible" to dissolution and the convulsions of death bespeaks a kind of despair—but not only despair: also a kind of heroic charge, a leap into the unknown. Echoes of the unmapped impossible resound in Fanon's call for people of color to enter through the process of psychoanalytically informed critique "a zone of nonbeing . . . an utterly naked declivity where an authentic upheaval can be born." We must be able to see, he suggests, "the advantage of being able to accomplish this descent into a real hell." What interests me is less the personal authenticity and the idea of being teleologically free from artifice that the "utterly naked" language evokes than its suggestion of a state of conscious privation—the willingness to examine the experience of abjection—en route to another state beyond. When speaking in these terms Fanon makes clear that the anger and rage intrinsic to this coming into consciousness is not an endpoint; he rejects the strategy of revealing truths that merely incite rage. "I do not trust fervor," he declares. Rather than generate such heat he "would prefer to warm man's body and leave him," with the effect, he hopes, that mankind might "retain[ ] this fire through *self-combustion.*" The incineration of the self is, I take it, "a real hell"—the very hell from which the Ex-Coloured Man understandably flees—but in Fanon's vision the inferno is as much a purifier and transformer as a destroyer, and something—the new man (ex-colored and ex-white)—yet survives.[65]

3

Slavery, Rape, and the Black Male Abject

Abjection and the "New" Sexual Encounter

How does the recognition—or the embrace—of blackness in its abjection play out? In the terms of the texts I have examined so far, in what further way can we adduce the abilities of the black/native in his state of productive muscle tension, and what shape might the Ex-Coloured Man's life take if he did not refuse traumatic (and traumatized) blackness but assimilated it, if he lived consciously in a black(ened) body that physicalized a self almost without ego? How might we imagine the unlived possibilities the Ex-Coloured Man eschews, especially as those possibilities seem insistently to be accompanied and constituted by possible transformations of gender and sexuality?

For always as we try to limn the qualities of racial vertigo (or the existential vertigo that provides psychic material for the production of racial identity), a measure and means of the disorientation are the possible reconfigurations of gender and reformulations of sexual expression that spin around that vertigo as if they were the phantasms of parallel universes. The Ex-Coloured Man cannot understand or attempt to enact his flight from black identity without relation to and introjections of ideals of masculinity and femininity defined by their whiteness, or without opposing relations to and projections of abject blackness that call up associations not only with death and the violability of the body but also with the feminine.

Similarly, Fanon describes the route taken by rebelling Algerians toward decolonization—in other words, becoming national Algerians rather than "natives," reshaping the meaning of race—as a journey that is confirmed by, and realized through, a metamorphosis in the way gender and sexuality operate. In the Algerian Revolution Fanon observes the transformation of Algerian heterosexual couples effected by their mutual and independent participation in the Revolution—and, in a sense, he charts too a transformation of heterosexuality:

> First and foremost is the fact of incurring dangers together, of turning over in the same bed, each on his own side, each with his fragment of

a secret. It is also the consciousness of collaborating in the immense work of destroying the world of oppression. The couple is no longer shut in upon itself. It no longer finds its end in itself. It is no longer the result of the natural instinct of perpetuation of the species, nor the institutionalized means of satisfying one's sexuality. The couple becomes the basic cell of the commonwealth, the fertile nucleus of the nation. . . . *There is a simultaneous and effervescent emergence of the citizen, the patriot, and the modern spouse.* The Algerian couple rids itself of its traditional weaknesses at the same time that the solidarity of the people becomes a part of history. This couple is no longer an accident but something rediscovered, willed, built. It is . . . the very foundation of the sexual encounter that we are concerned with here.[1]

Fanon's suturing of the heterosexual couple with the nation while at the same time explicitly disarticulating the heterosexual couple from both biological propagation and erotic sexuality runs counter to the usual way that patriarchal family and nation are ideologically conjoined,[2] and is a kind of nationalist vision that a feminist critique of nationalism might encourage. The couple becomes a "fertile" nucleus, but in a context where the patriarchal privileges of the father are being dismantled under the pressure of the exigencies of the revolution, which also require the wife to behave as something other than a traditional wife, this fertility is not about shepherding the progeny of the couple into the nation in a particular way: it is rather that the couple is a form of *ideological propagation*, a kind of proliferating example, or perhaps even a kind of social virus that founds cultural change: "it is . . . the inner mutation, the renewal of the social and family structures that impose with the rigor of a law the emergence of the Nation and the growth of its sovereignty."[3]

Even if Fanon's vision proved unjustifiably optimistic (it has been observed that the changes in Algerian gender relations were unfortunately mostly temporary, and arguably even ephemeral),[4] what is important for our purposes is that his theorization of possibilities which the revolution makes concrete links the transformation of race with that of gender and sexuality. Moreover, it is not only in the heroic scenes of Algerian women utilizing European colonialist fascination with the veil to conceal weapons or Algerian women breaking off from domestic duties to plan and take action with men not their husbands that these possibilities take shape; it is also in the suffering, the abjection that Algerian revolutionaries experience that the new citizen (ex-native) and the new spouse (ex-wife) "effervescently" emerge. Fanon observes that the depredations visited on the Algerians in internment camps that the French occupiers established to break their revolutionary will shattered traditional taboos governing proper conduct in sexual matters and violated some of the basic predicates on which gender identities are founded—and in so doing, actually also created opportunities for wholly different conceptions of gender and family relations: the woman raped "dozens of times" by soldiers and the man "more dead than alive, his mind stunned" by torture, Fanon writes, are the remnants of a family that through such violations has been destroyed, but "[i]n stirring up these men and women, colonialism has regrouped them beneath a single sign. . . . [T]his physically dispersed people is realizing its unity and founding in suffering a spiritual community."[5] Fanon's "single sign" is the nascent Nation, the rhetoric not unlike that of a doctrinaire revolutionary Leninist who asserts that all social distinctions will be smelted into classless new forms in the cauldron of revolution. But we might also see the single sign as the sociogenic analogue of a Freudian oceanic, a pre-ego, pre-object state, the not-yet-ego of incomplete or unstable gender differentiation: we might see it as racialization—or reracialization—under and as abjection.[6]

After all, what Fanon observes among Algerian revolutionaries is potentially true of the Antillean black as well, virtually as an always-already aspect of his blackness. Fanon observes that one profound effect of the invention of the category of blackness and of rigorous racial segregation is that the black family and the State are fundamentally disarticulated: "The family is an institution that prefigures a broader institution: the social or the national group. . . . The white family is the workshop in which one is shaped and trained for life in society. . . . Now, the Antillean family has for all practical purposes no connection with the national—that is, the French, or European—structure."[7] Whereas Fanon elucidates a process in which a patriarchal Algerian family under colonial domination serves as a kind of redoubt that throws up the walls of its privacy and difference against the cultural conquests of the colonizer, and thus becomes a kind of prerevolutionary cell of resistance under the guise of traditional (and therefore, for Fanon, "sclerotic") culture, what he observes in the Algerian Revolution is that these familial forms have already been shorn of the perpetuating reinforcements of the society in which they exist and are already thrown back, as it were, into the gap, the emptiness of *possibilities* that can found an entirely new "sexual encounter." The break between family (and concomitantly, all that family structures shape, most notably gender positions and sexuality) and nation that characterizes both black-ness and the Algerian native—the break that is made by what conquest, enslavement, and domination has broken (and for Fanon, all but erased) of traditional life, and that *is* abjection—restarts sociogenic processes and makes possible new nations, different families, different gender positions and sexualities.

By *"different"* gender positions and sexualities I mean here to invoke Hortense Spillers's argument that the Middle Passage and diasporic slav-ery produce gender and a host of other terms of relatedness, including sexuality, for those to whom blackness is ascribed, under different terms and/or with different meanings than those terms normatively appear. I would like, then, to examine an instance of how the process of racializa-tion through abjection plays out in a canonical work of African American literary imagination and to focus particularly on the way that this abjec-tion produces a "break" in gender and sexuality—a break that looks to all concerned like *broken* gender and sexuality—and how it therefore pro-vides an opportunity for different configurations of gender and sexuality.

How Things Really Appear

As Barbara Christian has argued, Toni Morrison in *Beloved* aims to create a kind of literary "fixing ceremony," both for the unremembered, unme-morialized African dead who perished in the Middle Passage and for those who survived it—and, by extension, for us as well, as Americans and Af-rican Americans who are the inheritors of the largely unspoken but none-theless persistently powerful experiences of the Africans who survived.[8] The novel's project is the recovery of painful and traumatic memory, of "what is not spoken and what is not seen."[9] In this sense the novel col-lapses the divide between questions of whether formative trauma is his-torical or universally constitutive. As in most of those 20th century nov-els we now call neo-slave narratives, in *Beloved* the past which originates African American and American culture—the practice of chattel slavery, and/as the crèche of racialization of black and white—lives on in repeated patterns, in present-day cultural epistemologies and hermeneutics, and in the personal and social lives that these epistemologies and hermeneu-tics underpin. Thus, the act of a sustained imagination of the slave past which these neo-slave narratives are is representative of a truth on which they commonly insist: that a purely linear sense of the temporal fails in the apprehension of reality; and synchronic, diachronic, or (following our West African ancestral practices) syndetic approaches to the temporal are necessary for understanding cultural reality and integral to the representational strategies aimed at reaching that understanding.[10] As we have already seen there is a dimension of human existence that lies in excess of narrative capture (trauma, the Real, anonymous or amorphous existence) and for which an insistence on linear historicity has the effect of suppression (or, as we shall see, repression). And as Marcuse suggests, the state of exception that legitimizes the authority of the sovereign is both structural (constitutive) and punctual (historical). Both a literary imagination and the goal of healing, of working with or through the inheritance of historical and constitutive trauma, require striking a balance between the assimilation and the defiance of historical narrative, between history and the individual, between history and, indeed, myth.

In the development of *Beloved*'s narrative, the strategies which the characters Sethe, Paul D, and Denver pursue of living only for the present or future, of holding the past at bay, constantly fail and, moreover, prevent the characters from attaining the freedom and integrity of self which seems to insist on coming into being despite all their attempts to maintain safe, partially lived lives. Morrison's narrative drives the characters to claim themselves in a way which perhaps seems at odds with many poststructuralist appropriations of psychoanalytic theory which emphasize the observation that identity is always a failure, always threatening to collapse against the pressure of what it has walled out. But in fact the "identity," if we can name it as such, to which the characters are driven to establish claim is never in the novel anything but divided and fractured from within, even when Sethe seems to glimpse a kind of coherence in the realization that she is herself her "best thing."[11] So, too, the "wholeness" which Morrison's novel offers to American readers by engaging in the exercise of a fixing ceremony; rather than providing an end, a complete satisfaction, a successful exorcism of the ghosts of the Middle Passage and slavery, the novel reopens wounds, to begin a healing that can only be understood as an ongoing process—a healing that *is* that process rather than the end of process, because Morrison's aim is above all to prevent forgetting.

Morrison vigorously engages in trope work—the reworking and reconfiguration of metaphor to create figures by which new knowledge can be transmitted. The novel's operative term is, to use Sethe's word, "*rememory.*" *Beloved* does not seek to give an "accurate" account of Margaret Garner's history (the woman on whom the character Sethe is based) but to mine that history for various possible meanings that, heretofore largely hidden from histories and absent from popular consciousness, seem available only in metaphor. The difficulty of this undertaking is evidenced in Morrison's handling of the Middle Passage. The Middle Passage experience is not, in Morrison's novel, actually figured; it is instead enunciated as fragment, as nonfigure, a collection of unpunctuated and seemingly hallucinatory words that do not cohere. The difficulty in transmitting knowledge of the Middle Passage is in part one of its virtual absence in language as an easily available trope. Therefore Morrison does not offer us a figure that is easy to assimilate but instead tries to force us to confront the outrage that is the erasure of that history, by figuring the Middle Passage as a point of resistance to being read in the text itself.

We can discern elsewhere in the text the difficulty of asking the questions that are not asked, of figuring what has not been figured, of representing those histories, those traumas that have been erased and forgotten. This problem is provocatively evident in what Christian has reported proved to be one of the most controversial parts of the novel: the sexual exploitation of Paul D and other black men on the chain gang in Alfred, Georgia.

The sexual exploitation of black women under slavery in the United States is to some degree acknowledged, however inadequately. Indeed, the "rape of black women" has become the trope around which questions of "black feminism" and "black female sexuality" arise without great controversy in discussions among sometimes contentious feminists, African Americanists, Americanists, and Afrocentrists. More prevalent still is the idea of the "emasculation" of the black male, another primary trope for various kinds of discussions about both blackness (because the masculine becomes conflated with the race as a whole) and "black manhood." The emasculation trope is, in effect, one of the most popular readings of the founding scene of African American male subjectivity, the reading which animates most discussions of men's experience of slavery. The emasculation trope has as its corollary the figure of castration, an image which does not remain only as a shadowy fear in the male mind as it does in Freudian theory but becomes a practice in the long and ugly history of the lynching of black men.

I will consider further the relation between rape and castration in the following chapter. For the present, I want to draw attention to the way these two tropes, "rape of black women" and "emasculation/castration of black men," are generally placed in parallel relation:[12] the rape is like the emasculation, the emasculation is what they did to men instead of rape, and so on—formulations which leave untouched the question of whether this "emasculation" of black men might have occurred *due to* or *through rape of men by other men.* That is, might this emasculation have been enacted, on a systemic level, not only by the physical (nonsexual) and psychological subordination of black men (i.e., they had to watch their wives being raped by the white master, etc.) but by sexual subordination as well, *to* white male masters *for* white male masters' sexual gratification or experience of dominance?

Morrison's *Beloved* attempts to imagine this possibility, in the incident on the chain gang in Alfred, Georgia.

> All forty-six men woke to rifle shot. . . . Three whitemen walked along the trench unlocking the doors one by one. No one stepped through. When the last lock was opened, the three returned and lifted the bars, one by one. . . . When all forty-six were standing in a line in the trench, another rifle shot signaled the climb out and up to the ground above, where one thousand feet of the best hand-forged chain in Georgia stretched. Each man bent and waited. . . .
>
> Chain-up completed, they knelt down. . . . Kneeling in the mist they waited for the whim of a guard, or two, or three. Or maybe all of them wanted it. Wanted it from one prisoner in particular or none— or all.
>
> "Breakfast? Want some breakfast, nigger?"
>
> "Yes, sir."
>
> "Hungry, nigger?"
>
> "Yes, sir."
>
> "Here you go."
>
> Occasionally a kneeling man chose gunshot in his head as the price, maybe, of taking a bit of foreskin with him to Jesus. Paul D did not know that then. He was looking at his palsied hands, smelling the guard, listening to his soft grunts so like the doves."[13]

Here, the forgotten possibility, the thing not said, is the tale of the sexual exploitation of black men by white men, under the system of total control which whites enjoyed over black bodies. Morrison attempts—almost in passing but as an inextricable part of the novel's larger project of excavation—to figure both the possibility of the sexual exploitation of men and the silence surrounding this possibility. The utter lack of spectacle, of sensation, with which Morrison describes this event also seems to suggest that it, like so many other tales of sexual exploitation in the novel, is what passes for normal under the circumstances: for example, the ex-slave Ella's year-long capture and rape by a father and son is also mentioned almost parenthetically.

It may be useful to recall in this context the well-known formulation that makes homosexuality the unspeakable, the crime or love which dare not speak its name. Though this is a key recollection for the character Paul D, and a primary basis of his "problem," the narrative source and substance of the dramatic tension the character plays out—it is a memory in which a host of other traumatic impacts and anxieties are cathected—it remains, in a way somewhat analogous to Beloved's unpunctuated and nonnarrative narration describing her past as that of the Middle Passage, an event hemmed with what it does not say. Its content is easily missed, so that its effect for the reader mirrors orthodox traumatic effects, in that the event is *recalled* but eludes willed access because Morrison's deliberate obfuscation disallows transparent reading. The solitary sentence following "Here you go" (itself almost invitational, lifting the reader up along the parabolic loop of a rising action that promises climax—a climax that, in a perverse way, Paul D is party to but that the reader is mostly denied) and the somewhat obscure phrase "taking a bit of foreskin with him" are all that betray the mechanics of humiliation in the scene; they are the heart of the drama but undramatically represented. It is as if what is being described is too horrible to examine closely without threatening to tip Paul and the readers over into an experience of extreme revulsion—which is to say, in accordance with the novel's overall project, that what happens is unspeakable.[14] Or, in accordance with Fanonian reading and with the example given by James Weldon Johnson's Ex-Coloured Man, the presentation of the event tracks the way that what happens seems to threaten total loss of self: the vertigo that contemplates death, the cessation of the existence of the subject (even if what momentarily ceases is really only an ego more masculine than feminine).

At the same time it might be that what is being described is too inconceivable, too absurd to believe, and it will fail to bear the weight of close examination. The narration retreats from what we call "graphic" description—a descriptive category reserved for descriptions of the sexual and the violent and curiously unapplied in, say, examples of dense detailing of the contents of a drawing room such as we find in high bourgeois realism. Thus, "graphic" becomes the cover, the code, for material that seems prospectively ordained, as though by a censor embedded in the conventions of usage of the language itself, to be treated as if it were traumatic, as if since it *should not* be spoken, it *cannot* be accessed. This strategy of retreat preserves the tenderness of our sensibilities on the one hand, and on the other refuses a spectacle that might too easily portray the suffering visited on black people as a prurient and sadomasochistic entertainment.[15] It is also in alignment with a representational strategy that Morrison prefers generally in her work—to "shape a silence while breaking it," to portray and make the reader feel something "like the emptiness left by a boom or a cry."[16] In any case, whatever the controlling reason or set of reasons for why the event is narrated as it is, it seems clear that the fact that it is "traumatic" for *readers* is as important, if not more so, than the fact that the event is traumatic for Paul D.[17]

That these culturally proscriptive and ostensibly protective layers of silence are in operation and that the excavation of this buried past is itself a kind of trauma is evidenced by Christian's reports of black audiences' response to the novel's account of black males as victims of sexual exploitation in the novel—an angry and disbelieving response that seemed quite out of proportion to the event's abbreviated appearance in the novel.

Part of what is at stake in the intense reactions to *Beloved*'s chain-gang episode, I think—reactions both convergent with and divergent from the homophobia and heterosexism of the dominant culture in the United States—is the very manliness of black men as a matter of fact and history: what is in jeopardy is African Americans' own investments in the "truth" of black manhood. African American critiques have long argued that any ascription of a kind of superior masculinity to black men is rooted in racist conceptions of the inherent savagery, the supposed authenticity and rapacious sexuality of black(male)ness. But that supposed authenticity, the vitality which racist discourse often projects onto the black male body, has also been used as a source of political strength, as a strategic essentialism of sorts; this was especially true in the late-1960s brand of black nationalism and its cultural arm, the Black Arts Movement, from which Morrison cannot be completely separated, and it is probably also true of 1980s–'90s Afrocentrism and hip-hop-flavored black nationalism.[18]

In a sense, Morrison's story threatens the stability of a history which has itself had to be painfully excavated—that of the heroic black male, who has been cast in white histories as a crafty, grinning coward at best and as a buffoon at worst. The figure of the black male has been recovered, in a long tradition of black historical scholarship, as a hero, on Civil War battlefields, in slave revolts, and as scholar/writer-warriors, such as Frederick Douglass or W. E. B. Du Bois. It is this painfully wrought history that exists almost as an affirming mantra in Paul D's mind as he ponders "where manhood lay": "he was a man and a man could do what he would; be still for six hours in a dry well while night dropped; fight raccoon with his hands and win; watch another man, whom he loved better than his brothers, roast without a tear just so the roasters would know what a man was like."[19] In this recitation the black man is, in effect, more of a man than the men who enslaved him. Yet the desperate coherence of this image, of this series of man-in-the-wilderness tropes which might do any mythical Euroamerican frontiersman proud, cannot ultimately provide Paul D (or American readers of all races with a stake, political, erotic, or otherwise, in the authentic masculinity of the black male) with a satisfying answer to the question of where manhood lies. History, acknowledged or unacknowledged, remembered or forgotten, returns: in the narrative, Paul D is first compelled to ask where manhood lies in order to resist being *controlled* by Beloved (she is literally moving him from the house to the shed, and she is by means unknown forcing him to have sex with her)—he asks in order to resist being controlled by the unspoken past, in other words. Though Beloved embodies Sethe's past, a haunting, maliciously active ghost plagues Paul D as well, for the traumas he has experienced continue to affect his life, forcing him to withhold himself from life and love.

Morrison figures Paul D's response to his past with the image of his heart encased in a rusty tobacco tin. Morrison is unyielding in her conviction that the wounds of the past, however heartbreaking, must be confronted. Paul D is free from the chains of the Georgia work gang, but the rusty tobacco tin that encases his heart, though of his own making, is another and perhaps more deadly kind of restraint. By playing out the trope of emasculation in a sexual scene that seems almost to be one of its logical conclusions (and therefore all the more shocking for remaining unspoken), Morrison disturbs the stable meanings which congregate around the idea of the emasculation of black men, with results that are both painful (hence the anger and disbelief of Christian's audiences) and, Morrison insists, potentially healing.

What I wish to emphasize is that this imaginary scene draws from the (largely) unspoken history of the various national cultures that originated in and participated in the enslavement of Africans in the Americas.[20] The audience reaction that Christian encountered indicates that the scene has the character of a repressed memory, in the Freudian sense.

The psychoanalytic paradigm indicates that at the heart of any such *scene* lies its symbolic coding of memories repressed by the psyche. Freud's theory (later modified, if not repudiated) about the so-called hysteria of his female patients was that the women's suffering arose from the repression of a memory experienced as so horrible that the patients were unable to speak it in language. In essence, the repressed memory was expressed by the unconscious where the otherwise unacknowledged memory continued to reside, and the unconscious, bereft of spoken language, in excess of language, spoke this memory through the hysterical symptoms of the body. This memory, moreover, was frequently one of the patient having been sexually seduced by her father. According to Freud, it was not necessary to ascertain the "truth" of this memory; the historical relation of the patient to her father was not important; it was rather the patient's relationship to a father figure or to the paternal metaphor that was salient, the Father as culture, society, regulation, law, and the gender role these various structures forced her to live out. This relationship was embedded in the symbolic "scene" which the patient held as memory and in which she was emotionally invested, and it is this scene which gave rise to the psychic and physical manifestations of sickness or unrest.

Regarding the concept of repressed memory in relation to hysteria-causing or other primal events, Freud's idea has been interpreted thus: there is the reality of parental seduction, on the one hand; and on the other, the seduction is fantasmatic. While the recollection may be fantasized, it is not simply dreamt up; it speaks to the difficult-to-unravel messages the child perceives. The parental seduction is what Kant called *transcendental illusion*—the child encounters the enigma and paradox of the other's desire, and fantasy comes into play to work with it, incorporate it, and make sense of it. (And of course, you never get rid of fantasy: adult sexuality is essentially infantile and requires fantasy's support.) The repressed memory concept thus elucidates neither a reality of seduction nor a fantasy; it instead points to *how things really appear* to the person or persons for whom the repressed memory is in operation.[21] In this light Christian's audiences respond to Morrison's scene, reacting as if what she points out to them in the text cannot have a purchase on reality, but their reaction has to do precisely with the fact that *it really does appear* to them that black men are or have been in some way placed in relation to white men in a way that is adequately represented by the image of Paul D and the chain-gang men forced to kneel before white jailers and performing fellatio or drinking their urine.

Again, I will revisit this matter in the following chapter, when I consider the recurrence of rape and castration as themes evoked in relation to black men and a precarious black masculinity that tend to show *how things really appear* to the authors who use these theme. For the present I want to focus on how the scene from *Beloved* is a scene of experience which Paul D holds as abjection; and it is a scene in which his blackness is partly established, his masculinity as he understands it undercut, and a *different* maleness engendered.

Arthur Flannigan Saint-Aubin, in an essay on black male sexuality, makes productive use of the terms of Freud's concept of the scene of repressed "sexual" memory.[22] Following the logic of Freud's theory of hysteria, Flannigan Saint-Aubin posits the existence of what he calls "testeria," neatly substituting the male testes for the female uterus as the metaphoric site of psychic disturbance. Testeria, he argues, can be understood as the response of black males to the position in which we are called into being in white supremacist patriarchy in the United States, where the sole subject, the sole being who is synonymous with human and whose experience counts axiomatically *as* experience, is the white male. "[I]nhabiting the untenable space of identification with yet dislocation from the Symbolic Order of the Father," feminized and other in relation to the White Father at the same time as he feminizes black women in particular and women in general, the black male is "simultaneously complicitous yet dissonant with and occluded by" the patriarchal power of the White Father.[23] The black male, in his history as African slave, is/was the object of control or desire for the White Father; the subjectivity imposed on him is as object—a position analogous to that occupied by women. He resists this imposition in various ways while (as Fanon emphasizes) nevertheless being simultaneously drawn into a vexed and emotionally invested identification with white male power.[24] This resistance and identification must be understood as coextensive with, and at times indistinguishable from, forms of desire: the urge to recover a lost (and ultimately fantastic) sense of wholeness. As Leo Bersani elegantly puts it, desire "combines and confuses impulses to appropriate and identify with the object of desire."[25] The rather provocative conclusion, then, of Flannigan Saint-Aubin's argument is that at bottom the crucible of black male subjectivity is the development of the black man's relationship to white men and/or to white male power and privilege; this relationship is characterized by hidden desire and the struggle for control—indeed, desire and a struggle for control which possibly can be understood as partly sexual, though not restricted to genital sexuality—and moreover, this desire replicates, mirrors, the white male's desire for the black male.[26] The repressed memory which is at the heart of testeria is thus the record or imagination of this complicated relationship of control and desire. Thus, the horror we might see in the audiences' reactions (and also acted out among black men, if Flannigan Saint-Aubin is on the right track, in the unspoken language of testeria) might not only be the horror of sexual exploitation as such (after all, one could always make the argument that black men were sexually exploited in that they were used as stud animals to produce slave progeny at their masters' whim); it might also be the horror of a repressed memory of homoerotic domination and the complex, contradictory set of desires—or, more properly, the set of perceived needs, inclinations, or wishes both impulsive and calculated that cannot be understood as the same as the desire of persons not enslaved or coerced—enacted by and engendered in sexual exploitation.

Power and/as Abjection: The Black in Black Masculinity

The particular horrors of the chain-gang experience and its challenge to black manhood are hinted at in the novel long before we as readers learn what occurred: Paul D does not pursue the subject of Sethe's jail tenure with her because "jail talk put him back in Alfred, Georgia"; Alfred, we learn on the previous page, is the place that left him "shut down." Other, more oblique references point to a specificity to the experience of black *men* in the slavery and postslavery United States that sometimes dovetail depressingly well with the contemporary discourse that flares up from time to time describing black men as an endangered species: Paul D, we learn, first accepts Beloved's status as drifter because of his own hard-won knowledge of the bands of mostly old and mostly female ex-slaves who wander the back country: "configurations and blends of families of women and children, *while elsewhere, solitary, hunted and hunting for, were men, men, men.*"[27] In a similar vein, Paul painfully relates to Sethe a moment in his captivity in which he watched the movements of a rooster that was freer than he was—the rooster being already, of course, a figure for a kind of strutting masculinity, and here doubly so, for the rooster's name is Mister.

Morrison in Paul D's character speculates on male gender formation under slavery and, importantly, also under the conditions of having a slave past—that is in part to say, under the specific conditions of blackness. Paul

D's question about where manhood lies is seemingly almost entirely formulated according to terms introduced to him as both the effect and the
substance of the enforced servitude into which he is born. Master Garner
delights in raising his male slaves as "men," giving them a certain degree
of freedom to move about on his land and teaching them to use guns, and
the like, for reasons that apparently have to do with his own aggrandize-
ment; doing so enables him to enjoy the shock of his fellow slaveholders,
whose intense debasement of their slaves, he seems to suggest, has to do
with an inordinate fear of black manhood and their own inferior masculinity.[28] "[W]hat did he [Garner] think was going to happen when those
boys ran smack into their nature? Some danger he was courting and he
surely knew it," observes Baby Suggs.[29] Thus, manhood as Paul D defines
it is a foreign and—because it depends so entirely on Garner's whims and
presence—precarious ideal (Sixo, by contrast, appears to follow his own
conception of manhood); while "nature" appears as a somewhat amorphous field of sexually expressive *possibility* that the otherwise highly perceptive Baby Suggs cannot quite suss out, and for which Garner provides
the genie bottle that gives it definite shape.

Morrison on one level presents Paul D's heterosexuality to us as "natural" to the character (as opposed to bisexuality or homosexuality). Yet at
the same time his sexuality is very clearly profoundly shaped by the physical and psychic limitations of his enslavement, in such a way that these
limitations become nearly constitutive—thus in part belying or undercut-
ting the presentation of his heterosexuality as the domain of "nature." The
relation of Paul's heterosexuality to nature is in fact given a rather sardonic
metonymic quality in the text: the original expression of his heterosexuality is in bestiality. Sethe is bought to replace Baby Suggs, and the Sweet
Home men, who in the absence of women have been having sex with
cows, spend an entire year waiting for her to choose. "A year of yearning,
when rape seemed the solitary gift of life. . . . All in their twenties, minus
women, fucking cows, dreaming of rape, thrashing on pallets, rubbing
their thighs."[30] Thus, Paul D's and the other men's heterosexuality takes
shape in large part—despite or as *underlined by* Garner's granting Sethe
(but not them) a "choice"—as a relation involving coercion, economic exchange, and animal husbandry. Sethe is bought to be a mare to someone's
stud; the men dream of rape constantly and rape cows.

That Morrison makes it appear that the Sweet Home men never
thought of having sex with one another to satisfy their "nature" accentuates the degree to which the practices on the chain gang are a violation.

This omission of voluntary or "natural" homosexual possibility on Morrison's part might indicate a certain cramped breadth of speculative vision in an otherwise flexuously free work of imagination. Equally, and perhaps more intriguingly, as a narrative choice it aligns her with Christian's audiences: for both Morrison and Christian's audiences, the chain-gang scene's register as the shocking trace of *how things really appear* (which, once its spectral presence is brought home to haunt, must either be denied or mutedly described, and is to be understood in any case as especially heinous) also suggests an awareness subtending conscious thought, and which we can thus think of as repressed memory: an awareness of how the terrors and degradations of abjection make available the "empty" possibilities that "we ourselves are." In this case, the possibilities are sexual.

These sexual possibilities take forms beyond Paul D's unstable claim to a manhood that is not of his own devising. Eventually Sethe chooses Halle, but the result is a husband-wife relationship that is loving but not normative by the standards that Morrison suggests prevail at the time or that probably serve as ideals for many contemporary readers: "Halle was more like a brother than a husband. His care suggested a family relationship rather than a man's laying claim,"[31] suggesting that the marriage has an incestuous quality. The bestial and the incestuous are of course ready markers for perverse, for other-than-norm, and they tell us clearly enough that sexuality is produced differentially under these conditions and is still experienced as such subsequent to the legal end of slavery.

Paul D's arrival at 124 reignites the desire that once potentially sparked between him and Sethe during the year of rape dreams, but the consummation is a disappointment. "Nothing could be as good as the sex with her Paul D had been imagining on and off for twenty-five years," it is explained.[32] The statement's meaning is more complex than it perhaps appears: the imaginary standard—a romantic or sexual ideal—against which the actual consummation is measured is itself troubled; Sethe's and Paul's disappointment not only lies in the gap between real and imaginary but is in fact all but compelled by the shape of the erotic and romantic imagination that gives rise to the sexual deed. The ideal of sexual desire's consummation, very much like the ideals of heterosexuality and manhood (and motherhood and fatherhood) that the characters hold—indeed, the ideal of Sethe and Paul D's sexual union is *itself* the consummation of the ideals they hold of heterosexuality, manhood, and so on—are ideals constituted in a system of (at least attempted) total exploitation of the black body and the black person's mind. A desire kindled under such a system is not likely to make possible fulfillments greater than or more perfect than its own limits and its own aspirations. The sexuality that takes form under those circumstances and that is practiced in relation to ideals formed under or even as the defiance of those circumstances will always partake to some degree of this origin. These origins do not describe the full breadth of sexual possibility, of course; and even if adhered to, they do not mean sexual expression under that aegis cannot be pleasurable, or even morally "good" or socially and politically productive or progressive. This is attested to by Paul D and Sethe's relationship soon after their disappointing consummation. It is also more epigrammatically suggested in the language describing Sethe and Halle's relationship, since their partnership is arguably freer and more equal than a traditional marriage exactly because it exists *without* the "laying claim" which living under the control of the Garners (living as abject) has made impossible to lay—and Morrison's calling into question of the phrase "laying claim" in Halle's case, with its play on the contemporary sexual connotations of "lay," indicates that all such paradigms of heterosexual relations ("lay" with its implicit references to the missionary position, to male-centered sexual pleasure, etc.) are, under the system of coercion which is slavery, altered, undercut, revised: differentially produced.

In this context Paul D's experience of something that might be called homosexuality appears not so much as the particular sign of sexuality perverted, since the "perversion" of sexuality—its being produced as different from the normative—exists along the whole continuum of sexual relations in the novel; homosexuality is more the means by which domination and torture are effected between white and black men, and, problematically, it is a measure of his abjection.[33] But precisely because of the latter, it appears also as the indication of and the window to, as it were, less definitely shaped—and thus at least momentarily more free—possibilities for sexuality and self.

The chain-gang experience is the location where Paul D believes that his manhood is lost, and this trauma speaks in bodily symptoms. In recounting Paul D's life with the chain gang in Alfred, Morrison begins by describing Paul D's uncontrollable trembling—a "flutter," a "rippling—gentle at first and then wild," a "swirl" and "eddy" within, that Paul felt powerless to control.[34] This feeling is, of course, fear, but these are also particularly descriptions of movement, of flux between states, of an unsettled position. And what is unsettled within him is, by his own admission and by the description of these bodily symptoms, gender: in a world in which the endlessly circulating trope of emasculation invites black men to be hyperconscious of a manhood which is always under attack or erasure, the language of "roiling blood" and of a "trembling" that migrates through the body bears a relation to hysteria—that bodily expression of a repressed memory held in the unconscious, a hidden knowledge of what has been done to you to compel you to fit a subordinate position. That hysteria is in popular if somewhat inaccurate interpretations of Freud a feminine disorder,[35] and that one might as easily claim this fluttering, rippling blood to have a relationship to familiar representations of female orgasm further suggests the precariousness of Paul D's "manhood" and the depth of his shame. The incapacity of Paul D's hands as a result of this trembling is first evidenced in the text by the fact that he cannot hold his penis to urinate. The trembling is elsewhere related to a "womanish need."[36] Thus, these swirls, eddies, flutters, and ripples can be read as figuring that state as yet undifferentiated along subject-object or gender lines that psychoanalytic theory attributes to abjection and that Spillers finds succinctly represented in the horrors of the Middle Passage.

The chain gang, in some ways like the emasculation trope, is an image that works to confirm the tale of the heroic black male. As Fanon argues, the black (male) body, in the various racist discourses which make the notion of blackness intelligible, is first and always corporeality itself: the black man *is* his body, is *the* body, is the excess of meaning associated with the body, above all the sexuality of the body.[37] The chain gang as figure situates this body within the folklore that makes the black male body most palatable: he is powerful but restrained; he sings even though he is forced to perform body-breaking labor; he endures heroically, but there hangs about him the lingering question of criminality. He is thus a body invested, saturated, with pathos, with the nonintellectual, the emotive, which is also the province of blackness in the black/white binary.

Into this familiar scenario, this well-worn page in what Morrison calls "the glossary of racial tropes,"[38] Morrison places an incendiary device: the "breakfast." That is, we are prepared for beatings, yes, and murder and mutilation and atrocity, because that is what one expects of these tales. The notion of breakfast, then, offered though it is by the hand of one who uses the word "nigger," seems merely diversionary, but for the inclusion of the mention of foreskin, which, along with the guards' "soft grunts," tells us that the black men are being forced to perform fellatio. Here the blackness = corporeality equation is transformed, its elements given different valences. We are accustomed to reading the emasculation of black men under slavery in the following fashion: to recur to Fanon, "In relation to the Negro, everything takes place on the genital level."[39] Fanon is of course performing his usual conflation—that is, the person of African descent is a man. The "genital level" of which he speaks, then, concerns the penis, and the penis, in its relation to the Phallus, is associated with kinds of sexuality, kinds of behavior, which are ascribed the relatively positive value of "active." The penis penetrates; it acts upon; as the stand-in for the Phallus and vice versa, it has and is power, dominance. The black genitalia in this schema is a focal point whose power radiates outward over the black (male) body, and however savage, frightening, and overwhelming that body becomes in this schema, it nevertheless carries the value of being associated with the Phallus. Even—or most especially—when the black (male) body is castrated, literally emasculated, its corporeal associations are with a certain kind of male power.

In Morrison's "breakfast" tale this corporeality is rendered "passive." The black man is *kneeling*; he is a *repository* for the white man's seed; he is a *mouth*, at best ("best" judged in terms of "action" and "power") he is merely *teeth*, an orifice dentata. His penis—so overwhelmingly present when black men are viewed through the lens of the racial-epidermal schema Fanon outlines—disappears. In this dismembering, his corporeality is divested of that which was perhaps its chief claim to power, to value: active sexuality. Whereas the black (male) body in its Fanonian incarnation is a surface on which white psychic needs and desires are projected, here that body satisfies the white male body directly and physically, as sexual play thing; it is the white guard's corporeality which now is the focus of interaction between white and black.

In this context, a rereading of Paul D's earlier (and somewhat odd) thought that "[c]ertainly women could tell, as men could, when one of their number was aroused" suggests a kind of intimate knowledge not only of female sexuality (which Paul D, as a man, might boastingly profess to have) but of a white male master's sexuality as well.[40] It is this knowledge, which in discussions of slavery is always and only imputed to black women, and the humiliation by which such a knowledge is acquired—again always said to be the province of black women—which has not been said, which remains hidden, and which the novel unflinchingly uncovers.

Moreover, Paul D's chain-gang humiliation has a mirror image in the novel: in the house of the formerly abolitionist and freedmen-friendly Bodwins, there is a piggy-bank black doll:

Denver . . . had seen, sitting on a shelf by the back door, a blackboy's mouth full of money. His head was thrown back farther than a head could go, his hands were shoved in his pockets. Bulging like moons, two eyes were all the face he had above the gaping red mouth. . . . And he was on his knees. His mouth, wide as a cup, held the coins needed to pay for a delivery or some other small service, but could just as well have been buttons, pins or crab-apple jelly. Painted across the pedestal he knelt on were the words "At Yo Service."[41]

The doll's filled mouth resonates with and echoes Paul D's full mouth on the chain gang, as does its submissive kneeling posture and involuntary offer of service (the doll, of course, is just *made* that way) and its concealed or suppressed phallic features (the doll goes without hands and fingers). The revealing irony of the figure is clear enough: this, Morrison suggests, is the way even "liberal" whites would see black people if they had their druthers, or when they are entirely concerned with their own pleasure; and further, what was done to Paul D continues in white people's fantasies and, in some form, in the social relations they practice with black people that respond to such fantasies. The humiliation in the piggy-bank figure is all the keener because it is a made object rather than a person, and thus it reveals an ideal of some kind that the Bodwins at the very least find amusing; others manufactured it, the Bodwins purchased it, it is an item in a system of exchange, as slaves, whom the piggy-bank fondly recollects, once were. It is positioned by the back door because this is where deliveries arrive but also because this is where the black servants are supposed to enter and leave, and there they will be greeted and bade farewell by this reminder. It is an image of the black male abject: the "blackboy"—one of Morrison's conjunctions that underline the thorough articulation of racial identifier to status in the black/white discursive universe of the United States. Thus, this is an image of horror, on the one hand; it confirms Paul D's horror at what has happened to him and Christian's audiences' shock and outrage.

The connection between Paul D's oral rape and the piggy-bank has a resonance in African American literature of the late 20th century: Morrison appears to have reprised an image in Ralph Ellison's *Invisible Man*, where we see a very similar bank. It is a possession of Men's House landlady Mary Rambo (a location that again underlines the way that the figure attends and mocks black manhood). This "very black, red-lipped and wide-mouthed Negro" has been ingeniously crafted so that if a coin is placed in its hand, it flips the coin into its grinning mouth.[42] The Invisible Man smashes it and tries to throw away its broken pieces and coins, but each time he attempts to throw it away someone returns it to him. And in Richard Wright's *Native Son*, Bigger Thomas describes the physical limitations of racial segregation in terms that would be all too literal for Paul D: "Every time I think about it I feel like somebody's poking a red-hot iron down my throat"[43]—a statement whereby, as Robyn Wiegman comments, "Wright casts Bigger's oppression in highly sexual and phallic terms, marking segregation, racism, and poverty as the symbolic phalluses of white masculine power burning in Bigger's throat."[44] In this sense Paul D's chain-gang experience is another in a line of representations of *how things really appear* regarding black masculinity.

At the same time Morrison's rendition of the figure indicates that though the bank is inanimate, a frozen representation of white people's hideous ideal for black people, it exceeds its signification as abjection, in a way that is suggestive for Paul D. The piggy-bank is *stuffed* with the leavings, the droppings, of its owners. The coins are not unlike the ejaculate of the chain-gang guards: potentially productive stuff yet cheaply produced and carelessly discarded. Paul D *is* to a degree stuffed and made, like the piggy-bank: he is stuffed with Garner's notions of manhood and molded by the privileges Garner doles out to suit his own vanity into a man-in-quotation-marks. As Fanon tells us, blackness itself is such a use-object on the cultural level, a thing stuffed and made—the invention of enslavers and conquerors and the offal-bin for their fears, especially about sexuality. (Morrison tells us this, too, in the novel: "Whitepeople believed that . . . under every dark skin was a jungle. Swift unnavigable waters, swinging screaming baboons, sleeping snakes, red gums ready for their sweet white blood. . . . The more coloredpeople spent their strength trying to convince them how gentle they were, . . . how human, the more they used themselves up to persuade whites of something Negroes believed could not be questioned, the deeper and more tangled the jungle grew inside. But it wasn't the jungle blacks brought with them to this place from the other (livable) place. It was the jungle whitefolks planted in them. . . . The screaming baboons lived under their own white skin; the red gums were their own.")[45]

But insofar as the ejaculate (and perhaps, the piss) of the guards is nonproductive, nongenerative because it is not used to produce a pregnancy, and insofar as it is humiliating because it underlines, enforces, substantiates the black man's lack of status as a "man," the transformation of ejaculate/piss into coins as the two moments in the text echo one another also suggests the peripheral capacity of that stuff with which the figure is bloated nevertheless to *become* generative and productive:[46] as coins, the stuff circulates as currency, and its value in the exchange system means it can pay for something in the economy in which it is itself a traded object, including paying for itself, in that the money could be pooled to pay the Bodwins for the piggy-bank—and even presumably, since this is in the house of an abolitionist family that continues to take an interest, however paternalistic, in the welfare of black folks, the money can in some minor way be put to projects supporting those goals. The figure's mouth *could* be filled with buttons and other detritus (each of which has its own uses), but it *is*, significantly, filled with coins. The image is not justified by these excessive or ancillary meanings; it does not receive the author's or the reader's forgiveness. But it is a figure suggesting that even in the abject there is something with which to work.

Paul D—predictably, perhaps, for a character obsessed with a rooster— regains his sense of manhood on the chain gang when he has a hammer in his hand. Wielding his hammer, he stills the trembling within. But ultimately the hammer is not enough: indeed, manhood, as such, certainly the manhood which he has been measuring himself against, is not enough. Even Sixo's example of relentlessly wily masculinity (which is just slightly reminiscent of a trickster figure, a Legba or Br'er Rabbit) does not describe the totality of Paul D's "nature" or provide a sufficient model for who he is and has been made to be. As Paul D himself remarks, "A man ain't a goddam ax. Chopping, hacking, busting every goddam minute of the day. Things get to him. Things he can't chop down because they're inside."[47]

The "inside"—figured by the red heart in the rusty tin, the "roiling blood" and trembling interior of his body, the softness (or at least the unshaped, unformed, inchoate) which the world says must be hidden behind the strain which is masculinity—must also, somehow, be acknowledged, grieved for, and reclaimed. The process by which this reclamation might be said to occur is, in both the novel and in readers' reception of it, far from complete or satisfying, far from an identity that coheres or a "wholeness" that heals without pain. At the novel's end, Paul D is grateful that Sethe, by *not mentioning* a part of their past together in which he was tortured, has "left him his manhood"—which suggests that though he knows that manhood to be something of a fiction, he also feels still, and will probably always feel, the pull of manhood, the seduction of the acts of denial, disavowal, and forgetting which constitute it.[48] This pull and seduction, and the conflict-ridden and unsatisfying nature of the seduction's goal, is the ancestral legacy, the knowledge, with which Paul D as figure, as bearer of an ambiguous trope, has endowed us.

Paul D's Double-Body

Paul D "could not say" to Sethe, "I am not a man"—which is to say that he *will not* do so, especially given Sethe's comparatively more steely, more normatively masculine character, which would make his failure to live up to the standard she actually meets more painfully apparent. But she knows. And Sethe's complicity in not speaking (her choosing, in the parlance of the novel, to "pass" on his story, as we the readers are given the choice to do in the novel's conclusion) is a recognition that mirrors and complements her own dawning recognition, given words by Paul, that she is her own "best thing."[49] By novel's end Sethe and Paul D understand that their subject positions, who they are, their having emerged from historical circumstances (that persist as present in the psyche, which ignores the dictates of linear temporality) that make unavailable to them the ego-ideal and defensive postures of the ego modeled by their enslavers and even by their dim "memory" of a preslavery past (which is a way of restating double-consciousness) endows them with the possibility of a *different* kind of identity: an identity which would acknowledge the full range—or at least a fuller range—of the extent to which it is not dependent on or shaped by ego defenses (the illusion of inviolability, wholeness, etc.).

For Paul D this "different" identity arises in and from the differential production of gender and sexuality. What is hinted at in Morrison's depiction of complicity between Sethe and Paul D concerning the mention of his "shame of being collared like a beast" is a partnering that underlines the playing of roles:[50] the manhood bequeathed by Garner that Paul D had believed in has proven hollow—it proved hollow, unable to sustain him, on the chain gang; indeed its very predicates, the limits that define it, made it possible for experiencing oral rape to shatter it. Subsequently he remained tethered to this broken ideal, holding on to it and preserving it in melancholic fashion through imagining his failure to achieve it. The trembling he still experiences is the bodily expression of the tension between this ideal and a different way of living in his body that is not in relation to the masculinity taught him by Garner: this is how Fanon's double-bodiedness diagnosis appears in Paul D. What unseals the binding between this empty ideal, his supposed failure, and his self—what permits him to shift, to move *between* the seemingly absolute binary split of masculine and not-masculine (i.e., *like* feminine, without masculine ego and thus *as if* nonexistent, dead) rather than remaining paralyzed by the tension between them—is actually his "rape" by Beloved herself.

Beloved moves him bodily by supernatural means from Sethe's bedroom to Baby Suggs's room, to the storeroom and then the cold room, so that his body is not his own—figuring both the conditions of enslavement and Fanon's double-bodiedness. She also makes him have sex with her and mimic the passion of lovers ("Call me my name," she demands; "No . . . Beloved") and brings him to orgasm (as we see in his repeated, rhythmic verbal ejaculation, "red heart")—so that though his pleasure is his, it is not mandated by him.[51] The forced movement figures the psychic movement that his healing requires; it is the physicalization of a psychic freedom that paradoxically only becomes apparent in being demonstrated as a repetition of slavery, a revelation of *how things really appear*. The forced sex recapitulates the conditions of slavery especially as *women* endure it and recapitulates the chain-gang fellatios that also repeat those conditions. But it is not until Paul D is raped again that the phrase "red heart," signifying the opening of his rusty tobacco tin, can occur. Emergence from the fragility and terror that the trembling seems to him to signify is to emerge *into* such fragility because of the evisceration of his ideal, and his being stripped down to what he is or can be without its essential defenses; it is to fall back into the empty gap of possibilities which he is.

That this enables possibilities to be imagined we can discern in the tentative but apparently pleasurable choice Paul D can make, now that he hovers in the space of the not-yet-ego. He becomes capable of making himself in the social, of joining with Sethe in a sociogenic process of sorts: her "tenderness about his neck jewelry" means that she knows he "is not" a "man" or, more properly, that he is a man differently than the norm. And he knows that she knows, and she knows that he knows she knows, but they will act as if none of this were true. The symptom of trembling follows the logic of symptoms in the usual way: a symptom is a particular truth that disturbs a false totality. Sethe's silence of complicity leaves Paul D his manhood, but their shared knowledge that this is what they are doing means the two of them have transformed a symptom that speaks from the unconscious into a fetish, for the logic of a fetish is that it is a particular lie that keeps truth at bay.[52] That the fetish of "manhood" has been chosen consciously, and is the coin of the agreement between them, is the work of sociogenesis, writ small. Within the bounds of their relationship they are in control of the logic of the fetish; it is their fetishism. And as with any such fetishism, its surer product is not safety (for as Baby Suggs admonishes both Sethe and Denver, there is no safety: "This ain't a battle. It's a rout") but some form of *pleasure*, however limited, however provisional, however attenuated: the pleasure of authoring choice, the pleasure of role playing, the pleasure of social making.[53]

. . .

Part of what *Beloved* implies is that for wholeness, the black body must be recovered, revalued (as we see in Baby Suggs's sermon, when she exhorts her congregation to love each part of their bodies). This black body is a part of and a stand-in for the black self or subject. The dismembered parts of the black self torn apart in slavery must be healed and reintegrated by the self-love of unflinching memory. This is a responsive strategy consistent with the logic embedded in the emasculation trope, which by focusing on what has been taken away urges us to take it back. The emasculation trope—the emasculation reading of the founding *scene* of blackness and African American male subjectivity—supposes that there is a natural, real, untainted, uncompromised black maleness which can be recovered if the effects of its emasculation are reversed; the trope emphasizes memory, but only to a degree. It recognizes the history of the exploitation of black bodies to the extent that it subsumes that history under the sign of a threatened manhood which can be recovered and defended.

By placing manhood at the center of its reading of the scene, by making manhood, lost or recovered, the *meaning* of the scene, the answer to the riddle of black male subjectivity, the emasculation trope repeats the Lacanian psychoanalytic notion that the Phallus, absent or present, is the marker of gender and thus identity. The Phallus is the symbol of patriarchal authority—those who possess it have within their power the exercise of mastery, over themselves, over "weaker" men not in possession of the Phallus, over women. In this sense the emasculation trope as a reading of black male subjectivity also buttresses Freud's postulate that the fear of castration governs the male child's relationship to his father and mother, and to men and women.

The emasculation trope's account of black male subjectivity tends toward a denial or erasure of part of the history of slavery: the sexual exploitation of enslaved black men by white men, the horror of male rape and of homosexuality—all of these memories are bundled together, each made equal to and synonymous with one another, and all are hidden behind the more abstract notion of lost or stolen manhood and are most readily figured by the castration which was so much a part of the practice of lynching.

This move secures black male identity by a denial which parallels and mirrors the denial that stands at the heart of white bourgeois heterosexual identity. I think here of Judith Butler's succinct reading of the psychoanalytic notion that any process of identification always involves a disavowal, a disidentification with something deemed to be opposite, something rendered abject: butch cannot be butch unless she throws out everything femme about herself; white cannot be white unless it throws out everything it considers black and projects it outward; man cannot be a man unless he abjects the feminine. Yet this disavowal holds the very thing being repudiated in intimate relationship to the identity; unresolved, the attempted abjection results in a kind of melancholy, a repressed but constantly returning wish for what has been repudiated.[54] Paul D's story in *Beloved* brings us a step further in the process of addressing that melancholy, by avowing what the emasculation trope disavows.

In Morrison's fiction, the heart must be liberated from its tin tomb: what is intimated in *Beloved* might be said to be a spiritual rather than a strictly psychoanalytic developmental trajectory, where some measure of wholeness is possible, is a necessary and worthy goal, and is not a fantasy. But this wholeness must be understood as a necessity in the context of an ongoing political struggle for black liberation and, moreover, as a *process* always ongoing, never quite complete. It must also be understood as a historical trajectory: in the text, past experiences produce blackness and black(male)ness and whatever distinctiveness these categories of identity might be said to possess; it is the history and the practices that respond to that history that found subjectivity; it is the encoding of that wider history in personal tales of loss and love, in *scenes* of memory whose importance lies less in their factual nature than in the knowledge they force us to reclaim, that founds subjectivity.

Thus, the ascension to a liberated black male identity must involve not only the recovery of the memory of the black male body's violation but also the recovery of the painfully acquired knowledge of other modes of being male than the model of phallocentric mastery.

The "other mode" figured in this scene encodes important aspects of African American history. As Hortense Spillers points out, under slavery both the law (in its sense as legislation) and the Law (the rules and regulations unwritten, circulating as culture) erase paternity and render virtually oxymoronic the position of the black father as holder of the Phallus.[55] (Correspondingly, Paul D is absent in the role of father in the novel. His presence is in relationship not to children but as a lover to Sethe and a brother of sorts to his fellow male slaves; moreover, his knowledge of himself is mediated by his memory of a particular relationship to white male power and white men, and thus to his own internal, idealized masculine image.)[56]

Psychoanalytic theory tells the story that white male subjectivity comes into being through the workings of the Oedipal triangle between son, father, and mother and in the mirror stage between son, mother, and the son's idealized image of himself. These give rise to the abjections, repressions, and taboos which structure heterosexuality and traditional gender roles. Yet the founding story of black male subjectivity in slavery is one in which the family as such does not necessarily—or frequently cannot—form the crucible of identity. As W. E. B. Du Bois observed, the black church preceded the black family, and here in this originary scene, as elsewhere in accounts of African American history, the position which a black male identity occupies is not necessarily one that is defined by a nuclear family structure, and it is not solely or primarily in the nuclear family that the black male forms the basis of his sexuality. Instead, his identity is formed in other kinds of relationship, other forms of connectedness, that vary from his partnership with black women to his brotherhood with other black men to his complex relationship to white men wielding near-absolute power.

There is a reading of this scene from *Beloved* that emphasizes its loss, its deprivation, its degradation, the outrage of it—and this reading we know in part because the emasculation trope has taught it to us. Another reading of this scene, not exclusive of the first and yet equally valid, is that in the horror which shattered African kinship groups on these shores, and in the convoluted and ridiculous and ugly ideology which justified and continually reproduces that shattering, we may nevertheless glimpse through this other mode of being male the model of another world, another form of connection between people: if we look more closely at the scene despite the inescapable hideousness of its context, it perhaps provides a glimpse of a kind of subjectivity in which we vault over the high walls that mark the limits of family and gender roles, in which we could recover what we have disavowed; it is a vision that moves beyond the merely parochial and constrained bonds of paterfamilias and everything that we build in imitation of paterfamilias, to begin to see connections that force us to embrace a wider community because to do so is the only way we can embrace and empower ourselves—a vision predicated on, perhaps all but impossible to see unless we look through, the translucent prism of blackness.

But this is only a glimpse; in this scene we see only a ghost, like Beloved herself.

And—alas—what we glimpse is not a utopia. Both psychoanalytic and existentialist theory tell us that the workings of identity and the unconscious will never settle or shelter us in a place of security but will always propel us toward the edge of a precipice, where the mere whisper of something not yet acknowledged in the light of day threatens to hurl us into the abyss—only then to force us to ground in a new place of continued struggle.

Notes on Black (Power) Bottoms

HOMOPHOBIA, MORE THAN heterosexism, on the part of readers (anticipated and actual) and perhaps even to some degree the author herself, cordons off Paul D's sexual humiliation by white men in *Beloved*. Paul D and Sethe *know* and yet choose not to take up fully the implications of Paul D's experience, and this choice is both a reflection and an emblem of what is effectively (though I expect not intentionally) a homophobic collusion between Morrison and her readers. This compromise acknowledgment of the painful, partially self-constituting past—the compromise being the decision, psychically agreed to as a foundation for Sethe and Paul D's heterosexual pairing, that they will name and shape a "manhood" with the chain-gang event at its back without examining that event explicitly, thus no longer "beating back the past" but nevertheless holding off the full investigation of the past—does not prevent them from exploiting the sociogenic *power* to which the abject past grants them access. But it should be clear enough to us that a further investigation of the implications of that past, an investigation that pulls out the *stop!*s, as it were, of homophobic reaction, would be useful in elucidating the abilities, the powers, inhering in blackness-as/in-abjection that are this study's object.

One question that arises when the barrier of homophobia is removed has to do with an assessment of the sexual in this scene of sexual domination. What is erotic for the white guards might be clear enough (though see the discussion later in this section), but in pursuing the implications of the scene, how do we account for the sexual, let alone the erotic, in the experience for Paul D, and for all whom he represents? Is it even possible, or productive, to do so? Or merely perverse?

A set of narratives and images that repeat in the discourses and imaginary of contemporary Western gay male identity cuts a tangent across Paul D's scene and finds erotic potential, fodder for lust, despite—and because of—the domination, degradation, and horror that are at its heart. Leo Bersani charts the political potential of the seemingly (and to some degree, actually) self-defeating "commitment to machismo" of gay male

desire, evidenced by gay male erotic practices and commercially circulating pornographic fantasies, which stoke sexual excitement by reiterat-
ing domination/submission scenarios in which the same despised faggot
that the dominant homophobic culture insists gay men are is demeaned
for the glory and ejaculatory satisfaction of the gay male participants and
consumers. For Bersani, this apparent self-defeat finds its value in its momentary abolishment of the fiction of the self, and in its endorsement of
powerlessness, even as it obsessively identifies with power—for no matter whether one enters the fantasy or scenario choosing the role of top
or bottom, that it is a fantasy mandates that all parts of it are occupied
and identified with by the fantasist/actor, who has distributed various aspects of his psychic needs and desires throughout. "If . . . gay men 'gnaw at
the roots of male heterosexual identity,'" Bersani asserts, "it is . . . because,
from within their nearly mad identification with it, *they never cease to feel
the appeal of its being violated*"—which is to say, of the *it* that is also *them*
being sexually violated (as the bottom) in the fantasy/scenario and of the
"self that swells with excitement at the idea of being on top" simultaneously becoming extinguished. This self-abolition is for Bersani an inescapable aspect of sexuality itself, which by his Freudian reading is constituted
as, or in, masochism: sexual pleasure occurs at a threshold of intensity
when the psychic organization of the self—the organization Freud gives
us as ego-centered—is "momentarily disturbed by sensations or affective
processes somehow 'beyond' those connected with psychic organization.
. . . [T]his sexually constitutive masochism could even be thought of as
an evolutionary conquest in . . . that it allows the infant to survive, indeed
to find pleasure in, the painful and characteristically human period during
which infants are shattered with stimuli for which they have not yet developed defensive or integrative ego structures."[1]

   Bersani in his discussion of the appeal of violation and powerlessness
is of course not consciously referencing the sort of scene that Morrison
writes for Paul D in *Beloved*, because he is not explicitly articulating the
real political histories of racialized domination and oppression to gay
male fantasies and scenarios. Nevertheless these fantasies and scenarios
draw on those histories, even if only by rough analogy. In fact, there is a
defining whiteness in Bersani's conception of gayness, since he makes the
all-too-common error of imagining "gays" and "blacks" as easily separa-
ble groups that can be opposed in order to provide illustrative contrasts.
Thus, elaborating on the pitfalls of gay men's fantasmatic investment in
machismo, Bersani notes, "blacks and Jews don't *become* blacks and Jews

as a result of that internalization of an oppressive mentality, whereas that internalization is in part constitutive of male homosexual desire"—a statement that seems to reserve for blackness either an ontological reality or a purely external origin, and which half the things Du Bois, Fanon, and even Black Panther Party dogma tell us should simply prevent being said.[2] In this sense Bersani stands parallel to Morrison's and Christian's audiences in reading Paul D's dilemma; they both see a near-absolute split between blackness and homosexuality, a perception that contributes to an intermittently prevailing discourse in the culture at large which ignores even the simple fact of the existence of black gay people. But if we bring these two perspectives into corresponding rather than parallel relation, if we see that Paul D's simultaneous racialization and engenderment as a *black man* proceeds in part from a combination of internalized oppressive notions having to do with manhood and oppressive actions that utilize sexual domination to impress upon him a racial identity confirming low social status—if, in other words, we see that he is pushed to the bottom of a racially defined social hierarchy by being made to perform as a sexual bottom and that we need not precipitately foreclose the possibility that this enforced position of sexual bottom bears a relation to the identity positions encompassed in contemporary male homosexuality as Bersani describes it—then a series of potentially productive questions arise: Is it possible to think about the question—to put this provocatively—of whether some part of Paul D could have "liked it"? What if Paul D experienced pleasure in being raped, including—or especially— that pleasure-from-pain that Bersani argues inheres in the development of the body as part of its evolutionary adaptation? Would such a pleasure be a form of the (black) *power* that we are investigating—which is to say, would such pleasure be a way to resist, or work with or work through, the challenges presented by a process of racialization through sexual degradation? And is this possible pleasure or power a window to, an access granted to, a *constitutive* masochism in human sexuality, as we could see Fanon's muscle tension as such an access to an anonymous or amorphous existence inhering in the body as it existed by consciousness? Or is this power/pleasure distinct from that masochism, perhaps analogous to it but different?

These questions bring us into an uncomfortable encounter with yet another dimension of the unspoken and unspeakable. Chiefly what is unspeakable here is the sexual or erotic pleasure of the human being in extreme conditions of coercion and nonconsent; or, rather than our being unable to speak it, we cannot *think* it, we cannot access it adequately. Hortense Spillers states the problem thus:

> Whether or not "pleasure" is possible at all under conditions that I would aver as non-freedom for both or either of the parties has not been settled. Indeed, we could go so far as to entertain the very real possibility that sexuality, as a term of implied relatedness, is dubiously appropriate . . . to *any* of the familiar arrangements under a system of enslavement. . . . Under these circumstances, the customary aspects of sexuality, including . . . "pleasure," and "desire," are all thrown in crisis.[3]

Saidiya Hartman adumbrates these complexities in her reading of Harriet Jacobs's *Incidents in the Life of a Slave Girl* (1861). As Hartman shows, for Jacobs's stand-in Linda Brent, it is better to "give" herself to a white male lover than to be "taken" by her master, though clearly the giving is a choice only insofar as it is an alternative to a threatened sexual coercion; and there is a strong element of market exchange in Brent's decision (she is stealing herself, appropriating herself as property within a system that mandates property as her only available category of being and only sphere of action), which further suggests that the notions of personhood underpinning our concept of choice are not necessarily in operation. Under such conditions agency is criminality and consent is constraint, thus problematizing and revealing the racial, economic, and social determinants of such putatively universal concepts as agency and consent. Just as "choice" thus presupposes a certain (implicitly male) bourgeois subject endowed with certain social status and political rights, the capacity of the slave to "have" his or her "own" sexuality, his or her own pleasure, is not something that can be assumed.[4]

There is a risk, however, that in being scrupulous about the *difference* the practices and conditions of slavery make for putative universalities such as pleasure and desire, we begin to conclude that what is different about this pleasure, desire, and so on is that it is virtually nonexistent. Of course, apart from the commonsense reality that pain and being victimized are not pleasurable and not desired, there are more than sound political reasons for tipping the balance in favor of this kind of evacuation of the pleasures that might attend experiences such as Paul D's. For one, there seems little to be gained in any emancipatory enterprise aimed at overcoming or reversing oppression—which African Americanist inquiry always already is—by dwelling on the ways that the oppressed participate or collude in their own defeat by somehow enjoying it; it is precisely for this reason that Fanon is keen to move beyond his native/black's tensed muscles and blackness, even as he signals their abilities. But I think Marcuse in his investigations of psychological tendencies toward surrendering to political authority, and in his insistence that the drive for pleasure which authority canalizes for its own purposes can be freed or redirected for a more liberatory politics, suggests the usefulness of such inquiry despite this objection.

Another reason not to pursue the possibility of pleasure in the Paul D scenario is that it is surely the case that an *excess* of pleasure on the part of the conquerors and enslavers is one root cause for the suffering that the blackened or feminized endure; thus, to dally overmuch in that arena is in some sense to contribute to the pleasure taken in the plundering of black bodies (by reproducing it as a spectacle for voyeuristic thrills disguised as horror or sympathy)[5] or to fall into the trap of maintaining relations of oppression as they are. In this regard bell hooks wonders "whether the law of sadomasochistic master/slave relationships is, finally, infinitely more sexual, more pleasurable and more erotic than freedom and decolonization, and . . . this is the difficulty we have in moving towards some kind of liberatory vision."[6] Generally I tend to agree with hooks's statement and her implicit exhortation to move beyond the compulsion to revisit slave/ master sadomasochistic scenarios; but even so I think there is still useful work to be done in examining the aspects of the "infinitely more sexual, more pleasurable, more erotic" problematics of those relations—because of the specific value Bersani gives to the mining of that material and because it seems possible to me that further explication of *how* or *why* that relationship is so hyperendowed with eroticism may, as in Marcuse's argument, help suggest still more ways (beyond what Bersani notes) that those endowments might be put to uses other than the reiteration of oppressive power dynamics.

The problem of an underemphasis on the pleasure in *different* pleasure is evident in a seminal text concerning these issues that it would be fruitful to take a moment to consider: Angela Davis's *Women, Race, Class* (1981) was among the earliest and most powerful assertions of the centrality of rape to the experience of enslaved black women in the Americas. In assembling the evidence for this assertion, Davis notes, "It would be a mistake to regard the institutionalized pattern of rape during slavery as an expression of white men's sexual urges. . . . Rape was a weapon of domination, a weapon of repression, whose covert goal was to extinguish slave women's will to resist, and in the process, to demoralize their men." Davis repeats this point: "Excessive sex urges, whether they existed among individual white men or not, had nothing to do with this virtual institutionalization of rape. Sexual coercion was, rather, an essential dimension of the social relations between slavemaster and slave."[7]

Davis's argument has the character of an intervention, offering its observations as much-needed corrective to trends in historical interpretation that have dithered in the fallow fields of essentially prurient interest in the sexual practices and mores of white or black men, to the detriment of a broader conceptualization of slavery and its legacies that would not demean or dismiss the positive contributions of women. As such, these observations have something of a preliminary air to them, a provisionality—which may in part explain her deemphasis of the sexuality in rape. (Other influences no doubt are in operation, too: an idea that circulated as a result of feminist interventions in the discourse about rape that worked—largely successfully—to establish rape as an act of violence rather than sex; and perhaps a strategy, well-known to our predecessors in post-Reconstruction black politics, of constructing arguments that give the lie to the relentless articulation between the sexual and black people.) Nevertheless it is not clear to me that rape, even or especially institutionalized rape, can or should be fully cleaved of its sexual dimensions when we examine it. Indeed, to deemphasize the significance of "sex urges" in the establishment and maintenance of such a virtual institution leads us to misunderstand a vital part of it: such rapes must have involved (as the evocation of them in representation in the present must also involve, in whatever tenuous form, as Bersani avers, and about which I will say more later) some degree of sexual excitation and arousal. This would be true physically if we understand the rapes to involve intercourse, but it would be true even if the only forms of penetration involved the use of inanimate objects. Sex urges must play a part: sexuality that lies precisely in attraction and/or the enjoyment and expression of domination. The key idea in Davis's formulation is the imbrication (or centrality) of rape with social relations, the way that racial domination (and thus racial *formation*) and gender domination (and thus gender *formation*) as organizations of the social through the differential distribution of political, economic, and social power historically did depend on rape in slavery, and on the cynical (and psychologically predictable) evocation and popular embrace of a mythic black male rapist figure in the post-Emancipation century. Rape is thus a key part of social relations in U.S. (and pan-American) culture, as Davis describes it.[8]

Thus, the organization of social and economic power through rape in these cultures might be profitably described in terms analogous—despite the obviously huge historical and cultural gap between them—to David Halperin's description of the relations between erastes and eromenos that were a key part of the formation of the social among the male citizenry of ancient Athens, and his description of the experience of pleasure therein:

> Sex is portrayed in Athenian documents not as a mutual enterprise in which two or more persons jointly engage but as an action performed by a social superior upon a social inferior. . . . Insertive and receptive sexual roles were therefore necessarily isomorphic with superordinate and subordinate social status; an adult, male citizen of Athens could have legitimate sexual relations only with statutory minors (his infe-riors not in age but in social and political status): the proper targets of his sexual desire included, specifically, women of any age, free males past the age of puberty who were not yet old enough to be cit-izens . . . as well as foreigners and slaves of either sex. . . . The male citizen's superior prestige and authority expressed themselves in his sexual precedence—his power to initiate a sexual act, his right to ob-tain pleasure from it, and his assumption of an insertive rather than a receptive sexual role. . . . Each act of sex was no doubt an expression of real, personal desire on the part of the sexual actors involved, but their very desires had already been shaped by the shared cultural definition of sex as an activity that generally occurred only between a citizen and a non-citizen, between a person invested with full civil status and a statutory minor.[9]

Thus, what is narrated and presumably experienced as a sexual and roman-tic relation in ancient Athens cannot be understood except as an expres-sion not only of "sex urges" as we understand them (by which we mean lust, pleasure) but also of social status or, more properly, of a relation be-tween a dominant social actor and a subordinate one. This would logically appear to have some purchase on our understanding of the institutional rape that was part of chattel slavery in the Americas, for the masters/rap-ists. Davis's cogent articulation of rape to racial and sexual terrorism and thus to social, economic, and political hierarchies must lead us to accept rather than to deny the sexually excitatory aspects of expressing (or try-ing to express) the dominant role in sexual relations, or performing the role of owner in relations of capitalist exploitation. At the very least, if we are to take these articulations as correct readings of the historical record, we would have to see that, in the ideal (and thus both in the realm of representations and in socially shared or socially transmitted fantasy), one has to get one's dick hard to rape to establish one's social position and terrorize one's enemy, and part of what gets one's dick hard is establishing one's social position and terrorizing one's enemy: the sex urge is as much the will (or urge) to dominate as it is an urge for something presumably more purely sexual; and the sexual cannot be understood to exist as part of this institution—and as part of any practices related to it or that make reference to it—except as *sexy* because it is an expression of sociopolitical power or status. We have not left the sex urge behind by identifying the political and economic determinants that make rape a virtual institution; we have instead identified part of what constitutes the sex urge.

If, then, we are to avoid deemphasizing the sexual and the pleasurable for the rapists in the virtual institution of rape central to chattel slavery, there is a corresponding observation—though clearly much more difficult, morally and intellectually—to make with respect to the raped slave. The barrier to understanding that renders unsettled the questions of sexuality and pleasure for our enslaved ancestors under conditions of coercion (under circumstances like Paul D's on the chain gang) is not unlike the barrier to our understanding of the sexuality and pleasure (if these are even appropriate terms) of all human beings at the point of the earliest formations of these dimensions of experience in infancy. We must be particularly careful in evaluating these dimensions for the enslaved because enslavement radically puts pressure on assumptions of personhood and conceptions of individuality that we take for granted as concomitants of our less obviously enslaved subjectivities; and similarly, we do not know how an infant processes those experiences we categorize under sexuality and pleasure because our own experience of them is greatly (though by no means completely) shaped by the psychic organization of the "I" around an ego and the perceptive split between subject and object that the infant—so we surmise—does not possess in the same way. I do not mean by this analogy to infantilize the enslaved. My point is simply that because a gap lies between our own widely shared assumptions about how our individual experiences are centered in a certain species of "I" and the underpinnings of the experiences of both slaves and infants, it would be wise to assume that dimensions of their experience such as sexuality and pleasure are *different*—but not necessarily (and not likely) absent.

If psychoanalytic conclusions are even partially correct, and the organization of the psyche around something that can be called a pleasure principle obtains for human beings generally, the condition of the infant—which, because of its radical dependence on parenting and because its psyche is organized to some significant degree *differently* from our own, is a condition at the very least of *not*-freedom (because freedom, like any other essentially political concept, would seem primarily to take its meaning in a world organized around and with the lived fiction of the "I")—is not without a domain of (something-not-unlike) sexuality, a domain of (something-not-unlike) pleasure. (This, too, becomes largely "unspeakable" in our common discourse, in which, for example, a morally correct horror of child molestation that extends its continuum of disapprobation to less clearly morally apt legal definitions of statutory rape always attributes solely to the adult in question the possession of sexual desire: which in hewing righteously to a focus on punishment of the adult runs the risk of failing utterly to address not only how the child in question does indeed experience something in the nature of sexuality and sexual pleasure in general, and might thus have done so in the acts of molestation, but also, most importantly, how that experience will thus give shape to the child's experiences of sexuality and pleasure as he or she matures.) Like the not-freedom of the infant, the "unfreedom" of the enslaved, even in those traumatizing moments when rape is being used as an instrument of domination—and *especially* as those traumatizing moments take on the character of the psychologically formative, as they inevitably must when they occur at an early age or as part of the early environment (like Frederick Douglass's witness of his Aunt Hester's sexualized whipping), and as they seem to do even when occurring in adulthood, as the literature on trauma tells us—cannot be assumed to be without a domain of sexuality, a domain of pleasure, however "warped" or *different*, however much such domains may be offensive to or apparently of disservice to our aspirations for ourselves or for our politics.

This is one description of what it means to be, live, or exist the abject. The example provided by the "evolutionary conquest" in Bersani's Freudian infant—that of an adaptation to conditions given (a whirl of sensations, ungovernable pain and not-pain, pleasure and not-pleasure; a radical dependence that is not freedom) through the recalibration of pain as pleasure, a degree of masochism that constitutes the sexual itself—would seem therefore to be of illustrative significance in understanding the implications of Paul D's sexual humiliation on the chain gang.

That said, it remains the case that a barrier obstructs our comprehension of what such experiences must have been like in their fullest dimensions for the enslaved and that the meanings we ascribe to "pleasure" and "desire" (which themselves are far from transparent or simple) probably cannot be ascribed to their sensations, cognitions, and psychic realities. This barrier and the crisis of these terms as they apply to our enslaved ancestors are not within the scope of this study; rather, I raise these questions with regard to slaves in order to expose some of the conundrums that lie coiled in the *representation* of black abjection in (what is at least apparently) a postslavery reality. When we ask the same questions we might ask of Paul D's experience of ourselves, as those who inherit such experiences as ancestral and/or cultural legacy (its persistence either as repressed memory or as the sexual violence of a dominant discourse founded on slavery), the barrier to understanding is more porous and the terms less direly in crisis—though the difficulty presented by the problem of pleasure and desire in and under conditions where racialization is enforced through sexual humiliation is such that the terms still need to be, as Fanon puts it, "slightly stretched":

Can we locate any "sex urge" in being raped? Does the raped experience sexual excitement at being violated in a way intended to terrorize him, and to establish his enemy's dominance over him? Is it possible to talk usefully about the choosing, desiring, or influencing person who is raped? Is it possible to locate choice, desire, or influence in that person? Is the object also a subject (much less an agent) *in* his or her own violation, or only *despite* the fact she or he is being violated, or neither (meaning that the very notion of subjectivity—or agency—must be revised, because it is in crisis)? If there is choice and desire, and if the object-victim is also a subject-actor, are these solely artifacts of self-hatred, or a kind of death instinct? Or is it possible that there is a *self-seeking* in the act (especially as the violating act becomes systematized, routinized), a subject questing after its own forms of relief and, in so doing, questing after the terms by which to know and to experience it*self*?

Such questions become legible, become *possible to answer*, even if the implications of answering remain disturbing, in contemporary contexts. Again, Paul D of course is not really a slave or ex-slave: he is a speculation on history and psychology of Morrison's, and a shifting point of identification for her readers—and thus he is not the "real" past but the past as we imagine and make it, as we work with that past in the counterlinear manner that Fanon prescribes and models. Paul D figures us in the guise of the past. It is important to recognize that while representations such as Paul D thus make these questions possible to answer for us, the questions tend to get bracketed or dismissed or seem simply impossible because of the way we think about rape, about rape victims, and crucially, also about blackness and femininity: because of the projection onto the victim—the victim of rape, of the subjugation that partly constitutes blackness and femininity—of total objecthood, of complete abjection. This is a projection that, again, stages a binary opposition between the narratable "I" and the self or not-yet-self that exceeds, falls somehow beneath or behind, or defies the requisites for that "I," in such a way that one figures as a surfeit so densely solid that it can support all that seems important about human experience (and which, not incidentally, is the chief politically salient locus), while the other undergoes complete erasure, and its already tenuous claims to being an inchoate precursor or a palimpsest fade into nonexistence (and thus this position is without political salience except as victim). That position or experience on the netherside of "I" remains an object and simultaneously a source of *shame*. Shame and defilement attend abjection, as Kristeva tells us.[10] Shame also, clearly, attends the position of blackness in a white supremacist reality—shame precisely in and as one of the terms for abjection in a white supremacist symbolic—as the Ex-Coloured Man demonstrates for us. And shame becomes the social badge and psychological reaction of a rape victim in a male supremacist reality, where what is considered a terrible violation is not so much violent treatment but to be penetrated as females (and bottoms) are routinely penetrated, an experience for which only (but by no means always) "consent" or wedded bond are satisfactory prophylactics against the most destructive insult. The attempted analysis here of the abject not-yet-self existing the black(ened) body has the benefit of dislodging some of these assumptions.

Representations of the sexual humiliation of black men by white men as the image of blackness in/as its abjection, and as representations that tell us *how* relations between white and black men, between whiteness and blackness, *really appear* in the ongoing now—specifically in African American texts from the 1960s and 1990s—are my subject in these concluding chapters. In particular, I aim to chart the ways that the invocation of such scenes illuminates those powers of blackness-in/as-abjection that I have been inquiring into. The power or ability I examine now has to do with *the creation and use of pleasure*: by this I mean the transformation of the elements of humiliation and pain, and the like, into a form of pleasure, the *taking* of pleasure out of the maw of humiliation and pain, and the utilization of that pain that windows into pleasure and back again for an experience of self that, though abject, is politically salient, potentially politically effective or powerful. And though I am of course working with literary representations, the (black) power I am attempting to reveal here is not only a cultural form in its usual sense but a bodily (and sexual, erotic) practice in which the experience of the body (pleasure/pain) gives to "'significance' a value which intellectualism withholds from it."[11] The taken or created pleasure/pain is a representation of political possibility. We might think of this as a bodily practice that arguably has synesthetic dimensions in that what is felt in the body is also produced as an impression, not of physicality or as an expression of an ego-ideal, but of a self not-yet-ego and, through that impression, of reconfigured social relations and culture.

And as I underlined Fanon's use of muscle tension to describe blackness's abilities in the midst of abjection, I use another, not unrelated metaphor in the two chapters making up this final section: the bottom. The "bottom" is evoked in the work of LeRoi Jones/Amiri Baraka, discussed later in this section; I use it to signify the nadir of a hierarchy (a political position possibly abject) and as a sexual position: the one involving coercion and historical and present realities of conquest, enslavement, domination, cruelty, torture, and the like; the other, consent/play referencing the elements of the former.[12]

To reiterate, Fanon repeatedly employs "tensed muscles" to represent an unconscious recognition of the colonizer's manifold injustices, a way in which the colonized knows and resists his historical subjugation; and the state of muscle tension or contraction simultaneously is a transitional precursor state to revolutionary action. This tension is represented as physical, but its full dimensions are psychic; and its form of knowledge is not fully intellectual because it inheres in the nexus between bodily sensation and perception, and in consciousness itself: what Merleau-Ponty refers to as anonymous or amorphous existence. Similarly, the figure of the bottom in this section links the political, the historical/temporal, the psychic or psychological, and the bodily.

We see this figure emerge in scenes or rhetorical evocations of the sexual humiliation or rape of black men or black male characters. Baraka and Eldridge Cleaver are drawn to the bottom, as a handy reference both to historically produced political realities and to its sexual connotations as a powerful signification for the harm that has been done to black men. But they understandably, if ineffectively—not unlike Fanon in relation to tensed muscles—and with highly problematic effects, work to banish or leap beyond the bottom in its sexual/bodily dimensions, for the now familiar purpose of shoring up an ideal masculinity (much like that prized by Paul D) as the basis for a phallocentric politics. Samuel R. Delany, by contrast, takes up gay male fascination with the sexual(ized) violation of the masculine to embrace the sexual bottom exuberantly, even as he mines the figuration of the bottom as reference to the history of the production of blackness; his representation of sexual humiliation as that-which-blackens turns that humiliation into a complex form of pleasure, and in so doing works on the bodily sensations and perceptions of readers, since Delany's text is pornographic. In Baraka and Cleaver by implication—against their intention—and in Delany explicitly, *bottoming* thus becomes a metaphor and a model for one of the black powers we are seeking in abjection: among its many inflections of meaning, it evokes the willed enactment of powerlessness that encodes a power of its own, in which pain or discomfort are put to multifarious uses.

.   .   .

Having just inveighed against the bracketing of uncomfortable questions, I nevertheless think some bracketing is important here and is indeed essential to understanding the way that these scenes or evocations of simultaneous sexual humiliation and racialization become stages for playing out the powers of blackness in/as abjection: I and the writers I am reading work with representation as the material stuff of the worlds we produce on paper. Black people existed and exist who have experienced horrific kinds of sexual humiliation and suffering. While these realities obviously cannot and should not be cleaved from the words that are meant explicitly to refer to or implicitly to suggest them, I am nevertheless dealing with how writers who are presumably *not* being sexually humiliated at the moment of their writing, and readers who are not sexually assaulted or humiliated at the moment of their reading, utilize these realities in representational strategies. Such essentially fantasmatic uses of the scenes of domination and humiliation in which blackness is born and which our ancestors suffered are at once a suturing of past to present and a declaration of independence from that history: as Spillers and Hartman warn, we cannot name what our ancestors experienced as pleasure. But we *can* name our reimagination and even our reenactment of what they experienced as pleasure (just as we could name it as pain or anything else, even, however morally or ethically bankrupt it might be to do so, as boredom). We can do so because we are not them *and* because they did suffer, because our legacy is both their suffering and their achievement of recovery from suffering (or, perhaps more accurately, their achievement of living-with-suffering) and the (relative) political advantages bought thereby. To represent blackness as/in abjection in such scenes is a way of working with the legacy of history.

In part I refer here to the unconscious, compulsive replay of painful or traumatizing experience. As Judith Butler remarks, "One does not stand at an instrumental distance from the terms by which one experiences violation. Occupied by such terms and yet occupying them oneself risks a complicity, a repetition, a relapse into injury, but it is also the occasion to work the mobilizing power of injury. . . . The compulsion to repeat an injury is not necessarily the compulsion to repeat the injury in the same way or to stay fully within the traumatic orbit of that injury."[13] This compulsion clearly operates to make scenes such as Paul D's an effective choice for how things really appear to us; that writers in the African American literary canon recur to such figurations is, presumably, the trace of cultural trauma. Yet at the same time there *is* a distance between the injury and its repetition, and for these writers, engaged in the both conscious and subconscious ordered dreaming that is literary production, that distance becomes precisely instrumental.[14] Their imagination of these scenes creates a way for them and their readers to identify with being violated or having been violated—and, in the manner of a willed (as opposed to developmental) identification, to do so from a position of power, relative to the real, historical, or present beings they might refer to, and thus to do so from a position better able to occupy or to utilize those otherwise hidden or overwhelmed powers that reside in the experience of (black) abjection.

In so doing, these writers affirm that there is a value to identifying with violated ancestors. This identification with violated ancestors is different from the positions into which one might slide down the slippery slope of self-hatred—those positions, as Bersani puts it, of "secretly collaborat[ing] with . . . oppressors, . . . that subtle corruption by which a slave can come to idolize power, to agree that he should be enslaved because he is enslaved."[15] Such positions are tirelessly policed by racial nationalists of whatever stripe. It is also different from the identification with or appeal of (apparent) powerlessness that Bersani notes runs as a strong current through the Western gay male fantasmatic and that depends on the bedrock notion that to be sexually penetrated is to be without power (a bedrock misogyny and masculinism, in other words)—again a notion shared by black nationalists[16]—although the identification I am discussing bears a relation to the appeal of powerlessness that Bersani illuminates, and I use Bersani's analysis of gay men as a useful analogy. This is instead specifically a pleasure-producing identification with being (sexually) violated in and as the process of racialization. Again because it is a process of willed identification, or a willed performance that operates both within and in excess of the performative as prescribed in and uncritically absorbed from the mandates of our culture, it occurs at a remove.[17]

This removal is key: it depends on a connection to a history in which people really were violated, people who, because of the effectiveness of racialization, are presumably of intimate (though at the same time far distant) relation to oneself. In this respect, since it is an identification that depends on someone else's suffering and pain, it is in some fashion an amoral (even immoral) form of identification, at least insofar as it could not exist without that suffering and it does nothing to alleviate it. On the other hand, there is *no choice* in the failure to alleviate the suffering. There is only a choice of how to make reference to this suffering in the crafting of a facet or dimension of oneself or of one's experience. That this identifying-with process can be harnessed to generate sexual or erotic pleasure in Delany's case, and arguably also in Baraka's and Cleaver's, makes it appear as if it is a sexual pleasure that derives from the subjugation of others who exist(ed) in the past—as if it is a violation of them or a violation of their memory. But even if there is some aspect of reviolating the violated here, the identification *with* those who are violated is both a moral choice—in that this identification is conscious, it is chosen, it does not flinch from recognizing and noting the terrible historical events from which it draws the materials for its own use—and it is *not* fully a choice, since we are all of us, as participants in a culture that like all cultures recycles and revises and repeats the narratives that have given it life and shape, the unwilling, unasked inheritors of that culture's terrors and suffering: the writer and the past victim are linked by travel in the same "traumatic orbit." The morality of this identification is in this light rendered all the more profound: it is a conscious decision not to deny that suffering but to work *with* the material of history bequeathed to us, where usually the masks of cultural ritual would allow and even require denial (a palliation without hope of producing healing).

To repeat, then, there is a value to the identification with being violated: if there is a value to *being* violated, it evades us—because the "I" necessary to assessments of a notion of value we can assimilate to our ego-structured world is difficult to locate under those circumstances. What "I" does an experience of violation that negates the ego possess? The subject may be formed from a violation, but insofar as it narrates or claims the violation it can only do so in retrospect or as a fantasmatic or willed identification: it recalls its violation from the "I"; when it is being violated, it recedes from narrative, it does not speak to us. The work of giving a narrative to this not-ego or not-yet-ego is the work of healing trauma; it is also the work of revealing and modeling a power of blackness in/as abjection.

A further caveat: I have explicitly quoted guides such as Bersani using the terms *sadism, masochism,* and *sadomasochism.* These may well be apt terms for the dynamics involved in the production of sexuality under conditions of slavery and of postslavery relations marked by Jim Crow. Marlon Ross notes that the continuum between *intimacy* and *possession* inherent to sexual mechanics can become manifest in same-sexual cross-racial interactions such as those in Paul D's scene as "the confused and confusing relation that sometimes adheres between sadomasochistic sexual pleasure and the sadomasochism required to administer and inhabit a totalizing regime of sexualized racial discipline," or as "possession [by] . . . intimate attack."[18] That such masochistic pleasure and its confusions might become the ground, the material, or even the expression, for the abilities or powers I am attempting to locate in blackness's abjection—as our encounter with Delany particularly will to some degree suggest—does not mean that this is properly a study of black masochism, however. Certainly I am not focusing here on masochism in its simplest definition (endowed us by the early sexologists), involving the derivation of erotic excitation from physical pain. Again, as I am working with writers producing representations here, physical pain is not likely to be at issue in the writing, and the written scene produces no such pain either. Insofar as the erotic practice of masochism is represented in these scenes, however, I do perhaps cross more than tangentially into the realm that interested Freud, the root articulation in the psyche between sexual pleasure and pain. Freud's analysis came to rest on a notion of primary masochism that, as Bersani elaborates, can be found in infantile sexuality: for Freud masochism arises from the death instinct (that is, the organism's instinct for equilibrium, for the cessation of sensation and agitation that characterizes living) in its early manifestation, when it is turned toward the subject itself and without the external object it will find in its subsequent development, and thereby, in that as-yet ill-formed subject-object trajectory, the death instinct is fused with the libido.[19] The ability to take pleasure *in* abjection, or in racialization through sexual humiliation (which, to be clear, is not the same thing as experiencing pleasure only because of such humiliation, or experiencing that humiliation as fully or immanently pleasurable), may well make use of this presumably universal psychic past, in the form of a skill set, as it were, that becomes readily available in the form and perhaps the misleading guise of a *racial* past. But as I am focusing on the representational strategies of people who have-been-blackened and carry abjection as a constitutive part of our racial identity, and on said strategies being adopted from mature (rather than infantile) positions defined by the social rather than by a dyad with mother,[20] Freud's primary masochism, like infantile sexuality, seems to me largely analogous rather than definitive in the final instance. The writers thus exploit dynamics in a black psyche produced by a cruel process of racialization that can be deemed masochistic—the compensations, like those of the sense-beleaguered infant, of turning pain into pleasure, transforming trauma into a source of enjoyment (because it is the norm rather than the exception)—rather than only illustrating those dynamics symptomatically.

The same relation of essentially uneven, jagged analogy applies to those forms of Freudian "secondary masochism" which become guilt, moral masochism, and the like, and which commentators have persuasively argued are part of the very structure of white male subjectivity as it was consolidated in western Europe during the early modern period. This form of masochism is a turning around of sadism against the subject's own self— an introjection of essentially paternal punishment for the ego's failures to police its instincts and appetites, an internal violence which becomes its own reward for the docile bourgeois servant of capitalist economies. This self-policing subject, abject before its tyrannical super-ego, is, as Fanon makes clear, dependent on black Others to hold the place of the threat of failure at self-policing. David Savran notes that "for a white male subject living in a pervasively racist and misogynist culture, a black positionality can function analogously to a feminine one insofar as both represent positions of abjection." Savran recognizes that of course the two positions are not identical, but "the masochistic fantasmatic is able to pose an implicit equivalence between them, . . . [and] this slippage . . . is one reason why masochistic fantasy has such enormous psychic power and is able to accomplish such an extraordinary amount of cultural work."[21] Obviously the question here has to do with certain dimensions of the subjectivity of these mirrored Others, for whom double-consciousness created by these very cultural functions must make secondary masochism of this sort exist at least in addition to, and more likely in a messily imbricated way with, those dynamics given rise to by both real and psychically imaged white male figures acting as the agents of *their* punishments.

This also raises the question of whether what we are really talking about is black castration—for which gender undifferentiation, the subject-object confusion of abjection, and the like are also somewhat descriptive. In this view what underlies the "power" that Paul D partly takes up and that he mostly refuses is the power that is intrinsic to a "castrated" position, which is either the power of the feminine (precisely as the Other to and threat against the self constituted as masculine in the masculinist assumptions of foundational psychoanalytic theory) or, as Bersani would have it, power*lessness* as such. There is a sadly obvious way in which the appearance of the term *castration* in African American contexts must, like so many other terms borrowed from a Eurocentric symbolic, register doubly. Ross on the subject: "From the viewpoint of race theory and African American history . . . [the standard psychoanalytic account of castration anxiety] reduces castration to an illusory anxiety afflicting transcendent male subjectivity by obscuring the *historical fact* of castration as a systematic instrument of torture and discipline practiced by white men against African Americans." In this sense *castration* is an inadequate term for this discussion. Moreover, in African American contexts castration raises the obscuring confusions I noted in the previous chapter, in which emasculation (of black men) and rape (of black women) become parallel and discontinuous practices. Even when this is not the case, as in the metaphor of "race rape," which Ross identifies in African American literature as a strategy of representing effects of racist domination that are not *just* castration or emasculation or suffering (I will return to this concept shortly), the equation between the feminine and castration not only has the clear effect of reinforcing sexist and misogynist epistemes but also works to marginalize women: "the curious thing about race rape is . . . the unspoken act of metonymy whereby black men, rather than women, become the improper tokens of the other race's raping desire, . . . erasing women as the routine targets of rape in order to metaphorize racial violence as the psychological desexing of black men."[22] Thus, it seems to me that castration, while not lacking in usefulness for this inquiry, limits our range of motion, as it were: we end up explaining everything as though its foundation were gender difference rather than being able to see gender in whatever form as one significant effect of—or one resource manipulated in—a process of racialization through sexual humiliation.

But at the same time I am not accepting powerlessness as the description of what we are examining without desiring to trouble that word: as I noted in the introduction, I want to talk about that which is not-power according to the ego-centric (and masculine and white) "I" definitions we have of power, but which is *some kind* of power, if by power we mean only ability, the capacity for action and creation in one or several spheres, be they internal or external to the empowered. This must be provisional, and to some degree described in vague and suggestive—which is to say *literary*—ways, as we shall see. Thus, though such familiar (if nevertheless endlessly fascinating and near limitless) terms as *masochism* and *castration* overlay, overlap, and even partly describe this power, they do not fully encompass it, adequately name it, or exhaust it.

4

The Occupied Territory

Homosexuality and History in Amiri Baraka's Black Arts

> You are not to touch other flesh
> without a police permit.
> You have no privacy—
> the State wants to seize your bed
> and sleep with you . . .
> You are not to touch yourself
> or be familiar with ecstasy.
> The erogenous zones
> are not demilitarized.
> —Essex Hemphill, "The Occupied Territories"[1]

THE CARTOGRAPHIC METAPHORS of zones, territories, and borders seem apt for examining representations of sexuality in the writing of Black Power and Black Arts Movement intellectuals during the Sixties. In the works of LeRoi Jones/Amiri Baraka, Eldridge Cleaver, and others—as for Frantz Fanon, at least in the early work *Black Skin, White Masks*—black sexuality is a terrain dominated by the history of enemy maneuvers, its capacities and limits delineated by the uses to which it has been put to serve white supremacy. The writers of the Black Power/Black Arts Movements identified sexuality as one of the primary means by which black subjugation was achieved and concomitantly as one of the primary arenas in which black liberation was to be won. Henry Louis Gates, Jr., endows the occupied territory with a topography when he reads Jones's early work and concludes that "[a] mid the racial battlefield, a line is drawn, but it is drawn on the shifting sands of sexuality."[2]

This line is drawn with an astonishing number of references to the figure of the homosexual, which, once evoked, is almost invariably ridiculed and castigated. The profusion of homophobic rhetoric in the works—Gates considers it an "almost obsessive motif"—has drawn attention from critics such as Lee Edelman, Phillip Harper, Dwight McBride, Robert Reid-Pharr, Marlon Ross, and Michele Wallace.[3] Generally these analyses work to identify the sexist, homophobic biases of the authors and the complicity of their arguments with the very forces they ostensibly oppose, and to read against the grain of the writers' attempts to demonize homosexuality, revealing instead the deeply intertwined, mutually constitutive relationship between racial and sexual identities in African American and American culture. I want especially to engage Edelman and Ross at this juncture, since their analyses of the homophobic rhetoric of Black Arts/Black Power thinkers provides a foundation for my investigation of how Baraka and Cleaver represent the power of taking pleasure in abject blackness.

Edelman demonstrates how literary representations of blackness frequently attempt to manage the challenging fact that racialization is accomplished through subjugation by containing or marginalizing threats of *penetration* to black male figures in the texts. Edelman's discussion of the overlap between homophobia and African American masculinist anticastration rhetoric—he uses Morrison's chain-gang scene as an example—pegs "internalization" as the threatening specter both for homophobic black nationalists and antihomophobic nationalists: the peril of racist domination is that the dominated black person internalizes a white or foreign ideology or belief or practice, thus compromising his claim to authentic blackness; for Edelman double-consciousness presents a dilemma wherein blackness is constituted by its compromise, by its constant oscillating struggle with the "foreign," with the occupying power that calls blackness its Other. Blackness is thus in its primary dimension—its very creation—*penetrated* or penetrable, and Edelman sees the recognition of this dilemma and the fear of its perpetuation metaphorically figured in the writings of Eldridge Cleaver et al. as the fear of being penetrated in homosexual sex—the compromised black male body being entered through a hole, invaginating the phallic invasions of its conqueror and enslaver who appears in the guise of a dominant lover, and thus becoming acquiescent to or, more disturbingly, desirous of what, given historical legacy, always threatens to be an essentially compromised (and thus defeated, even abject) black male identity. Thus, in Edelman's view, for Cleaver and Baraka white racism equals castration (or emasculation) equals homosexuality; white racists castrate black Others while homosexuals castrate themselves. In this vein homosexuality as intellectual or representative figure is both too passive and too active: its activity as threat lies in its involvement, its engagement, its struggling consent, to the "abjectifying denial of . . . 'masculinity.'" Edelman sees penetrability fears and the difficulties of maintaining the boundary between activity (racial and political resistance) and passivity (racial and political surrender) being distributed in the Paul D scene of the white guards and black forced-fellators: the guards under homophobic scrutiny are possibly "gay" and also "too active," and "the penetrated body is construed as acting contagiously to penetrate and thereby delegitimate the male body as such." As Edelman usefully reformulates the nationalist line of thought in psychoanalytic terms, to be regarded "as a tool" is to lose claim to "have a tool."[4]

Edelman's argument follows Lacanian theory to frame the doubleness of blackness as also—or yet another iteration, a kind of mapping, of—the (at least) doubleness that describes subjectivity, which is constituted as self in the cleavage between the Symbolic and the Imaginary: subjection to language makes one not one's "own" and produces, for black subjects, a fulcrum of identity that is the "discredited imaginary" that the alien Symbolic disavows and attempts to suspend. This discredited imaginary is what exists prior to clear subject/object relations—what we have been referring to as the space of abjection (though the abject does not seem to exhaust or adequately name this discredited imaginary for Edelman)— and is characterized by "irrationality, sensual immediacy, and an immature or narcissistic eros."[5] There is a "wholeness" (the obverse of the "hole") in the discredited imaginary that the Symbolic by the exclusions which constitute its ideal identities tries to compensate for, focusing on parts that substitute for the "lost" whole (the paradigmatic example being the Phallus itself, a part falsely standing in for a totality). Edelman's point is that the discredited imaginary which is identified with narcissistic eros and the like is a domain that the Symbolic both defends against and apes, attempting to effect the particular magic of "wholeness" through, paradoxically, its fetishistic and delirious obsession with parts. This fetish-produced wholeness is false, and even insofar as the discredited imaginary is, somehow, whole, its alien, surpassed, beyond-the-symbolic quality mandates that we will never be able to access it as whole; Edelman's argument is for a fractured, foreign-to-itself form of manhood that nevertheless maintains a cognizance or experience of its integrity. Edelman suggests that James

Baldwin, counter to the positions of Cleaver and, in his reading, of Morrison as well, represents the way that blackness-as-hole windows into that discredited imaginary, that lost whole which is never really whole.

There are overlaps and parallels between Edelman's observations and the argument I am attempting to advance here. But the possibility of different performances of identity or masculinity, while not incidental to the dynamics I am attempting to trace, is not my focus. While I am in part relying on a claim that I have derived through interpreting the metaphor of tensed muscles in Fanon's texts that abjection (as existential anguish and vertigo) provides an alternative to the tyrannies of our common realities which the Symbolic is one form of naming—a claim thus similar to that of Edelman, who locates this alternative as the discredited imaginary—my interest is not so much in claiming this realm or mode of existence as an alternative or escape in and of itself as it is in tracing particular ways that access to that realm operates or becomes manifest as an ability *in* the realities from which this other realm or mode is excluded. The quest for an alternative to the effects of dominant discourse arguably animates a hugely significant portion of work done in the academic world with any affiliation to progressive politics: Marcuse, of course, is centrally concerned with the potential for political alternatives presented by the narcissistic eros that Edelman identifies with blackness and the discredited imaginary. Reid-Pharr, for another example, discerns the sexually perverse homosexual functioning in the works of writers such as Cleaver as the scapegoat sign of boundary crisis whose exclusion manages both provisionally to secure black authenticity and simultaneously to escape "the systems of logic that have proven so enervating to the black subject."[6] But though the fact or possibility of such alternatives is a foundation of this inquiry, my primary emphasis is on some of the discrete mechanisms of the alternative's operation: its particular powers. These may appear to be simple abilities—nothing is more basic, more elementary to the human organism than its capacity to adapt psychically to the pain and terror of the inescapable vulnerability and violability of its existence, if Bersani is correct—but this does not, it seems to me, mean that the way the revenants of the alternative realm operate in the fields we know does not bear further observation and analysis. And these operations might redound to the credit of the claims that Marcuse, Edelman, and Reid-Pharr make for that "other" imaginary, that other eros and other logic.

Thus, speaking partly in Edelman's terms, while Baraka and Jones are busy erecting ramparts that support the repossession of a violently dispossessed and violated masculinity, I am interested here in the moments that the vulnerability to penetration are also moments of either power or pleasure, or power-as-pleasure. And moving somewhat beyond Edelman's argument, I am interested in how this penetration, while it is carried out by or represents the conquering Other, the "foreign," also intriguingly appears in these texts as penetration by ostensibly hostile fellow black males whose acts of sexual violation function as an indoctrination into black community—so that sexual violation is initiation into the resisting tribe, into the revolutionary nation, at the same time that it models submission to the oppressive alien social order.

Marlon Ross gives us insight into the latter phenomenon in his essay "Camping the Dirty Dozens: The Queer Resources of Black Nationalist Invective." Ross convincingly argues that Baraka's frequent and deliberately incendiary use of the epithet "fag" in his Black Arts work arises from his acquaintance with white gay men in his life as a Beat poet and playwright and from growing up in black neighborhoods in Newark. In black neighborhoods Baraka played the dozens, in which calling someone out of his gender or sexual orientation is a classic, almost reflexive, rhetorical move for belittling your opponent in the game; and among gay men, Baraka probably learned various camp rhetorical strategies for ridiculing hypocritical (and often powerful) white men who were homosexual but pretending not to be. Ross observes the sadomasochistic current in Baraka's liberal use of the street vocabularies of camp and the dozens, both of which contain, he says, "a tinge of identity-sadomasochism . . . whereby the participants both take pleasure in and inflict verbal pain on each other, acknowledging how they *share* maligned identities by pretending to malign those shared identities themselves."[7] Ross's articulation of identity formation to sadomasochism in Baraka's work delineates another way that the homosexual figure in Black Arts/Black Power rhetoric operates, and it is particularly useful for purposes of this essay because it provides a context in identity formation for the dynamic of pain-pleasure that I see as an ability, a power, at work in scenes of racialized sexual humiliation.

In this chapter, then, I want to extend these examinations of sexuality in the antiracist imagination of Black Power/Black Arts writers. I agree with Ross, Edelman, Reid-Pharr, et al., and take as a foundation for my inquiry their observation that homosexuality is one of the primary figures the writers deploy to serve as midwife for the birth pangs of a black national subject defended against the most insidious forms of racist domination (which is to say, the psychological dimensions of that domination).

I would extend this by arguing that the other figure so deployed is rape of men or male characters. Just as the exclusion of the homosexual figure continually fails in the ways that the aforementioned critics have shown, so too does the figure of male rape as a representation of racist domination at its worst paradoxically suggest that the historical subjugation to which the figure refers also endows its inheritors with a form of counterintuitive power, which shows itself in the assertion of *pleasure* within the scene of racialization and sexual humiliation. This pleasure is not only, and not necessarily, pleasure *in* homosexuality. The pleasure is of a broader dimension, being derived from the subjection to what is simultaneously a "foreign" influence and what is "one's own": it is the pleasure of introjecting and assimilating the alien (and perhaps, alienation itself), which is at once the pleasure of linking up and forming a community with ancestors whose legacy that *taking* of pleasure revises. It is taking pleasure in violent, exploitative, or painful events that are transmissions of tradition, of culture itself, even or most especially in culture and tradition's nationalist iterations. It is the transformation of the pain and terror that attends and is inextricable from the blackening process Fanon and Johnson describe, into a delight that is felt and is *known* in that formulation of bodily knowledge given us by Merleau-Ponty, at the nexus between body and psyche. But, given the slippages between homosexuality as figure and double-consciousness that Edelman, Ross, and Reid-Pharr detail, homosexual pleasure becomes a privileged representation—and access point—for that broader pleasure.

Rape and homosexuality in the texts are closely linked, in that they both are used as a kind of shorthand to signify the essential nature of white supremacy: that it is perverse and depraved and that it is enforced through forms of sexual domination. The Black Power/Black Arts invocation of the figures of rape and homosexuality is a way of referencing the history of slavery and, more importantly, the persistence of that history in the contemporary moment. The repeated use of these figures implicitly emphasizes that the history that produces blackness is a sexual history and that black sexual history (and, by extension, American history as a whole, since the production of blackness is such an integral part of its social, political, and economic fabric) is "queer." Black Power/Black Arts emphasis on the queer sexual history of American culture—however homophobic in its formulation—not only provides us with another local map for understanding the relationship between constructions of race and sexuality but also highlights the relationship between sexual liberation (by which

I mean, as modestly as possible, some degree of freedom from enforced sexual orthodoxy and prescribed sexualities) and more conventionally defined forms of liberation in the political realm, between sexual practice and power politics, which these last two chapters attempt to explore.

Sexual Revolution II

The demonizing of homosexuality in Black Power/Black Arts works—at times fiercely concentrated, often almost ingenuously flippant, but always thick with the spider's-web strands of the various queer histories to which it is attached—is a warning not to lapse back into a too-familiar habit of learned submission, as Eldridge Cleaver might argue explicitly. But the habit is not just familiar, not just the repugnant hallmark of defeat that Cleaver et al. would make it: it is a submission that also generates its own pleasures and that gestures unsettlingly toward a possibility of liberation extremely difficult and perhaps even frightening for the promoters of Sixties black nationalism to conceive. Though "black" because it arises from the specific histories of slavery and second-class citizenship in the United States, this possibility of liberation is not nationalist in the racial or territorial sense; and its black "power" might not be recognizable as such in a nomenclature in which power is chiefly defined by domination or the weapons to resist domination.

The forms of liberation and power revealed in readings of Black Power/ Black Arts writers help place the question of homophobic rhetoric in the work of the period in a broader frame: Black Power/Black Arts intellectuals and artists wrote during or on the cusp of the cultural developments that would become known as the Sexual Revolution, when what John D'Emilio and Estelle Freedman call the "liberal consensus" around sexual mores, practices, and public policies governing sexuality in America was disintegrating under the pressures of the massive social and economic reshuffling that occurred during the Depression and World War II and the resulting social upheavals of the Sixties. The link that Black Power/Black Arts writers drew between racial authenticity and (hetero)sexual practices relied on a set of assumptions (vulgar Freudian though they may have been) generally held by American intellectuals since the early part of the century that the truth of the individual self lay in sexual life;[8] and their arguments partook of a general conviction among many Americans who challenged the postwar social order that a sexually "liberated" society was fundamentally a more politically free society. In some ways, the swaggering machismo that links patriarchal, masculinist sexual power with political liberation in the writing of Baraka, Cleaver, and others reflected the profound shifts taking place in sexual attitudes in urban centers during the decade and anticipated the willingness of gay men and lesbians, feminist women, and participants in the counterculture to challenge customs and laws governing sexual choices. As a fellow traveler among the Beat poets in the late 1950s and early Sixties, LeRoi Jones was on the leading edge of the push for what Sexual Revolutionaries thought would be more open, less hypocritical sexual practice and discourse. Jones was prosecuted under the Comstock Act forbidding the mailing of obscene materials for his play "Eighth Ditch" (which later became a crucial chapter in his novel *The System of Dante's Hell,* discussed later in this chapter), and in arguing successfully against his imprisonment he struck a blow against government censorship of sexually explicit material.

Various changes in American society can be said to have been brought about at least partially because of phenomena associated with the Sexual Revolution. Women's liberation's challenge to marriage as an oppressive institution and gay liberation's challenge to the supremacy of heterosexual expression; Baby Boomer youth rebellion; the loosening of obscenity laws and the widespread commercial manipulation of erotic images in almost every corner of popular culture; the increasing availability of birth-control practices including abortion—all of these clearly had some impact on rising divorce rates, Americans choosing to marry later and postpone childbearing longer, and a general acceptance of nonmarital sexuality. Yet these developments, while expanding the freedom of daily life for the general populace, resonated differently when viewed from the perspective of nationalist black intellectuals and artists.

To read Amiri Baraka and Eldridge Cleaver working through the problem of black liberation in the Sixties is to encounter, again and again, *homosexuality* and *rape,* both as oscillating metaphors of history that meld one into the other and as opposing strategies for meeting the present emergency, either to be repudiated or embraced. Baraka in particular, as he transitioned from his position as Beat-style avant-garde poet and playwright to an ardent black nationalist and leader in the Black Arts Movement, emphasizes homosexuality and rape in such a way that his repeated usage of these figures—in the polemical shock-value fashion fairly common to Beat rhetoric—renders axiomatic the idea that perverse sexuality governs black-white social and political relations. In Baraka's work there is a conviction, not fully acknowledged but pervasive, that black identity is born in a matrix of sadomasochistic relations between whites and blacks. This sadomasochism is most readily represented in rhetorical incitements to action as sexual sadomasochism, though its mode was/is not only sexual. It is a sadomasochism that seems to be rooted in the memory of the founding scenes of race-creation on the plantation—race-creation in the discursive *and* the material-biological sense, that is, the creation of discourses and practices to justify slavery by positing the existence of an ontologically distinct group, and the literal breeding of a slave race through institutionalized sexual domination.

Baraka's declaration that "[m]ost white men are trained to be fags" from the 1965 essay "American Sexual Reference: Black Male" receives a great deal of attention in scholarship focused on the homophobia in Black Power/ Black Arts writing.[9] But this is just one of many such lines that appear in his essays: in 1964's "Last Days of the American Empire" white men are called "Hollow Men . . . the Closet Queens of the Universe," followed by a description of the "weak fag faces on those patrolmen arresting that beautiful chick."[10]

There are a number of aspects to Baraka's polemic: part of what inspires Baraka's flagellation of the white male homosexual figure is that it provides him with a white man who can be sexualized. If white men can be sexualized, they can become objects of (black) power: they can be praised or condemned in the very arena that black men are, according to racial myths, powerful and dangerous. Baraka repeatedly adopts a strategy in his writing that echoes a stance he urges his fellow black folk to use in political struggle. "The Negro must take an extreme stance," he says, "must attack the white man's system, using his own chains to help beat that system into submission and actual change." As a rhetorical strategy and a logic of argument, Baraka frequently draws deep from the well of (mostly sexual) stereotypes that liberals and integrationists of the day were attempting to combat, accepting and then tweaking the very figures of blackness used to justify the policing of black people. "[T]he average ofay thinks of the black man as potentially raping every white lady in sight. *Which is true*, in the sense that the black man *should* want to rob the white man of everything he has."[11]

Baraka asserts that the black-male-as-rapist "motif" is something black men consciously manipulate in bohemian, mostly white circles such as his own Greenwich Village haunts. He observes that white women choose black male sexual partners in order to experience the danger and pleasure of sex outside the (white) norm; and the choice to have that kind of sex is a tantalizing form of social and political rebellion against their construction as "the White Lady"—an act of sexual revolution. Baraka fully recognizes the allure of interracial sex coded as dangerous, perverse, and rebellious to be a function of white supremacist practices and ideology, on the one hand: "The black man is covered with sex smell, gesture, aura, because, for one reason, the white man has tried to keep the black man hidden the whole time he has been in America."[12] At the same time, as is almost always the case with the invocation of this myth, it is too fine a weapon to leave unused. "The black man, then, because he can enter into the sex act with less guilt as to its results is freer. Because of the rape syndrome, the black man will *take* the white woman in a way that does not support the myth of The Lady." And, "[T]he white woman understands that only in the rape sequence is she likely to get cleanly, viciously popped, which is a thing her culture provides for only in fantasies of 'evil.'"[13]

Thus, it is "true" that black men are rapists, but rape is, essentially, "freer" sex—and, since it is an act black men "should" commit as a blow against white men, it is a politically liberating act. Cleaver of course employs this latter spin on the black-male-as-rapist cultural figure in his much more notorious boast that he raped black women in the ghetto in order to practice raping white women. "Rape was an insurrectionary act," Cleaver writes. "I was defying and trampling upon the white man's law, upon his system of values. . . . I was defiling his women."[14] Cleaver cites Baraka's "Black Dada Nihilismus," in which the poet rails, "Rape the white girls. Rape their fathers."[15]

Yet for Baraka there must be some further political usefulness, some more incisive analytical gain that accrues from the manipulation of myths of black male sexual prowess; otherwise there is little or nothing to distinguish his use of the black male rapist figure from its employment in the minds of white bohemians who crave black stud service, or in the words of white men who justify lynching black men because they supposedly look at white women lustfully. His vague and almost clinical references to "the rape syndrome" and "the rape sequence" surely partake to some degree of shallow pop-psychology depictions of women's sexual fantasies (and prurient pop-culture pulp versions of the same) that had increasingly become a part of American public discourse as the rumblings of the Sexual Revolution began to be heard. But they also seem to reverberate with the sense that *rape* is the best—perhaps overdetermined—metaphor for the vicious inequalities of America's racial caste system. Rape as a "sequence" and "syndrome," rape that should be visited on the fathers of white girls, connotes the history of whites' brutal systemic domination of black people; as a choice of metaphor it points to the shadowy historical fact that sexual exploitation of black people has been intrinsic to the project of white supremacy in America, and it viscerally evokes the depth of the psychic damage done to black people by such a system of domination, because since the 1920s, sexuality had increasingly come to be understood as the arena in which one's deepest self was expressed. This is in accord with Ross's assessment of what he calls the "race rape" metaphor that he finds recurring—though critically underexamined—in postwar African American literature. Arguably, "rape" also evokes for Baraka as a writer the cognizance that white interest in fantasies of black sexuality as a representation of danger and/or as a representation of freedom have historically provided the economic ground on which black literary and cultural production can flourish, in the 1960s as in the 1920s (both moments when the dominant paradigms of American sexual mores underwent decisive change).[16]

D'Emilio and Freedman observe that white female sexual purity became the symbol used to consolidate (a distinctly white) American identity in the late 19th century, when the specter of hordes of black freepersons threatened the old social order as it attempted to right itself again after the dislocations of civil war; that same image of white female purity fed fears of "white slavery" when the social order was again threatened by the influx of southern European immigrants and rising working-class agitation in the early 20th century.[17] Of course, in a patriarchal culture in which the construction of male sexual desire as powerful and rapacious meant that men had to find sexual satisfaction somewhere, the sexual "purity" of white women depended on the enforced availability of all those women deemed inherently impure—and in the South, which had a history of sexual domination in slavery to rely upon, black women were frequently the targets of the various cultural practices (of which lynching was arguably a component) aimed at creating this sexual surplus. Both Cleaver and Baraka are very mindful of this. "I was very resentful over the *historical fact* of how the white man has used the black woman," Cleaver says when he justifies both his practice rape of black women in the ghetto and his attacks on white women.[18] Baraka has a similar view; his proof of the fact that black men in America have been "de-testicled" is that, "[i]n slavery times, *theoretically*, the slave master could make it with any black woman he could get to. The black man was powerless do anything to prevent it."[19]

Reshaping the black male rapist figure for ostensibly liberatory ends thus enacted a rhetorical (and in Cleaver's case, a too-literal) revenge in the sexual realm for a historical wrong, in which the oppressed would do unto others what had been done to "their" women. But the rapist figure carried within it the power to effect another form of redress: it also had the power of sexual reproduction, the power to wipe out a history in which blackness was created through white sexual domination, by generating the black race anew in terms deemed conducive to black liberation—as the Black Nation. Baraka writes, "Black creation is as strong as black flesh. If the raped white woman has a child (or the raped black one) it is a black child. The black woman can bring forth nothing out of her womb but blackness, the black man can send out no other kind of seed. And that seed, anywhere, makes black. The black shows through, and is genetically dominant."[20] The value of the "true" myth of black male sexual prowess, a value that finds its apotheosis in the rapist figure, is procreative fecundity. When Baraka endorses the "freer" sexuality of the black male, he appears not to be greatly interested in pleasure or even in the kind of freedom from social constraints that notions of orgasmic abandon conjure in the rhetoric of sexual revolutionaries: his clearest interest is in nation-building, in propagating a race.[21] Baraka is deeply concerned about whether black men are sufficiently motivated to bestow their genetic gifts on the ready wombs of black women. "It is only recently that any currency has been given in the mass media to the idea that a black man and a black woman might actually feel sexually attracted to each other," he says.[22] Of course, Baraka was married to a white woman, Hettie Cohen, and the tone of complaint in this observation is indicative of his own sense of having been led astray from what he deems should have been his more natural inclinations; but it is indicative, too, of a larger anxiety about the propagation of the race, an anxiety historically shared by the would-be architects of nations.[23]

This anxiety has a particular slant for African Americans in the 20th century: in the South, state officials with little interest in promoting contraceptive use or family planning among their white populations actively tried to persuade black couples to practice birth control; the Birth Control Federation of America went so far as to develop a "Negro Project" in 1939 because, it argued, "the mass of Negroes . . . particularly in the South, still breed carelessly and disastrously." Medical professionals throughout the country used compulsory sterilization laws to perform tubal ligations on poor women—mostly women of color—at a far higher rate than surgical birth-control procedures performed on white women.[24] For Black Power/ Black Arts intellectuals, the compulsory sterilization of black women exists on a continuum with the history of the rape of black women. Both are components of white power enacted through the control of black people's sexuality. From their perspective, a sexual revolution would not so much involve the freedom to make sexual choices unconstrained by compulsory heterosexuality and marriage—the primary institutions that we think of the Sexual Revolution as challenging—for these were rigorously promoted by state power and the dominant social class for white people. African Americans were expected, and forced, to define "freer" and more "perverse" forms of sexuality.

It is therefore in worries about propagation that we can discern one of the roots of the recurrence of homosexuality in Baraka's cosmology as an evil (or an object of ridicule), bound up with rape as the metaphor of black history and its redress. He writes, "It is in the 'individualistic' ego-oriented society that homosexuality flourishes most since the Responsibility of bearing one's generations is not present among the kind of decadent middle class such a society creates."[25] It is part of the project of white supremacist representational practices to sterilize, in a sense, the figure of the black male even as he is hypersexualized as the rapist-stud; hypersexualization is the justification for sterilization, in representation and beyond—the "freer" sexuality of black folk makes them breed "carelessly and disastrously," and they must be stopped. This has to do with a problem that of necessity surrounds the notion of racial supremacy or any race-based nationalism; such a project stakes its claim on biological ground, but it is precisely in the central predicate of biology—reproduction—that race itself cannot be sustained. A race cannot be reproduced if there is "mixing," if women make sexual choices that bring Other fathers beyond the designated boundaries of the clan into the gene pool.[26] Thus, for the white male supremacist, white women and black men have to be limited in their sexual choices—hence the massive juridical and social edifice built to stoke fears of the predatory black male rapist and to prevent and punish "intermarriage" (meaning, primarily, unions between men of color and white women).

Baraka's demonized homosexual therefore positions a figure that serves as the projection of his fears and outrage about the sterilization of black men and women that is embedded in white supremacist discourses and state-sanctioned practices. The homosexual is supposedly nonproductive, antiprocreative; similarly, white supremacy limits, attempts to suppress, black (re)productivity—especially, in Baraka's view, the (re)productivity of black men. The governing trope in black nationalist discourse for this constellation of white supremacist practices generally shows up as emasculation or castration, as we have seen, and as both Edelman and Ross discuss—but given Baraka's focus on both the metaphor and the reality of procreation, sterilization seems to me an operating trope as well. This sterilization has various effects that Baraka flags: there is the kind of sterilization that under the institution of American slavery rendered the father's issue not the father's but the mother's; and there is the kind of sterilization whereby mass-media images render black men and women sexually unattractive to one another. In either case the generative power of black sexuality (but especially black male sexuality, of course) is denied or constrained. The patriarchal power that Baraka assumes should flow from male status is diluted; the very foundation of a race, or a nation, or any society (if it is reasonable to assume Freud and Levi-Strauss in their work on exogamy and the incest taboo have purchase on nationalist thought) is taken from black men's hands because rather than being *actors* in the exchange of women, they are themselves gifts and pawns. For Baraka and Cleaver, the sign of patriarchal power regained is the liberation of black male sexual prowess in the form of the rapist-warrior in at once cultural and biological combat; while the sign of the patriarchal power denied to black men in the specific history of American slavery and segregation emerges as homosexuality.

The choice of rape as a figure for incitement is dangerous for black nationalists, and the homosexual figure is brought in to manage its pitfalls. Rape as an overarching metaphor for black history feminizes black people in relationship to a masculine white predatory power. The rape of black women points to the powerlessness of black male ancestors to fulfill the patriarchal expectations their descendants would demand of them and occasions a sense of historical shame. This history is thus effaced by the white male homosexual (and by his counterpart, the black homosexual suborned by white domination, for whom James Baldwin seems often to stand as an easy example). Just as the black male rapist figure is imaginary for the most part, a creation used to shore up the notion of white female purity that was itself used to consolidate white America's image of itself and its hierarchical social relations, Black Power/Black Arts writers imagine a weak white faggot *as well as* a predatory white faggot "master" whose mastery is belied by his supposedly inherent lack of masculinity. Homosexuality does double duty: it is a figure that shouts a warning about the end-point of a capitulation to white supremacy, because the homosexual fails to procreate; simultaneously, it is a figure that represents the crippling legacies of slavery, for homosexuality—especially homosexuality with a sadomasochistic slant—emerges in Baraka's fiction and essays as the mode of transmission of white supremacy. As Marlon Ross observes, evoking homosexuality transfers the "historical fact" of the rape of black women (and the history of white domination through sexual control for which the rape serves as a handy metaphor) into a male-only domain— where would-be patriarchs Baraka and Cleaver are more comfortable and believe the real battle for liberation is to be fought.[27]

The use of this figure has its own perils, of course. Nonprocreative sex, which homosexuality represents for Baraka, is to be shunned; but nonprocreative sex is also "freer" sex, promising unruly pleasures, and the hypersexed black male stud that Baraka wants to deploy in the battle for liberation also carries the promise of those pleasures and their tendency to slip beyond control with him. Baraka acknowledges the affective power of the kind of sexual liberation that both black male sexuality and homosexuality can signify. He describes the sexual energy that white people repress as a tremendous natural force—"a dirtiness, an ecstasy, which always threatens the 'order,' i.e., 'rationalism,' the ahumane asexual social order the white man seeks with all his energies to uphold." But this power must be distinguished from the debility that results from indulgence in "decadence," because "luxury reinforces weakness" and makes a people "effeminate and perverted."[28] Since both blackness and homosexuality play the part in Western culture of sexual libertines, they can march too closely together, bleed one into the other; therefore the border between them must be vigilantly policed: blackness as the sign of the pleasure of nonprocreative sex is at once something to beat white men over the head with—they do not know how to give their women a "clean, vicious popping"—and also something to keep under strict control.

Baraka's suspicion of sexual pleasure also seems to gesture toward historical injuries in another way: the use of sadomasochistic homosexuality as a rhetorical and fictional figure, at a time when the Sexual Revolution is happening in urban America, seems to recall that not only have black men historically been controlled and limited in terms of their sexual choices, but black men were used for sexual pleasure, by socially and politically dominant white men. Bringing the tropes of rape and homosexuality together in an analysis of black history and as incitements to act in the contemporary emergency casts the shadow of a history that does not exist because it is not well recorded, that history that Paul D's chain-gang scene wrestles to the surface in the manner of a repressed memory: the sexual exploitation of black men by white men, whether in the sexualized realm of beatings and whippings of black male bodies or in sex with black men. The *first* sexual revolution, as Sharon Holland usefully reminds us, occurred under the auspices of American slavery, and the memory of it is "lodged in the psyches of all Americans."[29] In that revolution, black men as well as black women were the sites, the ground on which that revolution was waged.

Systems and Transmissions

I turn now to consider a couple scenes from Jones's 1965 novel *The System of Dante's Hell*, which recapitulates Dante's Pilgrim's journey through the circles of the Inferno by tracking the journey of main character Roi, who is clearly an autobiographical fiction of Baraka himself, from sin—defined, in Baraka's words, as "the abandonment of one's local (*i.e.*, place or group)"[30]—to salvation (reimmersion in home, the womb of blackness). The authentic blackness that Roi has lost and that the author sets him on the road to find again is marked by its sexual qualities. In the novel, sexuality is the means by which or the medium in which blackness is lost and betrayed, and by which it is regained and secured: paradise lost is signified by degrading homosexual experiences, while the nearest approximation of paradise regained for Roi is figured in a (somewhat abortive) sexual union with a black woman.

I discuss these scenes in relation to the location in Baraka's Inferno which they occupy.

Fifth Ditch of the Eighth Circle: Grafters (Barrators)

Grafters are those who use their position to extort from others, and the barrator participates in the sale or purchase of Church or state positions. While Dante was very much concerned with the idea of right relations between the Church and state and the individuals whose souls and bodies these institutions governed, Baraka's concerns are with the relation of the black male individual to his authentic self. The positions and favors that are being extorted or sold by grafters and barrators become, in Baraka's translation, the true self being sold or bartered. The authentic self, again, is that which is endowed by birth and location, one's native tradition. Homosexuality figures prominently as a representation of this perversion of one's relation to oneself; Baraka appears to make it the mark of inauthenticity.

Baraka's autobiography mentions that while he was in the air force he was stationed in Illinois and spent a good deal of time in Chicago. While in Chicago he began to immerse himself in the works of Joyce, Pound, and Eliot.[31] The reference to his immersion in the Western high-modernist canon appears in the fictional account in *System of Dante's Hell*, in which the character Roi spends some time in Chicago, and these authors' names function as a kind of password into the eyries of the high-culture cognoscenti—which are also, not at all incidentally, the secret enclaves of a succession of gay men. "In Chicago I kept making the queer scene," Roi tells us.[32]

To the "first guy" he encounters Roi gives his name as Stephen Dedalus (James Joyce's fictional protagonist), and he extols the virtues of Proust and Eliot. In the extreme abbreviation of the stream-of-consciousness form the narrative takes, it is as if the names of Proust, Eliot, and Joyce grant Roi entry into the man's bed and, by extension, into a world where he can worship and learn from these literary works. If Roi has any lustful desire to have sex with these men it is not signaled. Only the lure of belonging to a high-culture club that is by its nature exclusive draws him. In a 1991 interview, Amiri Baraka explored the link between sexual seduction and the appeal of participating in America's myth of itself in a discussion of his play *The Dutchman*.

> *The Dutchman* . . . is not just a tale about being seduced by a white woman; it's a tale about the kind of seduction the black middle class, particularly black intellectuals, experience. It's not simply like, say, Spike Lee's *Jungle Fever*. I was really talking about a false welcome into society. . . . [I]t doesn't have to be a black man; it doesn't have to be a man, as opposed to a woman. . . . No matter the sexual nature of the seduction represented by Lula, the seductive nature of America is inarguable: come be an American, come be a citizen, come join the party.[33]

For Roi the price of this ticket is prostituting his body to men. Physical pain is the central component of these experiences. "To be pushed under a quilt, and call it love. To shit water for days and say I've been loved," he reflects.[34] The implication is always that Roi is a kind of victim, rather than an initiator or eager participant, in these sexual scenes; the dominant and dominated roles are very clearly delineated.

The effect is that the deacons of the Western canon become, through Roi's lovers, his tutors, in exchange for sex. In effect, Proust, Eliot, et al. fuck and fuck over Roi, culturally, intellectually, and morally. This recalls the classic erastes and eromenos relationship, in which the young Athenian male citizen is prepared to assume his role in the ruling class by a sexual relationship with an elder in which he is supposed to receive no pleasure. Baraka of course means the application of this model to Roi, as a black man, to be ironic. By placing this part of Roi's life in the Barrators' circle, Baraka makes clear that Roi has bartered his body and his manhood in order to belong in the company of writers that the dominant culture hails as its best. He has sold himself, become indentured. The relationships represent cultural domination and recapitulate a historical context in which black male bodies are sexual/economic commodities. They also suggest that cultural domination—in part demonstrated by the style of Roi's narration, which is insular in its reference, opaque and mannered as though trying to be hailed as a "black Joyce"—is the internalized, psychic, and contemporary expression of that history when black bodies were owned.

At the same time, while physical pleasure and lust seem largely absent in these encounters, there is the hint that something beyond the empty cultural products of an alien conqueror's tradition is also being bought with the currency of Roi's body. "Another bond. You miss everything. *Even pain*," he observes—suggesting that there were other kinds of connections that Roi sought and found, even if the context later appears tainted to the author looking back on his fictional younger self. Indeed, later in the novel when this period is recalled, Roi remembers, "The books meant nothing. My idea was to be loved. . . . And it meant going into that huge city melting." "I thot of a black man under the el who took me home in the cold," he says, unable to shake the memory of the preacher's kindness. "And how he listened and showed me his new suit. And I crawled out of bed morning and walked thru the park for my train. Loved. Afraid. Huger than any world."[35]

The sense in which homosexual male relationships provide a space of intimacy for Roi is not fully evacuated. The unruly character of the figure of homosexuality, its proximity to the pleasures of "freer" sexuality and the political (possibly nonnationalist, or antinationalist) possibilities liberated sexuality might represent, renders even the physical pain of submission in sex that seems sadomasochistic in its dynamics rewarding in a way Baraka does not deny, though he cannot account for it or theorize it. This psychic pleasure—and its relation to traditions alien or native which both subjugate and make the subject, which violate and initiate at once—expands in later segments of the novel.

Eighth Ditch of the Eighth Circle: Fraudulent Counsellors

Written as a play, "Eighth Ditch" was, as Baraka later described it in his autobiography, "about a homosexual rape in the army." Some associates of Baraka's lover, Beat luminary Diane di Prima, asked Baraka if they could produce the play—"probably," Baraka speculates, "because they were gay."[36] The police closed the play down after a few performances at the New York Poets Theatre, and Jones himself was arrested and charged with sending obscenity through the mail. At trial he convinced a federal grand jury to dismiss the charges, apparently without the benefit of counsel.

Baraka's brief summary of the short play and his emphasis on its depiction of homoerotic scenes is intriguing, for though the rape that occurs is its central plot development, "Eighth Ditch," especially when read in the context of the rest of *System*, seems, like the novel, to be about the difficulties of coming into one's own cultural tradition, if it is about anything. The homosexual rape, at least as Baraka scholars Kimberly Benston and Werner Sollors have read it, largely has a symbolic or metaphoric function and is to be understood as illustrating a division between Roi's body and mind, or as being *like* an aspect of the problem of cultural transmission for a middle-class bohemian black boy.[37] Yet the literal reading of the play that Baraka gives us seems to me useful: we might thus read the rape as the point, the primary focus, for the chapter, that all other thematic considerations mirror, rather than the other way around.

The two main characters, 46 (Roi) and 64 (Herman Saunders), both black males in the army, are figures for Baraka's divided consciousness. The older 64 represents Baraka as a disillusioned bohemian and fan of jazz who intensely regrets his choice to abandon "the fundamental and profound" learning of his youth. The younger 46—the numbers are of course mirror-images—figures Baraka as the young middle-class boy evincing a hungry interest in white bourgeois artistic forms that his elder self now views to be a quest of folly. Consequently the issue of naming is prominent in the piece. When 46–Roi asks, "Who are you really?" 64–Herman answers, "The Street! Things around you. Even noises at night, or smells you are afraid of. I am a maelstrom of definitions."[38] 64's embodiment of definitions is at once menace and beneficence. According to Sollors's reading, since Baraka proposes that definitions are the means by which one ends up in hell,[39] 64 desires to show 46 "a world that is 'clearer' and 'more easily definable' than the 'hell' of his early misguided 'definitions.'"[40] Yet 64's identification with definitions suggests that he himself is hellish and that any intimacy he has with 46 could be to 46's detriment; he radiates an aura of threat. "I want you to remember me," 64 demands, "so you can narrate the sorrow of my life. . . . I want to sit inside yr head & scream obscenities." At the same time, to possess the knowledge of names is, in shamanic cultures, to be a wizard and to know the deepest self. "I know names that control your life that you don't even know exist. Whole families of definitions," 64 says, dangling the prospect of knowledge that 46 might do well to know.[41] The tone of this latter statement differs from his earlier boastful assertion; here 64 does not claim to embody the definitions but to know them, the suggestion being, perhaps, that he speaks as one who has been subjected to definitions that have harmed him. Further complicating the picture, however, 64 chooses this moment to mount 46; and before, when he boasted that he embodied definitions, he began to unbutton his shirt. The context for both these announcements, then, is suggestive of sexuality, and they are, as we learn, preparatory of 64–Herman's forced anal penetration of 46–Roi. Thus, naming and defining are linked with sexual exploitation.

The Narrator of the play tells the audience that the hero of the piece is a "foetus" and that the play is a "foetus drama."[42] This, along with 46's statement in the midst of being sexually violated, "I guess I'll get pregnant," suggests that 64's action somehow impregnates the spiritually wayward 46—evidently, given their linked but developmentally staggered positions, 64 impregnates 46 with the potential for growth *into* 64.[43] 64 rapes 46, impregnates him with knowledge that is meant to produce a new Roi: the impregnated 46, the receptacle of 64's seed, is also the product of this transformative, creative ejaculation. 64 retains the procreative powers that 46 has either not acquired or has abandoned. The rape of 46 is almost, as Sollors terms it, an exorcism.

Unlike the well-meaning rapists in the Fifth Ditch, 64 is not initiating Roi into the canon of high-modernist writers; his munificence is to make Roi himself, to transform him into who he is to become. As in Baraka's contemporaneous essays, to impregnate is the black man's native power; to propagate the race, his national duty. The difference between Roi and 64 is 64's compendious knowledge of the blues, a knowledge which presumably makes 64 closer to authentically black than 46, who is still, like the Roi of the Chicago interlude, enamored of European culture. The blues as 64 describes them are a kind of Mystery worthy of mystical initiation, an apparent amalgam of European and African American forms: 64's blues incorporate everything from "Abstract Expressionism blues" and

"Kierkegaard blues" to "poetry blues," "Hucklebuck Steamshovel blues," "White buck blues," and "blues blues." "All these blues are things you'll come into."[44] On one level there is a kind of nonsense quality to these blues that 64 lists, suggesting the incoherence and the oppressiveness of the Afro-European position that 46 yearns for. 46's adoration of European culture and forms of expression figures what Baraka in his autobiography calls "cramming . . . imbibing, gobbling, stuffing yourself with reflections of the Other."[45] On another level blues are a creative expression of this position that both calls attention to its basic incoherence, its double-consciousness, and that creates musical figures which for the duration of their performance and their effects make the incoherent cohere: they are an adaptation in cultural form that 46 must make psychically. In effect, 64 attempts to give 46 one kind of knowledge of what it is to be a black man in white supremacist America. 64's blues are thus laments for various forms of subjection and alienation and the necessity of creating something out of the muck of those experiences of the abject, delivered, as if the point were not clear enough, via an act of forced anal penetration.

Further complications ensue as the scene of this rape/seduction is then replayed. When 64 rapes 46 the second time, the now more resigned 46 asks, "Is this all there is?" 64 answers, "Yes. And why do you let me do it?" 46 replies, "Because you say it's all there is . . . I guess."[46] Both characters view their relationship as instrumental, unequal, and adversarial. Insofar as *System* and so much of Baraka's work during the period of his transition from Beat to Black Arts stages the difficulties of his ideological rebirth, this exploitative, top-bottom relationship reflects, possibly, Baraka's insistence on looking at each step in his personal evolution as necessarily conflictual with previous steps: change does not occur unless the wiser, newer self conquers and subdues the mistaken, previous self. More broadly, however, to the degree that Baraka's ideological transitions participate in and map dynamics at work on the level of the culture itself, neither 64 nor 46 can perceive any other mode of the transmission of tradition or any other way to belong *with* others, to build a socius, than to interact as conqueror and conquered, because that is the model offered to them as they have absorbed the lessons of their racial and class backgrounds, and of Western cultural traditions.

Homosexual rape, erastes and eromenos, serves as the easy figure for this model: it is not only that indoctrination by the dominant culture is like a rape but that rape, literal and metaphorical, material and psychological, is the very mode by which black men become black in the terms of white supremacy—that is, they become abjected, they become objects: they become acculturated (which is to say, dominated), in history and in the present as history relentlessly recapitulates itself. 64's sexual abuse of 46–Roi ends the play and the chapter, but it is just the beginning of an act that repeats. At curtain, an excited member of the troop catches 64 and 46 in the act, and other members of the troop begin gathering to get their turn riding 46's acquiescent bottom.

The character Roi ends the novel in a scene that stages the same dynamics involving cultural transmission through sexual violation and violence, distributing the roles somewhat differently: there Roi, as Marlon Ross observes, is essentially raped by Peaches, a black female whore (who is also, in the novel's translation of Dante, an angel); her "rape of Roi . . . becomes a purifying manhood ritual," as Peaches taunts Roi for being a "faggot" and as her sexual voracity temporarily grants Roi access to the blackness from which his betrayal of his origins has barred him.[47] Subsequently, when Peaches's rescue proves insufficient for Roi to abandon his love of the "demons" of white European culture that so enrapture him, he is attacked by three "[t]all strong black boys." The black men ostensibly want Roi's money, but the better part of their speech with him is an interrogation of his identity, a testing of the strength of his now-collapsed resolve to claim himself as one of them. They demand to know where he comes from and tease him about the U.S. Air Force uniform he wears (Roi serves in the air force, as Baraka did); they call him "Half-white muthafucka" and then, when he refuses to give them money, beat him senseless.[48] Where Peaches's taunts are meant to make Roi meet the challenge of being a "real black man" and have sex with her, the three young men are also offering a last chance for him to keep faith with his origins by compelling his submission. Their violence is the counterpart to Peaches's sexual invitation; but Peaches is as violent with Roi as the young men are (she slaps Roi, tugs viciously at his genitals), in some way, sexual with him: the beating is another form of gang rape in the universe of the novel, where sex and violence or coercion are closely linked, and where Roi's relations with other black men are frequently mediated by an ostensibly improper sexual desire. (For example, Roi enters the final circle of the Inferno with his fellow air force serviceman Don, and at one point—just prior, in fact, to meeting Peaches and being offered the opportunity to change his ways—he has to fight the temptation to make a sexual pass at Don.)[49]

The fraternity of black(male)ness, the "freemasonry of the race," is in Baraka's symbolic entered into through violence that is sexual, through

sexuality that is violent: "The Alternative," a story from Baraka's 1967 collection of short fiction *Tales*, features a clandestine relationship between
a male Howard University student (it is noted that the character is an actor who has appeared in "Jimmy's play"—perhaps a reference to Baldwin)
and an older gay man from D.C., who at the story's end are set upon and
threatened with gang rape by a group of howling Howard men.[50] Given
the particular resonance of rape and its relation to history in Baraka's texts
during this period, the rapelike quality of the three young men's beating of
Roi in *System* seems to be underlined by the character's final words. The
three men apparently leave Roi "with white men, screaming"[51]—for this
is the counterpoint, the nadir and proof par excellence of Roi's failure to
achieve that movement into Black Art that Baraka himself makes (by ex-
orcising Roi?) so successfully:[52] left to be fucked by white men instead of
black.

I will return to the novel's final scenes shortly. Reading Baraka and
Cleaver together allows us to understand Baraka's recurrence to the figure
of male rape in relation to brotherhood and the cultural transmission of
blackness through Cleaver's highly prurient speculation about homosexuality among African Americans. "[M]any Negro homosexuals, acquiescing
in . . . [a] racial death-wish, are outraged and frustrated because in their
sickness they are unable to have a baby by a white man. The cross they
have to bear is that, already bending over and touching their toes for the
white man, the fruit of their miscegenation is not the little half-white off-
spring of their dreams but an increase in the unwinding of their nerves—
though they redouble their efforts and intake of the white man's sperm."[53]
Given such a view, that 64's rape of 46 in the Eighth Ditch and Peaches's
rape of Roi and the three young men's beating of him function each as attempted rescues makes logical sense. How else does a suborned black man
who has "gone white" get brought back into the fold unless he increases
his intake of a *real* black man's sperm, in lieu of, or even as necessary com-
plement of, sex with a black woman?

In Baraka's symbolic, the desired sense of belonging in blackness that
Baraka understands specifically as an intimate, sexual bonding cannot be
experienced except as a sexual violation that itself stands for the depredations, psychic and physical, visited on black men by white men. It
is as though Baraka cannot envision such fraternity without attaching
it to, fusing it with, the oppressive actions of the alien other who historically created (inseminated, birthed) blackness as a category of being.
These rapes and gang rapes appear to reenact conquest and enslavement

symbolically as sexual violation, both as the compulsion to repeat a trauma—a working with sexual violation as repressed memory in the Freudian sense—and as a therapeutic adaptation: the harm done by the foreign becomes the harm done by "one's own." And moreover, *pleasure* is found in it—not only the pleasure of being raped by Peaches and thus, in the contradictory terms that Ross has outlined, discovering real manhood. Just as in Roi's painful surrender in the Fifth Ditch, there is a disturbing pleasure to be found in conforming to the habit of submission taught by the history that 64–Herman represents and reenacts. In the closing lines of "Eighth Ditch," 46 begs 64 to tell him exactly "what kinds" of blues he will give him, an entreaty that reads almost as if 46 were trying to get 64 to "talk dirty," as though 64's lists of blues—of laments and creative transformations of the injustices being lamented—function to arouse the bottoming 46. The ecstatic 64, drawing near to orgasm, is oblivious to the need to parse out his gifts. He simply moans, "Oooh, baby, just keep throwin it up like that. Just keep throwin it up"—so that we can see how 46 is experiencing his own ecstasy, one that is figured as a quest for knowledge (definitions) and for physical pleasure: 46–Roi is not a passive bottom but one who willfully and greedily moves in rhythm, "throwing it up" for Daddy.[54]

Whether bonding paid by such a price and pleasure thoroughly suffused with pain are the only options for working with the history of conquest and enslavement that constitutes blackness is not certain in this transitional moment of Baraka's oeuvre: 46's uneasy "because that's all there is . . . I guess" response to 64's question bespeaks some inkling that this mode of transmission, this way of relating, is not, in fact, all there is. That 64 is, compared to 46, at least, the more putatively authentic of the two modes of blackness the characters represent suggests some skepticism about such traditions. It suggests skepticism about blackness itself, which despite its promise of returning Roi to a lost sense of being whole also is attached to the oppression that has helped make blackness what it is and, in being passed down to its inheritors, recapitulates that oppression: 64, after all, is a creature of "inadequacies" and "the deepest loneliness."[55] When LeRoi Jones definitively becomes Amiri Baraka (and reads Fanon), he believes he has solved the problem of how to be with other black people in a way that loves them and himself: he has done so by banishing the ambiguities and bottling up the powers of blackness-in/as-abjection that his transitional work reveals—with all the problematic effects of cultural nationalism that later critics and Baraka himself have detailed.

For our purposes, as we excavate the powers of abject blackness that Baraka despises or, not unlike Fanon, believes he can surpass, it is interesting to observe that, where the complexities of cultural transmission— confronting the legacies of blackening—are represented as *rape* or sexual violation, this symbolic turn, always already in the African diasporic case also a historical reality, even for black men, permits that legacy to be transformed into a source of erotic pleasure—if we understand eros as Marcusian and as encompassing those libidinal drives both to the sexual and to the communal. This relation to the ancestral past is at least partly exploitative and is at the same time partly an illustration of the fact that violence and culture are midwives for one another: as noted earlier, the history of most sets of practices, beliefs, and ideologies we deem cultures, if those histories can be traced back far enough, are likely to show an *imposition*, through some form of unequal influence and therefore at least some structural degree of violence, on some other practice, belief, or ideology.

The total effect of 46 and 64's interaction, like that of *System* in general, is unsettled; the entire experience of the Eighth Ditch, after all, is located in hell as the example of fraudulent counsel, "possibly because the author cannot rid himself completely of all hellish definitions," Sollors speculates.[56] Baraka makes no clear decision as to how to position himself or the audience with respect to this drama. Who is the fraudulent counselor, 64 or the shadow-figures of the Western canon? What is the fraudulent counsel? There is no certainty, and it seems to me that this lack of clarity *is* the point signified by the rape as a reference both to a history of subjection and the transmission of the means to create community in relation to that subjection—the rape, like the history, is brutal but productive of an exchange, exploitative but protective in its attempt to work with or through the pains bequeathed by the past, creative but fundamentally fraudulent.

The Sixth Circle: Heretics

The cartographic and the sexual metaphors with which I began this reading of Baraka and Cleaver cohere in the Bottom, Roi's final destination and the location where heretics (those who betray their origins) are punished in Baraka's Inferno. The Bottom is at once a black neighborhood in Shreveport, Louisiana, that Roi visits while on furlough and an existential rock-bottom where Roi must finally confront the core of his self- (and race-) betrayal to define himself anew. It is not coincidentally also the point where a novel which has been largely narrated in a surrealistic, deliberately idiosyncratic and opaque high-modernist fashion suddenly takes on a measure of narrative transparency: as Baraka notes of the process of writing *System,* "I was living in New York then and the whole [Robert] Creeley–[Charles] Olson influence was beginning to beat me up. . . . The two little warring schools that were going on then were what I call the Jewish-Ethnic-Bohemian School (Allen Ginsberg and his group) and the Anglo-German Black Mountain School. . . . [T]he very fact that at the end of the novel I could write plain narrative meant that I had achieved, to a certain extent, my goal: to get away from those influences. At the end, I felt comfortable with the narrative for the first time."[57] The Bottom is thus the space within *System* where Baraka's "own" voice finally asserts itself, the voice that, in his own terms at that time, is most authentically black.

That the Bottom bears this name seems to owe more than a little to Norman Mailer's 1959 essay "The White Negro." I am following here Michele Wallace's argument that Mailer's lionizing of black musicians and hustlers as American *cultural* representatives of an *existential* truth—the fundamental universal confrontation with death and mortality—"had a profound effect on such black leaders as LeRoi Jones and Eldridge Cleaver."[58] Two figures which emerge as distillations of the hipster ethic of politically radical " philosophical psychopathy" that Mailer hopes will, by example, save a bankrupt and necrotic (white) civilization are the Negro—the model par excellence of the ethic, whose experience provides a screen for projecting the possibilities of social transformation and individual transformation—and the homosexual, who is a psychopath because he is a sexual outlaw and a representative of the complete abdication of the ability to act or move (since in the parlance of the day as Mailer understood it, to "flip" and be "beat" in the most extreme way is to be "queer") and thus also closer to the bedrock reality of death. Mailer's view of black people, typical primitivist cant, runs thus: "Knowing in the cells of his existence that life was war, nothing but war, the Negro (all exceptions admitted) could rarely afford the sophisticated inhibitions of civilization, and so he kept for his survival the art of the primitive, he lived in the enormous present . . . relinquishing the pleasures of the mind for the more obligatory pleasures of the body." And "psychopathy is more prevalent with the Negro. . . . [I]n the worst of perversion, promiscuity, pimpery, drug addiction, rape, razor-slash, bottle-break, what-have-you, the Negro discovered and elaborated the morality of the bottom." These descriptions apply almost perfectly to the ethos and lives of the denizens of *System's* Bottom and to what they present to Roi in the novel. The fact that "bottom" appears in a couple phrases in Mailer's essay ("a cultureless and alienated bottom of exploitable human material"; "At bottom, the drama of the psychopath is that he seeks love") buttresses Wallace's assertion in Baraka's case (Cleaver, of course, explicitly praised Mailer and preferred him to Baldwin).[59] Wallace writes that Mailer captured the imaginations of Baraka and Cleaver because he "articulated so well the nature of the white man's fantasy/nightmare about the black man," and "that fantasy/nightmare, through an Americanization process of several hundred years, had become . . . the black man's as well."[60]

Of course, such a genealogy undercuts the project of both Baraka's and Cleaver's burgeoning nationalism, insofar as they are eager to cast off white cultural influences that appear to them as domination: that this shared fantasy of blackness becomes the expression of Baraka's authentically black voice again demonstrates the way that culture is always already penetrated (as Edelman would put it), that the terms of self are not ever really "one's own," and that the transmission of those terms, even (or most especially) of putatively independent self-assertion, will not be cleaved from the domination that instantiates them. Baraka's imagination of the Bottom, the socioeconomic and moral bottom raised to political and existential summit, is, as viewed through the lens of his own homophobic or antihomosexual project, a function of *being* a (cultural) bottom or being the descendant of ancestors who, in the manner of repressed memory, *really appear* as (sexual) bottoms. Which—in some ways despite Baraka's intentions—is not to say that to be or to appear as a bottom is without power.

In the novel, the Bottom, because it is an all-black community, is the site where Roi is tested—and, somewhat curiously, and very much like James Weldon Johnson's narrator in contradistinction to Johnson himself, Roi fails the test. The failure, predictably, has to do with homosexuality; Baraka tries to disarticulate blackness from the partner it is given in "The White Negro," which pairs (but hearteningly for Baraka and Cleaver does not overlap) the Negro with the homosexual. But the perhaps somewhat less predictable shape homosexuality takes for Roi in this final chapter is that of receiving what is at once sexual attention and fraternal welcome from a greedy oral bottom who willingly performs as Paul D is forced to.

Upon Roi's arrival in the Bottom he is immediately confronted with an omen that this is a site that will test the masculine power he has willfully cast aside. The smell of the air in the Bottom is like "mild seasons and come," with the "simple elegance of semen on the single buds of air."[61] The semen in the air presages the narrative and thematic developments of

Roi's visit to the Sixth Circle that Baraka places in the deepest regions of hell; it suggests that, according to the authorial design of the universe in which Roi lives, the Bottom will provide conditions for Roi to be "seeded" or impregnated as 64 attempted to impregnate him in the Eighth Ditch, and he will again be given the opportunity for a new, more successful re-birth into authentic black masculinity. Yet, though the Bottom and its folk remind Roi of a ward in Newark (where the lower-class black folks lived, away from the domicile of his middle-class family), he sees them as dis-tant, other than himself, and he continually struggles with this distance.

In one of the novel's final sequences, just subsequent to the sexually harrowing would-be initiation he receives at Peaches's hands, Roi goes walking in the darkness. "I slipped out into Bottom," he says. The absence of the definite article of course proves prophetic, as Roi, at this point, having failed to satisfy Peaches sexually and having become lost in his memories of his homosexual Chicago interludes, has reached a kind of nadir. In his perambulations he encounters a man calling to him from un-derneath a house. The man is described as repulsive: "Round red-rimmed eyes . . . and teeth for a face, . . . his dripping smile and yellow soggy skin full of red freckles, . . . [an] Irreligious spirit." This man is Baraka's version of a demon. "Comere a second," the man begs. "Lemme suck yo dick, honey."[62]

Roi is presented with an opportunity to turn his back on his hereti-cal homosexual past. Roi's response is decisive—he runs away. Next he encounters a dying soldier in the street, who is also an image of his in-creasingly irrelevant old choices, since the soldier is by definition a stooge for the white supremacist government. Roi runs from this figure as well. But while fleeing, Roi ruminates, "I wondered if 'sweet peter eater' would show up. (He'd told me his name.)"[63]

No such conversation or exchange of names is narrated in the previous telling: in that version of events, Roi describes the man under the house screaming in frustration, and then transitions to the next occurrence this way: "*finally* when I had moved and was trotting down the road . . ."[64] Roi's "finally" opens a lacuna in the sequence of events, also suggesting that we have not been told the whole story of the characters' tête-à-tête, that, in the space between parentheses, there has been an exchange between Roi and "sweet peter eater," the character and dimensions of which we can only guess.

"[S]weet peter eater—he'd told me his name" reads as mocking, con-temptuous, even—sweet peter eater is no name but at best a mocking title that might be bestowed in the dozens (it also allows Baraka to take a satiric swipe at Christianity, since "sweet peter," with the elimination of three letters, becomes "St. Peter"). Yet there is the strong suggestion of intimacy in the declaration: peter eater is "sweet"—and the appearance of their encounter in parentheses gives it a kind of cozy parallel-universe feel, something that occurs in its own little hearth-warmed space where only the two of them exist. Baraka's narrative voice switches from "he" in referring to Roi to "I" when the exchange of names is recollected.

The rhetorical belaboring of the moment when Roi recalls it is comically absurd and yet almost touching. "[S]weet peter eater"—why does Roi mention that the man told him his name except to emphasize that there is something shared between them? What is shared is their past: the declaration is of a past interaction, and at the same time, their past is common. Roi, too, once ate peter—and, in a sense not entirely metaphorical, so did their enslaved ancestors. The nostalgic sweetness of this bonding occurs in a context meant to be horrific, the man with whom Roi bonds described as screaming "like some animal[] . . . , some hurt ugly thing dying alone."[65] Thus, the event seems meant to demonstrate the extent to which Roi is lost and decadent. But the nostalgia is there, nonetheless; Baraka does not or cannot fully purge it.

There is an unaccounted intimacy between black men in homosexual encounters in the novel, in the shared memory and reenactment of a trauma lodged in the psyche, an intimacy that generates its own pleasures in the recollection and reenactment of sexual submission, and in coming into one's identity in master-slave ritual. The demonic man beckoning from the darkness beneath the house raised on stilts is a personification of Roi's heresy and of the sin being punished in the Sixth Circle: he is the bottom of the Bottom, apparently excluded from the lives of the Bottom's other inhabitants. He is a figure for what Roi has been and could yet become: his appearance as an offered mouth-hole, which, when denied, screams like an animal, is of course the very image of a Paul D who has internalized and become the abject not-man his jailors intend him to be, and the personification of the Bodwins' "blackboy" and the Invisible Man's piggy-bank.

Roi's manhood is under question throughout the novel, his penis that is not a Phallus a cause for anxiety: at the outset of his journey into the Bottom, Roi recollects, "Thomas, Joyce, Eliot, Pound, all gone by & I thot agony at how beautiful I was. And sat sad many times in latrines fingering my joint." Thus, heresy, the betrayal of one's origins, figured by Roi's immersion in the Western canon, is linked to masturbation, a figure for nonproductivity and the waste of creative potential. That Roi *fingers* his penis suggests female masturbation and, if we go a step further, hints too at a small penis (like a clitoris), capable of being stimulated by a single finger. Later in the visit to the Sixth Circle, Roi in growing embarrassment at his inability to have sex with a whore refers to his penis as "my tiny pecker"—which also, of course, figures Roi as a less-than-successful model of the masculine.[66]

In the encounter under the house—assuming the so-called name "sweet peter eater" accurately describes otherwise untold events—Roi's questionable penis is *received* in the demonic man's hungry mouth; Roi is fellated as he has fellated others, in a sense fellated by another version of himself, much as 64 relates to 46, though the demon under the house is both a younger Roi, immersed in his former sins, and an older one, the warning of what he could yet become. These ministrations grant to Roi the ability and resolve he has lacked to return to Peaches and (temporarily) be the man she desires him to be; they make his penis into a Phallus of sorts, though Roi does not admit that receiving a blowjob from a man has such an effect, and Baraka only hints it. The "sweet" blowjob is also pleasure and intimacy.

But these are secrets, not admissible into the narrative of Roi's journey back to blackness. This is so even though that journey clearly *fails*. Since Roi does fail it might seem to benefit the exposition of that failure for Baraka to elaborate on the dimensions of Roi's relapse here, rather than allow it to remain an ellipse within a parenthetical. Roi's encounter with his demon lover is perhaps unspeakable for the usual homophobic reason, because it is shameful. But the shame of what counts as sin is the putative point of all Roi's infernal adventures; the sin of betraying one's origins is what is being revealed and worked through. Thus, the obfuscation of the events does not seem to serve the overall project of shaming Roi into correct cultural, political, and personal choices.

Perhaps that the event occurs without its being held up clearly as an indication of Roi's failure suggests that this encounter, too, like the encounter with Peaches, is a part of what blackness *is* in the space of the Bottom. To be able to take this pleasure and to receive it is one of the powers of Roi's lost blackness, though it is also one that Baraka refuses to detail even as he references it by an elaborate omission. In this light the language of Roi's nonnarration of the encounter can be put under possibly revealing pressure: "As I moved back he began to scream at me. All lust, all panic, all silence and sorrow, and finally when I had moved and was trotting down the road, I looked around and he was standing up with his hands cupped to his mouth yelling into the darkness in complete hatred of what was only some wraith."[67]

This "all" list, which on first reading we might assume describes the man's screams only, becomes a possible attempt to capture without detailing the range of emotion and action at play in the encounter, for Roi and the demonic man both: lust, panic, and sorrow describe one set of possibilities within an abject sexuality, where boundaries between self and other are collapsed or on the edge of doing so, unlike the kind of sex where, as Bersani puts it, "the self . . . swells with excitement at the idea of being on top."[68] The "silence" of this list must belong to Roi; it is clearly not, in the end, his demonic lover's silence, since that man pierces the night with screams of "complete hatred." These apparently inarticulate screams speak deliriously to "what was only some wraith." I read the screams as extensions of and even reflections on the acts the two men have shared and what it meant—a representation without a clear symbolic for acts with meanings and effects that perhaps are foreclosed by the cultural symbolic. Their address is to something not tangible, not recognizable within the terms Baraka has established for Roi's explorations of his blackness. The screams might be representations, performances, of a violated consciousness that revels in and at the same time is outraged by its violation. The demonic man has given a blowjob and thus taken *his* pleasure, and the screams seem to demand more satisfaction—to insist that, in fact, the demon (himself, and also as he is the demon of desire) has not been satisfied—but simultaneously, without temporal or narrative separation, to bespeak pain and misery, to rail against all the ways in which he has been deprived. The "wraith" he hates might well be the unseen organizing structure mandating that there be a Bottom and that he be at the bottom of it, rather than be permitted simply to act, pleasurably, as a bottom in it. These screams can encompass such targets in the sequence of fictional events because they exceed the terms of Baraka's narrative, and he chooses to signify them—or can *only* do so—by reference to absolutes or pervasive and therefore nonrational, even chaotic, emotional states ("*all* lust, *all* panic"), which themselves appear to stand for and gesture toward immaterial but nonetheless powerful larger forces. At the same time, these screams are the figure for what I have referred to as a literary imagination. The screams bespeak, and activate in our reading of the text, apparent contradictions: degradation that is delight and delight that is degradation;

pain that is pleasure; a demand for communication and a claim to representation that are not symbolized; a demand for revenge that is also a demand for justice; a love absolutely saturated by hate. Such are the representational powers of blackness-in/as-abjection, which Baraka sketches the lineaments of but disavows.

5

Porn and the N-Word

Lust, Samuel Delany's The Mad Man, *and a Derangement of Body and Sense(s)*

The ability to regard as an honor and a joy what society has declared to be an insult and a defilement bespeaks an agile mind—often one that loves learning for its own sake.

—Samuel Delany, *Phallos*[1]

Porn and Praxis

I have been attempting to develop an understanding of the qualities and abilities that become available through (or which themselves partially constitute) blackness-in/as-abjection. Yet the relation between blackness and abjection, while effected historically and in the present primarily by economic, military, and political means, is experientially *lived*, as a psychic reality and as a material reality, especially for the inheritors of the events that bring blackness into being, at that site and product of culture which is the nexus between psyche and body. We have been able to see this nexus and access to both it and its powers, represented textually in the metaphor of muscle tension, in a lynching scene and in narrative scenes of the sexual violation of black men. Courtesy of the French existential phenomenology on which Fanon relies, I have referred to at least one aspect of this nexus as anonymous or amorphous existence, and I have argued that it is accessible through existentially defined states of vertigo or anguish. This body-psyche nexus wherein the relation between blackness and abjection is experientially lived, and the various qualities it might be said to possess, enter representation, as I noted in the introduction, vexed by particular challenges: they do not so much defy or resist narrative as simply pose a problem for narrative machinery, because the marvelous fictions of I, self, linear temporality, or the coherent perspective on which narrative usually depends are in the state of abjection awash in those fictions' opposites, their negations and what is in excess of them. I have argued that the (black) power I am attempting to reveal here is an experience of the body-psyche nexus that gives to "'significance' a value which intellectualism withholds from it," wherein an impression of self not-yet-ego takes some kind of form, and that this impression itself potentially offers corresponding impressions of human relations (and thus, culture and society):[2] the synesthesia of a perceived pain and loss in abjection that is also felt or can become known as political possibility.

In this final chapter I wish to traverse the difficulties narrative machinery encounters in blackness-in/as-abjection by visiting a kind of text that generically aims to work with (and to work) psychic-bodily responses: pornographic writing. Pornography (or erotica)[3] as a genre of writing is meant at the very least to arouse the reader—arousal being a state of difficult-to-measure mixture between the physiological, the psychic, and the psychological; and porn is an intended impetus to masturbation, either while reading or in response to what one has read.

Samuel R. Delany's 1994 novel *The Mad Man* is, in his words, "a serious work of pornography. . . . Those who say it is not a pornographic work (and that I am being disingenuous by saying that it is) are, however well-intentioned, just wrong."[4] I do not reference this comment of Delany's to defend his particular pornographic work or pornography itself against an all-too-customary dismissal of porn as a "low" cultural form without complexity;[5] here I will assume, with admitted tendentiousness, that no such defense is required post-Foucault, and I take it as a given that even a work that everyone could agree was "only" about sex or solely intended to arouse sexually would not fail to warrant serious attention, since sex and sexual arousal are often entwined, often inextricably, with many if not all the elements of the worlds humans have made—so that, for example, it is certainly possible to read the ways sex informs politics even in its buttoned-down electoral form, just as electoral politics informs sex.

I summon Delany's authorial imprimatur here in order to underline how Delany's novel works with the body-psyche nexus that I have been gesturing toward throughout this study, since the novel operates in the way that porn works with that nexus: in *The Mad Man*, a pornographic work, arousal and climax are achieved for *The Mad Man*'s protagonist— the protagonist being a position that functions as a prescribed point of identification as well as resistance to identification on the part of the reader—by and because of his inheritance of specifically racialized (i.e., black) abjection. Thus, arousal and potential sexual climax or satisfaction is produced, or meant to be produced, in a way utterly shot through with the racialized political, social, and economic hierarchies that (however sloppily or incompletely) structure contemporary American living. This is a more or less generic truth—all porn, like all representation, is thus saturated. Pornographic writing, in its working with and manipulations of and *education* of the bodily and psychic responses constituting arousal, demonstrates a method for working with racialized abjection, a method for effecting the abilities or powers of that otherwise seemingly powerless state of being.

The Mad Man's John Marr is a black gay male character who feverishly seeks out the pleasure of sexual acts that involve some form of apparent humiliation or degradation, often in conjunction with the enjoyment of watersports and scat (excrement), so that the acts—the fantasies that get represented as acts in the novel, and the fantasies the characters have—are often soaked and stained by those hallmarks of the abject, urine and feces.

In this and in other ways the ante of what I might have too hastily supposed (at the risk of exposing a stubbornly Puritan sensibility) to be the *shock* of men being sexually violated in Morrison and Baraka rises significantly. The way Morrison's Paul D brings the hidden logic of Baraka's and Cleaver's rhetorical figures to its apparent fruition gets extended in directions Morrison, Baraka, and Cleaver have not failed to signal but which they did not choose to imagine explicitly (for what we may assume at least partly are the usual homophobic reasons). The role play in the sexual acts that *The Mad Man* depicts for John Marr's pleasure and ours is frequently explicitly racialized—Marr's partners call him (and other black characters) "nigger" repeatedly. The depiction of these scenes references the (mostly) undocumented sexual exploitation that is part of the history of racialization in the Americas that Morrison and Baraka point toward. What the texts we looked to in the previous chapters gingerly suggest or hint against the grain of their larger narratives, Delany's novel—insofar as this is possible in the mode of fiction—proposes nearly outright: Delany's protagonist navigates the position of sexual/racial "bottom" as a complex, empowered political persona and potentially demonstrates how a history of sexual domination endows the figure of blackness with nimble abilities, with a form of power. John uses his activities and fantasies and their historical resonance of racial subjugation, and the intense pleasure these acts give him largely *because* of that resonance, to open the way to a sense that he operates within a greater sphere of freedom and power than he did before engaging in his sexual practices. John Marr *does* "like it," as Baraka and Cleaver and their fictional brother Paul D might fear. If the rather Victorian homoeroticism of the Ex-Coloured Man's admiration of the Southern lynchers sets up, as a kind of unclosed parenthetical, the question of erotic attraction to one's racial enemy and the ripple effects of such attraction on identity and subjectivity and, more importantly for our purposes in this study, on perceptions of personal and political power, Delany dilates on this question with John's attraction to mainly white and sometimes Southern hillbilly lovers. The agreements John makes with his sexual partners—his seizure, like Paul D's, of the fetishes of blackness and manhood, his participation in the sociogenic processes giving meaning to those fetishes as core constituents of his sense of self and the persona he performs in social relations—amounts to a somewhat different mode, and a different result, of "making a race." Delany holds in simultaneous tension degradation, racial power dynamics, political analysis, and sexual pleasure in such a way that all these often contradictory elements are available to both the narrator's and the reader's consciousness, becoming resources for a narrative that represents the possibility of defeating the internalized defeat demanded by the legacies of history. The novel attempts to achieve what it represents through a sexual or erotic practice—in this case, primarily, an erotic and sexual *reading* practice—of Marcusian exuberance.

The relation between these contradictory elements is not smooth or mapped by symmetries in the novel. A monstrous chimerical dream-creature—in unequal parts bovine, canine, avian, reptile, human, and (of course) horse-hung, which farts, shits, and pisses on whom it visits—presides as though it were a profane divinity over the proceedings. This figure represents the fusion of the diverse elements with which the novel works as *ugly*, as messy—the monster's aesthetic lack of appeal condensing everything about the text that interrupts narrative expectations. Yet the ugly fusion is dynamic and politically productive. The monster is most resistant to assimilation within the terms by which we imagine the "reality" of the story as we read, at the far end of a continuum in which characters and sexual acts, however surprising in content or shockingly indefatigable in ardor they may be, are by comparison far more "real." The monster is, Delany says, a figure of and for desire itself, and "the content of desire . . . if [that content is] anything other than itself, is that tiny part of the freedom of language associated with abjection."[6]

This jarring conjunction of freedom (even freedom "only" as an artifact of language) and abjection should now be familiar to us. In *The Mad Man* the combination between the evocation of the history of racialization through humiliation and the pornographic form itself doubly represent the apparent paradox of power in abject blackness: we find what Morrison and Baraka et al. suggest is most recalcitrant to the politics of black empowerment—black men sexually violated or degraded, homosexuality, masochism—in the realm of what common hierarchies of discourse assigns as one of the sites most unlikely to demonstrate anything "redeeming": porn.

Delany describes what he is creating in *The Mad Man* as a "pornotopia"—his term for "the place where all can become (apocalyptically) sexual, . . . where every relationship is potentially sexualized even before it starts."[7] That ugliness and monstrousness (which of course appear as such only because they are not easily bludgeoned into the conforming shapes at once recognizable as, and comfortably invisible to, convention) preside over his pornotopia makes clear for us that the praxis represented in the novel ought not to be too readily confused with utopias, those golden Edens imagined by emancipatory narratives: here the erotic and sexual are not liberating as some hoped they might prove to be in the midst of the Sexual Revolution, though they are of course political in their work in and with human relationships. We do not find emancipation here; but we find movement toward it, however ponderous, along a particular asymptotic curve. This is so due to the likelihood that most and perhaps all pornotopic representations emerge from something similar to a utopian imaginary. The idea of pornotopia, in its distinction from and overlap with utopia, has intriguing ramifications. Though imagining utopias is frequently under attack as a viable or reasonable part of political theorizing in light of any number of species of poststructuralist critique,[8] perhaps an imagination that takes as a first step nothing more or less than its vision of unlimited sexual satisfaction and working its way backward is a politically useful method. What kind of social, political, and economic conditions might be necessary for such a vision to be realized? Might we not have a clearer focus on the kinds of political changes necessary *especially* where the fantasies envisioned both attempt to address and exploit the shame and outrage arising from—for example—racialized abjection?

Also it seems important at the outset not to weigh too heavily in the scales the reality effects of bodies' materiality and the palpable nature of physiognomic events: that is, I am not positioning *The Mad Man* as prescribing the sexual practices it describes or as offering such practices as comparatively more "real" solutions for the problems they reference and textually attempt to address because the text works on its readers' bodies.

We have to bear in mind that pornographic representation underlines the *fantastic* dimension of all representation: it operates on and with the fantasies of its consumers; and the shaping of fantasies we experience individually or share in dispersed or mass collectives is of paramount value in the sociogenic process being carried out by this and other texts. In this sense the sexual arousal such fantasies open us to is one way to observe and chart the reshaping of those fantasies; that the fantasies become a part of individual consciousness or of societal discourse is important in itself, without the component of their being practiced or materialized.

Even so, to complicate matters I need to say that at the same time we ought not lose sight of the *possibility* of actually practicing what *The Mad Man* describes; we should not, simply because this is a work of fantasy, be seduced to cushion our discomfort with the relieving reminder that these perhaps-disturbing representations are "not real." What is represented in the novel is not prescriptive but also is not without material referent or "real" implication. The novel begins with Delany—leading us by the bridle, as it were—offering readers an extensive "disclaimer," which clearly anticipates the shock the novel's descriptions might arouse (and which declares hands-off to any other kind of arousal it might conjure) in asserting that *The Mad Man* is highly imaginative fiction detailing "a set of people, incidents, places, and relations among them that have never happened and *could never happen*."[9] But Delany also states that the novel is not about "safe sex"—not because it fantasizes a pornotopia in which HIV infection does not exist but because the relative safety vis-à-vis HIV infection of the sexual acts described in the novel are from a certain point of view not "safe," and from Delany's vantage have not been sufficiently studied to determine what degree of risk they pose for the disease's transmission. Thus, the sexual *acts* described—which again, must envelop in their penumbra, as they are enveloped in turn by, the fantasies and desires that are in some fashion always already part of them—are preserved from the reach of the novel's general disclaimer: they *could* happen. Note that acts and "incidents" are not the same, and the sexual acts, or at least the possibility of their being practiced, are in fact acclaimed, endorsed even, as against the easily outraged norms of safe-sex piety. This sleight of disclamation goes hand in hand with Delany's statement in an interview that "[a]s far as my own experiences, suffice it to say that, without reproducing any of them photographically . . . , *The Mad Man* covers a great enough range of them so that a reader who bears in mind that it is written by a fifty- and fifty-one-year-old man about a twenty- to thirty-five-year-old man, and thence allows for . . . novelistic exaggeration . . . , would probably not be too far off in most of his or her assumptions about my own sex life."[10]

It is this smudged and traversable line between representation and fantasy on the one side and practice on the other—the projection and reflection (or refraction) of the mind and the body's relation—that we need to keep in view and that I would argue permits me to say that what is represented in *The Mad Man* is something in the nature of a rough model of working with the legacies of history—with blackness, with having-been-blackened—through an erotic or sexual practice, much of which involves the transformation of erotic/sexual fantasies.

ISO Black Bottoms, White Tops

> DOMINANT ARYAN WHITE MEN wanted. Totally submissive, boot licking, butt kissing Black boy is looking for a dominant, verbal White man to service. Should include heavy verbal abuse, dog training, degradation, humiliation. Have a foot fetish—love to lick boots. If you're dominant, White and into White power, leave a message.
>
> BITCH BLACK BOY. Totally submissive, boot licking, cock hungry, cum hungry, oral Black pig ISO dominant White master. I'm 6'4", 200 lbs, 30, shaved head, hazel eyes, looking for LTR with dominant, verbal, politically incorrect White man who is into humiliating and degrading Black cocksuckers. If this is you, leave me a message. Live in LA and looking to move to SF.
>
> —two personal ads in the June 1999 issue of *Frontiers* magazine

I would like to contextualize my discussion of Samuel R. Delany's literary pornographic novel *The Mad Man* with a consideration in very general terms of what we can probably safely call conventional (and also, therefore, *non*literary) North American gay male porn. (Since most product identified and marketed as gay porn has historically originated in the United States, which appears to have had until recently a Hollywood-like dominance of the market—though this is rapidly changing as homegrown porn industries in Europe, South America, and Asia proliferate—many of these considerations apply generally to what has become known as gay male porn or to the general gay male porn paradigm established by North American product.)

Of course, the reputation of *The Mad Man*'s author and the work's conscious engagement with various themes that we generally associate with literary fiction set it some distance apart from the vast majority of other pornography. Nevertheless, it will not be surprising or controversial to take note that though the novel's aforementioned depictions of sex acts involving feces and urine do not appear in the majority of gay male pornography, the eroticization of such elements—especially urine—appears with sufficient frequency in written and video gay male pornography which take domination and submission dynamics as their primary theme (or as added spice, as a dash of color, in otherwise "vanilla" sexual scenarios) that *The Mad Man* is by no means unique in this regard. I will discuss *The Mad Man* from the angle of its participation in commercially circulating gay male sexual fantasies centered on BDSM further later; initially I want only to signal its minority, though by no means singular, position vis-à-vis the universe of those fantasies in which such thematic elements place the novel.

Several factors place *The Mad Man* in the minority of gay male porn: the bulk of North American gay male pornography, written or visual, does not feature characters of identifiable African descent at all, though of course there is a significant market niche of porn videos centered on African American, Puerto Rican, Cuban, and Brazilian actors. Gay male pornography centrally featuring African American men and other men of color might be said to constitute a slice roughly equal to or only slightly greater than that of BDSM of the work produced.[11] Depictions, let alone explorations that rise to the level of the thematic, of *interracial* or cross-racial sexual play in the general category of gay male porn, BDSM and non-BDSM, occupy a still smaller portion of the market—though in this relatively small group, black-white interracial pairings may well be in the majority. The three groupings (men of color, interracial, BDSM) are generally separate: there are some African American, Latino, or Asian men who appear with white men in BDSM porn fiction or video, but vanishingly few, and all-black or all-Latino porn will sometimes feature the paraphernalia or, less frequently, the explicit evocations of BDSM practice; but these depictions or themes are marginal to arguably already marginal spheres of porn. The proportions and numbers of the depictions of men of color or interracial sex decline significantly in the case of written porn—though my impression is that BDSM erotic fiction seems to hold a fairly large segment of the written porn market.

Such, then—again in rough general terms—is the position of *The Mad Man*, as a literary porn novel depicting and thematizing domination/

submission dynamics and something in the nature of BDSM practice, with an African American male protagonist involved in predominantly interracial (black-white) couplings. Delany's novel is distinct in the way that it combines these elements generally constructed and represented as separate. *The Mad Man* is distinct not only because such a combination shines a critical light on the routine and largely unremarked nature of such separations in the universe of pornographic representations, and not only because Delany, in a novel meant in part to give us erections or orgasms, chooses unflinchingly to examine the legacy of racialization (of blackness) through sexual exploitation or humiliation, which any contemporary combination of BDSM thematics with depictions of racial dynamics seems necessarily to evoke whether or not its author wishes to acknowledge them—but also because it accomplishes these ends through the depiction of a *black bottom*.

I will briefly take as a contrasting example another work—importantly, *not* North American—that stands in that marginal position of the already marginal in commercially circulating gay male pornographic fantasy: Alex Von Mann's *Slaves* (1997), a porn novel published by the British company Prowler Books, follows Jack Mallard, a white American involved in historical research of some kind (the research is quickly forgotten in this pornotopia), who travels to Zanzibar. Zanzibar is a not-quite-fictional country, having once been an independent sultanate and a British protectorate before becoming a region, island, and city in present-day Tanzania. The imaginary national site thus collapses historical pasts of conquest, domination, and colonization into the present—which of course is very much to the point of the fantasies the novel explores. In Zanzibar Jack lingers in a museum that houses an exhibit commemorating Dr. Livingstone's colonialist adventures and also a display cabinet containing "chains, manacles, yokes, shackles, handcuffs, fetters, stocks and bonds, whips, a whipping post," and a pillory. Jack meets his tourist-bureau guide in the museum, Konoco Fassal, whom Jack sizes up lustfully. Konoco has a personal story to tell about the pillory.

> "The Arab who owned my grandfather . . . put him in one of these [pillories] on a regular basis. He'd drop my granddaddy's drawers and beat my granddaddy's bare butt with a whip much like that one." . . . [Konoco] indicated a cat-o-nine-tails a little less vicious than its metal-studded companion. "After each beating of my granddaddy's ass, the Arab fucked it. . . . Happened regularly . . . whenever the Arab suspected

granddaddy was getting a bit too uppity and needed to be taken down a peg or two. According to granddaddy, the Arab never did learn that my grandfather liked getting his ass whipped and fucked."[12]

Konoco departs—but not before revealing to Jack that because of the currency exchange rate where one American dollar buys a pair of brand-new black-market Nike shoes, the sexual opportunities in Zanzibar are abundant for an American tourist. Jack then returns to the display cabinet, where this revelation of the inequities of economic (and national and racial) power in post-/neocolonial Zanzibar and the sexual license they afford him make highly apparent the simultaneity of past and present. "Jack imagined what it had been like for that Arab who'd had the unquestionable power to command Konoco's grandfather to . . . offer up neck and wrists for the pillory, to offer up black ass to the skin-blistering strokes of a cat-o'-nine-tails, to offer up the funky depths of black asshole to fucking Arab cock, and to have it all happen, without a hitch." Later in his hotel room, overtaken by this fantasy—which quickly becomes a scenario in which Konoco stands in for his grandfather, Jack for the Arab master— Jack strips in front of his mirror and promptly engages in masturbatory exercise fecund for Lacanian dissection, as he pretends he is Konoco and shouts orders to his own image. "Drop your pants, you black bastard!" he says, and "Shuck it all, blacky!"

> So what that it was a white and not a black ass? This was fantasy time! "Maybe, this time, I'll grab that big black prick of yours and whip it for white cream, even while I fuck the shit out of your cat-o'-nine-tails whipped black ass with my lily-white dick," Jack said. "Would you like that?"
>
> No pillory in the hotel room, but Jack imagined Konoco secured in one. If Jack laid on the hotel bed, the mildew on the bedspread clammy beneath his butt and back, he was, in his mind, standing behind Konoco, his cock ready for the hot plunge up restrained Negro's funky ass.
>
> "My cock is at your door, black man," Jack said and shut his eyes. "I'm going to fuck my pale cock up your inky asshole, and there's nothing whatsoever you can do about it."[13]

This particular scene appears as the commercial teaser prior to the title page, advertising to the reader the kinds of fantasy available at length within.

It is not clear to me what the extent of the audience for this work is, though it seems from my own nonsystematic anecdotal survey to be, from the point of view of the publishing industry at least, a fairly small and specific readership, since this kind of depiction is marginal to the marginal paraliterature of gay male erotica. Nevertheless, it is the case that the zealous hyperbolizing here of imagined visual opposition between the two characters in Jack's fantasy—the rain of blackys and black bastards, the inky assholes and big black pricks that contrast in such overdetermined fashion with "lily-white" cocks—is common enough in written pornographic representations of interracial sex. (However, such hyberbolic verbal staging of fantasy in live-action visual porn is very uncommon—though the language of sexual banter is sometimes similarly racialized in black-Latin films, or even all-black films, as well as, of course, the black-on-white gang-bang genre.) Generally, the more commercial and mainstream the black-white porn story (i.e., the more likely you can pick up a magazine from the rack in a store and read a porn story in it), the more muted such racial hyperbole is, though there is still built into the convention of such tales an obsessive underlining of the race of the black character(s)—references to the character's "ebony" beauty and the like. This is a representational strategy which no one deems very necessary in stories about white characters, and which also of course makes abundantly clear that the fantasy is assumed to be a white man's fantasy, the porn-story reader constructed as a white person beholding the electrifying alienness of black skin and black bodies.

It may well be, too, that BDSM-themed porn stories are more likely to engage in this hyperbole, precisely because a black-white pairing in domination/submission fantasies cannot avoid the historical underpinning of such scenes, the fact that a history of enslavement makes the pairing possible and legible—and the BDSM stories might even, as in the case of *Slaves,* own up to the fact that it is this very history that is the source of erotic fantasy. David Savran observes that "S/M pornography . . . unequivocally remains the product of an imperialist fantasmatic and often appeals (like most pornography, and . . . like most American cultural productions) to racial and ethnic differences in constructing its erotic scenarios."[14]

Yet despite this, it is rare to find erotic fantasies of white male sexual domination of black men. The image of the black top—which shades fairly swiftly into the familiar cultural imago of the big black stud/rapist—and the white bottom is the more familiar pairing in the universe of gay male pornography, especially in North America.[15]

This pairing, especially since it not infrequently is accompanied by more or less explicit narration that finds the black top "taking revenge" on the white bottom for the injustices inflicted on black people (and this is often doubly signified by some attention being paid to the class differences between the two sexual partners: the black top being usually poorer and less educated)—has the effect of accentuating racial difference in an erotic scenario just as Savran describes, with the apparently at least somewhat erotic side effect of assuaging liberal guilt. Through such devices, the appearance of the racial Other, the black male constructed in opposition to the assumed white consumer of porn, amid the manifold and mostly unconscious complexities of erotic and/or masturbatory fantasy, is neatly managed: one is permitted, as Michele Wallace said of Richard Wright's *Native Son*, to enjoy the pleasures generated by the black buck image without feeling terribly guilty about it, because, presumably, the white consumer of pornography is getting "punished" for his enjoyment of white privilege, for being the inheritor of the injustices committed by his ancestors, in what is probably as a psychological matter inaccurately presumed to be his singular identification with the white bottom. Certainly one effect, perhaps intended, of drawing attention to and exaggerating the spectacle of skin-color difference in the usual black-white porn narrative is to inoculate the (white) reader against the messiness of a cross-racial identification (though we see such inoculating strategies rather insouciantly cast aside by Von Mann—only to facilitate the mobilization of others). And, to make everyone happy—the white reader, the fantasy black presence, and maybe even the black or person-of-color reader who presumably has also been led by the nose to the appropriate racial identification—the punishment is an orgasm.

Of course, black-top depictions are closely related to the large number of porn movies available in which you find a single white woman, or (more rarely, but increasingly in the past few years) a single white man, being enthusiastically gang-banged by multiple black actors. They are clearly related, too, to the straitjackets of relative passivity and desexualization that have in the past tended to condition the representation of black men in performances in the mass media of movies and television, a convention of representational castration that began to become less prevalent (while other strategies of representational containment rose to the fore) only with the infusion of hip hop into mainstream popular culture in the last decades of the 20th century.[16] While it was and often still is deemed necessary by the producers of images for mass consumption to corral the threat that the fantasy of black men presents in contexts where sexuality is an undercurrent, the fantasy worlds of pornotopia generally take the opposite tack. The threat black men pose in the fantasy that constitutes "real life" and consensual reality as it appears to us in media-disseminated images is appealingly accentuated in the fantasy that constitutes sexual and erotic excitation: the black male imago as the fantasized hyperpossessor of the Phallus can run wild when all who watch him can use the fantasy of someone possessing and wielding that Phallus for their pleasure. Fears that require a production of black men as passive victims in general media thus fuel, or are merely obversely related to, the enjoyment of porn-fantasy black men as hyperstuds. In both iterations we recognize the validity of Fanon's basic observation in *Black Skin, White Masks*: that blackness is the West's preferred sign for nonnormative human sexuality and that there is a strong cultural investment that stands as belief, whether conscious or unconscious, acknowledged or repressed, that black maleness is significantly different from white maleness and that black men *do* "have" some *it* that makes a tangible sexual difference.

Given this set of contexts, in effect the black-top/white-bottom sexual fantasy scenario masks the history of oppression and slavery that it on the other hand evokes and palliates. By contrast, in Von Mann's novel, it is almost as if Jack has to be guided by historical example demonstrating that a lighter-colored or nonblack man *can* sexually dominate a black African, in order for his fantasies—as well as the fantasies of the European or American reader of the novel—to ignite successfully. While the black-top/white-bottom pair holds the history it depends on for erotic sustenance at a distance that it measures by willful ignorance or desperate disavowal, the white-top/black-bottom pair seems not to be able to do so: the fact of there having been a process of blackening (conquest, enslavement, and colonial exploitation) in the past is unavoidably *present* in the visible enactments of "play" and "fantasy," directly mirroring—or seeming to do so—an extant and thus palpable distribution of social and class status along racially determined lines. The white top in such a scenario is instantly and inescapably tethered to this history; his whiteness is revealed as the specific product of a historical and present domination (rather than his whiteness being, as it usually is, unraced, invisible, and baseline human) which he is now, for the pleasure of the participants in the scenario (which means anyone taking on the fantasy, as reader or player), supposed to enact sexually. Thus, the pairing of white-top/black-bottom, especially if the racial differences and a dominance/submission dynamic are brought to the fore, has less in the way of the palliative of disavowal or guilt-assuagement to offer; it cannot occlude the history's framing presence but instead evokes it—and demands, or reveals, that this history become for the participants sexually and erotically pleasurable. The white-top/black-bottom BDSM scenario is how things *really* appear, the manifestation in the economy of circulating sexual fantasy images of the same white supremacist dynamic that obtains when black men are represented in black-white interracial narratives in the various media sans overt erotic or sexual reference—and most porn writers seem to know this, which might be one reason they tend to avoid the white-top/black-bottom depiction or to assume that their readers will not readily find pleasure in it.

What Delany's *The Mad Man* suggests is that in avoiding this depiction most porn writers not only avoid the unwelcome intrusion of certain kinds of possibly arousal-killing racial reality into fantasy, but they also miss a complex opportunity that arises from the likelihood that arousal is not suppressed but stoked by this history: the possible palliating, or even politically progressive, effect of rendering a terrible history not only sexy[17] but as directly productive of powerful bodily and psychic pleasure in the present; and concomitantly, the possibility that this way of working *with* that terrible history immerses you *in* it rather than necessarily working you *through* it—which is potentially to effect a metamorphosis, an evolution, a transformation, but not a recovery or a remission: a tender scar, not a hard scab. The white-top/black-bottom BDSM scenario means that if there is going to be an erotic fantasy played out—which is to say, if we are going to partake of the pleasure afforded by imagining or playing out what is in part supposed to give pleasure because it is "not real"—participants have either to acknowledge, or to cultivate, the derivation of sexual and erotic pleasure from the history of blackening: we have to address the historical (or little-r "real") in the mode of the fantastic and to invest the fantastic with a consciousness of the painful, horrific historical reality that makes the fantasy appealing (precisely in its also being appalling). And for the black bottom, this means deriving sexual/erotic pleasure specifically from the history—as well as from the present enactment—of an abjection that gives rise to the racialized subject-that-is-also-an-object.

.   .   .

Though more extreme only because these scenes insist on explicitly, rather than mobilizing in coded fashion, the histories of racist domination for erotic fantasy, and though at the margins of a marginal field of representation, the elements of this particular sexual or erotic scene—white male top in bondage or domination relation with black bottom—do circulate and do sell as commodities in a transnational economy (perhaps a transnational libidinal economy) and/or in a transnational erotic Imaginary.

I have encountered the surprise, the unsettling challenge of this pairing: in Marlon Riggs's use of cartoonist Tom of Finland's image in his documentary *Tongues Untied,* in which a black character of typically Tommish robust physique, his wrists bound overhead to a tree branch in a stance and setting highly suggestive of a lynching, spews semen from his terrifyingly large and erect penis and appears to gasp in pleasure while a naked white character, of nearly identical physique and ejaculating erect endowment, rears back to apply a whip to the already striped back and buttocks of the black character. This image, ballooned on screen, drew a gasp from the Castro Theater audience in San Francisco where I first saw it screened circa 1989.

In a similar vein I find myself recoiling, unable to finish reading, when I encounter a couple stories in the Alt.Sex.Stories.Gay.Male.Moderated website collection, one of which is called "Enslaved," the other "Black Sperm Engines." In "Enslaved," a young black college student is kidnapped by white Southern fraternity boys dressed in Klan robes, who—to draw almost at random from a long list of richly imagined misadventures—orally rape him while hurling racial epithets at him, paint "nigger" on his chest, and make him crawl on his knees, clean them with his tongue after they defecate and urinate, and most memorably, clean his own ass with a corncob after defecating and then fuck himself with it, all as steps in "nigger training." In "Black Sperm Engines," ingenious tortures are applied to a young black character's testicles and nipples by an older white man instructing a group of white adolescents who fondle their erections while watching his flesh burn and perforate and listening to his squeals of pain. Dale, as the writer of "Enslaved" identifies him- or herself online, prefaces his story thus:

> [T]his story is being written to respond to a request by several African American readers who find this type of scenario erotic. It is a fantasy. A good piece of erotic art will turn off as many people as it turns on. . . . [T]hat's because our imaginations are so fertile and diverse. We must keep the line distinct between fantasy and reality, otherwise our country and our freedom is at stake. In Japan where they

have tremendously abusive and violent comics and films . . . there is a very low crime rate . . . because they can distinguish between what is real and what is not. I hope that we can too.[18]

When I first read that disclaimer, I suspected it was a lie: Dale, I was instantly certain, was in fact the alias of someone affiliated with some Aryan Nation–like group, distributing undercover evil fantasies for closet racists. But I now strongly doubt my initial conclusion.

Robert Reid-Pharr writes about the shock of the late Gary Fisher's journals, published posthumously by Duke University Press, that detail Fisher's encounters with dominant white tricks and his erotic fantasies of racial degradation.[19] Reid-Pharr argues that the shock of Gary Fisher is that, ultimately, blackness is always in some part, in some echo, distant or near, niggerness—which is to say that Fisher's announced interest in being dominated and called a nigger by a powerful white top reveals that black self-definition is always to some extent produced with and through the summoned totemic presence of the abusive white master/stud and that the ritualized suffering of the black body sought in sexual encounters by Fisher is in fact a paradigmatic mode of psychically joining the modern African American to his enslaved ancestors. Thus, Fisher can be read as excavating the history of the concept of blackness in the Americas: his journals tell us that for African Americans racialization was/is humiliation and subjugation, the experience of being dominated, and all claims to black identity created through that repeated, entrenched process of domination partake, to one degree or another, of that process. They repeat it, drive its meanings a bit more deeply into the individual psyche, fasten those meanings more securely within the cultural Imaginary and Symbolic.

Might we say, then, that it is the case that black-white sexual relations— or black-white relations as they become revealed in the sexual dimensions that the very invention of blackness as whiteness's opposite has made inherent to them—are always shot through with the primal scenes of slavery that establish their historical conditions? Is it always already BDSM? Clearly a certain cultural nationalist anti-interracial dating line of thought, exemplified by Baraka's and Cleaver's rhetoric (and both buttressed and violated by them in practice), says yes. I think that position is on one level absurd[20]—absurd, but not untrue: human relationships cannot be effectively or even productively analyzed on such a reductive basis; but à la Heisenberg, such a reductive assessment becomes true if you *look* at any such coupling, because in looking you influence or alter what you see so that it is, in fact, seemingly always true. The technology of seeing and observation is as much discursive as biological—and at the level of analysis it is entirely discursive. We *can* see only what the set of representations we have been given teach us to see, even when that set of representations is meant to cloak or dismiss yet another set that is brought into being as its unclaimed remainder, its newly drafted palimpsest-like shadow. In this regard Baraka and Cleaver are not wrong or overwrought: if you *look* at the obsessive sexualization of blackness and recognize what *practices*—sexual domination—bring the equation between blackness and sexuality into being, then the BDSM scene inevitably looms up. Again, then, the presence of that scene does not necessarily show us what *is* in the inevitable complexities of any individual or collective set of human relationships, but it does genuinely show us how those relationships must *really appear* to us, given a paucity of discourse for examining the weblike interconnections between race, sexuality, and romance/attraction. The only other set of terms and images readily available to us—that any such black-white pairing is a relation between equals, absolutely soluble in the great ocean of romance—is the denial of the BDSM scene without being its more truthful or complex corrective. The seeming inescapability of this BDSM scene, then, raises the question of what lived realities this scene does manage to represent and what aspects of those lived realities it in turn conceals—for our purposes, what powers, what nimble abilities—and which themselves might bear yet another level of dissecting examination.

In any case, our responses of shock, offense, and anger or squeamishness to what are, after all, fantasy representations are in part, of course, shields against uncomfortable experience and the knowledge—the recognitions—that might accrue from the examination of this discomfort.

As I noted at the outset of this discussion of scenes of rape, an impassioned argument can arise about both representations of such sexual domination and how analysis of them should be handled: Saidiya Hartman, for example, suggests that the deployment in criticism of scenes of black people or black characters suffering, especially criticism or scenes evoking "the slave's ravaged body"—such as the very scenes I have alluded to—has the effect of numbing us to that suffering, of assigning to the black body a lesser capacity to recognize pain; and by continually greasing the rails on which these stories and scenes circulate, such deployments perniciously interpellate us as readers/critics into positions too close to thrilled spectatorship, in which we ravage the black body fantasmatically and thus extend the dominating work begun by our common ancestors. "[D]oes the pain of the other merely provide us with the opportunity for self-reflection? . . . In light of this, how does one give expression to these outrages without exacerbating the indifference to suffering that is the consequence of the benumbing spectacle or contend with the narcissistic identification that obliterates the other or the prurience that too often is the response to such displays?"[21]

Hartman's solution to this problem is to draw attention to quotidian aspects of domination and to psychic rather than physical suffering. But even if the spectacularization, narcissism, and prurience she identifies are the results of reproducing these scenes, to heed her warning may foreclose the identification of other effects—which, whether less, more, or equally pernicious, might complicate or even undermine such voyeuristic and politically quietist effects as much as buttress them. There may be something of use to understand, or even worthy enough strategies to discover, precisely in consciously considering the enticements of such scenes as their vicious pleasures become *explicitly* erotic and sexual, and the possible political effects of these enticements. In the realm of the explicitly rather than covertly pornographic, strategies of respectful silence or hesitant, muted reference around representations of suffering and degradation that Hartman's observation taken in this context might seem to invite is rather too easily aligned with discursive conventions that enforce sexual reticence. The depictions with which I am dealing here are in fact of the suffering visited on black people, produced as a prurient and sadomasochistic entertainment. They are of the ravaged black body, which is also at the same time, and, in the mode of fantasy, for the same reason, *because* of that ravaging, affirmed or avowed as the very instrument and vehicle of black (and nonblack) sexual enjoyment. They are of a black sexual enjoyment *and* suffering meant to produce for its observers some form of climactic sexual and physical pleasure: they are consciously *spectacular* representations produced for the (sexual) excitement of those who consume them that call attention to, as *part* of the excitement, the historical processes of the production of racial difference through humiliation and domination.

To develop further a line of thought I began to establish in the introduction to this section focusing on representations of so-called male rape, it is perhaps the case that our relation to what Fanon calls the "burning past" cannot be utterly purged of amorality or even immorality, whether our approach to it is rigorously intellectual or sloppily sentimental or greedily prurient. It may well be that as inheritors of this past, if we take on the task of consciously working with that past, we cannot help reproducing in some measure the false, pernicious, discursively achieved "fungibility"—the commodification, the reduction to a value of use or exchange—of the black enslaved body. Marcuse argues that a genetically and culturally inherited tendency to the perception of linear time necessitates a stance of transcendence toward that aspect of the temporal which is called the past (a transcendence which is, in essence, the constitution of the historical)—distancing to master—and therefore, potentially, it necessitates a stance of exploitation with respect to the past and those who lived it. If so, it may be at the nexus of the psyche and the body that this transcendence, mastery, and exploitation can be mitigated: through the imagination (which might or might not be strictly literary but which entails all the psychic processes inherent to reading of identification and disidentification, of the play of discourse-as-the-text with the play of discourse-as-the-imagined-"I") intimately linked to bodily response (arousal) that the pornographic text provides.

If one *exists* a black body, then it is already the case that the suffering of the past is, or at least can be, held in one's body simply by dint of being the inheritor of the circumstances established by the past, as Fanon's muscularly rigid patients indicate; thus, the suffering from this perspective is not merely spectacular—though we need not claim it is utterly without spectacle—but also one's own, or what one is. As I claimed earlier, in the pornographic mode, then, there may be through the body-psyche nexus some partial access to what we have been referring to by Merleau-Ponty's term "anonymous existence," with its counterlinear perception of the temporal—which is to say that this mode perhaps grants us one of the powers of blackness. Is it not possible, then, to locate something as unexpected as an ethics in the attempt to identify with the suffering black ancestor, precisely in fantasies aimed at producing pleasure that are fantasies of their suffering which, like all erotic fantasies, must of necessity involve an identification with both perpetrator and victim? What if the attempt is not to *empathize* in that putatively liberal way that Hartman argues effaces the suffering of the black enslaved person and occludes their sentience but to address one's own pleasure and, at the same time, one's hurts as inheritor, even if precisely by transmuting the consciously or unconsciously imagined suffering of the ancestor into personal pleasure? This might be an ethics of erotic and sexual pleasure.

Delany at least sees something politically ethical about it. Certainly he is not interested in maintaining a respectful silence or adopting a strategy of muted reference to his contemporary fantasies that evoke as shadow the imago of the ravaged black body. In the essay "Pornography and Censorship," Delany argues against publishing-industry timidity about the supposedly limited, conservative tastes of reading audiences (the most prevalent and most dangerous form of bona fide censorship, in Delany's view), as well as against the more sincere concerns of antiporn feminists and high-culture gatekeepers that porn leads, in essence, to male readers' arousal in ways that will promote behavior harmful to others. He makes the same political claim for pornography that he might make for art in general: "limitations on the aesthetic presentation of what the body may undergo, either in pleasure or in suffering, immediately and *a priori* restrict what the mind is allowed to contemplate: For nothing encourages the practice of political torture and sabotages the pursuit of happiness more than blanket restrictions on speaking, in precise, articulate, and graphic terms about either."[22]

Delany's reference to the depiction of *suffering* here speaks to Hartman's objection, even though, of course, she is not writing about pornography but about the harms that arise from the covert eroticism of slave-narrative readers' interpellation as voyeurs. But it is particularly his reference to *pleasure* that seems important in this context, since he is referring explicitly to the pleasure of fictional bodies as, implicitly, the prompt to the pleasure of the readers' bodies. Delany notes, "despite the autobiographical accuracy I've almost never striven for in my fiction, the overwhelming majority of the situations of arousal I've experienced . . . have been relaxed, friendly (when other people were involved), pleasurable—and largely free of guilt. . . . And for me this forms the context that all new situations of arousal enter, even when, from time to time, in specifically pornographic texts, the material is violent or disturbing or generally unpleasant."[23] Thus, if Delany's project in *The Mad Man* is anything, it is a flouting of liberal or conservative imperatives to ignore or downplay racialized roles and the part those roles play in both the suffering that results from domination and—much more prominently, since *The Mad Man*'s world is pornotopia—in the forms of pleasure and power that can be derived from that domination as well, and to do so in such a way that the very meaning of suffering, pleasure, and power takes on very different valences than are encompassed in the understanding of our common vernacular.

What, then, are ways we can think about reading this (largely suppressed) black-bottom/white-top BDSM scene, its explicit erotic and sexual appeal, and, most importantly, its erotic and sexual ways of working with the real histories of conquest, enslavement, domination, and discrimination that the scene so disturbingly evokes? In what ways does Delany's novel perform its intervention in the rendering of such a scene?

Lusting for the N-Word

Delany's text addresses the messy imbrication of blackness with a queerness that expresses itself through the main character John Marr's developing delight in being both physically dominated and *verbally* insulted—abused—in explicitly racialized terms, mostly by white male characters, while he gives them enthusiastic and skillful blowjobs. The playing out of being simultaneously sexually dominated and *blackened* (where, as we have already seen, these two effects, domination and blackening, must be understood as mutually constitutive) is increasingly for John a source of great pleasure and, moreover, productive of a profound psychic satisfaction that becomes at least suggestively the foundation for a kind of politicized, liberatory way of living.

John Marr is an African American, middle-class philosophy graduate student living in New York City in the early 1980s, whose sexual adventures, following the slippery-slope trajectory of most extended erotica tales, graduate from an early interest in anonymous sex in men's rooms, movie theaters, and "Wet Nights" at a local bar to increasingly charged encounters in both public and private spaces with a number of homeless men—all of whom are in one way or another, along with John, the "mad men" of the title. But the novel is also about a range of other concerns, in particular the erotic foundation for intellectual production and creativity: it is, as Delany says, an academic novel, depicting the intellectual and financial struggles of graduate students; and its principal plot (apart from the sex) concerns John's attempt to unravel the mystery of the life and death of a Korean American genius philosopher named Timothy Hasler—a Michel Foucault, Douglas R. Hofstadter, and Pier Pasolini figure—who was murdered in the '70s in a New York hustler bar, while, as it turns out, accompanied by the acknowledged chief top stud of the homeless men Marr himself encounters, Mad Man Mike.

In the most extended of John Marr's encounters, the word "nigger" is used: that is, John is routinely called a nigger by his white partners (and the occasional black one as well). As this is consistently a component of his fulfilling sexual encounters—and as John never really objects to the word—"nigger" seems to be, or to become in the course of the novel, a powerful sexual incitement. It is inciting partly *because* of its meaning as a slur, or as a word that provides an expression of the domination/submission dynamic that gives him pleasure and that opens the way to his most powerful ecstatic experiences. In an overall sense, though not always explicitly in a given sexual act or encounter, the word "nigger" dominates John; and domination excites him and gives him pleasure.

Many of John's partners express a particular preference for sex with black men. John's first love, Michael Bellagio, announces, "I only came to Enoch State for one reason, John: that's to eat out as many black assholes as I can"—an enthusiasm which leads Bellagio to cry out in the midst of having sex with John and three or four black friends whom John invites to join them, "Fuck me, you goddam black bastards—fuck the shit out of me, you fuckin' niggers!" One of John's first connections is with a homeless man whose nickname is Piece O' Shit, who says, "I love me a nigger—you know, a colored feller—suckin' on my crank." Piece O' Shit claims he prefers black women: "what I like, see, is a big, nasty, smelly, runny, drippy, sweaty, funky black pussy!"—but he good-naturedly accepts John's lips, mouth, and throat as a substitute and, as he orgasms, cries out, "you are one *fine* black bitch . . . God *damn*, nigger." Another character, Tony, has a tattoo that boasts, "I'm Ruff, Tuff, Eat Nigger Shit for Breakfast, and Piss Battery Acid!"—and Tony does in fact find eating the feces of black men gives him the greatest satisfaction. Crazy Joey (my favorite character), a rather simple-minded young homeless man whom John meets when Joey gets thrown out of Burger King for masturbating, has an enormous penis that he assumes must be the inheritance of a black father whom he never knew. In addition to calling John "a nasty black suckhole," he chants, "I wanna come in your mouth; I wanna come in your face; I wanna come all over your nigger-nappy hair." The character who becomes John's lover and ideal companion, Leaky—so nicknamed because he loves urinating and does so constantly—says, "Nigger, you're a low-down fuckin' piss-guzzlin' jigaboo." Leaky's description of his and John's relationship, a description intended to excite both him and John, is the following: "That's the way it should be. . . . I like a nigger doing for me—little things: getting me a fucking beer, opening it for me, rubbing my feet, playing with my balls when I beat off, licking the cheese from out my fuckin' yoni when my dick gets *too* fuckin' filthy. . . . Ain't nothin' nicer than waking up with some nigger sucking on your dick, so you can just lie there and drop the first one of the day without even having to think about how you gonna get off." There are numerous similar examples.[24]

The n-word is also part of ordinary exchange in the novel; yet, since the novel is a pornotopia, and all exchanges between men are potentially sexual, there is always a sexual element in the use of it. Indeed, none of the few female characters use the word in speaking with John, nor does anyone in whom he does not have a sexual interest. In almost every "nigger" there is a covert or overt sexual—and oftentimes intensely romantic—charge. John tells Dave, a white guy he meets and has sex with who has a pronounced (and for Dave, troubling) preference for black men, "You'd tumble with any nigger who looked at you funny, wouldn't you, white boy?"[25]

Similarly, Tony has an exchange with John when he asks for money, and John replies, "I'm good for a meal—and a blowjob. . . . But I can't do money. I'm a poor nigger—white man. Not a rich one." The contrast in this conversation between "poor nigger" and "white *man*" illustrates the circular path that the n-word takes in the text—the nigger/ man hierarchy operating as a form of vicious semantic oppression in the world, taken up as enunciations of sexual/racial roles giving pleasure to consenting partners, then migrating back to the "ordinary," nonsexual conversation where John identifies himself according to its semantic terms, with a nod—incipiently erotic—toward the hierarchy, but fraternal and romantic in tone, without any overt oppression. That the history of domination both is and is not in operation in its familiar form is evident, too, by Tony's reply: tenderly, he touches John's cheek and says, "You're a good nigger, professor"—wherein we can read several layers of signifying at work:[26] Tony's "professor" is his partly awestruck, partly mocking, and always affectionate nickname for graduate student John and an acknowledgment of the considerable economic, educational, and therefore social-status divide between them, which places Tony decidedly on the lower rung of any hierarchy that structures their relations. At the same time, this acknowledgment, couched in language that is a clear echo of Jim Crow discursive practices of racial domination that divide black people into "good" and "bad" niggers and that, both during and postslavery, assert the right of the white person to own and to value the black person through such labeling, indicates that the racial hierarchy remains stubbornly extant, though here its terms are transformed into mere masks of play and insignia of flirtation and genuine affection—simultaneously, then, suggesting that play, flirtation, and affection are nevertheless radically limited at least in *how they can be enunciated* (though not in how they can be felt or experienced) given the inescapable history of inescapably racialized partners.

Thus, these are not the "niggas" of intra-black-community camaraderie and insult, or even of multiracial hip hop generation parlance—though assuredly as a set of enunciations they overlap with the use of the term in those contexts. These are inevitably "nigg*ers*," which usually issue from the mouths of white men—often white men from the South—and seem to imprint themselves in the auditory imagination of the reader with a telling drawl. The usual verbal incitements one sees in BDSM erotica fiction combine with the n-word in such a way that plantation and Middle Passage slave-ship scenes—certainly as those scenes have been evoked by the likes of *Beloved*, for example—hover, ghostlike, behind. White character Tony (who is not Southern), says, "I'm gonna do something nasty to you, nigger," and pisses in John's face and mouth. Leaky, who is Southern, surprises John by urinating in his face in a theater, saying, "*Drink* my fuckin' piss, you low-down no-account shit-suckin' nigger shithole."[27]

The deployment of the term "nigger" is made even more hyperbolic by the addition to the roll call of characters of two especially randy outback Marylanders named Blacky (a humpbacked and mostly toothless pig bottom, who especially lusts for the urine and ejaculate of white boys) and Big Nigg (his older brother, a foul-mouthed top who has a longtime lover relationship, or self-described "marriage," to a hillbilly self-described "nigger-lover"). These two characters' names, descriptions (Blacky is once called a "blubber-lipped bastard"), and exploits add a dose of helium to the novel's insistent play with racialized sexual roles, ballooning the narrative beyond all the boundaries of taste or conventions of restraint and thus dispersing some of the discomfort generated by the n-word into the realm of the absurd and comedic.[28] By the time we meet Blacky and Big Nigg we are well past offense, or so absolutely suffused with the experience of it that fresh occasions for offense skim off the surface like raindrops on the windshield of a speeding car.

In Delany's oeuvre this joke repeats: in his 1973 porn novel *Equinox*, there are two aggressive characters who make their living in pornotopia as "rape artists," a biracial half-brother pair named Nig and Dove, both in the employ of one Sambo.[29] In both *Equinox* and *The Mad Man* a comedic reading of these names seems significant: the names of Big Nigg et al. point to, underline, and mock the very conventions in porn of descriptions of interracial black-white sex which Von Mann's *Slaves* typifies—so that constantly to describe inky assholes and obsidian penises is, certainly, a lot like calling the characters Nig and Sambo.

One might be inclined to cordon off the proliferation of the n-word in *The Mad Man* as *only* making such a point, especially when reading a footnote in Delany's recent novella, *Phallos* (2004). *Phallos* is also pornographic, a kind of book-within-a-book that is a playful illustration of Lacanian notions of the Phallus, in the form of a fictional synopsis of an imaginary gay porn novel in which the action takes place in the Roman Empire of Hadrian. The imaginary porn novel, "*Phallos*," like the mythical Phallos sought after (in between accounts of epic sex) by the characters in the story, constantly eludes those who seek it: the preface finds one Adrian Rome (i.e., Hadrian/Rome), "a young African American," searching for the book but losing it to homeless men who filch it from a garbage pile where his landlady has deposited it, then having to settle for a synopsis—the text we have as readers—posted on the Internet by a man bearing the porn-star-reminiscent name of Randy Pedarson. The elusive erotica, written, the preface claims, by "an elderly black man of letters,"[30] is in part a fictional avatar for another of Delany's porn novels, *Hogg*, which, like the "*Phallos*"-within-*Phallos* was first completed in draft form in 1969 (to be completed for publication in 1973) but, due to a long history of editorial censorship, was not published until 1995.[31] (*Hogg*, not incidentally, narrated by an eleven-year-old boy who is the sex slave and companion of *another* rape artist—named Hogg—also features liberal use of the descriptive term "nigger," along with "wop" and "spic" and others, and another character named Nigg, along with a character named Dago.) There is a resonance, too, between the fictional "*Phallos*" and *The Mad Man*—not only in the library-despoiling acts of homeless men and the kinds of sex described (mostly, to greater and lesser degrees, having domination/submission dynamics) and in the fact that Adrian Rome goes searching for *Phallos* in 1994, the publication date of *The Mad Man*, but also in the content of a footnote on page 94 of *Phallos*: there, Randy Pedarson acknowledges having chosen to omit from his synopsis long passages involving "'the ebony orgy' with the Arabian slavers, the black tribal slavers, and *their* black slaves," about which editor Pedarson comments, "I confess, all those S&M jungle bunnies bouncing about, buggering and being blown, no matter how eloquent, passionate, or poetic, hit me as hopelessly racist. . . . In a document whose main purpose is advocacy, I saw no reason to stress it."[32] Pedarson might possibly be Delany distancing himself from the apparent racism of the language in *The Mad Man* and *Equinox*—but instead it seems likely that he is imitating, and gently elbowing, readers who recoil from *The Mad Man* (and *Equinox* and *Hogg*) with just such a criticism, as well as, more seriously, skewering the censorious responses and unacknowledged racism of such dismissive readings, which Pedarson's flippant, overheated use of "S&M jungle bunnies" underlines. In this way, though the n-word has no place in the ancient-world setting of *Phallos*, a space is reserved for it in that pornotopia as well.

Thus, the recurrence of this device—and, to be sure, the bona fide exuberance that seems to characterize the use of it—strongly suggests that comedy and mockery as analyses are incomplete (leaving aside what Freud has to say about the significance of jokes, which we need not repeat here). We have strong reason to suppose this as well because Delany notes, "One of the self-imposed constraints on the writing of *Equinox* was that I would write none of it unless I was actually in a state of sexual arousal, even for the nonsexual parts."[33] This evidence suggests that "nigger" is a highly important, perhaps even indispensable, part of Delany's written (i.e., consciously ordered and selected, rather than semispontaneously generated as in everyday fantasy) erotic scenarios, which, after all, we do not generate primarily to make ourselves laugh, and/or that its use takes on a political meaning. This is to say that, apart from being comedic, in *The Mad Man* as in *Equinox*, the word "nigger" is *erotic*, and this eroticism has political meaning.

.   .   .

Two of the few literary critics to engage Delany's porn novel, Ray Davis and Reed Woodhouse, briefly note but do not discuss the historical and social resonances of the racist language used in the novel and the implications of the novel's articulation of that language to cross-racial BDSM sexual encounters.[34] Davis does, however, intriguingly summarize *The Mad Man* as "a realistic novel where sex involves fantasizing oneself into cartoonish roles"—and it is this very "cartoonishness" I wish to adumbrate here, since Davis's adjective may accurately state the *result* of the laborious work Delany does with "nigger" and racialized sexual role play, but it does not adequately reveal—or even has the effect of dismissing or containing—the difficulty of that labor and the breadth of its implications.[35] Jeffrey Allen Tucker's monograph on Delany addresses the proliferation of the n-word in *The Mad Man* and even contextualizes this usage with reference to the Paul D scene from *Beloved*, discussing how Delany's novel "interrogates anxieties about black gay masculinity and race conscious-ness." His reading, however, tends to resolve these anxieties by finding in the text a definite "difference between the sexual and the social," between "mere 'perversion'" and harmful derogation. Nevertheless this demarca-tion between sexual and social meaning is sometimes, Tucker notes, dif-ficult to locate—he asks, and does not answer, "Because iteration implies *both* identity and difference, are they ever truly released from their histo-ries as brutal linguistic weaponry?"[36] This is a question I want to answer here by arguing that Delany pointedly does *not* release his slurs from their histories, that in fact it is precisely their histories that Delany summons to the scene, for the character John Marr's erotic pleasure and, indeed, for the reader's; the continuum between the sexual and the social is useful, then, to highlight, but only to weigh their relative emphasis in a given mo-ment of eroticized enunciations of the n-word, not to settle on one rather than the other.

Another critic, Phillip Brian Harper, zeroes in on the racial dynamics at work in the novel, succinctly examining John Marr's and two other black characters' "highly motivated, eroticized engagement with the fact of their fetish status." For Harper, John exemplifies a way (though not necessarily a method Harper would emulate) to negotiate complex and uncomfortably dissonant dynamics of social, economic, and racialized power, identity and erotic fantasy, a way to "*mobilize* identity in relation to power for the sake of maximally intense erotic effect." Harper dis-cusses how John Marr illustrates a motivated occupation of the status of racially fetishized object that reveals how being a racial fetish object can be central to black gay men's sense of self. I concur with this observa-tion and would like to expand on it, though my interest is in tweaking the emphases of Harper's statement:[37] Delany's John Marr mobilizes a history of racialization through sexual/erotic exploitation and humili-ation—thus plugging in, as it were, to an existing framework of erotic effect—and uses this already-operative erotic effect "for the sake of" a kind of power, that is, as both the means and the end of the achieve-ment of an empowered sense or impression of self. My interest here is in how being the inheritor (and thus, both consciously and unconsciously, the reenactor, the re-actor) of a historical practice of sexual domination becomes the centerpiece of a fictional black gay male character's erotic imagination and arousal—and by extension, because *The Mad Man* is porn, a part of the imagination and arousal of readers by no means bound by those demographic descriptives—and also how it becomes the platform or foundation for that character's explicitly politicized choices of community and his political stance in general.

Certainly Delany's "niggers" can be read as just another occupation in the long career of the word. As Randall Kennedy details, while the word is primarily an insult, "nigger" also has satirical, affectionate, and racially nonspecific meanings (i.e., the word is not used to refer to a black person) in the mouths of different speakers in different contexts. "[N]igger can mean many different things, depending upon, among other variables, intonation, the location of the interaction, and the relationship between the speaker and those to whom he is speaking," Kennedy notes. Satirical or affectionate uses of the word without apparent intent to injure overlap with but are not the same as those more politically acceptable uses—by, say, comedians who are black or have otherwise signaled their opposition to bigotry—which are sometimes explained as being aimed at reclaiming the word or diminishing the sting of the insult. Kennedy concludes, "despite the costs, there is much to be gained by allowing people of all backgrounds to yank *nigger* away from white supremacists, to subvert its ugliest denotation, and to convert the N-word from a negative into a positive appellation. This process is already well under way."[38]

To some extent the "niggers" of *The Mad Man* are satirical, as the outlandishness of names like Big Nigg makes clear, and undoubtedly, too, they are used between sexual partners and lovers in the novel with affection as well as lust. But they are not, by and large, racially nonspecific—they refer to black men who are the objects of sexual desire or are spoken by those men referring to themselves as such objects. And as the use of the word tends to arise in sexual contexts exclusively (though of course there is an abundance of those, this being a pornotopia), the question of whether they are negative or positive seems to put the question misleadingly: Delany's "niggers" are not generally spoken by white supremacists (at least, not by characters who are consciously or threateningly such), but as the exchange between John and Tony suggests, the n-word's "ugliest denotation" is being invoked, exploited for its sexual power, in a way that seems not to be fully captured by the notion of subversion Kennedy describes and endorses as doing socially progressive antiracist work.

That these n-words refer vociferously to the history of enslavement, humiliation, and domination in which they originate, that the "niggers" of *The Mad Man* are not ever "innocent" jokes or simply resignified endearments completely drained of pejorative content, is made evident in various ways. As we have seen, "nigger" is often only one term—usually the more heavily weighted and more often repeated one—in an exchange of insults between sexual partners in the novel. But Delany does not spare us the implications of this, depicting the ease with which such apparently agreed-upon, lust-producing uses of insults that we see at its greatest clarity with John and Tony can slip toward less fully consensual, nonsexual uses—that is, the ease of "nigger" being used in a way that seems largely or only offensive, without clear sexual reference. In one Wet Night at the Mine Shaft exchange, a man named Tex yells, "*Suck* my dick, black boy!" Later, Tex explains that he means no offense by using the term *boy*. "I ain't callin' you boy 'cause you a nigger; I'm callin' you boy 'cause to me you look like a fuckin' *kid*! . . . No offense then, nigger . . . ?" John narrates: "It kind of made me start. Then I laughed. 'No offense, you fart-faced old toothless piss-drippin' scumbag honky!'"[39]

The n-word is never without its teeth. At one point in the story, having sex with Tony (the one who likes eating black men's feces), John, having defecated for Tony's consumption, summons up and articulates the racist and homophobic discourses that underlie both his and Tony's mounting excitement:

> "You wanna make a nigger come in his pants?" I said—surprising myself. . . . "You ask fifty guys what the lowest thing in the world is. They'll tell you, it's a cocksucker. Ask them what's lower than a cocksucker, and they'll tell you it's a nigger cocksucker—right? And that's a nigger cocksucker's *shit*—that *you're* gonna eat! . . . [W]hich makes you the fucking lowest scumbag around, right? Well, see, not only is it a nigger cocksucker's shit, man. It was a nigger cocksucker who was sucking on *your* fucking dick, drinking *your* fucking piss! That means it's gotta be even fuckin' *lower*—and the only way you could be lower, . . . dog, is if you ate my fuckin' shit . . . [i]n front of the fuckin' nigger himself."[40]

Here John is in rhetorical charge of how the low status accorded by racism and homophobia gets distributed—he is the locus point, the proudly announced cocksucker, the nigger who speaks his occupation of object-status as its own value, as a reveled-in prize—but both he and his white partner acquire putatively degraded positions and experience corresponding levels of excitement because of the status they, by dint of the magical use of words in conjunction with action (sucking cock, drinking piss, eating shit), occupy. There is never really a question in the way Delany portrays this character that John really *believes* himself to be "low" (though Tony does, for a time) or that John even ascribes to a notion that low and high are fundamentally truthful descriptive categories in the world—but certainly it excites him to *say* that he is, to recognize that the world cognizes such hierarchies, and to *say* that he is at the bottom of it.

Leaky, who has never learned to read or write and has apparently been told he has a learning disability, admits that he finds sexual satisfaction in being called "stupid" and "dummy." His erotic interest in these words is parallel to John's interest in being called a nigger, and as a result he and John toss "niggers" and "stupid morons" at each other in both sex and conversation:

> [Leaky] . . . said: "When I was in school, in the second grade, they said I was a slow learner—borderline retard. Even niggers can call *me* dumb." He looked pleased, even proud. . . .
>
> "Man," I said, "you're so fuckin' stupid, you don't even known enough to come in out of the rain. You're probably the stupidest whitey running around homeless in this fucking neighborhood. You're so fucking stupid you'd piss on a nigger in the middle of the street then let him suck your fucking dick. You fucking retard. . . ."
>
> . . . So I leaned over his leg, got half a dozen fists in my face, before his other hand clamped the back of my head and he pushed me down on him. Within my mouth, he erupted, thick and copious.[41]

As in the conversation between Tony and John, here the names Leaky and John call one another are truly insulting names. Though Delany does not imply here that stupidity and niggerness are equally insulting, they are both salient, for the characters and the readers, in easily identifiable, different but overlapping ways.

The pleasure to be had from hearing insults, from verbal abuse—in the exchange just quoted, accompanied by play-angry blows to the face—as part of the sex act, derives from at least two simultaneous, tightly entwined, and yet somewhat contradictory transformations of the insults:

1. The erotic context and the fact that someone who is the character's sexual partner is speaking, rather than, say, a chain-gang guard, takes the sting out of the insult—since its trusted intent is to deliver or accentuate pleasure, it potentially removes the hearer from the effects and the reality of the ways in which such words effect domination or oppression in their lives because, within the intimacy and implicit agreement of

partners playing roles, the words are, in a sense, spoken out of context. Leaky offers evidence for this effect when he makes known his political antiracism. "I been all over, man," he tells John. "I do not like the south though. I was born there. . . . But, you know, I can't take the way they treat black people. I'm serious. You'd think with me, gettin' off on black guys what get off on bein' called 'nigger' and stuff, that wouldn't make somebody like me blink an eye. But I can't take it. It fucking turns my stomach." Leaky compares the South to the North, finding the latter only marginally better: "at least everybody isn't joking about lynchin' [black people] . . . and cuttin' their balls off and expecting you to laugh your head off." John replies, "it makes sense to me that, if you like some group sexually, and you want them to be around and happy and fuck with you a lot, you might be concerned with how they're treated socially—and politically."[42] In this sense the insults in a sexual context seem to be a corrective, a healing of past hurts.

Reading the insults along these lines corresponds with a certain viewpoint in BDSM communities that tries carefully to balance between a commitment to the fullest range of sexual play containing elements of hierarchy and oppression, and antiracist politics. The editors of *The New Bottoming Book* discuss race play, that is, "playing cultural trauma, . . . play that involves enacting some of the horrors of our cultural past" as a "kind of play that is particularly controversial for many individuals and groups within the BDSM communities."

> We know bottoms who belong to recently oppressed minority groups and who have found tremendous healing and excitement in building scenes around that historical oppression. One African-American friend says, "Playing a consensual scene in which my top called me 'nigger' made me much better able to handle hearing it in the real world. Before, when I heard the word, I'd become irrationally, reflexively furious. Last week a panhandler called me that and I laughed in his face—'now *there's* a smart way to ask for money, bozo!'"
>
> . . . We suggest extreme care in negotiating and enacting such scenes, similar to precautions for playing around a history of personal trauma such as rape and abuse. . . .
>
> And when you and your top can work together to reclaim parts of yourself that have been wounded by humanity's sad history, what a great and worthwhile gift that is—a perfect example of how the darkest corners of BDSM can bring the greatest illumination.[43]

Such assertions of self-reclamation and empowerment may well strike us as tenuous at best, as achieving an effect so difficult to assess and so insular and individual as to appear of vanishing significance. This is so not only because of our stubborn Heisenberg-principle-like inability, when viewing such play from the outside, to perceive anything other than the bloody operation of power in that "sad history" which enables and seems to require the enactment of these scenes. David Savran brings an additional criticism to such claims, when he observes of lesbian S/M,

> Becoming (or introjecting) the one she fears, the lesbian S/M subject lays claim to the pleasure and the power that have been denied her historically. . . . S/M practices and narratives . . . allow consenting subjects control over the production and reproduction of these most important fantasmatic points of identification . . . thereby facilitating the subject's negotiation . . . of those insecurities and fears that come into play around questions of power and sex. *Without fundamentally altering the social structures that produce oppression,* they perform a kind of psychic alchemy . . . and offer a genuine, if *limited,* sense of empowerment to subjects who, in many cases, have been denied power as social actors.

Savran adds that "the performance of victimization enables a mastery of subjection. Rather than reinforcing submissiveness, the act of *choosing* humiliation, *performing* subjection, allegedly reactivates . . . individualized control and agency."[44]

Savran's skepticism, easily enough extended to race play in general, might equally apply to the characters John and Leaky and to the project *The Mad Man* makes of their sexual fantasies. But Delany does not write John as someone seeking the healing of hurts;[45] and significantly, while Delany gives us Leaky's account of his past (always in something of a comic vein), and while other characters, generally John's sexual partners, allude to theirs, Delany never produces a family narrative or elements of a bildungsroman for John—eliminating the chance of reading the character as any more or less "damaged" or traumatized than we the readers are. Rather, John seeks the answer to a mystery surrounding the death of a fellow human being with whom he shares a number of interests and characteristics (both he and Hasler are gay, persons of color, sexually interested in feces, urine, dirt, etc.)—so that John is really on a quest for knowledge of himself and for the kind of understanding of oneself and others that either permits or is required for building community.

Moreover, it seems to me that Savran's faint-praise damnation of lesbian S/M's "limited" empowerment given that the social structures have not been fundamentally altered is not saying enough: all forms of empowerment must be accepted as having their limitations—is power only ever absolute, or nothing? Also, the critique Savran articulates of S/M practices has to be recalibrated as we make the crucial shift from practices and play to a porn text using or adopting an aspect of S/M practice for its thematic: the depiction of John's excitement in racialized verbal abuse becomes less a private therapeutic tool, bound up within and conditioned by the various idiosyncrasies of consenting partners, than *also*, because we are reading it, an occasion for private participation in a socially shared reimagination of such abuse (interestingly, *without* our consent, or at least without consent of the same kind that partners participating in play can offer—about which I will say more shortly) and an option for public (political) posturing.

The public, political implications become apparent as we examine the second source of John's pleasure, which partially contradicts the palliative, empowering, or pain-mitigating source of pleasure we first identified.

2. Deploying the insults as sexual patter intensifies reference to the historical context from which the words emerge. The ugly historical contexts of domination, of oppression, of abjection, are a fundamental substance of the sexual and erotic excitement—it incites sexual pleasure for Leaky to be called a moron as he has been throughout his life by various teachers and members of governments' social welfare networks, for John to be called a low-down, no-account nigger as his ancestors have been and as he might sometimes *really appear* in his current life, with all its racially determined inequities and injustices, and for both to be called these names by partners who because of one characteristic or another can represent the very persons or forces that have used such insults as instruments of domination in the past (John is very well educated and therefore "smart"; Leaky is white and Southern). In essence, the traumatic past is exacerbated as it is also soothed, the wounds both bandaged and bled; and it is in that body-psyche nexus wherein what we call the sexual operates that this contradiction is held and that both psychic pain and the effects, if not the content, of language undergoes a transformation.

The enthusiasm with which John's partners manhandle his head and neck elicits textual references that demonstrate the connection between John's pleasures and the history of the display cabinet in Von Mann's fantasy, with its many instruments of torture: frequently the men's large hands make a "cage" around John's head as they thrust his mouth back and forth on their penises. And at another point, in the hands of Crazy Joey, John chooses a telling metaphor for the loving forcefulness of Joey's actions: "He grabbed the base of his cock, and began to slam in hard with each blow. His fist made a *collar* I couldn't get past." Later, Leaky insists that as a pledge of their new relationship, John should buy him a dog collar and, in accordance with the rituals of his coterie of homeless friends, also buy Leaky himself for a penny. The collar of course is a standard leather BDSM accouterment, the sale of submissives a standard part of BDSM fantasies if not practice, but the reference to American racialized chattel slavery is not lost on John. As he is making the purchase in a pet store, "Suddenly it had hit what I was doing. All this stuff about paying a penny, about collars—suddenly it was all frightening. My heart beat, thudded, banged the inside of my ribs. You crazy black bastard, I mouthed. *What are you getting into . . . ?*" When Leaky puts the collar on and says that it makes him feel "pretty good, . . . [l]ike now I'm where I'm supposed to be," John agrees: "It would be a real head-fuck . . . if this is what buying and selling slaves turned out to be all about."[46]

Here John, the bottom sexually, is the "owner." Leaky insists on this despite John's protest, because John rents the apartment and has a job—signaling that Delany is always aware of the overlapping and contradictory ladders of hierarchy operating in any interaction across lines of socially recognized difference. The idea or pretense of one character "owning" the other becomes a sealing metaphor for their relationship; and later, Tony, a participant in the practice of buying and selling sexual favors among the cadre of mad men, explains that the penny paid has nothing to do with the measure of labor power but only with "owning" as a vague conceptual tent for all the peculiarly satisfying aspects of the intimacy of a mutual relation in which top stud and pig bottom are roles. By this many-layered resignification of the slave auction and the collar (Delany has an extensive rumination on the slave collar and its erotic properties in his fantasy series *Return to Nevèrÿon*),[47] Delany acknowledges—he refuses to ignore or to be carefully silent about—the history of ravaged black bodies that underlies, prescribes the terms of, and makes possible John Marr's sexual interests and his love; and in the process of acknowledging this history rather than repressing it, he redistributes the meanings cathected in the symbol of the slave collar for a contemporary use, for a partially liberatory use.

John ruminates,

I have put the collar on you that allows you to roam and, because the collar is a *true* sign of belonging, of ownership, of the genitive in its possessive mode, lets you return . . . to what comforts, what privileges, what rights, what responsibilities, what violences?

Historical, political, and bloody, in a land built on slavery, what appalling connections were inscribed within that phatic figure . . . ?[48]

The connections John makes across race and class, between men, between top and bottom, are indeed "appalling"—at least the history of injustice that makes all these terms legible is—but they are strong, productive connections. Putting the collar on Leaky does, John admits, make him "feel better." The "head-fuck" that might be what buying and selling slaves is all about *for John* is, after all, not only a figurative, intellectual, and emotional degradation/exaltation that disturbs him even as it gives him pleasure but also literally descriptive of his favorite, voraciously sought-after sexual act. This is clear when we place alongside "head-fuck" the following sentence John generates while blowing Crazy Joey—as Joey is pissing in John's face: "And because that thing feels so good plugged into your head, I threw myself back on his cock again."[49] What feels so good is not just the cock but—of course—what the cock represents: not only its usual referents (masculinity, the Phallus) but also here, because the head-plugging resonates so strongly with the head-fuck of historical slavery, a history of racialization, of blackening, through domination, humiliation, and exploitation, a history that John can literally stroke with his mouth, that he can manage, give pleasure to, and take pleasure from, pleasures he can stroke in and *as* his body.

John describes this "feeling good" as something more than the physical relaxation that comes after orgasm. It is, rather, he says, a "psychological peace, which, were I religious, I'd describe by saying, it feels like you're doing what God intended you to do—like you're filling the space God intended you to fill, . . . not want, or need, or yearning, but desire itself—satisfied. Finally satisfied. Not a God believer, I'm willing to accept the God in that feeling as a metaphor . . . [and] here I'd found the point where the metaphor and the thing it's a metaphor for *might* be one."[50]

This psychological and emotional peace, this "knowledge," as John refers to it, obtained through the acts of the body and the catalysis provided by words (insults, abuse), is the material and psychic trace of a shift in discursive activity that comes from working in the present with the legacies of slavery, with the historical process of racialization as sexual domination and sexual humiliation. It is a kind of transformed body, or rather a transformation of consciousness that could not occur without (and possibly could *only* occur as) a bodily transformation, a working with embodied consciousness.

"Leaky," John narrates, "probably went back to sleep, even while his waters ran within me. . . . His gut lifted and dropped my forehead. I lay there, his furry warmth against me, *feeling very much like someone who was in his right and proper place.*" If we unpack this statement and the one about the God metaphor quoted earlier, we see that the language of a "proper place," especially as it describes John resting against Leaky's body, with Leaky "above" him, Leaky having previously been "[r]ubbing . . . [John's] head" and Leaky urinating in John's mouth as it pleases him to do so, evokes the history in which a white man tells a black man to "know his place."[51] The urination surely must echo for us Morrison's scene with Paul D and Beloved's brutal recollection of Middle Passage slave galleys, where the "men without skin" feed their captives their "morning water."[52] In this sense the history of racialization through humiliation, of blackness as and in abjection, is reenacted, performed as sexual play—with all the offense to the correctness of a Black Power– or Civil Rights–identified discourse that such a play entails. This history is not denied; it is not detached from the sexual and romantic acts being described. At the same time, these acts and this evocation of the domination of *knowing* one's *place* is, in fact, romantic, but not only in that sense of romance in which the lover and the loved cease to feel the boundaries between them—an intimacy figured here in the simultaneously physical and psychic experience of "his waters running within me"—but also, and more importantly, in the soldering of the constitutive split of subjectivity that Delany presents to us: for John, in this moment at least, the circle of desire is closed—desire *itself* is "finally" satisfied. John *lacks* nothing; and we know this, too, because Delany tells us that for John at this moment language itself, the culprit of self-division which also makes the self, presents no obstacle to knowing or experiencing, for John has arrived at "the point where the metaphor and the thing it's a metaphor for *might* be one." Thus the phrase "filling the space God intended you to fill" acknowledges and exploits a history of domination that white supremacist discourse has tried to justify with divine imprimatur, but it rapidly nonetheless extracts from John's experience both God and the notion of a place that is a form of subordination: John, as Delany imagines him, has come to a point where the mystery of who he is (a mystery his quest for the circumstances of Timothy Hasler's murder only externalizes) is not mysterious. Language—and God and Law and Father—presents no obstacle to the thing it ushers into being; there is no slippage between signified and signifier, between desire and fulfillment, between what would pose as the divine (which is will, authorship) and the human.

What Delany imagines is a scene where it is as if to be interpellated is not *only* to be corralled into a subjugating internalized surveillance but also to become who you "really" are, in your "right and proper" place—precisely through a combination of language and acts that enact or perform that interpellation. The italicized "might" here tries to hedge bets and reduce John's moment to the provisional and evanescent (and how could we think of the complete satisfaction of desire as anything other than a passing experience?), but the audacity of the claim—of Delany's imagined solution and of the suggestion that the solution to what I have elsewhere called the problem of history lies in an enactment and embodiment of imagination—remains. It is significant, too, that the *place* where metaphor and the thing a metaphor signifies draw so near to one another as to be fully coextensive is a "place" John enters through his association with Leaky and other men who are all homeless; in this sense the resonant meaning of the "right and proper place" is no-place, is, in fact, utopia.

It clearly is also pornotopia, "the place where all can become (apocalyptically) sexual"—or at least, it is through apocalyptic sexuality that the closing of the circle of desire can be accessed. The *apocalyptic* in Delany's definition of pornotopia acquires a more substantial meaning as we repeat it in light of these scenes: at the conclusion of Timothy Hasler's own climactic sexual experience, he writes *ekpyrosis* on a mirror in his apartment. This is the Greek root of the English word "apocalypse," which Delany employs in the scene just as he employs the English word in his description of pornotopias—the sense in which apocalypse indicates an unveiling: it is in the realm of the sexual that this unveiling occurs.

Delany provides another example of how eroticizing or sexualizing a painful event can be (at least partially) transformative in his semiautobiographical novella *Citre et Trans*. *Citre et Trans* takes place in Greece during the 1960s. A narrator called "Chip"—Delany's own nickname—is anally raped while staying overnight with a friend. The friend brings home two Greek sailors as tricks, a squat one and a tall one, but is only able to hold the attention of the taller of the two. The squat one, bored, decides to take advantage of Chip as he tries to sleep and, despite Chip's protests—and eventually with the other sailor's help—forcibly fucks him. Chip chances to meet the sailor again on a train platform as he departs Greece, and they have a tense but not particularly confrontational conversation—the sailor seems largely unaware of having misbehaved and, when he does seem to intuit that Chip is wary of him, offers him his knife and declares that they are "friends." This peculiar conversation opens the way for Chip to address the experience of his rape in a different way, which seems more powerful and more important, ultimately, than the nonconfrontation—though the unexpected platform encounter appears to make it possible.

> That night, in my couchette, while we hurtled between Switzerland and Italy, in the dark compartment I thought about the two sailors; and *when my body told me what I was about to do*, I had some troubled minutes, when it was easy to imagine the armchair psychiatrists . . . explaining to me . . . how, on some level, I had liked it, that—somehow—I must have wanted it.
>
> While I masturbated, I thought about the thick, rough hands on the squat one, but grown now to the size of the tall one's; and the tall one's hazel eyes and smile . . . ; and about sucking the squat one's cock, with all its black hair . . .
>
> . . . I used my waking up with the sailor beside me, his leg against my arm, his hand between my legs. I did it first with fear, then with a committed anger, determined to take something from them, to retrieve some pleasure from what, otherwise, had been just painful, just ugly.
>
> But if I hadn't—I realized, once I'd finished, drifting in the rumbling, rocking train—then . . . I simply would have found it too bleak. I'd have been defeated by it—and, more, would have remained defeated. That had been the only way to reseize my imagination, let go of the stinging fear, and use what I could of both to heal.[53]

In this account, Chip responds to a specifically sexual trauma with an attempt to "reseize" his imagination sexually, and the emphasis is on healing, on reclamation of pleasure. By contrast, as I have noted, the character John is written as not having suffered any particular acute trauma, sexual or otherwise, and his interest is not in healing but in knowing, and in pleasure. Nevertheless there is a clear resonance between this scene and John's experience, in that if John has been hurt at all, his hurt has almost nothing to do with an individual narrative and rather to do with a societal narrative about racial difference and racial hierarchy; he *has* been traumatized, but in that sense in which we are all traumatized by the distortions imposed on us by living race as reality, the at once frustratingly remote and painfully intimate trauma of historical determinations, the trauma that makes S/M how black-white relations *really appear*. (Delany thus takes up the Fanonian challenge, to view properly what would improperly be individualized as a neurosis arising out of family relations: as a societal neurosis arising out of social conditions, to see the patient and his subjectivity as fundamentally sociogenic.) Chip follows what his body tells him to do, as does, in his own way, John. The smaller-scale healing address of sexualizing a sexual trauma for Chip in a "real-life" story models, in the wider scope of imagining a fictional pornotopia, a more universal—and perhaps more complex—address to working *with*, if not precisely *through*, history.

John's sexual practices, Delany's representations of his sexual proclivity and compulsion, might be said aggressively to eroticize racial difference, racialized roles: this is of course a refusal of the usual liberal humanist position, which—being mostly shell-mouthed on the question of sex and eroticism, anyway—habitually and insistently disavows the salience of racial difference and argues that any recognition of it taints the "purity" of "real love" or "real desire." A corresponding argument comes from the harder left, especially one strain of the feminist left that is (or was once) deeply committed to rooting out the vestiges of domination in sexual practices and sexualized interactions. Delany's characters render hyperbolic racialized roles and emphasize domination; and in doing so they insist on the relation of white-top/black-bottom BDSM play to the history of conquest, subjugation, and violence that instantiated the roles and established the terms and modes of domination. The process here is one of *sublation*, that sweet dream of philosophy—a fitting concept and practice for a literary character who studies philosophy—of historical, political, bodily defeat: the simultaneous, dialectical, and progressive destruction *and* preservation of that history.

Black Power

The domination, and the violent history that undergirds and makes possible domination, does not emerge only in the realm of the verbal or purely as the pleasures of arousal and orgasm. There is an act of sexual violence in the text—an incident when John Marr does something sexually that he absolutely does not wish to do, and does not enjoy. This is when Mad

Man Mike, Leaky's guide in the world of slave collars and slave sales, an elusive man who is almost a cult leader of many of the sexually prodigious homeless men that John encounters, is finally found.

Mad Man Mike—who, not incidentally, is black—is the missing puzzle piece in the mystery of Timothy Hasler's violent death. He did not commit the murder, but Hasler became enamored of Mad Man Mike as John has become enamored of Leaky. In an extended sexual session intended to "turn out" Hasler—to initiate him into the group and to welcome him into the place of belonging that John begins to experience with Leaky— Mad Man Mike and his crew defile Hasler's apartment with shit and piss, and later, when Hasler is killed in connection with a dispute at a hustler bar, Mad Man Mike returns to the apartment and, in a grieving rage, completes its destruction. In essence this defilement and destruction repeats in John Marr's life; John is turned out in an extensive party that includes Crazy Joey, and subsequently, through yet another series of mishaps and a dispute at that same dangerous and ever-contentious hustler bar, Crazy Joey is murdered. After Crazy Joey's death, Mad Man Mike returns to John's already befouled apartment and throws down all the bookshelves before raping John.

"He raped me before he left," John narrates. "In the mouth . . . There's no point in my describing it with any detail that might suggest even the vaguest eroticization; because there was nothing vaguely sexual in it—not for me. . . . (It really *was* a rape!) But I hold nothing against him for it. Because I also knew that if he ever returned to me in the same state, I'd service him again. (Or let him service himself on me—and I'm only lucky that he did it orally and not anally. Because I would have let *that* happen too. And that's madness.)"[54]

In this scene the relation between racialization and humiliation, between blackness and abjection, and our quest for *power* in this set of relations where we should not expect to find it reveal themselves in the mode most similar to the Paul D scene: utterly without pleasure. But not without a will, a desire, to *give* or *give up*—to become, at least in the conventional sense of the word, abject—if what is gifted or surrendered is John's own body for the use of someone else (which of course is a way of describing enslavement), or if what is gifted or surrendered is, in some way, the self itself—certainly the self that presents itself in the form of the defended ego and the masculine. The transformations of the "burning past" achieved in the realm of the erotic and of pleasure here threaten to presage physical destruction and to consume the self completely, to transform without sublation but through destruction. John knows that this particular trajectory downward into the abject is "madness," but this knowledge does not bar his willingness to experience it and to risk enduring or failing to endure it. The domination is not a game, not role play; it is no longer the domain of language but of physical hurt and psychic violation—"certainly his act was entirely beyond my own moral boundaries and even any sense of my own safety," John says.[55] It is, like Chip's experience, "just painful, just ugly"[56]—but for Mad Man Mike's sake John would allow it again, if it "meant, for him, even the slightest inward relief."[57]

That this rape occurs at the hands of a black man could possibly be read to cushion the blow for the reader of John's willingness to surrender to the risk of his (masculine/ego) destruction. But it does not do so in any sustained way. Mad Man Mike's racial position is slightly ambiguous—he is, curiously, blond—the acts he engages in with John only distinguishable from those engaged with Leaky and Crazy Joey and others by the intensity of the violence; and Mike's own play with verbal abuse, like Big Nigg's and Blacky's in Leaky's stories, makes gleeful use of the n-word, too. After the rape, John actually seeks out Mad Man Mike, and he desires, though ambivalently, to give him a blowjob. This second oral scene with the Mad Man indicates the powerful insistence of John's craving for abjection. The penetration of Marr's throat on this second occasion draws blood and leaves his shoulders and arms bruised: these are essentially the same physical effects of the rape. Thus, the rape is only a rape because of Mad Man Mike's emotionally needy intention to hurt Marr as an expression of his rage, a rage that seems partly to be intended to punish Marr for the relative privilege he enjoys in having an apartment and books while Mike (like the deceased Crazy Joey) is homeless. But the effect is that this sole act of sexual violence is not really cordoned off from the other sexual acts in the novel, and the fact that a black male character is its perpetrator suggests rather that, as Kobena Mercer argues, the violence of enslavement and racist domination has "no necessary belonging" in our cultures, which are pervasively the inheritors of its legacies.[58]

When John experiences the profound peace that surprises him in his relationship with Leaky, he observes that "[t]he fantasies of it may be drenched in shame, but the act culminates in the knowledge no one has been harmed, no one has been wounded, no one has been wronged."[59] But in fact the subsequent rape by Mad Man Mike suggests that harm and wounds to the body and to the psyche are not far removed from the pleasurable acts that fulfill John's fantasies: that what shapes the fantasies—which is in part and centrally the history of enslavement, and racialization through and as humiliation, which *is* (but not en toto, not *only*) harm and wound—lies very close, even dangerously close, separated by gossamer, from the more empowering, fulfilling sublation of that historical material in contemporary, conscious reworking.

"[A] nigger pissin' on a nigger. A fuckin' revolutionary act!" Mike cries out when he urinates on and in John.[60] This is Delany's comic and provocative revision of the 1980s slogan that "black men loving black men is a revolutionary act," a political formulation associated with *In the Life* editor Joseph Beam and documentarian Marlon Riggs that both settled black gay identity politics firmly within the rhetorical and conceptual traditions established by the Black Power and Civil Rights Movements and, as the motto was often interpreted, cast a deeply skeptical eye on black-white sexual and romantic relationships. As Delany's depiction of John's sexual interests departs radically from the Beam/Riggs vision of the confluence between liberation politics, romance, and sexuality, so does he, in Mad Man Mike's mischievous sloganeering and in John's willingness not only to play the abject but to risk *being* it, suggest an altogether different form of politics and social bonding: a politics that does not organize itself around a stance of defense or aggression, a politics that assimilates to itself racial identities and the history that makes them, knowing and naming the injustice of those identities and histories but choosing not to battle against them but rather to let them, as it were, flow through the self—even overwhelm the self—and yet become transformed. And perhaps it would be useful for us to imagine that transformation occurring within, or being enabled to transform by the very amorphous form of, the swirling cauldron of what Merleau-Ponty describes as "that gap which we ourselves are."[61] It is thus a position that takes on board race without having at the same time to take up its fellow traveler, so often mistaken for the thing itself, ego.

Is it possible to have race without ego, without defensive postures, without boundaries to police and ramparts on which to stand watch? The character of John Marr tries to model for us this position: Delany imagines him living his black body in its collective, sociogenic dimension, in which the demand to self-protection of that seductive individual *I* is refused in favor of one's becoming immersed in, lost in what it is to *be* the race, precisely as to be black means to have-been-blackened, to have been rendered abject.

Whereas Fanon laments in *Black Skin, White Masks* that the cry of "Look, a Negro!" makes him (in his rhetorical guise as Black Everyman) "responsible at the same time for my body, for my race, for my ancestors" and that he finds himself "battered down by tom-toms, cannibalism, intellectual deficiency, fetishism, racial defects, slave-ships,"[62] John, by almost greedily and with the fierceness of erotic hunger imbibing these associations as language, as insults and verbal abuse, and crucially, doing so in conjunction with sexual acts, transforms the meaning of this "responsibility" and is not battered down but transported to the experience of "feeling good," of being or meeting whatever God actually is or is a metaphor for. This is his *black* power, a power of blackness-in/as-abjection which John utilizes. This abjection is not only abjection, but abjection always appended to, the obverse of, and at the same time coextensive with pleasure and, through pleasure, power—a relation of contradictory elements already modeled for us in Fanon's relation of death to life and action to injury in his native's tensed muscles, in Sartre's discovery of freedom (choice) in imprisonment (limitation), and Merleau-Ponty's vision of the self in the gap of nothingness.[63]

And is this not, finally, a sister iteration to the seemingly pitiless advice Baby Suggs gives to Sethe and to her granddaughter Denver in *Beloved*? "'Lay down your sword. This ain't a battle; it's a rout.' Remembering those conversations and her grandmother's last and final words, Denver stood on the porch in the sun and couldn't leave it." Baby Suggs laughs at Denver's fear, and then lists only a few of the many losses and pains she and Sethe have had to endure. "But you said there was no defense," Denver says. "There ain't," Suggs answers. "Then what do I do?" Denver asks. "Know it, and go on out the yard. Go on."[64]

What emerges, then, from such a process for John Marr is an experience of identity that feels *new* because it is, at any given moment, an identity without the customary defenses against history, a way of living a black body without patrolling and ever mending the brittle edges of its ego: in the midst of his newfound connection to Leaky, and having found his "right and proper place" taking a hillbilly's piss, being called a nigger, and calling the hillbilly a dummy, John, not unlike Denver but for almost the opposite reason, finds himself reluctant to venture out of his apartment barefoot. "I felt like I didn't want to be seen. . . . I thought: Is all this good for you? It leaves you kind of raw and unshielded to the world— so that it's more comfortable thinking of yourself as a 'you' than an 'I.'"[65] The identity that is unshielded, that is a you, the object of a relation more so than its subject—or a subjectivity that stands, wobbling, in its object-status—is what John acquires through his apocalypse, the unveiling of histories of sexualized domination and defilement and his inheritance of them, through his surrender to the monstrous antidivinity of desire, the no-place he travels to through the muck of racialized abjection. The "madness" of John's willingness to self-abnegate is, of course, linked to the madness Mad Man Mike already occupies and lives, as a homeless uneducated black bisexual man on the margins of margins; it is the madness of living, of being that consciousness existing a black(ened) body, what Morrison calls "the desolated center where the self that was no self made its home"[66]—and perhaps also, what Fanon refers obliquely to as that "zone of nonbeing," that "utterly naked declivity where an authentic upheaval can be born."[67]

Mad Man Mike's grief and rage that expresses itself in rape reminds us that extant social and political conditions render as punishable offenses the decision to take the position of abjection-embracing or abject-performing madness and to practice its politics. Mike is a shadowy figure even in the world of *The Mad Man*, and though as the title suggests, what he represents is at the heart of its fictional universe, structuring that world, whether as boundary or as a core truth, Delany does not allow us to imagine that Mike's madness is acknowledged or embraced, except by initiates. John, however, models the integration of this black-and-abject self in the world that would reject or punish it. His experience of desire satisfied and of fulfillment is initially evanescent and momentary, but once Leaky, the partner to deliver the transformative, apocalyptic abuse, becomes permanent, becomes institutionalized, as it were, in John's life, John moves into something like happiness. This happiness we might define, à la Herbert Marcuse, as the refusal of the multiple repressions and renunciations enforced as a matter of political history by the ruling or hegemonic powers and then regularly introjected into the psyche and reinforced by a variety of cultural pressures. Marcuse's broad concept of the erotic as that creative energy that extends well beyond sexual or genital experience clearly finds its place here in *The Mad Man*, in that John's progressively more extensive repetition of the sexual scene he enjoys corresponds to prolific cultural and intellectual production: suddenly he publishes numerous essays, edits collections, completes (in the margin of the action of the text) his first academic book and is well on his way to a second. He becomes the ideal academic critic (not unlike Delany himself, who has been startlingly prolific in his production as a writer).

John's integration of pornotopic world with academic world— as well as the novel's melding of the two genres—points to the political import of

Delany's public enunciation of this kind of erotic fantasy: it is not so much that the fantasies here are necessarily transgressive but that they insist on highlighting, eroticizing, working with the political histories and positions that give rise to sexual and racial identities (and potentially gender identities). They do the strange and, from the viewpoint of our standard understandings of power and weakness, perpetrator and victim, perhaps almost *unrecognizable* work combining, collapsing, conflating in some jarring or beautiful or shocking way things and ideas that were heretofore not placed in contiguity or not placed in contiguity in that precise way—which, of course, is the work of metaphor and the work of a literary imagination. In Delany we find an almost unrecognizable conjunction between "dominated" and "powerful," "humiliated" and "exuberant." We also find a different way of thinking of something we imagine ourselves to understand fully: the conjunction of "racialized" and "powerful," "black" and "powerful" that we know as "black power"—for here we have a black power that is queer, powerful because it is queer, queer precisely because it insists on a confrontation with, a use of—a confrontation and use partly formulated as a surrender to—power.

A Politics of the Bottom

Delany gives us a disquisition on the use of curse words and insults in sexual contexts in *Neveryóna*, a novel from his Nevèrÿon fantasy series, which I will quote at length. In this conversation, Gorgik, a former slave who has become known as the Liberator because of his efforts to free slaves throughout the empire that gives the series its name, talks with Pryn, a young woman whom he befriends. Gorgik queries Pryn whether she has ever heard the inventive and vigorous curses of camel drivers. Pryn, aware of the camel drivers' foul-mouthed reputation, nods. Then Gorgik asks,

> "Are you too young to have heard . . . that some of these same men, alone in their tents at night with their women, may implore, plead, beg their mistresses to whisper these same phrases to them, or plead to be allowed to whisper them back, phrases which now, instead of conveying ire and frustration, transport them, and sometimes the women, too, to heights of pleasure?"
> . . . [Gorgik continues:] "Now there are some, who . . . say that to use terms of anger and rage in the throes of desire indicates some great

malaise, not only of camel drivers but of the whole world; that desire itself must be a form of anger and is thus invalid as an adjunct of love—"

"*I* would say," Pryn said, who after all had heard her share of camel drivers . . . , "the sickness is using terms of desire in the throes of anger and rage. Most curses are just words for women's genitals, men's excreta. . . ."

[Gorgik responds:] ". . . But both arguments are very much the same form. Both assume that signs thought about in one way and felt to mean one thing mean other feelings that are not felt and other thoughts that are not in the mind. Since the true meanings in both arguments are absent from the intentions of the man or woman speaking, one finally ends with a world in which neither love nor anger can really be condoned, since neither is ever pure. The inappropriate signs do not enrich the reading; they pollute it. . . . But there's another way to read."

. . . [Gorgik continues:] "Enriched pleasure is still pleasure. Enriched anger is still anger."[68]

The nature of the enriched pleasure that the character John Marr feels hearing the word "nigger" is, I hope, fairly clear. How, though, might we think of the possibilities of Delany-style enrichment for the reader in his or her response to John's pleasure and to the simple use of the word in sexual contexts? What is the effect of *The Mad Man*'s public, pornographic use of "nigger"? Or, to put it differently, how do we read these n-words in a text meant, among its various aims, to arouse us sexually, to make us jack off? My sense is that we can answer these questions by locating within the possible reader responses aspects of those same powers and abilities we find in examining Fanon's figurative uses of muscle tension and in James Weldon Johnson's Ex-Coloured Man, Toni Morrison's Paul D, and Amiri Baraka's various fictive selves.

The proliferation of "nigger" in *The Mad Man* achieves an astonishing density, which I have tried to reproduce some sense of here through extensive quotation. This density has (perhaps) surprising effects: "nigger" is the refrain, the rhetorical intensifier and punctuating epithet of so many sexual encounters of John Marr's that it has an alternately, indeed rhythmically, *de*sensitizing (we read the word and "hear" it in our heads so much that it ceases to jolt) and *re*sensitizing effect (as "nigger" gets enunciated in contexts of increasingly inventive play with the various excretions of the human body). But it functions more subtly as well: just as it is an incitement or punctuation for ever more heightened and frenzied experiences of pleasure for John, the reader, too, begins to experience the repetition of this locution with a bodily response, a regulation of physical tension that rises and falls with reading. The discomfort and resistance the word generates as it appears in a particular scene, the painful history it summons to the scene of erotic fantasy and possible sexual pleasure, becomes a source of tension that demands release. This craving for psychic release from that discomfort is complicated by the tremors of sexual arousal—a building tension of another sort—that from time to time can make themselves known in the reader. And whereas the climax of such a scene, literally its ending, in representations of happiness and relief (just as happiness describes the ending of the novel as a whole), provides a narrative pleasure (or just relief) for us as we read, the tension and the fleeting or sustained moments of arousal also present themselves as something to be read. This tension and arousal is the body responding to some collusion in the amalgam of conscious and unconscious historical elements that compose the psyche, the body perhaps *knowing* something about "appalling connections" the conscious mind refuses—in the way that Delany suggests when his narrator Chip says, "when my body told me what I was about to do."

Arousal can proceed from discomfort, if by arousal in this sense we mean stimulation, excitation, the marshaling of bodily stress responses in reaction to stimuli. This form of arousal-through/as-discomfort, brought on by reading about sex acts that may themselves stimulate arousal which we might more readily identify as sexual desire or as erotic frisson, (1) simply foregrounds the ways in which what we do call sexual arousal is always already partly indistinguishable from what we also call stress and (2) provides an opportunity for one form to transmogrify into the other, for our stress and tension related to the use of "nigger" to take on an erotic frisson or become sexually arousing as it is for John, and for our sexual arousal to be defined by, or saturated with, the tense discomforts arising from the inescapable political and historical material that the n-word brings to the scene.

Regarding arousal and stress we can look to Marcuse redacting Freud to limn the relation between Eros and Thanatos, where we find, as Marcuse says, "the erotic component in the death instinct and the fatal component in the sex instinct." For Marcuse, the erotic, that is, the life instinct, and the death instinct (it is important to note that for Marcuse as for Fanon, instinct is mutable rather than essential, because it is an artifact of historical development) demonstrate their mutual interpenetration in that both fundamentally tend toward an aim for *relief*; this relief, moreover, is something that we can read becoming refracted in the political and social realms as an aim toward freedom. This is clear in what Freud discusses as "perversions," which Marcuse defines as those expressions of sexuality or Eros that cannot be assimilated into the project of organization, rationalization, and domination that is "civilization" (or hierarchically organized society) itself; the perversions are expressly nonprocreative forms of sexuality, in which pleasure is the end rather than a means tending toward a use (the production of more workers). Marcuse describes the death instinct as the instinct to return to the placid, untroubled nirvana of the womb; it is the instinct to release all tension—and thus to be *free*. "The death instinct is destructiveness not for its own sake, but for the relief of tension. The descent toward death is an unconscious flight from pain and want," he argues. The death instinct, in a way disjunct in trajectory but conjunct in foundation with the life instinct, is therefore a psychic expression of "the eternal struggle against suffering and repression."[69] It is then in the so-called perversions that the conjunction in aim toward relief (which, again, is also freedom, and precisely in a political sense) and the disjunction in method (cessation of life vs. sexual practice) are apparent.

We have seen these death/life combinations in Fanon's many references to the black's and the native's muscular rigidity—and in Fanon, too, the action that propels the black or native out of his tension toward release is either short-term relief or, if it is to achieve its true aim in Fanon's view, long-term reconstitution of political life (which is to say, revolution). It seems reasonable to imagine as similar, and as an example of what Fanon and Marcuse both describe, the partly conflictual, partly harmonious relation between tension and erotic or sexual arousal that *The Mad Man* may produce for its readers, that text's ability to immerse us in the psychic and physical processes that hold simultaneously and in the same space (the body/mind which is the self) tension and release, rigidity and action, the craving for life and the longing for death—and perhaps, too, disgust (rejection of sexuality) and lust—as these putative opposites virally rewrite the content and expression of each other. The effect in *The Mad Man* is to call up and coagulate racism and sexual arousal, rape trauma and sexual excitement, racism and sexual arousal or sexual or sexualized "degradation"—which is, more broadly, both to theorize and to enact the mutually constituting relations between the definition and content of race and the definition and content of sexuality.

It is possible to turn this coagulum to view another of its faces or another set of connections fundamentally related to the foregoing discussion.

Marcuse points out that the perversions are linked to *fantasy* (which for Marcuse is principally that component of the conscious/unconscious not subordinated to the reality principle, and which is attached to the pleasure principle alone). He writes, "the perversions show a deep affinity to phantasy," and "[p]hantasy not only plays a constitutive role in the perverse manifestations of sexuality; as artistic imagination, it also links the perversions with the images of integral freedom and gratification."[70] Thus, for Marcuse the imagination of freedom finds its home and partial satisfaction in fantasy and in the nonnormative, nonprocreative sexual practices that are linked to these fantasies. This is in part the ground on which sexual liberation and political liberation are linked, a connection for which Marcuse is famous (and infamous) for asserting.

What is important to note for purposes of this discussion, however, is the illumination Marcuse provides here for thinking about the implications of Fanon's arguments, and vice versa: since, as Fanon asserts, blackness is positioned in Western culture as one of the primary signs of perversion, of nonnormative sexuality, blackness itself might already be said to be a vehicle ready-made for *imagining freedom*. This is particularly true insofar as Fanon is correct, and blackness, rather than being a material truth, is a *psychical reality* produced by historical and material events—which is to say, it is, in the fundamental sense that Freud uses the term, very much like fantasy.[71] Fantasy's connection to perversion and perversion's connection to the foundational instinct for freedom in both life and death instincts, blackness's connection to perversion and its nature as psychical (and thus political) rather than material reality—these connecting bridges and overlapping territories seem to correspond with the blueprint of Delany's project in this pornographic novel: which is to run the labyrinth-tracing thread between blackness, perversion, and (the will to, the imagination of) freedom, all through the arena of abjection, as abjection participates in and informs each, wherein we can discern blackness-as/through-abjection *and* blackness-as-power.

That there is a power or ability in this experience of body-mind tension and arousal is indicated, too, in the way that the psychic and physical tension and drive for relief that the text prods us toward potentially enables a working with temporality, with the problem of history, for us as readers as for John as character. The word *nigger* in the novel achieves a kind of temporal dispersal, or a collapsing of linear temporality. For us even more than for John, it calls up the history of domination and racialization in sexualized terms, in bringing that history to bear as part of the sex act (for the characters) and as part of arousal (for the reader). Its density in the novel provides a textual analogue—and perhaps even access to—the potentially self-dispersing experience of sex itself which Bersani describes. So many "niggers" thrust us so out of expectations or requirements for reading porn, as sex thrusts us to the edge of the membrane of our skins, and *out* of self as well as *in* the body. The reporting and building of arousal around the word *nigger* unsettles current reader expectation even of sexual fantasy in such a way as not only to deliver abjection as sexual arousal but, in a manner available to intellect but more viscerally "known," à la Merleau-Ponty, in that arena in which the body grants significance a value that intellectualism withholds from it, to give us also that history of our ancestors that is our legacy, to put us *in it*, in the part of blackness that is, as Reid-Pharr warns, always niggerness.

But this blackness-niggerness is not quite a shackle or a binding; the way that it operates to bring the past into the present for us does not determine for us that the historical events will play out as they did in the past. Rather, it is as though blackness-as-niggerness, at least as something encountered in reading for sexual pleasure, were a flat plain we could move across and settle in (or, as it were, project or explode across) at will—which is to say, we are given a *perspective* not unlike that of the three-dimensional person in a two-dimensional world, as though the terrain of linear temporality, with its high mountains barring us from the future and its irretrievable lost continents beyond the sundering seas of the past, had become a flat, open *traversable* plain. This plain is not homogeneous; it has none of the false emptiness of that triumphal temporality that relies on historical violence but suppresses the recognition of this violence, which Benjamin identifies in its perniciousness—rather, not unlike the Benjaminian Jetztzeit, it exposes and names the traumatic cuts of the past in the present and, working in the medium of physical and psychical which constitutes sexuality, takes the past down a different path and to a different end.

I think here of Hortense Spillers's analysis of Ishmael Reed's satirical and comic rewritings of *Uncle Tom's Cabin* and the universe of tropes one enters through the maw of that text's black hole. Reed, she says, produces an "eternal present" in which "the past is subject to change": "Reed's stunning anachronisms resituate variously precise portions of cultural content so that we gain a different cartography of historicized fiction. These radical displacements sever *event* from a desiccated spatial focus so that it comes to belong once again to the realm of *possibility*, the possibility of *movement*."[72]

The tensions and pleasures of reading Delany's *The Mad Man,* and the tensions and pleasures of John the character, are not necessarily touted as *healing* or as politically *effective* (though this pleasure and tension clearly is shot through with the political, the realm of history from which the players derive the roles that give them pleasure). Nevertheless it is clear that the *claim* to pleasure in such a context itself carries an identifiably political weight—if not as strategy, then as philosophy, for it explodes our notion of the political in the sexual, the sexual in the political. The position here is different from Bersani's proposal of a radical gay male politics, which lauds gay male sexuality's potential to discard the self and to refuse the privileges of masculine identification. First, Delany's characters indulge, stroke, luxuriate in those parts of the self (or those masks of the self that are the self) that no political program will embrace (or, mostly, even acknowledge, except as the sign of counterrevolutionary backsliding or self-hatred, etc.). Second, whereas Bersani upends and undoes masculinity, here masculine identification is never fully discarded, though it is given a thrashing in the shit-strewn and urine-soaked spaces of abjection. Masculinity remains as a role—a role that is *used* by another role player not identifying with, or indifferent to, his own masculinity. This is a politics of the bottom, a desire to (a will to) love and live the bottom for its bottomness without surrendering to or ceding the lion's share of the pleasure or power to the top—indeed, in a way flamboyantly, exuberantly *ignoring* the top except insofar as he dutifully presses on the levers of pleasure. In this sense, while Delany's pornotopia in *The Mad Man* is an all-male club, the politics of the bottom that it begins to describe is genuinely queer—since the bottom can be occupied by man or woman, though the specificities of that occupation and the histories they invoke will differ, as they do when we consider persons of different races occupying top or bottom.

It is possible, of course, to circumscribe Delany's bottom politics under the rubric of BDSM—and thus butt against the limitations of that practice. Savran notes, "The laws of (S/M) desire ensure that one will always . . . both identify with and desire one's oppressor."[73] But again, Delany's fiction takes on BDSM tropes and themes but transforms them. The scenarios of the intertexts—*The Mad Man,* the Nevèrÿon series, and *Citre et Trans*—all suggest a process of relationality that "identification with the oppressor" inadequately describes. They suggest specifically a use of that oppressor as a (usually foul-mouthed) *him,* as an object of desire. Of course, desire combines and confuses impulses to appropriate and identify, but these representations or reproductions of desire in a literary frame already hold a distance between the object and one desiring (that is, it is not *sexual* desire itself but the incomplete satisfaction of that desire that writing, especially writing porn, is): one responds to the desire experienced by writing about it, in part to satisfy the desire by, in a sense, controlling it as one does in fantasy, but since the conventions of language always write us as we manipulate them, such control fails, so that the desire becomes ever more elaborated, it proliferates, and its relation to an object and to identifications that could maintain the clarity of oppressed and oppressor become ever more attenuated. Most important, insofar as an identification with the oppressor is part of what is operating, such identifications seem, within the realm that Delany has created, a universal condition, in that, in a sense, everyone has an oppressor both external and internalized. Delany suggests that this is an inescapable aspect of existing in a social world: we are always in some way objects of interpellation in claiming subjectivity or agency. This complicates or gives us another window on claims such as Bersani's, that it is a *danger* or *risk* that gay men become gay men by identifying with their oppressors: Delany seems to say, who doesn't? Is not the process of identification always just such a process of forced reception of authority? And moreover, it is precisely as *object* of interpellation that insults such as "nigger" taken on as sexual incitement function; that these are sexually exciting suggests the way they have been internalized, but that they constantly underline the receiver of the insult as object, as receiver, brings attention to the process of interpellation, of power-making-its-object, a recognition it helps fix on some layer of consciousness by repetition—especially, it seems to me, for readers. The naming of interpellation, calling it out, that this repetition effects, makes it, like "nigger" itself, amenable to various uses and transformations.

Conclusion

Extravagant Abjection

ALL OF WHICH is to say: power works abusively, but not only in the ways that we might expect. That the abusiveness of power should be generative, just as the constraints and repressions of power are, is no surprise; but *what* exactly is generated *in* abuse *for* the abused is harder to limn. To perform that illumination we struggle to bring within the ambit of language an experience, a state of human being, that—at least for the moment—is so unable to hold the defenses which constitute the subject who speaks that language in its essence seems an expression of that state and experience's opposite: language seems to erase that state; it seems, like the Lacanian Real in relation to the Symbolic, at once to create it as an excess and remainder and yet to extirpate it as an enunciable possibility. This is the space, the place, and the being of the abject: a subjectivity that does not or cannot claim its subjecthood (much less its agency), an "I" without clear demarcation or referent, that does not or cannot speak *as* "I" except, perhaps, after the fact. Blackness, in one of its modes—and, following Fanon's formulations, *the* very mode through which blackness comes into being in the world—takes us to and describes that abjection, at least in our deliriously racialized reality. Clearly the long history of African peoples since the rupturing advent of diasporic slavery indicates that there are many modes of blackness, in everyday cultural practices, in demands voiced in the recognized sphere of the political, in community creation, in a dizzying array of artistic endeavor, which do *not* describe abjection and, far from taking us there, strive, often successfully, to rocket far beyond it. But the project here has to been to investigate blackness in what we could think of as a fundamental or ontological or existential mode—the mode of abjection—and to map the beginnings of pathways outward from it which tend toward the cultural, political, social, and artistic, even if the meanings we attribute to those vast spheres must be "slightly stretched" when they are approached by that peculiarly objectlike (it is easier, as

John Marr says, to think of it as "you" than as "I"), and frequently spectacular, abject black subject.

In the most basic sense, *Extravagant Abjection* draws on three now-familiar tenets of "identity" analysis: blackness is a construction, not an essence, which serves to shore up white identity and superiority; categories of race are intimately connected to categories of gender and sexuality; philosophy needs literature to embody, and thereby better envision, its concepts. In *Extravagant Abjection*, I have tried to bring the *power* that is a product and substance of powerlessness and defeat within the ambit of description by addressing these tenets in the following ways: (1) I have read Fanon's account of blackness as a being-*blackened*, a process that substantially affects fundamental categories of subjectivity (consciousness, temporality, body-imago). From this standpoint I have elaborated concepts in Fanon that are undertheorized even by him—principally the psychic lineaments and physical manifestation of historically located and culturally perpetuated defeat, especially as these concepts define what it is to *exist* a black consciousness (and a black-ened body) in Western societies. These concepts I have demonstrated to be referenced in Fanon via a recurring metaphor in his work, the black's or native's tensed muscles. (2) I have enlisted scenes and figures in the work of canonical African American literary authors that investigate what has not yet been adequately theorized in African Americanist criticism as exemplifying responses to white supremacist domination—racialization through sexual humiliation; male rape—in part because these scenes and figures generally appear to offer little beyond the representation of racism's most destructive effects. In contrast to this neglect, while I am not claiming to provide anything like a survey of 20th-century literary treatments of blackness-in/as-abjection, I have selected texts that stage a kind of progressive relay of scenes of increasingly sexualized abjection, which offer their increasingly intensified incoherences as capabilities. And (3) I have attempted throughout my analysis to enact the need for a *literary* imagination to render the black power that I discern in blackness in the mode of abjection, because the literary's primary reliance on slippage and evocation of excess, and jarring combinations of contradictory elements which are inherent to metaphorical representation and theorizing-in-metaphor, both enacts what blackness *is* as a cultural figure and at least points toward the existential elements of abjection that language otherwise effaces.

Each point of address depends on *Extravagant Abjection's* alignment with the subordinated term of each tenet (black, gay, literary). For me, the combination results in, and necessitates, a black power that theorizes *from*, not against, the special intimacy of blackness with abjection, humiliation, defeat. Affirming this form of black power keeps its subjects from being (re)subjectified to an identity politics that, in its penchant for strong ego formations, ultimately serves white, masculinist, retrogressive nationalist and heteronormative regimes. In this sense, *Extravagant Abjection* tries to recover the revolutionary promise of 1960s Fanonian theoretical formulations and the Black Power and Black Arts Movements' appropriations of those formulations by aligning itself psychically, not just politically, with the experience of being on the bottom of every psychosocial hierarchy. I am positing a counterintuitive black power—counterintuitive as that phrase was understood and taken up by Black Power/Black Arts advocates and counterintuitive, too, in dominant readings of Fanon: a way of having, doing, and being blackness, with its myriad possibilities of political organization and for social romance—though, again, the focus here has been on *beginning* to move toward those—without necessarily having also to have a racial ego.

The principal elements of this race-without-ego, this (black) power, are the following: access to *anonymous existence*, to indeterminacy and a kind of freedom in the form of anguish and vertigo, as Sartre and Merleau-Ponty define these terms; experiences of temporality as interarticulated, counterlinear rather than linear, which, by the light of Marcuse, we can understand as key to conceptualizing freedom from the constraints we accept due to the loss inherent to the perception of linear time; access to constituents and forms of gender and sexuality which are nonnormative and *queer*, and thus access to the resources available for sociogenic "stretching" of the normative forms; and, in part because the foregoing elements are often best described and most clearly experienced as components of experience or of existence highlighted by embodiment, that is, they inhere in the nexus of body and mind rather than solely as creations of consciousness and discourse—and in larger part due to the obsessive sexualization of black bodies in the cultures that make blackness legible— the power of blackness-in/as-abjection also lies in its providing ways to confront the problem of history by transforming that history and that problem into the basis for pornotopias, such that the eroticizing of *every-thing* in our worlds, but most especially its ugly history of the production of races, becomes a useful practice.

.   .   .

In a project heavy on close reading of literary scenes, I admittedly risk capsizing the boat by concluding with more. But by way of illustration of these points I want to look quickly—call it an only-so-close reading—at a scene from Gayl Jones's provocative novel about the persistence of slavery in the present, *Corregidora* (1975), and at a brief, arguably literary formulation in the preface to the 2004 edition of President Barack Obama's certainly literary memoir, *Dreams from My Father* (1995).

Whereas *Beloved* has been the ur-text and beginning of this inquiry, I would like to use the following passage from *Corregidora*—a novel published under Morrison's editorship—as an extended coda. The speaker in the following scene is known as Great Gram and at other times as "the coffee-bean woman," a name used by both her owner and her descendants, signifying her skin color for both, and her status as a piece of property for the former. She was a slave in Brazil, and her master, Corregidora, used her as both prostitute and favored mistress. Having eventually relocated to the United States after Brazilian slavery was abolished in 1888, in this scene, taking place sometime in the early decades of the 20th century, Great Gram recalls one of the many crimes committed against her body and her psyche. Corregidora, she is explaining, was especially vigilant against his coffee-bean woman forming romantic or sexual liaisons with any men other than Europeans:

> [Corregidora] wouldn't let me see him [a young, black, male fellow slave], cause he said he was too black for me. He liked his womens black, but he didn't wont us with no black mens.... I was only talking to him [the black fellow slave] once, all Corregidora did was seen us talking, and I guess he figure the next step was we be down in the grass or something, I don't know, but they said he did something, and they were goin to beat him real bad. He was young too, young man, so he run away.... I think he woulda run away anyway, cause he had this dream, you know, of running away and joining up with them renegade slaves up in Palmares.... I kept telling him that was way back before his time.... You know, Palmares, where these black mens had started their own town, escaped and banded together. I said the white men had killed all of them off but he wouldn't believe me.... I said he couldn't know where he was going because Palmares was way back two hundred years ago, but he said Palmares was now. But they claimed he did something, and he had to leave before he planned to.... They sent this whole mob of mens out after him.... But it was

only because Corregidora thought he'd been fooling with me when he hadn't, . . . cause all that was uncalled-for. . . . [H]e [the young man] had this dream he told me about. That was all he wanted me for, was to tell me about this dream. He must've trusted me a lot, though, cause I could've been one of them to run back to Corregidora with it. But I wouldn't. It was because he seen us out there talking. I wouldn't even go tell him, cause I would've been seen telling him. And I kept feeling that all that time he was running, he kept thinking I'd told something when I didn't. And then there I was kept crying out, and ole Corregidora thinking it was because he was fucking so good I was crying. "Ain't nobody do it to you like this, is it?" I said, "Naw." I just kept saying Naw, and he just kept squeezing on my ass and fucking. And then somehow it got in my mind that each time he kept going down in me would be that boy's feets running. And then when he come, it mean they caught him. . . .

When they came back, they said they lost the boy at the river. . . . We was all glad. . . . Three days after that somebody seen him floating on the water. What happened was they chased him as far as the river and he just jumped in and got drownded. Cause they didn't know nothing till three days after that he rose.[1]

We are again, as with Sethe and Paul D, not listening to the testimony of a former slave but reading a contemporary writer's imagination of a former slave's voice. Through Jones we imagine a relatively near past as the listening post from which to hear recollected a past far more remote. The *act* being described—a fucking, a brutal, possessive, punishing fuck punctuated by compelled verbal affirmations of the well-settled always-already and yet threatened, ever in need of *proof,* white mastery of black bodies—comes to us with an array of frissons that Delany's evocations of the slave past have made familiar: horror and outrage, tension, as well as voyeuristic attentiveness and titillation. Summoning these sensations (which are also, à la Merleau-Ponty, forms of bodily knowing) to our minds and bodies as we read, the imagination of the sexual act makes almost palpably present the remote past, traverses the breach and rupture between the often untranslatable slave past and the "free" present. This conjuring of time not as a line but as a loop might be a minor effect, except that this effect resonates with the elements of the novel's resolution: there Great Gram's great-granddaughter Ursa, the story's protagonist and heir of the histories of her foremothers' violations, asserts her break from being determined by that "body of history" from which Fanon wishes to shake free, by re-enacting in the present a *sexual* act she imagines Great Gram performed on Corregidora (and this too is an act refusing either end of a continuum between pain and pleasure, erotics and violence, empowerment and domi-nation: it is fellatio with teeth).

But how is anything that Great Gram narrates "powerful"? How might we say it is *black* power? Great Gram's telling of what has happened in the past is an accusation levied against Corregidora and his ill use of her and of the young man; like all of her recollections in the novel, it is "evi-dence" being given for a judgment to be made in the present. It is there-fore the present form of what was suppressed and repressed at the time of the event: Great Gram's yearning for the basic freedom to build intimate connections with whomever she chooses, which, because this freedom is denied her due to her legal and racial status, is also a yearning for po-litical change. The political dimension of what Corregidora's actions are aimed at crushing is symbolized—a space is held for it even in the midst of its punishment and suppression—by evoking Palmares, the great ma-roon community that resisted slavers' attacks for almost the whole of the 17th century in northeast Brazil, and which had become, by Great Gram's time, a legend. This space is held even though she denies the presence of Palmares, tendentiously reading the history as evidence of defeat ("the white men had killed all of them off") and the inevitable failure of re-sistance or escape: for Great Gram, although the story is about the cru-elty visited on her and the young man, and how she was prevented from forming friendships with black men, her repetition of the name and the quilombo's history, and of the young man's insistence that "Palmares was now," maintains within the story the impossible promise of reaching the past as a dim possibility of reaching a place of refuge *now*—and though the young man fails, she herself narrates her story from such a position of (relative) refuge. The tether between the impossible and possible free-doms gets tightened through a kind of physical and psychic nonce-ritual created to meet the extremities of suffering: Great Gram, without solid belief that Palmares exists or that refuge can be found, gives her body over to being forcibly taken so that the young man can escape, partaking in, mentally and verbally underlining the way that she is being harshly fucked by Corregidora. Corregidora is thrusting his body into hers to claim her as his piece of property, while she imagines those thrusts as propelling the young black man's feet. She takes "blows" (unlike in kind but like in sen-sation to those John Marr receives as he fellates Leaky); she receives and participates in an attempt to negate her will and her freedom, and this is not only compensation, a protective mask for her unspoken inner rebellion and outrage, but something she does *in order* to save the young man.

All of this transformation in her consciousness, and her telling, of the words and sensations of her being defeated into the elements of the young man's escape, of course, is magical thinking—the harm Corregidora does to her does not speed the young man on his way. Her imaginary associations incorporate this recognition—"And then when he come, it mean they caught him"—thus building failure into the fantasy of achieving freedom. Her cries of "Naw" have a double, even a triple, meaning: "Naw," no one fucks her as Corregidora does—a recognition of mastery Hegel probably did not imagine but which the reality of chattel slavery would seem to make routine; "Naw," in refusal, rejection of what is being done to her; and perhaps "Naw" as a cry of apparently existential woe, the despair that she will not reach a place other than the abject. Indeed, everywhere we look in Jones's scene there are doubles and triples ghosting the events in the foreground. The report of the young man's death which confirms Great Gram's conviction of the inevitability of defeat is itself undercut— they discover his body in the river "three days after . . . when he rose," a reference that in the telling, in the use which Great Gram makes of the history of her own suffering and his, seems to complete the magical nature of her ritual by symbolically giving him a resurrection. Her own Christ-like sacrifice, her suffering for the young man's having chosen her for an intimate, as well as for the guilt she worries he wrongly imputes to her for passing information on to Corregidora, redeems the young man; and the fact that this is a figurative, only discursive redemption also resonates with the looming figure of Palmares, which, in the young man's figurative resurrection, he *can* be said to have reached, since both lie beyond the grasp of anything but storytelling, in the symbolic realm that is dead.

We can discern the *blackness* of the *power* to work with symbolization depicted here—indeed to work extravagantly, to build a fretwork of meaning toward which this somewhat fretful reading can only gesture— because the layering of the story, its different and competing registers, is an effect of double-consciousness and double-bodiedness, and one way of describing the very substance of that doubleness. Great Gram frames her story with Corregidora's praise of her beauty and his assertion of her special place (not to be touched by black men); the story also appears to be told as a cautionary tale warning of the perils of associating too closely with black men and aimed at her granddaughter, Ursa's mother, who had recently taken up with Ursa's father, a black man. The tale of Great Gram's abjection and Corregidora's crime is also, then, a justification for colorist pride, a story of self-aggrandizement. She is being sexually humiliated and rendered abject—she is being thrust into the condition of being a black enslaved woman, where racialization, gendering, and enslavement are all occurring in conjunction, as one physicalized event. At the same time she is following the lessons of Corregidora's devaluation of blackness by, in telling the story, expressing pride in the fact that she was not to be touched by black men—thus she casts away and disowns, ab-jects her own blackness. Great Gram dissociates herself from dark-skinned black men even as she affirms her strongly ethical attachment to one whom she also thinks of as representative of the group. Each aspect of the story she tells—being harshly fucked and yet specially desired by Corregidora; being kept from black men and, in fact, never openly admitting to any desire for them but being scrupulous in the maintenance of ethical and supportive relations with the young slave, treating him as confidant and compeer; and magically assisting in the young man's escape—contributes to building an antiblack self-regard and black political solidarity. She crafts one racialized identity with ego—not-dark, or not-black, or desired-by-white-men: the normative ego, the ego that claims just to be ego when it is, really, at least in our world, white—and another seemingly without it—black; and she has, is, and *makes* them both.

In sum, we see operating in this imagined portrait of the abjection of enslaved black people a survival strategy or adaptation: taking the "blows" and making something of them simply to survive; an inchoate, churning, as-yet-unshaped resistance that is characterized by intense, even extravagant meaning-making, by intense symbolization—elements we have seen also in Fanon's muscle tension and in Kristeva's account of the abject. We see, too, elements which should remind us of Bersani's description of the infant's adaptive transformation of pain into pleasure: for in the midst of Great Gram's affirming and denying cries of "Naw" there is another repressed or suppressed possibility, that Corregidora's punishment also provides occasion for a psychic if not a physical pleasure. Ruminating on the lives of her great-grandmother and grandmother, both born slaves, Ursa says, "*Sometimes I wonder about their desire, . . . Grandmama's and Great Gram's. . . . You know how they talk about hate and desire. Two humps on the same camel? . . . Hate and desire both riding them.*"[2] If on one hand Great Gram hammers together an unspoken wish and demand for freedom out of the sensations of sexual assault, on the other she could be making her imagined certainty that the young man will fail and be captured erotic and pleasurable, at least by way of the rising surfeit of tension associated with arousal. Thus, as in Delany's novel, even horrors are part of the topography in pornotopia; because she is routinely hypersexualized, Great Gram can sexualize and eroticize everything in her world.

That this illustration of the *black power* in abjection centers a female character's story, unlike the stories of men under various kinds of sexual and psychic pressure with which this book has been concerned, underlines and extends a point I began to discuss in the introduction. There is not a necessary connection between black masculinity or black maleness and abjection, since it is clear that women can be—and by the normative or traditional definitions of gender, often are or supposed to be—"bottoms," too. Thus, my discussion of the relation between blackness and abjection might have focused largely on scenes of abject black women, or it might have been divided more or less equally between women and men. However, given my alignment (and, I assume, my readers') with feminist politics that combat normative gender and labor to establish a human dignity for women that does not *enforce* or reinforce the definition of the feminine as the abject, I think that focusing on the more counterintuitive association between black maleness and abjection—which is also, as so much of our history indicates, the more fiercely resisted association—is, for this project, more politically useful, or at the very least somewhat less hazardous to our common political struggles. To ferret out and disclose abjection in the case of black maleness reveals the abject which is—of course—part of masculinity per se, but which is rejected (ab-jected) and cast out under the names of femininity and of blackness. To focus on the abject in its relation to black women too easily might appear to be a confirmation of the defeat with which abjection works rather than a complication of it, without the kind of framing which demonstrates the abjection of black men that precedes this reading of *Corregidora*.

I hope that what I have done in the bulk of *Extravagant Abjection*, and my turn here at the last to a female character, will be understood as contributions to the notion that the abject does not inhere in femininity and blackness to the exclusion of its inhering in masculinity and whiteness and any other -ity or -ness we perform and embody. The operation of meaning-making in our discourses and given substance in our practices certainly means that socially subordinated categories such as black and female will more readily reveal their dimensions of psychic abjection: the categories are, after all, *created* precisely for the purpose of bearing and demonstrating that burden so that those not included in them will have the privilege of pretending that their shoulders are free of it. But the dominant observation here is that abjection informs humanness and that, in this light (or, since this truth is so denied and so elusive, in this darkness), the conjunction of a subordinated categorical name, *black*, with a privileged name, *male*, is one of the best ways to show us abjection's pervasive presence all along the continuum of the human world. Such a conjunction's illumination of universal conditions is precisely one of its "powers"—about which I will say more, after a final reading.

.   .   .

What the character of Great Gram and Jones's imagination of her story illustrates for us are the powers of blackness in its abject mode. In making a final plea for the usefulness of *knowing* more than we like to know about blackness in its abjection I want to turn here to the words of someone who must, at least at the moment of this writing, seem to all the world to represent the very opposite of black abjection: Barack Obama.

In the 2004 preface to his 1995 memoir, *Dreams of My Father: A Story of Race and Inheritance*, Obama reflects on the near decade between the editions and remarks on some salient events in the interim, including the 9/11 terrorist attacks on the United States. He offers a brief sketch of how that event highlighted for him the binary cleavage by which so many in the world now understand and articulate themselves—"the underlying struggle . . . between worlds of plenty and worlds of want; between the modern and the ancient"—and also how 9/11 made clear to him again the necessity of exposing the falsity of that cleavage. His memoir, Obama observes, sets forth this same struggle, as well as its apparent resolution, on the smaller stage of his own life. "I know, I have seen," he writes, "the desperation and disorder of the powerless: how it twists the lives of children on the streets of Jakarta or Nairobi in much the same way as it does the lives of children on Chicago's South Side, how narrow the path is for them between humiliation and untrammeled fury, how easily they slip into violence and despair."[3]

It seems to me that this narrow path is another way of speaking of the abjections defined by race, class, and status—these are Sethe's choices, again. Thus, the proximity of humiliation to violence, fury and despair could be mapped this way: the abject is the receiver of humiliation—it is the experience of violence at the core of the self, violence run so rampant that it is, in the moments of its being, what the self is; and violence and fury are that abjection turned outward, visited on others. The terrible ease of the fit, the fit that is almost a lock, between these two halves of a binary, Obama attempts to disassemble in a telling of his life story; and obviously what his example models with dazzling success is a set of possibilities that partake of neither evident option within the deceptively narrow confines of abject realities.

But, acknowledging that Obama's example—of full-throated participation in oppressive political and economic systems that make us who we are in order to change them (or at least benefit from them rather than simply being trodden down by them)—is not an example readily available to all those children he observes, or to us, and leaving aside the sometimes fully appropriate response *of* violence directed outward, which Fanon describes for us so compellingly in *The Wretched of the Earth*—with these provisos, one way we can slip, and one way we have slipped, the lock between the seemingly narrow confines of the abjection Obama describes is by seizing hold of the various components and effects of the psychic and physical violence which constitutes abjection. I have already named these components and effects, as powers, as extravagant rather than impoverished, and as wider in capacity than we might guess: access to the indeterminacies of anonymous existence; perceptions of temporality as interarticulated; access to a wider range of gender and sexuality configuration; the capacity to turn pain into pleasure; and the activation of a pornotopic imaginary. When these are identified, activated, enacted, are "desperation and disorder" accurate descriptions of what results? Do these terms describe what Great Gram comes to?

The recognition of the kinds of resources of which Great Gram makes use opens out a series of questions which current scholarly endeavor (as outlined in this book's introduction)—and, if Obama is any judge, current politics—now struggles with, poised as we are at the seeming exhaustion of radical or liberatory or reformatory politics organized on the slippery ground of identity. How then does, say, a black nationalism that takes account of, and makes a central element of, such resources, such power as I have outlined, operate? We have surveyed possibilities of the individual's relation to, his momentary living out of, the concept of race in its abjection and viewed there a transformation of the notion of black power itself. But what becomes of the concept of nation, which traditionally resists any notion of adulteration,[4] which promotes the fantasy of itself as an extended family, bound to reproductivity, to future, and thus would appear to be antithetical to powers such as these? Is it possible, and productive, to conceive of *nation* in terms that undermine the ways we traditionally understand it, and demand, as it were, a new constitution?

The attempt here has been to suggest, in the manner and along the avenues opened by queer theory, that even if identities by their nature undo themselves, that it is in the processes that effect this undoing (and that—to keep ourselves as firmly as we can within the maelstrom of the paradox—also are vital to constituting, also *do* and make the falsity that is identity), processes which traditions of understanding and working with identity and nation attempt to transcend, that we can find possibilities as yet untapped by our politics. The *practice* of such a politics along these untapped trajectories we have seen clearly in one instance, in the form of literary pornography, and elsewhere only peripherally, since the texts, literary, philosophical, and political, are working with the traditional concepts of nation/identity which, in part because of those very texts, are known to us and appear to have reached their limit. If the form of literary pornography provides an instance of both revealing and making use of these as-yet-unexplored potentialities in identity and nation, then the shape of that politics—in this instance, consciously deployed aspects of blackness-in-and-as-abjection in a white supremacist context—may mean that the powers available here are, in the end—at bottom—powers over *ourselves*, strategic manipulations of *our* self- and race-conceptions. Such a politics does not grasp toward politics' traditional object, which is power over objects (the organization of the social world) and over others conceived as adversaries. The proliferating use of strategies such as those modeled within and by Delany's text, precisely because these strategies are not yet exhausted, promises to move in directions and to shape political practices, and perhaps even political subjects, not imagined in that text or this book.

.   .   .

Sartre notes, "'The terrible thing about Death,' said Malraux, 'is that it transforms life into Destiny.' By this we must understand that death reduces the for-itself-for-others to the state of simple for-others. Today I alone am responsible for the being of dead Pierre, I in my freedom. Those dead who have not been able to be saved and transported to the boundaries of the concrete past of a survivor are not *past*; they along with their pasts are annihilated."[5]

One meaning of this observation that when a person dies his survivors fully assume power over him (by the means of whatever way they maintain the memory of him) is that only ending, only loss, confers meaning: certainly in Sartrean terms, when there is choice, meaning is indeterminate; and when there is a present from which we flee into the future and a past whose possibilities have been taken out of play, meaning cannot be settled. But meaning becomes possible (not inevitable, perhaps—or perhaps so, as a result of the inescapable operations of living consciousnesses) in loss. Here, then, we might conceive of the "power" of a blackness that is conceived in and *lived* as what it loses, has lost, what it suffers: that in this loss and suffering is the opening to *meaning*—the meaning, in fact, of those qualities of which it is putatively (or momentarily) deprived, qualities which we understand to be ideals rather than concrete realities, evanescent moments rather than eternal verities: full humanity, the autonomous and healthy body, citizenship within a socius, the esteem or love of others. It becomes possible to *know* what these things are, by inhabiting the space (the bottom), the experience (in the body) of being violently dispossessed of them; it is a power not to name, necessarily, since this is the province of power—but the power to *know* what the name signifies by living, consciously, the negation that defines the name.[6] In living one's death—or to say it differently, living the apparent loss of what is sure to endow you with the happiness of not suffering what you suffer—you know fully or uniquely what is the meaning of that which you lose. And you know this because it is only in the experience of the opposite of it that its meaning becomes apparent.

According to the phenomenologists, the structure of consciousness is such that it relates to what it knows as object, as not-self; as Marcuse observes, this problem is usually wrestled with in the annals of Western philosophy as a bedeviling frustration: you are always separated from the world, and therein lies the conundrum of it, and therefore from Plato on down you are required to create abstractions and speculative ideals to mirror and render accessible the experience of knowing and being simultaneously. Eastern philosophical currents purport—from the point of view of the West, which is the East's younger imitator—to solve this by a rigorous methodical practice (meditation) of coming into the present moment and experiencing this moment as the all and the everything. Western subjects may become initiated into such teachings but have difficulty reaching such a resolution on their "own" terms. But the invention of blackness, Fanon and my writers suggest, is an instrument permitting those who exist within or as it simultaneously to occupy the body (in physical or psychic suffering and/or loss—in abjection) and to confer meaning on that suffering and loss, almost precisely by the window the loss opens onto what-is-being-lost, the window onto what is being denied it (again, the healthy body, humanity, etc.—Western ideals). It is as if the Eden that St. Augustine and Boethius yearn for cannot be returned to except in the inevitably finite moment, be it fleeting or elongated, of being deprived of it, of being made—in the case of the black(ened) by an act of mass collusion that is represented and lived as "natural" reality: racial delirium—to occupy, by definition, being deprived of it (which is blackness).

Yet this loss is not possible unless the one suffering loss already possesses the lost thing; otherwise what it loses could not be known. This is the paradox within the paradox: the power is to know what is being lost, that which can only be known by losing it (for having it, it has no palpable meaning, or its meaning is insubstantial), but to lose it and know you have lost it is truthfully to recognize that you always had it in the first place—and, by turns, therefore to make it possible to see that you *still* possess "it." This is what Johnson's Ex-Coloured Man cannot bear, what Baraka's characters and essay personas refuse to acknowledge, what Paul D perceives and hides from, what Delany's John Marr transforms into sex play in order to work with and to domesticate.

This power is not to be celebrated, necessarily; but it is available for use. As I hope I have shown, these resources are rich, and not without effective capability; and there may be something to gain from the recognition of them as we try, as ever, to meet the challenge of the defeat already imposed on us (the defeat that *makes* us) by the problem of history.

Notes

Notes to the Introduction

1. Toni Morrison, *Beloved* (New York: Knopf, 1987), 165.

2. See generally Ashraf H. A. Rushdy, *Neo-Slave Narratives: Studies in the Social Logic of a Literary Form* (New York: Oxford U P, 1999), especially chapters 1 and 2.

3. Sharon Patricia Holland, *Raising the Dead: Readings of Death and (Black) Subjectivity* (Durham, NC: Duke U P, 2000), 120.

4. David Halperin provides several both succinct and elaborate descriptions of abjection in its relation to gay male sexuality. See David M. Halperin, *What Do Gay Men Want? An Essay on Sex, Risk, and Subjectivity* (Ann Arbor: U of Michigan P, 2007), 64.

5. Our two projects overlap most clearly in Stockton's explorations of what she refers to as "debasement": "I want to ask of my texts what they imagine debasement produces, at certain moments, for those people who actually undergo it," she writes. "How does debasement foster attractions? . . . What does it offer for projects of sorrow and ways of creative historical knowing?" Kathryn Bond Stockton, *Beautiful Bottom, Beautiful Shame: Where "Black" Meets "Queer"* (Durham, NC: Duke U P, 2006), 24. Though all but the introduction and conclusion of *Extravagant Abjection* were written before I encountered Stockton's book (in 2007), the two sometimes follow similar directions, while emphasizing different stops along the way. For example, my chapter on Baraka's *The System of Dante's Hell* might well be described just as Stockton describes the overall aim of *Beautiful Bottom*, which, in her words, "investigate[s] shame (and shameful states) as an invaluable if also painful form of sociality even when debasement seems lonely and interior" (ibid., 26). At the same time, shame as a complex affect is not what I investigate in Baraka's novel; instead I am interested in the "painful form of sociality" arising from what she calls debasement and what I call abjection that I find there, and this sociality, rather than being a central object of discovery as it is in *Beautiful Bottom*, is of secondary importance in my inquiry, being just one example of the "power" I find in black abjection.

Stockton and I also share an interest in scenes of the sexual humiliation or rape of black men and in a figure, the bottom, which we both find to be a metaphor useful for illuminating the discursive correspondence between descriptions of the penetrable male anus (or, more simply, getting or being "fucked") and

descriptions of black folks' enforced occupation of the lowest rungs of socioeconomic hierarchy. Stockton, however, uses the bottom figure to elaborate—beauti-
fully, as her title suggests—on anality and anal eroticism; *Extravagant Abjection*
does not engage much with anal eroticism, focusing instead on the bottom as a
sexual role.

6. Stockton, *Beautiful Bottom,* 7–8.

7. One example of such an argument is Hazel Carby, *Race Men* (Cambridge,
MA: Harvard U P, 1998).

8. Lewis R. Gordon, T. Denean Sharpley-Whiting, and Renée T. White, "In-
troduction: Five Stages of Fanon Studies," in *Fanon: A Critical Reader,* ed. Lewis
R. Gordon, T. Denean Sharpley-Whiting, and Renée T. White (Cambridge, MA:
Blackwell, 1996), 7, 6, original emphasis.

9. Both the dating and the titles of these works, originally published in Fanon's
native French, are slightly more complicated than the listing I am providing for
purposes of this introduction to the project. I address these matters explicitly in
chapter 1.

10. Lewis R. Gordon and Jane Anna Gordon, *Not Only the Master's Tools: African-American Studies in Theory and Practice* (Boulder, CO: Paradigm, 2006), 41.

11. James Weldon Johnson, *The Autobiography of an Ex-Coloured Man* (1912;
New York: Vintage, 1989), 187–188.

12. Frantz Fanon, "The 'North African Syndrome,'" in *Toward the African
Revolution,* trans. Haakon Chevalier (New York: Grove, 1967), 4.

Notes to Chapter 1

1. It flows easily as well because, as Robert Reid-Pharr puts it, the fact of "our
eager, greedy reception of Fanon" (the implied *we* here comprising African American intellectuals from the mid-Sixties until today) is "a matter almost beyond
comment"—though I hope my own commentary will prove to be other than
redundant. Robert Reid-Pharr, *Black Gay Man: Essays* (New York: New York U P,
2001), 80.

2. Kwame Ture and Charles V. Hamilton, *Black Power: The Politics of Liberation*
(1967; New York: Vintage Books, 1992), xix–xx.

3. Huey Newton, "The Founding of the Black Panther Party," in *The Huey P.
Newton Reader,* ed. David Hilliard and Donald Weise (New York: Seven Stories
Press, 2002), 50; Huey Newton, "The Correct Handling of a Revolution," in ibid.,
145; William Van Deburg, *New Day in Babylon: The Black Power Movement and
American Culture* (Chicago: U of Chicago P, 1992), 60, 61, 321n84. David Hilliard
relates that Newton referred to *The Wretched of the Earth* as "the black bible." David
Hilliard and Lewis Cole, *This Side of Glory: The Autobiography of David Hilliard and
the Story of the Black Panther Party* (Boston: Little, Brown, 1993), 120.

4. LeRoi Jones, "The Legacy of Malcolm X, and the Coming of the Black Nation," in *Home: Social Essays* (1966; Hopewell, NJ: Ecco, 1998), 246.

5. Amiri Baraka, *The Autobiography of LeRoi Jones* (1984; Chicago: Lawrence Hill Books, 1997), 295, 271.

6. I can find no evidence that either Jones/Baraka or Newton read Fanon in French. David Hilliard writes specifically of his first baffling encounter with Fanon in Newton's copy of *The Wretched of the Earth*: he required a dictionary, he notes, and found the experience of reading the text frustrating initially; but he read the text in English. See Hilliard and Cole, *This Side of Glory,* 119–121. Note that William Van Deburg quotes Dan Watts, the editor of *Liberator* magazine, saying, "Every brother on a rooftop can quote Fanon." Van Deburg implies Watts made this comment in the late 1960s, by the time that sales for *The Wretched of the Earth* were reaching 750,000. Van Deburg, *New Day in Babylon,* 61, 321n85.

7. Newton, "Founding of the Black Panther Party," 50.

8. Jones, "Legacy of Malcolm X," 246.

9. See especially Fanon's essay "Algeria's European Minority," which appears in *A Dying Colonialism,* trans. Haakon Chevalier (1965; New York: Grove, 1970).

10. Frantz Fanon, *The Wretched of the Earth,* trans. Constance Farrington (1963; New York: Grove Weidenfeld, 1965), 144. A subsequent translation, by Richard Philcox, was published by Grove in 2004. Also, a new translation of *Black Skin, White Masks* by Philcox was published by Grove in 2008. I sometimes reference the newer Philcox translations in the notes as Philcox, *Wretched,* and Philcox, *Black Skin.*

11. Jerry Gafio Watts, *Amiri Baraka: The Politics and Art of a Black Intellectual* (New York: New York University Press, 2001), 255.

12. LeRoi Jones, "American Sexual Reference: Black Male," in *Home,* 225.

13. Baraka writes in his autobiography, "Nationalism . . . does not even serve the people. . . . In the U.S., since White nationalism is the dominant social ideology, reactionary Black nationalism merely reinforces the segregation and discrimination of the oppressors" (Baraka, *Autobiography of LeRoi Jones,* xiii).

14. Fanon, *Wretched,* 216.

15. Ture and Hamilton, *Black Power,* 6.

16. David Macey, *Frantz Fanon: A Biography* (New York: Picador USA, 2000), 29.

17. See bell hooks, "Feminism as a Persistent Critique of History: What's Love Got to Do with It?" in *The Fact of Blackness: Frantz Fanon and Visual Representation,* ed. Alan Read (Seattle: Bay Press, 1996), 76–85; and Hortense J. Spillers, "'All the Things You Could Be by Now, If Sigmund Freud's Wife Was Your Mother': Psychoanalysis and Race," in *Black, White, and in Color: Essays on American Literature and Culture* (Chicago: U of Chicago P, 2003), 376–427. hooks and Spillers provide precise considerations of Fanon's distortions of the

"inner" and "intra" of black life—that is, the individual black person's psyche and black-on-black family and community relations.

18. See Henry Louis Gates, Jr., "Critical Fanonism," in *Rethinking Fanon: The Continuing Dialogue,* ed. Nigel C. Gibson, 251–268 (New York: Humanity Books, 1999).

19. Frantz Fanon, *Black Skin, White Masks* (1952; New York: Grove, 1967), 231.

20. See Ronald A. T. Judy, "Fanon's Body of Black Experience," in Gordon, Sharpley-Whiting, and White, *Fanon: A Critical Reader,* 53–73.

21. Fanon, *Wretched,* 224.

22. See Homi K. Bhabha, "Day by Day . . . with Frantz Fanon," in Read, *Fact of Blackness,* 186–205.

23. Fanon, *Black Skin,* 226.

24. Ato Sekyi-Otu, *Fanon's Dialectic of Experience* (Cambridge, MA: Harvard U P, 1996), 76.

25. Fanon, *Wretched,* 224, 227, 246, 247. National consciousness "is not nationalism," Fanon says, even though "the most elementary, most savage, and most undifferentiated nationalism is the most fervent and efficient means of defending national culture"; thus, a "national period" is probably necessary for national consciousness to take hold (ibid., 247, 244).

26. Frantz Fanon, "Racism and Culture," in *Toward the African Revolution,* trans. Haakon Chevalier (New York: Grove, 1967), 34.

27. Fanon, *Wretched,* 218.

28. Fanon, *Black Skin,* 226.

29. Fanon, *Black Skin,* 225, 226, 230, 229, original emphasis.

30. Spillers, "Peter's Pans: Eating in the Diaspora," in *Black, White, and in Color,* 36.

31. Paul Gilroy, *Against Race: Imagining Political Culture beyond the Color Line* (Cambridge, MA: Harvard U P, 2000), 336.

32. Abdul R. JanMohamed, *The Death-Bound Subject: Richard Wright's Archaeology of Death* (Durham, NC: Duke U P, 2005), 300.

33. Sonia Kruks, "Fanon, Sartre, and Identity Politics," in Gordon, Sharpley-Whiting, and White, *Fanon: A Critical Reader,* 132.

34. Francoise Verges, "Chains of Madness, Chains of Colonialism: Fanon and Freedom," in Read, *Fact of Blackness,* 63, original emphasis.

35. Sekyi-Otu, *Fanon's Dialectic of Experience,* 76.

36. Spillers, "Peter's Pans," 36.

37. Fanon engages Lacan extensively only once, in the long footnote 25, discussing Fanon's revisions of Lacan's ideas concerning the mirror stage, in "The Fact of Blackness" chapter of *Black Skin,* which runs from page 161 to page 164 of the cited edition. There are four other mentions of Lacan in *Black Skin,* two of which are footnote references without further explication (61n26 and 141n1);

the other two are brisk dismissals of ideas attributed to Lacan which Fanon feels the need to note but explicitly does not agree with and does not bother to argue against (Fanon, *Black Skin,* 80, 152).

38. See Jacques Lacan, "The Function and Field of Speech and Language in Psychoanalysis," in *Ecrits: A Selection,* trans. Alan Sheridan (New York: Norton, 1977), 103.

39. Spillers, "Peter's Pans," 36.

40. Lacan, "The Function and Field of Speech and Language in Psychoanalysis," 52.

41. Ibid., 86.

42. Fanon, *Black Skin,* 227.

43. Such musings on the temporal perhaps put many of us in the contemporary moment in a Benjaminian state of mind—though there is no evidence Fanon read Benjamin. Regarding Walter Benjamin's "Theses on the Philosophy of History," Slavoj Zizek argues that Benjamin's historical materialist method and his use of the concept of messianic time turns on the notion of the redemption of the past, on the dimension of the "will have been." "The oppressed class appropriates the past to itself in so far as it is 'open,' in so far as the 'yearning for redemption' is already at work in it—that is to say, it appropriates the past in so far as the past already contains—in the form of what failed, of what was extirpated—the dimension of the future." Slavoj Zizek, *The Sublime Object of Ideology* (New York: Verso, 1989), 138. "The actual revolutionary situation is *not* a kind of 'return of the repressed.' . . . The actual revolutionary situation presents an attempt to 'unfold' the symptom, to 'redeem'—that is, realize in the Symbolic—these past failed attempts which 'will have been' only through their repetition, at which point they become retroactively what they already were" (ibid., 141, emphasis in original). This sounds much like the Sartre-influenced way that Fanon is working with temporality. However, Zizek says that there is a distinction between an "evolutionary idealism" that "always implies a hidden, disavowed teleology" (and which Zizek identifies with Stalin) and a Benjaminian "creationist materialism" that "always includes a *retroactive* movement: the final Goal is not inscribed in the beginning; things receive their meanings afterwards; the sudden creation of an Order confers backward signification to the preceding Chaos" (ibid., 144). Fanon's view of temporality is avowedly teleological, and yet also not: because the past is not necessarily the unrecognized form of the future so much as it is the analogical model for how futures can be produced (see main text following this note). And Fanon's emphasis is not so much on any retroactive conferral of meaning on the past as itself a revolutionary action, though he implies or allows for this.

44. See Lewis R. Gordon, *Her Majesty's Other Children: Sketches of Racism from a Neocolonial World* (Lanham, MD: Rowman & Littlefield, 1997), 144.

45. Fanon, *Black Skin,* 112, 140.

46. Ibid., 116.

47. Ibid., 98, original emphasis.

48. Ibid., 95, 97, 110.

49. Fanon, *Wretched,* 238, 244.

50. Ibid., 51, 210, 50, emphasis added.

51. This is partly to say that Fanon here takes a view that seems *antidialectical,* because dialectics are at the heart of post-Hegelian Western notions of historical progress. Samira Kawash argues that Fanon's conception of violence is similarly antidialectical, at least in the Hegelian sense; but Kawash asserts that Fanon's notions of violence encode an idea of symbolic rupture that is close to the kind of dialectic that Walter Benjamin describes as "divine violence" or, more familiarly, as the messianic or redemptive. See Samira Kawash, "Terrorists and Vampires: Fanon's Spectral Violence of Decolonization," in *Frantz Fanon: Critical Perspectives,* ed. Anthony C. Alessandrini, 235–257 (New York: Routledge, 1999). Lou Turner argues that, within Fanon's insistence on a Negritude that he otherwise disparages as precisely the minor term he criticizes Sartre for labeling it to be, and within Fanon's statement that Hegel's description of the master-slave dialectic does not quite apply in the case of the Caribbean Negro, one can nonetheless read a powerful reliance on the operation of Hegelian dialectic. See Lou Turner, "On the Difference between the Hegelian and Fanonian Dialectic of Lordship and Bondage," in Gordon, Sharpley-Whiting, and White, *Fanon: A Critical Reader,* 134–151.

Yet Fanon is not doctrinaire in his approach to dialectics. In a 1960 essay (late, therefore, in Fanon's development) for *El Moudjahid* called "Unity and Effective Solidarity Are the Conditions for African Liberation," Fanon notes, "It is rigorously true that decolonization is proceeding, but *it is rigorously false to pretend and to believe that this decolonization is the fruit of an objective dialectic which more or less rapidly assumes the appearance of an absolutely inevitable mechanism.*" He says also, "Africa shall be free. Yes, but it must get to work, it must not lose sight of its own unity. . . . We must arm ourselves with firmness and combativeness. Africa will not be free through the mechanical development of material forces, but it is the hand of the African and his brain that will set into motion and implement the dialectics of the liberation of the continent." Frantz Fanon, "Unity and Effective Solidarity Are the Conditions for African Solidarity," in *Toward the African Revolution,* 170 (emphasis added), 173. But even if the dialectic does have the inescapable explanatory power Turner finds in Fanon, my interest here lies in the investigation of the properties of the black subject where its dialectical turn to revolutionary work has not yet become fully manifest. "It is not the meaning of black misery and wretchedness out of which the torch is shaped 'with which to burn down the world,'" Turner declares; in the abject lies only a trap that will get the Negro no further than the self-limiting revolution that an overreliance on Negritude affords. This may be so. Nevertheless my sense is that the abject, even in its failures, has a range of lessons to teach us that will be useful both in making the turn to revolution and in orienting us as we go about the work of dismantling the material conditions that gave rise to blackness and the abjection that constitutes it. Turner, "Difference between the Hegelian and Fanonian Dialectic," 138; Turner is quoting from Fanon, *Black Skin*, 134.

52. Fanon, *Wretched*, 246.

53. Fanon, *A Dying Colonialism*, 130.

54. Fanon, *Wretched*, 203, 147.

55. See again Kawash, "Terrorists and Vampires."

56. Fanon, *Wretched*, 304–305.

57. Fanon, "Racism and Culture," 34; Fanon, "The 'North African Syndrome,'" in *Toward the African Revolution*, 4.

58. Fanon, *Black Skin*, 95, original emphasis.

59. Ibid., 228, 230.

60. Gilroy calls them both "prototypical black European[s]." *Against Race*, 343.

61. See Van Deburg, *New Day in Babylon*, 272–280.

62. Toni Morrison, *Playing in the Dark: Whiteness and the Literary Imagination* (Cambridge, MA: Harvard U P, 1992), 33.

63. Fanon, *Wretched*, 237, 236, 224, emphasis added. An extended consideration of this kind of cultural transformation can be seen in Fanon's discussion of the veil, the chapter "Algeria Unveiled," in *A Dying Colonialism*, 35–68, as well as in the chapter "The Algerian Family," in *A Dying Colonialism*, 99–120.

64. Fanon, *Wretched*, 139, 138.

65. Ibid., 139, 138. The Richard Philcox translation of the "mirage of his muscles' own immediacy" phrasing is, "the mirage sustained by his unmediated physical strength" (Philcox, *Wretched*, 88).

66. See generally Judith Butler, *Bodies That Matter: On the Discursive Limits of "Sex"* (New York: Routledge, 1993). See also Lewis R. Gordon, "Fanon, Philosophy, and Racism," in *Her Majesty's Other Children*, 25–50. Regarding the distinction between *flesh* and *body*, see Hortense J. Spillers, "Mama's Baby, Papa's Maybe: An American Grammar Book," in *Black, White, and in Color*, 203–229, where Spillers defines flesh as "that zero degree of social conceptualization that does not escape concealment under the brush of discourse or the reflexes of iconography" (206).

67. Fanon, *Wretched*, 139.

68. Fanon, "West Indians and Africans," in *Toward the African Revolution*, 27.

69. Fanon, *Wretched*, 313.

70. Ibid., 290; Fanon, "The 'North African Syndrome,'" 7.

71. Fanon, *Black Skin*, 111.

72. Ibid., 110, 111.

73. Maurice Merleau-Ponty, *Phenomenology of Perception*, trans. Colin Smith (1958; New York: Routledge, 2003), 173.

74. Diana Fuss usefully teases out and clarifies Fanon's concept of "triple-consciousness" in her "Interior Colonies: Frantz Fanon and the Politics of Identification" chapter of *Identification Papers* (New York: Routledge, 1995), 141–165.

75. The white male experiences a similar breakdown of corporeal schema, though at a different point of contact: "The Negro, because of his body," Fanon writes—which is to say, because of the what has been projected onto the Negro's skin, because of the body that he has been made—"impedes the closing of the postural schema of the white man . . . at the point . . . at which the black man makes his entry into the phenomenal world of the white man" (*Black Skin,* 160). Fanon uses the example of a group of boys competing in the high jump, when the fifth jumper surpasses all the others in a display of athletic ability that shatters the other boys' sense of what their own bodies can do. Thus, in the presence of this Negro body that has been made to represent the body at its extreme—an extremity whites can fear or admire or both—the white male himself experiences a corporeal "destructuration" (ibid., 161).

76. Ibid.,139, 161n25, 140.

77. Verges, "Chains of Madness, Chains of Colonialism," 61, 65.

78. Fanon, "The 'North African Syndrome,'" 9.

79. Fanon, *Black Skin,* 161n25, 161 (original emphasis).

80. Merleau-Ponty, *Phenomenology of Perception,* 273.

81. Jean Paul Sartre, *Being and Nothingness,* trans. Hazel E. Barnes (1956; New York: Washington Square P, 1984), 409, 428.

82. "The body is what this consciousness *is;* it is not even anything except body" (ibid., 434).

83. Fanon, *Black Skin,* 225.

84. Sekyi-Otu, *Fanon's Dialectic of Experience,* 82.

85. Fanon, *Wretched,* 40.

86. Sekyi-Otu discusses Fanon's revelation of the failure of various forms of movement (interracial desire, acquiring the language skills of the colonial power, etc.) in *Fanon's Dialectic of Experience,* 87–100. Homi Bhabha also parses Fanon's description of the Manichean zones of the colonial world as being split without "a higher unity" to reach a similar conclusion, quoting Lacan, "When one is made into two, there is no going back on it. It can never revert to making one again, not even a new one. The *Aufhebung* [sublation] is one of those sweet dreams of philosophy" (Bhabha, "Day by Day . . . with Frantz Fanon," 197).

87. Fanon, *Wretched,* 53.

88. Sartre, preface to Fanon's *Wretched,* 24, 23, 17, emphasis added.

89. Fanon, *Wretched,* 57, emphasis added; Sartre, preface to *Wretched,* 19; Fanon, *Wretched,* 57, emphasis added.

90. Julia Kristeva, *Powers of Horror: An Essay on Abjection,* trans. Leon S. Roudiez (New York: Columbia U P, 1982), 51, 49.

91. Fanon, *Black Skin,* 231.

92. Frederick Douglass, *Life and Times of Frederick Douglass* (1881), in *Frederick Douglass: Autobiographies*, ed. Henry Louis Gates, Jr. (New York: Library of America, 1994), 596, 595, 594. For a discussion of the mutually constituting relationship between the permitted pleasures of American slaves and their subjugation and subjectification *as* slaves, see the chapter "Innocent Amusements" in Saidiya Hartman, *Scenes of Subjection: Terror, Slavery, and Self-Making in Nineteenth-Century America* (New York: Oxford U P, 1997), 17–48.

93. Fanon, *Wretched*, 56, emphasis added. Philcox translates this passage thus: "In the colonial world, the colonized's affectivity is kept on edge like a running sore flinching from a caustic agent. And the psyche retracts, is obliterated, and finds an outlet through muscular spasms that have caused many an expert to classify the colonized as hysterical" (Philcox, *Wretched*, 19).

94. Fanon, *Wretched*, 252 (emphasis added), 292.

95. Cf. J. Laplanche and J.-B. Pontalis, "Hysteria," in *The Language of Psycho-Analysis*, trans. Donald Nicholson-Smith (New York: Norton, 1973), 194–195. Fanon did not think conversion hysteria was always a misdiagnosis, but he seems consistently to have taken the view that traditional psychoanalytic talking cures—especially the Lacanian version sometimes dominant in hospitals where he practiced—did not address the problem adequately. While working in Tunis (after his sojourn in the hospital at Blida), Fanon, along with his colleague Lucien Levy, conducted clinical trials in which they attempted to administer a muscular relaxant to treat patients who had been diagnosed with conversion hysteria, or minor depression that was manifested with physical symptoms. The trials did not indicate success for conversion hysteria but did show promise for minor depression. See Macey, *Frantz Fanon: A Biography*, 324–325.

96. Fanon, *Wretched*, 291, emphasis added.

97. Fanon, "The 'North African Syndrome,'" 4.

98. Fanon, *Wretched*, 294, emphasis added.

99. Ibid., 237.

100. Ibid., emphasis added. Philcox translates, "This persistence of cultural expression condemned by colonial society is already a demonstration of nationhood. But such a demonstration refers us back to the laws of inertia" (Philcox, *Wretched*, 172).

101. However, nonlinear or counterlinear temporality is not the absence or nullification of temporality itself. Sartrean orthodoxy dictates that consciousness—the for-itself—requires a body and that an ontological characteristic of consciousness is that it temporalizes nature and itself. "Temporality must have the structure of a selfness," Sartre notes. "Not that the For-itself has an ontological priority over temporality. But Temporality is the being of the For-itself in so far as the For-itself has to be its being ekstatically" (*Being and Nothingness*, 195). I see no reason to believe Fanon departs significantly from this view. Thus, there is no nontemporal consciousness or identity, or even a nontemporal

consciousness—which is not to say that consciousness could not comprehend the idea of nontemporality or even perceive it, merely that it cannot be coincident with nontemporality; it cannot enter the nontemporal because its existence is by its nature temporalized, and consciousness constitutes and thus temporalizes the world.

102. Fanon, "Racism and Culture," 41–42.

103. Fanon, *Black Skin,* 109.

104. Fanon, "The 'North African Syndrome,'" 13, emphasis added.

105. Fanon, *Wretched,* 292–293.

106. Samira Kawash reads Fanon's descriptions of such symptoms (in relation to the figure of the vampire) in the following terms: "If living depersonalization names the attack on the ego characteristic of life under colonialism, then the corresponding name for its corporeal manifestation might be *living death*" (Kawash, "Terrorists and Vampires," 247).

107. Fanon, *A Dying Colonialism,* 127, 128, emphasis added.

108. Fanon, *A Dying Colonialism,* 180, emphasis added.

109. Fanon, "Decolonization and Independence," in *Toward the African Revolution,* 101. See also, in the essay "Mr. Debre's Desperate Endeavors," the following: "Conquest, it is affirmed, creates historic links. The new time inaugurated by the conquest, which is a colonialist time . . . because deriving its *raison d'etre* from the negation of the national time, will be endowed with an absolute coefficient." In *Toward the African Revolution,* 158.

110. Fanon, *A Dying Colonialism,* 134.

111. Fanon, *Wretched,* 220. Philcox's translation gives this passage a slightly different emphasis, indicating that Fanon is referring to the native intellectual's muscular reaction as purely metaphorical, though Philcox accentuates the choice of that metaphor through repetition: "This movement of withdrawal, which first of all comes from a petitio principi in his psychological mechanism and physiognomy, above all calls to mind a muscular reflex, a muscular contraction" (Philcox, *Wretched,* 157).

112. Fanon, *Wretched,* 241, emphasis added.

113. Fanon, "The 'North African Syndrome,'" 4, emphasis added.

114. Sartre, *Being and Nothingness,* 179, original emphasis.

115. Fanon, "The 'North African Syndrome,'" 9.

116. Ibid., original emphasis.

117. Spillers, "All the Things You Could Be by Now," 391.

118. Fanon, *Wretched,* 253. Philcox translates this a bit differently—and less lyrically, to my mind: "But can we escape vertigo? Who dares claim that vertigo does not prey on every life?" (Philcox, *Wretched,* 185n23).

119. Fanon, *Wretched,* 253.

120. This is David Macey's euphonious translation of a recollection reported

by Francois Jeanson in his afterword to the 1965 French edition of *Peau noire, masques blancs*. See Macey, *Frantz Fanon: A Biography,* 159, 535n22.

121. Fanon, *Wretched,* 242.

122. Ibid., 253.

123. Sartre, *Being and Nothingness,* 64, 65.

124. Ibid., 186.

125. Fanon, *Black Skin,* 140.

126. Sartre, *Being and Nothingness,* 65.

127. Ibid.

128. Ibid., 66 (original emphasis), 68.

129. Ibid., 68, original emphasis.

130. Ibid., 69, emphasis added.

131. "Everything happens as if the Present were a perpetual hole in being—immediately filled up and perpetually reborn" (ibid., 208).

132. "The before and after are intelligible . . . only as an internal relation" (ibid., 195). "Temporality is a dissolving force but it is at the center of a unifying act; it is less a real multiplicity . . . than a quasi-multiplicity, a foreshadowing of dissociation in the heart of unity. . . . There is no priority of unity over multiplicity, nor of multiplicity over unity. . . . Temporality [is] a unity which multiplies *itself*; that is, temporality can be only a relation of being at the heart of this same being" (ibid., 194). And again: "Temporality *is not.* . . . This means that temporality can only indicate the mode of being of a being which is itself outside itself. Temporality must have the structure of a selfness. . . . Not that the For-itself has an ontological priority over temporality. But Temporality is the being of the For-itself in so far as the For-itself has to be its being ekstatically" (ibid., 195).

133. Merleau-Ponty, *Phenomenology of Perception,* 273, 196, 197–198, 247.

134. Ibid., 278–279, emphasis added.

135. Ibid., 162, 279, 280, emphasis added.

136. Ibid., 279.

137. Ibid., 250–251.

138. Ibid., 279, 241. This corresponds with a line of Sartre's: "Everything happens as if the Present were a perpetual hole in being—immediately filled up and perpetually reborn" (*Being and Nothingness,* 208).

139. Merleau-Ponty, *Phenomenology of Perception,* 404, emphasis added.

140. Ibid., 277, 246.

141. Fanon, *Wretched,* 56–57, emphasis added.

142. Fanon, *Black Skin,* 109–110.

143. Sekyi-Otu, *Fanon's Dialectic of Experience,* 76.

144. Sartre, *Being and Nothingness,* 434.

145. See ibid., 462–470.

146. Fanon, *Black Skin,* 150.

147. Ibid., 110–111.

148. Merleau-Ponty, *Phenomenology of Perception,* 251.

149. Sartre, *Being and Nothingness,* 437, 438–439, emphasis added.

150. Fanon, *Black Skin,* 232.

151. Sartre and Merleau-Ponty both insist that the body and consciousness are constituted in dialectical relation with others. See again Sartre, *Being and Nothingness,* 462–470.

152. Merleau-Ponty, *Phenomenology of Perception,* 277.

153. Fanon, *Black Skin,* 134.

154. Gates, "Critical Fanonism," 266, 267.

155. See Macey, *Frantz Fanon: A Biography,* 230.

156. Diana Fuss, "Interior Colonies: Frantz Fanon and the Politics of Identification," in Gibson, *Rethinking Fanon,* 318, 319.

157. Kobena Mercer, "Busy in the Ruins of a Wretched Phantasia," in Alessandrini, *Frantz Fanon: Critical Perspectives,* 197.

158. T. Denean Sharpley-Whiting, "Fanon's Feminist Consciousness and Algerian Women's Liberation: Colonialism, Nationalism, and Fundamentalism," in Gibson, *Rethinking Fanon,* 351n5. Fanon did in fact evidently experiment with psychoanalytic technique at Blida-Jounville, but he considered it to be a failure and abandoned the attempt. See Macey, *Frantz Fanon: A Biography,* 230.

159. For a critique of the antibody position in Fanon, see bell hooks, "Feminism as Persistent Critique of History," 83.

160. Fanon, "The 'North African Syndrome,'" 4.

Notes to Chapter 2

1. Fanon, *Black Skin,* 111.

2. Robert Stepto, *From Behind the Veil: A Study of Afro-American Narrative* (Chicago: U of Illinois P, 1979).

3. Johnson, *Autobiography of an Ex-Coloured Man,* 211.

4. See generally Carby, *Race Men.*

5. Phillip Brian Harper, *Are We Not Men? Masculine Anxiety and the Problem of African-American Identity* (New York: Oxford U P, 1996), 108–113; Siobhan B. Somerville, *Queering the Color Line: Race and the Invention of Homosexuality in American Culture* (Durham, NC: Duke U P, 2000), 111–130.

6. Kristeva, *Powers of Horror,* 51.

7. Harper and Somerville discuss the mirror incident extensively. See *Are We Not Men?* 108–109, and *Queering the Color Line,* 112–122.

8. Johnson, *Autobiography of an Ex-Coloured Man,* 186, 185, 186, 185.

9. Ibid., 27.

10. Ibid., 143. Somerville discusses Red Head, and the narrator's various ho-

moerotic investments in white masculinity, at length. See *Queering the Color Line,* 113–122.

11. Johnson, *Autobiography of an Ex-Coloured Man,* 56, 61, 62, 121.

12. Ibid., 189, 186, my emphasis.

13. Ibid., 189, 170, 189.

14. Fanon, *Black Skin,* 161.

15. Johnson, *Autobiography of an Ex-Coloured Man,* 187, 186, 187, emphasis added.

16. Ibid., 190.

17. His concessions to difference in appearance are that he does not grow a beard and that he is of course not blond, though later he claims an Italian complexion.

18. Johnson, *Autobiography of an Ex-Coloured Man,* 190, 150, 74, 181.

19. The narrator's inclination toward this object, and Johnson's canny observation of it, can be understood in relation to the way that Western cultures, in their enshrinement of images of the European as the racially unmarked standards of beauty, renders everyone in those cultures, in a particular parlance, a snow queen. See Kobena Mercer (with Isaac Julien), "Black Masculinity and the Sexual Politics of Race," in *Welcome to the Jungle: New Positions in Black Cultural Studies* (New York: Routledge, 1994), 131–170.

20. Sigmund Freud, "'A Child Is Being Beaten' (1919): A Contribution to the Study of the Origin of Sexual Perversions," in *Sexuality and the Psychology of Love* (New York: Simon & Schuster, 1963), 97–122. I want to thank Lauren Berlant for suggesting the use of this essay in this context.

21. Ibid., 98.

22. Johnson, *Autobiography of an Ex-Coloured Man,* 200.

23. Ibid., 211.

24. Ibid., 104.

25. Stepto, *From Behind the Veil,* 125, 124.

26. This is an understanding of abjection that relies heavily on Kristeva. "Abjection preserves what existed in the archaism of pre-objectal relationship. . . . Obviously, I am only like someone else: mimetic logic of the advent of the ego, objects, and signs. But when I seek (myself), lose (myself), or experience jouissance—then 'I' is heterogeneous." Kristeva proposes that abjection can be properly understood if it is analogized to a point in the development of the subject prior to effective achievement of the ego. Thus, abjection is or is like primal repression, narcissistic crisis: primal repression is the ability of the speaking being to "divide, reject, repeat" prior to any single division or separation having been enacted; it involves the "earliest attempts to release the hold of the maternal entity even before ex-isting outside of her." The father-figure (who or which heralds the arrival—and triumph—of the Symbolic) helps root the embryonic

self in its struggle against the mother (and helps make the introjected part of her abject). But primal repression is not able to repress what it seeks to banish, and it depends on the pervasive presence of the Symbolic, which is not yet rooted (this is "the instability of the symbolic function in its most significant aspect—the prohibition placed on the maternal body (as a defense against autoeroticism and incest taboo).") Narcissistic crisis refers to a different take on the classical image of narcissism; rather than the "wrinkleless image of the Greek youth," this so-called contemplation of self is a throwback to the place of the "not yet" ego, where what exists are the life and death drives. "The abject shatters the wall of repression and its judgments. It takes the ego back to its source on the abominable limits from which, in order to be, the ego has broken away—it assigns it a source in the non-ego, drive, and death." Kristeva, *Powers of Horror*, 10, 13, 14, 15, emphasis added.

27. Johnson, *Autobiography of an Ex-Coloured Man*, 16, 17, emphasis added.

28. Butler, *Bodies That Matter*, 180–182.

29. Fanon, *Black Skin*, 162n25.

30. This would qualify Butler's assertion, to make it clear that the ego is a racialized ego in societies in which racial identifications are core forms of social organization and core terms in the Symbolic.

31. Merleau-Ponty *Phenomenology of Perception*, 250.

32. Fanon, *Black Skin*, 10.

33. Johnson, *Autobiography of an Ex-Coloured Man*, 17, 124, 190.

34. Fanon, *Black Skin*, 226.

35. Cathy Caruth, "Trauma and Experience: Introduction," in *Trauma: Explorations in Memory*, ed. Cathy Caruth (Baltimore: Johns Hopkins U P, 1995), 3–12. "The impact of the traumatic event lies precisely in its belatedness, in its refusal to be simply located, in its insistent appearance outside the boundaries of any single place or time" (9).

36. Ibid., 6.

37. Merleau-Ponty, *Phenomenology of Perception*, 246.

38. Bessel A. Van Der Kolk and Onno Van Der Hart, "The Intrusive Past: The Flexibility of Memory and the Engraving of Trauma," in Caruth, *Trauma*, 158–182. "One extreme post-traumatic state consists in living in the unremembered past. . . . A different state consists of continuously switching from one internal world to another, as described by a survivor of Auschwitz . . . : 'I live in a double existence. The double of Auschwitz doesn't disturb me or mingle with my life. . . . Without this split, I wouldn't have been able to come back to live'" (177–178).

39. "Ontology is merely the repetitiveness of custom and habit that at some level gets hypostatized as the epochal recursiveness of 'civilization.'" Turner, "Difference between the Hegelian and Fanonian Dialectic," 137.

40. "The Real constitutes the very kernel of the subject's being, the kernel that is simultaneously created and extirpated by the advent of the signifying order.

Lacan does not imply that the order of the signifier robs the subject of some pre-vious (and full) possession of her being—this being is utterly coextensive with the symbolic order and yet it is separated from it by a gap that can be described as existential." Alenka Zupancic, "Ethics and Tragedy in Lacan," in *The Cambridge Companion to Lacan,* ed. Jean-Michel Rabate (Cambridge: Cambridge U P), 174.

41. Fanon, *Black Skin,* 140.

42. Herbert Marcuse, *Eros and Civilization* (1955; Boston: Beacon, 1966), 231.

43. See David Allyn, *Make Love, Not War: The Sexual Revolution: An Unfettered History* (New York: Routledge, 2001), 196–199, 202–206.

44. Marcuse, *Eros and Civilization,* xvi. Marcuse was also, of course, Angela Da-vis's teacher at the University of California. See also Marcuse's references to the Black Power Movement in his 1968 lecture "Beyond One-Dimensional Man," in *Herbert Marcuse: Towards a Critical Theory of Society: The Collected Papers of Her-bert Marcuse,* vol. 2, ed. Douglas Kellner (New York: Routledge, 2001), 111–120, especially 112 and 116.

45. Marcuse, *Eros and Civilization,* 56.

46. Ibid., 16, 231.

47. Ibid., 120.

48. Ibid., 232.

49. See Laplanche and Pontalis, "Castration Complex," in *Language of Psycho-Analysis,* 56–59.

50. Merleau-Ponty, *Phenomenology of Perception,* 278–279.

51. The link between the suspension of linear time, blackness, abjection, and sociogenic possibilities has been discussed in other terms by Hortense Spill-ers, and her analysis has been a very useful guide and jumping-off point for me. Spillers observes that the relentless process of unnaming and renaming captured Africans while enslaving them, routine disruptions of mother-child dyads, and banishment or theft of the paternal function, along with Middle Passage ungen-dering of newly enslaved Africans in the holds of the slave ships (where the ships' logs made no distinction between men and women except in terms of weight and space), essentially render both the historical experience of diasporic slavery (becoming black) and the symbolic significance of blackness as "nightmarish un-differentiation"—undifferentiation in the Freudian pre-ego, pre-object-relations, pre-gender-identification sense, which is also abjection ("Peter's Pans," 23). "Those African persons in 'Middle Passage' were literally suspended in the oce-anic, if we think of the latter in its Freudian orientation as an analogy on undiffer-entiated identity," she remarks ("Mama's Baby, Papa's Maybe," 214). In this sense we can view "the whole career of African-Americans . . . as a metaphor of social and cultural management"—a statement we can reasonably align with Fanon's proposal of the sociogenic principle and the idea that blackness is produced by its operation (ibid., 227). This state of undifferentiation is marked and represented

in narrative, according to Spillers, by the failure to count time: "in short, the failure to make the leap into contemporaneity, either time as progressive halting and puzzling, or time as the creative demarcations of what is becoming and overcoming moment by moment. . . . Because one needed to start *counting* in time." Spillers's readings suggest that at the heart of blackness—in the crèche of racialization—linear time and its concomitant and constitutive counting is suspended; and in that suspension the range of possibilities we see mapped by Sartre as his everyman wobbles vertiginously at the edge of a precipice become available ("Peter's Pans," 23, original emphasis).

52. Johnson, *Autobiography of an Ex-Coloured Man*, 211, 133–134, 135, my emphasis.

53. As in Spillers's reading of the trope of incest in African American literature, its appearance raises the specters of nightmarish undifferentiation and the terrifying rich possibilities that attend that collapse of boundary. See note 50.

54. Fanon, *Wretched*, 253.

55. Johnson, *Autobiography of an Ex-Coloured Man*, 143.

56. Ibid., 203.

57. I am relying for this conception of the erotic as the basis for a collective politics on Herbert Marcuse's *Eros and Civilization*.

58. Stepto, *From Behind the Veil*, 126.

59. Salome's dance is a sexual seduction, and the sometimes disturbing, often compelling appeal of sexuality is one of the tactics, the strategies, of the text's dance of revelation as well.

60. Stepto, *From Behind the Veil*, 97.

61. See Sigmund Freud, *Totem and Taboo* (1913; New York: Norton, 1950), especially 28.

62. Johnson, *Autobiography of an Ex-Coloured Man*, 211.

63. Fanon, *Black Skin*, 218, my emphasis. Richard Philcox's translation of this line is, "In a fierce struggle I am willing to feel the shudder of death, the irreversible extinction, but also the possibility of impossibility" (Philcox, *Black Skin*, 193).

64. Kristeva writes that abjection is at its peak when the "subject . . . finds that the impossible constitutes its very being, that it is none other than abject. . . . There is nothing like the abjection of self to show that all abjection is in fact recognition of the want on which any being, meaning, language, or desire is founded" (*Powers of Horror*, 5, original emphasis).

65. Fanon, *Black Skin*, 8, 9, emphasis added.

Notes to Chapter 3

1. Fanon, *A Dying Colonialism*, 114, original emphasis.

2. See David Lloyd, "Adulteration and the Nation: Monologic Nationalism

and the Colonial Hybrid," in *An Other Tongue: Nation and Ethnicity in the Linguistic Borderlands,* ed. Alfred Arteaga (Durham, NC: Duke UP, 1994), 53–92. See also Rey Chow, "The Politics of Admittance: Female Sexual Agency, Miscegenation, and the Formation of Community in Frantz Fanon," in Alessandrini, *Frantz Fanon: Critical Perspectives,*34–56.

3. Fanon, *A Dying Colonialism,* 179.

4. Fanon biographer David Macey reports, "women with political ambitions, or who wanted to be the equals of their 'brothers,' had a particularly hard time of it. Their desire for equality was interpreted as meaning that they were 'loose women.' . . . After the Battle of Algiers, an unknown number of these ambitious young women . . . were massacred by their 'brothers.'" Fanon, Macey concludes, "mistook temporary changes born of extraordinary circumstances for a permanent revolution." Macey, *Frantz Fanon: A Biography,* 406. But Fanon does himself remark in the same discussion of changes he observed that I quote in the main text, "but no revolution can, with finality and without repercussions, make a clean sweep of well-nigh instinctive modes of behavior" (*A Dying Colonialism,* 113). See also Sharpley-Whiting, "Fanon's Feminist Consciousness," 329–355, especially the discussion on 330–334.

5. Fanon, *A Dying Colonialism,* 119–120.

6. As Spillers sees the Middle Passage. See previous chapter, note 50. Regarding the abject "not-yet ego," see Kristeva's *Powers of Horror,* 13–15.

7. Fanon, *Black Skin,* 149.

8. Barbara Christian, "Ancestral Worship: Afrocentric Debates in Toni Morrison's *Beloved*" (lecture, "Issues of Feminism, Gender and 'Race'" series, Stanford University, April 23, 1993).

9. Angelita Reyes, "Reading a Nineteenth-Century Fugitive Slave Incident," *Annals of Scholarship: Studies of the Humanities and Social Sciences* 7 (1990): 465.

10. See generally Rushdy, *Neo-Slave Narratives.* For a discussion of syndetic approaches to interpretation and temporality in relation to David Bradley's neo-slave narrative *The Chaneysville Incident,* see Edward Pavlic, "Syndetic Redemption: Above-Underground Emergence in David Bradley's *The Chaneysville Incident,*" *African American Review* 30.2 (Summer 1996): 165–184. For a discussion of traumatic temporality in relation to Gayl Jones's neo-slave narrative *Corregidora,* see Elizabeth Swanson Goldberg, "Living the Legacy: Pain, Desire and Narrative Time in Gayl Jones' *Corregidora,*" *Callaloo* 26.2 (2003): 446–472.

11. Morrison, *Beloved,* 273.

12. There is a significant exception to this parallelism, in the recurring metaphor we find particularly in postwar African American literature written by men, of what Marlon Ross calls "race rape." See Marlon B. Ross, "Race, Rape, Castration: Feminist Theories of Sexual Violence and Masculine Strategies of Black Protest," in *Masculinity Studies and Feminist Theory: New Directions,* ed. Judith Kegan Gardiner (New York: Columbia U P, 2002), 305–343. Ross finds this metaphor

operating in texts by Richard Wright, James Baldwin, Chester Himes, Eldridge Cleaver, and George Wylie Henderson. That such a textual current runs through the literature and arguably includes the scene from *Beloved* I examine here does not obviate the claim that emasculation and rape are generally gender-specific paralleled tropes in discussions of African American history. Ross observes this very tendency and frames his discussion as an intervention examining a phenomenon "rarely commented on" (ibid., 325). See also his extensive quotation and discussion of comments by bell hooks, on page 317–318. I will consider "race rape" further in the following chapter.

13. Morrison, *Beloved,* 108–109.

14. See Anthony S. Parent and Susan Brown Wallace, "Childhood and Sexual Identity under Slavery," in *American Sexual Politics: Sex, Gender and Race Since the Civil War,* ed. John C. Fout and Maura Shaw Tantillo (Chicago: U of Chicago P, 1993), 19–57. These researchers studied early 20th-century interviews with African Americans who had been slaves as children and found that despite the relative frequency of sexual exploitation of slaves, slave children were generally quite insulated from direct knowledge of sexuality. This silence as to sexual matters in a context accented by forced sex, the researchers suggest, was a suppression of knowledge which, predictably enough, generated a range of psychological conflicts and crises for the ex-slaves.

15. The latter is the danger Saidiya Hartman sees in the portrayal of graphic "scenes of subjection" such as Frederick Douglass's oft-reproduced memory of his aunt's bloody whipping. See Hartman, introduction to *Scenes of Subjection.*

16. Toni Morrison, afterword to *The Bluest Eye* (New York: Plume, 1993), 216, 215.

17. Indeed there may be reason to question whether Morrison writes the event as truly registering for Paul D as *trauma* in the technical sense that it is used in the psychoanalytic and psychological lexicons from which literary criticism borrows the term. The earliest clear references to Paul D's memory of the chain gang surrounds Alfred with elements of the technical traumatic: Paul D is "shut down" and "put back" in a way that seems to correspond with the past-presence of traumatic temporality (Morrison, *Beloved,* 41, 42). We know that figuratively he encases his emotional self in a tobacco tin. But at times Paul D's references to Alfred, Georgia, and even to his having worn the bit indicate that though these experiences certainly have been extremely harmful, there is a freely willed and consciously self-defining way that he accesses the memory of them. In these instances it seems that the meaning of the memory is all too clear to Paul D, and it is this meaning that causes him great fear; thus, he relates to the memory as an act of *will,* and the memory is his object rather than his being a *"possession"* (in Caruth's words) of it: he shuts down—not *during* what happens to him, in contrast to the trauma patient, who is "never fully conscious during" the traumatizing event and for whom "the traumatic event is not experienced as it occurs"—but *after*: "After Alfred he shut

down"—again suggesting a different cognitive process. What characterizes trauma as such is a relation to the event that, as literal memory, is characterized by its failure to be grasped, its having been "forgotten" in the very sense of its not being available to meaning. Caruth, "Trauma and Experience," 4, 7, 8, original emphasis.

18. See Scott Paulson-Bryant, *Hung: A Meditation on the Measure of Black Men in America* (New York: Doubleday, 2005).

19. Morrison, *Beloved,* 125, 126.

20. The history of the sexual exploitation of African or black men, like the history of sexual exploitation of African or black women or children, and indeed sexual history period, has little in the way of the usual archival evidence, an absence of record which fiction such as Morrison's works to correct. And like other forms of sexual exploitation or sexuality, historiography in this realm must usually rely on (1) logical deduction and (2) oblique digressive references in slave narratives or little-known mentions that may appear in records of the odd legal adjudication. This is true, at least, regarding the archive in English. On the other hand, the records of the Portuguese Inquisition and its sedulous investigations of acts of sodomy in the Lusitanian universe from the mid-16th century to the 18th century does provide detailed testimony concerning acts of rape, forcible sex, or coercive sexual liaisons between slaveowners and enslaved black men and boys in Brazil. Academic research concerning, and summaries of, this testimony has recently been translated into English. See generally Harold Johnson and Francis A. Dutra, eds., *Pelo Vaso Traseiro: Sodomy and Sodomites in Luso-Brazilian History* (Tucson, AZ: Fenestra Books, 2007); and in particular, Ronaldo Vainfas, "The Nefarious and the Colony," trans. Harold Johnson and Francis A. Dutra, in ibid., 337–367. Here is "proof" that the repressed memory I discuss in the main text indicates not only *how things really appear* but to some extent how they actually were.

21. I take this account of repression of the memory of parental seduction from a presentation by Slavoj Zizek during a faculty seminar held at the University of California Humanities Research Institute at UC-Irvine called "Psychoanalysis and the Event," held in August 2004. See also an entry in Laplanche and Pontalis that Zizek referenced in his lecture: Laplanche and Pontalis, "Primal Scene," in *Language of Psycho-Analysis,* 335–336.

22. Arthur Flannigan Saint-Aubin, "Testeria: The Dis-ease of Black Men in White Supremacist, Patriarchal Culture," *Callaloo* 17 (1994): 1054–1073.

23. Ibid., 1069.

24. See ibid., 1067. Also Fanon, *Wretched,* 39.

25. Leo Bersani, "Is the Rectum a Grave?" in *AIDS: Cultural Analysis, Cultural Activism,* ed. Douglas Crimp (Cambridge, MA: MIT Press, 1987), 209.

26. Fanon, as discussed in the previous chapters, maintains in *Black Skin, White Masks* that Negrophobia is a sexual fear and that white men who hate black men are in effect displacing or masking a homosexual desire for black men.

27. Morrison, *Beloved,* 42, 41, 52, my emphasis.

28. "Garner's smile was wide. 'But if you a man yourself, you'll want your niggers to be men too.' . . . 'I wouldn't have no nigger men round my wife.' . . . It was the reaction Garner loved and waited for. 'Neither would I,' he said. 'Neither would I,' and there was always a pause before the neighbor, or stranger, or peddler, or brother-in-law or whoever it was got the meaning. Then a fierce argument, sometimes a fight, and Garner came home bruised and pleased, having demonstrated . . . what a real Kentuckian was: one tough enough and smart enough to make and call his own niggers men" (ibid., 10–11).

29. Ibid., 140.

30. Ibid., 10–11.

31. Ibid., 25.

32. Ibid.

33. For a discussion of rape in relation to torture, see Goldberg, "Living the Legacy," 448–451.

34. Morrison, *Beloved,* 106.

35. See Jacqueline Rose, *Sexuality in the Field of Vision* (New York: Verso, 1987), 94–99. Rose argues that Freud's radical intervention was to challenge the prevailing late 19th-century northern European hygienic notion that women were essentially "diseased" by claiming that the central dynamic of hysteria was at the center of everyone's consciousness.

36. Morrison, *Beloved,* 117.

37. "What is important . . . is that with the Negro the cycle of the *biological* begins. . . . For the Negro is only biological" (Fanon, *Black Skin,* 161, 176).

38. Toni Morrison, "Introduction: Friday on the Potomac," in *Race-ing Justice, Engendering Power: Essays on Anita Hill, Clarence Thomas, and the Construction of Social Reality,* ed. Toni Morrison (New York: Pantheon, 1992), xvi.

39. Fanon, *Black Skin,* 157.

40. Morrison, *Beloved,* 64.

41. Ibid., 255.

42. Ralph Ellison, *Invisible Man* (1947; New York: Vintage, 1980), 319.

43. Richard Wright, *Native Son,* (1940; New York: HarperPerennial, 1993), 20.

44. Robyn Wiegman, "The Anatomy of Lynching," in Fout and Tantillo, *American Sexual Politics,* 235.

45. Morrison, *Beloved,* 198–199.

46. Stockton highlights the *non*productiveness of the black male figure in reading representations of anality in another Morrison novel, *Sula.* Glossing Eva's desperate attempt to remedy her baby son Plum's life-threatening constipation, Eva shoves beets up his rectum to loosen his bowels. "Here looms Morrison's clearest figuration of the black male's quandary in relation to the white . . . economy: he can't produce—either feces or coins," Stockton observes (*Beautiful Bottom,* 91).

47. Morrison, *Beloved,* 69.

48. Ibid., 273.

49. Ibid., 128, 273.

50. Ibid., 273.

51. Ibid., 117.

52. This succinct formulation of symptom and fetish I owe again to Slavoj Zizek's lecture in the "Psychoanalysis and the Event" seminar. See note 21.

53. Morrison, *Beloved,* 244. This is one way we can see Spillers's observation in "Mama's Baby, Papa's Maybe" that terms of implied relatedness such as "sexuality," "pleasure," or "desire" are terms "thrown in crisis" where kinship systems based on patrilineal heritage and opportunities for mothering are so ruthlessly destroyed as they were in slavery (Spillers, "Mama's Baby, Papa's Maybe," 221).

54. Butler, *Bodies That Matter,* 121–140.

55. See Spillers, "Mama's Baby, Papa's Maybe."

56. The possible significance of this fictional *scene* as a pathway to useful knowledge has an unpleasant contemporary resonance. As of 2007, a tenth of all black men between ages twenty and thirty-five were in jail or prison; and one in three male African Americans in their thirties had a prison record. See Orlando Patterson, "Jena, O. J., and the Jailing of Black America," *New York Times,* 30 September 2007, natl. ed., "Week in Review," 13. Also see Fox Butterfield, "More Blacks in Their 20's Have Trouble with the Law," *New York Times,* 5 October 1995, late ed., A18. These grisly statistics in important respects echo the story of Paul D and his experience as a slave and as a member of a chain gang: what is common to all is the submission of black men to the near-absolute rule of a white-controlled system of surveillance and forced labor. The experience of being imprisoned is, as we well know, characterized by widespread male rape as well as consensual same-sex sexual encounters.

Notes to Notes on Black (Power) Bottoms

1. Bersani, "Is the Rectum a Grave?" 208, 209, 218, 217, original emphasis.

2. Ibid., 209, original emphasis. And regarding Jews, Bersani might reconsider in light of Sartre's *Anti-Semite and Jew,* in which he argues that it is the anti-Semite who makes the Jew, and the Jew who becomes what he is by internalizing the anti-Semite's prejudices (even if mostly to combat them). Fanon relies heavily on Sartre's argument in his own theorizing about blackness. See Sonia Kruks, "Fanon, Sartre, and Identity Politics," 122–133.

3. Spillers, "Mama's Baby, Papa's Maybe," 221.

4. This argument is in chapter 3 of Hartman, *Scenes of Subjection.*

5. Hartman makes this argument in the introduction to *Scenes of Subjection.*

6. "Dialogue: bell hooks, Lyle Ashton Harris, Gilane Tiwadros, Homi K. Bhabha, Members of the Audience," in Read, *Fact of Blackness,* 182.

7. Angela Y. Davis, *Women, Race and Class* (New York: Vintage, 1983, 1981), 23–24, 175.

8. For a discussion of the relationship between rape and lynching, see Wiegman, "Anatomy of Lynching," 223–245.

9. David M. Halperin, "Is There a History of Sexuality?" in *The Lesbian and Gay Studies Reader*, ed. Henry Abelove, Michele Aina Barale, and David M. Halperin (New York: Routledge, 1993), 418–419.

10. See Kristeva, "On Filth and Defilement," chapter 3 in *Powers of Horror* (53–89). Shame is also, of course, a primary object of Stockton's investigations in *Beautiful Bottom, Beautiful Shame*. See note 5 of the introduction to this volume.

11. Merleau-Ponty, *Phenomenology of Perception*, 246.

12. Stockton also makes central use of the figure of the bottom, though her deployment of it generally emphasizes the resonance between black folks' occupation of the lower rungs of social and economic hierarchies and anal eroticism (Stockton, *Beautiful Bottom*).

13. Butler, *Bodies That Matter*, 124.

14. See chapter 2, "Basic Skills, Genre, and Fiction as Dream," in John Gardner, *The Art of Fiction: Notes on Craft for Young Writers* (New York: Vintage, 1985), 17–38, especially 30–32.

15. Bersani, "Is the Rectum a Grave?" 209.

16. See Lee Edelman, "The Part for the (W)hole: Baldwin, Homophobia, and the Fantasmatics of 'Race,'" in *Homographesis: Essays in Gay Literary and Cultural Theory*, 42–75 (New York: Routledge, 1994). I discuss Edelman's argument in greater detail in chapter 4.

17. I am not here specifically referring to identification in the psychoanalytic sense, as a process that produces as an effect the noun identity. Certainly there are conceivable identity effects of this identification with the violated and working with abjection that I am describing—a particular kind of identity might well be a *power* that I am attempting to elucidate, but the psychoanalytic notions of identification are not being engaged and traced here. For example, Diana Fuss in her engagement with Fanon tracks a Lacanian identificatory process in which there is an abject that attends the terror of alterity en route to subjectivity that identification describes. I am tracing access to an abject analogous to but not the same as that, access to something *like* the not-yet-subject or the object-subject. See Fuss, "Interior Colonies," 294–328.

18. Ross, "Race, Rape, Castration," 322.

19. Laplanche and Pontalis, "Masochism," in *Language of Psycho-Analysis*, 244–245.

20. The mother-child dyad is a relationship for black folks that in any case was systematically disrupted in the historical events of racialization and, because of the repetition of these original, constituting violences in the discursive forms of our cultural black-white symbolic, remains continually in crisis or threatened by such crisis, as Spillers tells us. See generally, Spillers, "Mama's Baby, Papa's Maybe."

21. David Savran, *Taking It Like a Man: White Masculinity, Masochism, and Contemporary American Culture* (Princeton, NJ: Princeton U P, 1998), 33. The other commentator I refer to in the paragraph of the main text from which this quotation comes is Kaja Silverman, with whom Savran engages extensively. See Kaja Silverman, *Male Subjectivity at the Margins* (New York: Routledge, 1992).

22. Ross, "Race, Rape, Castration," 312, 314.

Notes to Chapter 4

1. Essex Hemphill, "The Occupied Territories," in *Ceremonies* (1982; San Francisco: Cleis, 2000), 80–81.

2. Henry Louis Gates, Jr., "Looking for Modernism," in *Black American Cinema*, ed. Manthia Diawara (New York: Routledge, 1993), 203.

3. See Ross, "Race, Rape, Castration"; and Marlon B. Ross, "Camping the Dirty Dozens: The Queer Resources of Black Nationalist Invective," *Callaloo* 23.1 (Winter 2000): 290–312. See also Harper, *Are We Not Men?* 39–53. One of the earliest and most influential assays of sexuality in its relation to black nationalist politics is Michele Wallace's controversial *Black Macho and the Myth of the Superwoman* (1978; New York: Verso, 1990). See also Dwight McBride, "Can the Queen Speak? Racial Essentialism, Sexuality, and the Problem of Authority," *Callaloo* 21.2 (Spring 1998): 363–379; Robert Reid-Pharr, "Tearing the Goat's Flesh," in *Black Gay Man*, 99–134.

4. Edelman, *Homographesis*, 56, 57, 52.

5. Ibid., 72.

6. Reid-Pharr, *Black Gay Man*, 134.

7. Ross, "Camping the Dirty Dozens," 304, original emphasis.

8. John D'Emilio and Estelle Freedman, *Intimate Matters: A History of Sexuality in America*, 2nd ed. (Chicago: U of Chicago P, 1997), 301–325. D'Emilio and Freedman write in *Intimate Matters* that "sex was becoming, in the view of modern theorists, a common characteristic that motivated both men and women, and expressed one's deepest sense of self" (233–234).

9. LeRoi Jones, "The Last Days of the American Empire," in *Home*, 216. Michele Wallace was one of the first to call attention to Jones's essay in *Black Macho and the Myth of the Superwoman* (62–69).

10. LeRoi Jones, "The Last Days of the American Empire (Including Some Instructions for Black People," in *Home*, 193.

11. LeRoi Jones, "What Does Nonviolence Mean?" in *Home*, 151; Jones, "American Sexual Reference," 227, my emphasis.

12. Jones, "American Sexual Reference," 226. This line seems to echo closely Fanon from *Black Skin, White Masks*: "The Negro . . . gives off no aura of sensuality either through his skin or through his hair. It is just that over a series of long days and long nights the image of the biological-sexual-sensual-genital-nigger

has imposed itself on you and you do not know how to get free of it." *Black Skin,* 201–202.

13. Jones, "American Sexual Reference," 228, 227.

14. Eldridge Cleaver, *Soul on Ice* (New York: McGraw, 1968), 14.

15. Ibid. The quotation from the poem may be found on page 99 of "Black Dada Nihilismus" (1964), in *Transbluency: Selected Poems of Amiri Baraka /LeRoi Jones,* ed. Paul Vangelisti (New York: Marsilio, 1995), 97–100.

16. See generally Baraka's 1964 essay "LeRoi Jones Talking," in *Home,* 179–188.

17. D'Emilio and Freedman, *Intimate Matters,* 186, 208–214.

18. Cleaver, *Soul on Ice,* 14, emphasis added.

19. Jones, "American Sexual Reference," 221, emphasis added.

20. Ibid., 233.

21. Baraka notes, "Nations are races. (In America, white people have become a nation, an identity, a race.) Political integration in America will not work because the Black Man is played on by special forces. His life, from his organs, *i.e.,* the life of the body, what it needs, what it wants, to become, is different—and for this reason racial is biological, finally. We are a different *species.* A species that is evolving to world power and philosophical domination of the world. The world will move the way Black People move!" ("Legacy of Malcolm X," 246).

22. Ibid., 229.

23. See Stuart Marshall, "The Contemporary Political Use of Gay History: The Third Reich," in *How Do I Look? Queer Film and Video,* ed. Bad Object-Choices (Seattle: Bay Press, 1991), 78.

24. D'Emilio and Edelman, *Intimate Matters,* 247–248, 255.

25. Jones, "American Sexual Reference," 231.

26. See Chow, "Politics of Admittance," especially 46–49. Also see Samuel R. Delany, "Some Queer Notions about Race," in *Dangerous Liaisons: Blacks, Gays and the Struggle for Equality,* ed. Eric Brandt (New York: New Press, 1999), 259–289, especially 270–272.

27. Ross writes, "Again, the curious thing about race rape is . . . the unspoken act of metonymy whereby black men, rather than women, become the improper tokens of the other race's raping desire" ("Race, Rape, Castration," 314).

28. Jones, "American Sexual Reference," 233, 220.

29. Holland, *Raising the Dead,* 198; see also ibid., 120.

30. Jones, "The Myth of a 'Negro Literature,'" in *Home,* 108. Baraka notes in his 1996 preface to the second publication of his revised autobiography that a number of the dramatic changes he made in his life during his transition from Greenwich Village to Harlem involved a desire to "be able to struggle with my whole heart and soul, with my whole being, for what was deepest in me, which I took, then, as Blackness" (Baraka, *Autobiography of LeRoi Jones,* xiv).

31. Baraka, *Autobiography of LeRoi Jones,* 149.

32. LeRoi Jones, *System of Dante's Hell* (New York: Grove, 1965), 57.

33. Amiri Baraka, "An Interview with Amiri Baraka," in *Conversations with Amiri Baraka*, ed. Charles Reilly (Jackson: University P of Mississippi, 1994), 256–257.

34. Jones, *System of Dante's Hell*, 139.

35. Ibid., 58 (my emphasis), 124, 140.

36. Baraka, *Autobiography of LeRoi Jones*, 251, 275.

37. See Kimberly Benston, *Baraka: The Renegade and the Mask* (New Haven, CT: Yale U P, 1976), 14–17. See also Werner Sollors, *Amiri Baraka/LeRoi Jones: The Quest for a "Populist Modernism"* (New York: Columbia U P, 1978), 139–146.

38. Jones, *System of Dante's Hell*, 80.

39. Baraka concludes the novel with a coda called "Sound and Image" which begins, "What is hell? Your definitions" (ibid., 153).

40. Sollors, *Amiri Baraka/LeRoi Jones*, 97.

41. Jones, *System of Dante's Hell*, 82, 84.

42. Ibid., 84. The spelling is a deliberate repetition of the word Stephen Dedalus sees carved on a desk in the anatomy theater of Queen's College in *Portrait of the Artist as a Young Man*. There the "sudden legend" seems to be obscenely associated with perverse or unnatural or illicit sexuality, and this appears to be the resonance Jones wishes to import to "Eighth Ditch." James Joyce, *A Portrait of the Artist as a Young Man*, ed. Seamus Deane (1916; New York: Penguin, 1992), 95.

43. Jones, *System of Dante's Hell*, 84, 87.

44. Ibid., 85, 86, 85, 86.

45. Baraka, *Autobiography of LeRoi Jones*, 174.

46. Jones, *System of Dante's Hell*, 89.

47. Ross, "Camping the Dirty Dozens," 303. Melvin Dixon also makes this observation, as Ross notes (see reference to Dixon in ibid., 302, and endnote 21 of the essay).

48. Jones, *System of Dante's Hell*, 151.

49. "I . . . looked thru my wallet as not to get inflamed and sink on that man screaming of my new loves. My cold sin in the cities" (ibid., 125). The "cold sin" of course refers to his sexual interludes with men in Chicago.

50. LeRoi Jones, "The Alternative," in *Tales*, 5–29 (New York: Grove, 1967). The reference to "Jimmy's play" is spoken by Lyle, who is referred to as a "real D.C. queer" (19); it appears on page 25.

51. Jones, *System of Dante's Hell*, 152.

52. Fred Moten glosses these relations for us nicely in an endnote to *In the Break*: "The black arts are, in part, the cultural vehicle of return to a certain moral fundamentalism, one based on (the desire for) African tradition rather than white/bourgeois normativity. This is to say that they would enact a return to the former after having enacted the bohemian rejection of the latter. *The embrace of the homoerotic is, here, an opening and not an aim.*" Fred Moten, *In the Break: The Aesthetics of the Black Radical Tradition* (Minneapolis: U of Minnesota P, 2003), 281–282n102, emphasis added.

53. Cleaver, *Soul on Ice,* 102.

54. Jones, *System of Dante's Hell,* 91.

55. Ibid., 82, 83.

56. Sollors, *Amiri Baraka/LeRoi Jones,* 98.

57. Amiri Baraka, "Amiri Baraka: An Interview: Kimberly W. Benston/1977," in Reilly, *Conversations with Amiri Baraka,* 106–107.

58. Wallace, *Black Macho,* 39.

59. Norman Mailer, "The White Negro: Superficial Reflections on the Hipster" (1957), in *Advertisements for Myself,* 337–358 (1959; Cambridge, MA: Harvard U P, 1992), 341, 348, 347.

60. Wallace, *Black Macho* ,46.

61. Jones, *System of Dante's Hell,* 122.

62. Ibid., 141, 142.

63. Ibid., 145.

64. Ibid., 142, emphasis added.

65. Ibid.,

66. Ibid., 119, 131.

67. Ibid., 142.

68. Bersani, "Is the Rectum a Grave?" 218.

Notes to Chapter 5

1. Samuel R. Delany, *Phallos* (Whitmore Lake, MI: Bamberger Books, 2004), 80.

2. Merleau-Ponty, *Phenomenology of Perception,* 246.

3. I am aware that some are invested in arguing for a difference between the two, but I do not count myself among them, and throughout this chapter I use the terms indiscriminately.

4. Samuel R. Delany, "The Thomas L. Long Interview," in *Shorter Views: Queer Thoughts and the Politics of the Paraliterary* (Hanover, NH: Wesleyan U P, 1999), 133–134.

5. See Laura Kipnis, *Bound and Gagged: Pornography and the Politics of Fantasy in America* (Durham, NC: Duke U P, 1999), 177, and her argument generally in the chapter "How to Look at Pornography," 161–206.

6. Samuel R. Delany, "On the Unspeakable," in *Shorter Views,* 66.

7. Delany, "Thomas L. Long Interview," 133.

8. I am thinking particularly of the strong current in contemporary queer theory that generally positions itself as opposed to utopian politics. See "Forum: Conference Debates: The Antisocial Thesis in Queer Theory, MLA Annual Convention, 27 December 2005, Washington, DC," *PMLA* 121 (May 2006): 819–828.

9. Samuel R. Delany, *The Mad Man* (1994; Rutherford, NJ: Voyant, 2002), ix, emphasis added.

10. Delany, "Thomas L. Long Interview," 132. Reed Woodhouse and Ray Davis also skeptically discuss, in different terms than I, though reaching similar conclusions, Delany's disclaimer. Their conclusions possibly give rise to Delany's protest against being called disingenuous for labeling the work pornography, though it is not the pornographic nature of the work that arouses Woodhouse's and Davis's skepticism; it is the claim that the novel is purely fantastic. Ray Davis, "Delany's Dirt," *New York Review of Science Fiction* 7/8.12 (August 1995): 181; Reed Woodhouse, *Unlimited Embrace: A Canon of Gay Fiction, 1945–1995* (Amherst: U of Massachusetts P, 1998), 220–221.

11. See my discussion in "Black Gay Pornotopias; or, When We Were Sluts," in *Best Black Gay Erotica*, ed. Darieck Scott (San Francisco: Cleis, 2005), ix–xiv. See also Dwight McBride, "It's a White Man's World: Race in the Gay Marketplace of Desire," in *Why I Hate Abercrombie & Fitch: Essays on Race and Sexuality* (New York: NYU P, 2005), 88–131.

12. Alex Von Mann, *Slaves* (London: Prowler Books, 1997), 30–31.

13. Ibid., 34.

14. Savran, *Taking It Like a Man*, 236.

15. Though my sense is that such depictions, both of black-white interracial sex and of white tops, occur more frequently in works from Britain, where if you peruse, for example, Alan Hollinghurst's elegant novel *The Swimming-Pool Library* or Isaac Julien's short film *The Attendant*, both meditations on the centrality of homosexuality (and its attendant anxieties) to British identity and British empire, you find reflected there a more sharply defined taste than in North America for scenes of the domination of dark-skinned persons, much as you see a more explicit obsession with class difference as the ready-made markers of top and bottom sexual roles. Black-white—or at least dark-light—interracial sex and white (or light) tops also seem to occur more frequently in porn films made by French studios—Citebeur, for example—and in Brazilian films.

16. See Donald Bogle, *Toms, Coons, Mulattoes, Mammies & Bucks: An Interpretive History of Blacks in American Films*, 3rd ed. (New York: Continuum, 1994). See also Nelson George, *Buppies, B-Boys, Baps, and Bohos: Notes on Post-Soul Black Culture* (New York: HarperCollins, 1992); and Edelman, "Part for the (W)hole," 53.

17. A master/slave dynamic viewed from a distance often becomes sexy, on some level, whether or not it is racialized. Recall hooks's comment about the sexiness of the law of sadomasochistic slave/master relationships, which I quoted in the main text of "Notes on (Black) Power Bottoms." hooks, "Dialogue," 182.

18. Dale, "Enslaved," *ASSGM.com*, 7 June 1999, 10 August 2001, http://www.assgm.com/Enslaved-01-07.

19. Reid-Pharr, "The Shock of Gary Fisher," in *Black Gay Man,* 135–149.

20. I have considered this matter at greater length in my essay "Jungle Fever? Black Gay Identity Politics, White Dick, and the Utopian Bedroom," *GLQ* 1 (1994): 299–321.

21. Hartman, *Scenes of Subjection,* 3.

22. Samuel R. Delany, "Pornography and Censorship," in *Shorter Views,* 297.

23. Ibid., 295.

24. Delany, *Mad Man,* 15, 21, 25, 34, 196, 235, 301, 324, all emphases in original.

25. Ibid., 123.

26. Ibid., 199–200.

27. Ibid., 283, 355.

28. Ibid., 334.

29. Samuel R. Delany, *Equinox* (New York: Masquerade, 1994). Rpt. of *Tides of Lust,* 1973.

30. This elderly black man of letters is Arnold Hawley, the protagonist of Delany's 2007 novel *Dark Reflections.* Hawley recounts his unhappy experience writing *Phallos* in the novel. Samuel R. Delany, *Dark Reflections* (New York: Carroll & Graf, 2007).

31. I am relying on the account of publication history produced in Rob Stephenson's introduction to the 2004 reissue of *Hogg* and on Samuel R. Delany, "The Making of *Hogg,*" in *Shorter Views,* 298–314. Rob Stephenson, introduction to *Hogg,* by Samuel R. Delany (1995; Normal, IL: Fiction Collective 2, 2004), 7–10.

32. Delany, *Phallos,* 94n9, emphasis in original.

33. Delany, "Pornography and Censorship," 295.

34. Woodhouse remarks, a bit blandly, that "the racial mixing of *The Mad Man* is one of its compelling charms" (*Unlimited Embrace,* 215). Davis notes that *The Mad Man* accomplishes a "transfiguration of values, in which hell's lost pleasures are regained via the hostile terminology of the angels. 'Nigger,' 'piece of shit,' and 'dummy' are endearments; the 'top' wears the dog collar while the 'bottom' has the power; what is 'low' is desirable" ("Delany's Dirt," 183).

35. Davis, "Delany's Dirt," 182.

36. Jeffrey Allen Tucker, *A Sense of Wonder: Samuel R. Delany, Race, Identity, and Difference* (Middletown, CT: Wesleyan U P, 2004), 252, 251, 248.

37. Phillip Brian Harper, "'Take Me Home': Location, Identity, Transnational Exchange," *Callaloo* 23.1 (Winter 2000): 471, 470. Harper does not discuss in detail, though he implicitly invokes, the historical resonances of Marr's BDSM practices, nor does he expound at length on Delany's deployment of the word "nigger," focusing rather on other insult names Marr assumes or plays with, such as "cocksucker" and "piece of shit."

38. Randall Kennedy, *Nigger: The Strange Case of a Troublesome Word* (New York: Pantheon, 2002), 54, 175.

39. Delany, *Mad Man*, 101, 109–110.

40. Ibid., 286–287, emphasis in original.

41. Ibid., 302–303.

42. Ibid., 326.

43. Dossie Eaton and Janet W. Hardy, *The New Bottoming Book* (Emeryville, CA: Greenery, 2001), 148–149.

44. Savran, *Taking It Like a Man*, 232–233 (emphasis added), 237 (emphasis in original).

45. Tucker observes, "Marr is no one's sexual servant; nor is he a victim who is coerced into indiscriminately catering to other's lusts" (*Sense of Wonder*, 246).

46. Delany, *Mad Man*, 238, 352 (emphasis and ellipsis in original), 354.

47. Delany describes the Nevèrÿon series as dealing with slavery by staging a number of reversals of the usual way the story is told in an American context: black/brown people have the money; white/blond people are often the slaves. He notes that Gorgik, the series's main character and a crusader against slavery, is racially mixed and "is also sexually attracted to the accoutrements of slavery—whips, chains, and the iron collars that, traditionally, slaves in Nevèrÿon are made to wear. . . . But what paradoxes do these situations create for Gorgik? Does his own desire somehow contaminate his political project of abolishing slavery? Does it intensify it?" Samuel R. Delany, "The *Black Leather in Color* Interview," in *Shorter Views*, 118.

48. Delany, *Mad Man*, 364, emphasis and ellipses in original.

49. Ibid., 354, 301.

50. Ibid., 344, emphasis in original.

51. Ibid., 345, 344, emphasis added.

52. Morrison, *Beloved*, 210.

53. Samuel R. Delany, *Atlantis: Three Tales* (Hanover, NH: Wesleyan U P, 1995), 206–207, emphasis added.

54. Delany, *Mad Man*, 428, emphasis in original.

55. Ibid., 429.

56. Delany, *Atlantis*, 207.

57. Delany, *Mad Man*, 428.

58. Kobena Mercer, "Decolonisation and Disappointment: Reading Fanon's Sexual Politics," in Read, *Fact of Blackness*, 129.

59. Delany, *Mad Man*, 345.

60. Ibid., 371.

61. Merleau-Ponty, *Phenomenology of Perception*, 241.

62. Fanon, *Black Skin*, 112.

63. The relation of these contradictions of course runs the other way as well: does not abjection also make you cling more forcefully to an I? The abject strictly speaking is denied, forcibly (and mistakenly, misleadingly) transcended, but the reaction *against* abjection is of course not without the abject; it carries its denied content as the inextricable excess or shadow, as a haunting.

64. Morrison, *Beloved*, 244.

65. Delany, *Mad Man*, 361.

66. Morrison, *Beloved*, 140.

67. Fanon, *Black Skin*, 8.

68. Samuel R. Delany, *Neveryóna* (1983; Hanover, NH: Wesleyan U P, 1993), 179–180, emphasis in original.

69. Marcuse, *Eros and Civilization*, 51, 29; see also ibid., 55.

70. Ibid., 50.

71. Laplanche and Pontalis, "Phantasy (or Fantasy)," in *Language of Psycho-Analysis*, 314–419. Laplanche and Pontalis write, "the expression 'psychical reality' itself is not simply synonymous with 'internal world,' 'psychological domain,' etc. If taken in the most basic sense that it has for Freud, this expression denotes a nucleus within that domain which is heterogeneous and resistant and which is alone in being truly 'real' as compared with the majority of psychical phenomena. 'Whether we truly attribute *reality* to unconscious wishes, I cannot say. It must be denied, of course, to any transitional or intermediate thoughts. If we look at unconscious wishes reduced to their most fundamental and truest shape, we shall have to conclude, no doubt, that *psychical* reality is a particular form of existence not to be confused with *material* reality'" (315, emphasis in original).

72. Spillers, "Changing the Letter: The Yokes, the Jokes of Discourse, or, Mrs. Stowe, Mr. Reed," in *Black, White, and in Color*, 200, emphasis in original.

73. Savran, *Taking It Like a Man*, 236.

Notes to the Conclusion

1. Gayl Jones, *Corregidora* (1975; Boston: Beacon, 1986), 124–128.

2. Ibid., 102, emphasis in original.

3. Barack Obama, preface to *Dreams from My Father: A Story of Race and Inheritance*, rev. ed. (1995; New York: Three Rivers, 2004), x, x–xi.

4. See Lloyd, "Adulteration and the Nation."

5. Sartre, *Being and Nothingness*, 165–166, emphasis in original.

6. Lacan's Master's Discourse schematizes this sort of "knowledge" on the part of the Slave.

Index

Abel, Elizabeth: *Female Subjects in Black and White*, 22

Aberrations in Black (Ferguson), 15

abjection: anonymous existence and, 89; avoidance as subject, 4–5, 14; black embodiment of, 17–18, 27, 38–39, 59, 97, 104–105, 113, 126, 137, 173, 195–196, 204–205, 224, 259, 266–267; body tension and, 67; "bottom" as, 28; castration anxiety and, 117–118, 170–171, 173–174; concept of nation and, 128; disowning knowledge of, 104; docility and, 54, 100, 143–146; as heroism in disguise, 5–6, 107–109, 119–120, 122, 124, 207; identity and, 150; impossibility of, 125; Kristeva's views on, 283–284n26, 286n64; learning from, 6; lies and, 7; living within, 66–67; lost wholeness in, 174–175; memory erasure and, 129–131, 135–136, 138, 148; "new" sexual encounter and, 126–129; optimism and, 78; pleasure in, 12, 15, 28, 30–31, 94, 153–171, 177, 195, 202–206, 249–250; political transformation and, 9; pornographic portrayal of, 12, 165, 205–206; power and, 9, 18, 19–20, 29–30, 39, 93–94, 124–125, 170, 222–223, 246, 265, 270; productivity and, 247–248; racialized, 205–210, 212, 230–231, 239–240; sadomasochism and, 106, 154, 155–171, 176, 180, 185–187, 214, 235–236, 242; self-hatred and, 165–166; self-knowledge and, 235, 299n63; sensory impressions of, 101–103, 105; shame, defilement and, 163, 204; Stockton's study of, 271–272n5; as survival strategy, 264–265; as term, 4, 14–24; transformation through, 217; word "nigger" and, 218–219

Afrocentrism, 131, 134

Algerian Revolution, 33, 49–50, 59–60, 65, 69, 73–74, 126–129, 287n4

alienation, 13, 30, 77, 81, 88–89, 93, 117, 177, 192

"All the Things You Could Be by Now . . . " (Spillers), 22, 273–274n17

"Alternative, The" (Baraka), 194

Alt.Sex.Stories.Gay.Male.Moderated website, 218

American exceptionalism, concept of, 54–55

"American Sexual Reference: Black Male" (Baraka), 180–182

anguish: abjection as, 175; of Johnson's character, 97, 103, 118–119, 120; Sartre's concept of, 26, 51, 76, 79–83, 88, 118, 204, 259

anonymous or amorphous existence: abjection and, 89; colonialism and, 40–41; Merleau-Ponty's concept of, 25, 85–86, 88, 97, 98, 115, 118,

About the Author

DARIECK SCOTT IS Assistant Professor of African American Studies at the University of California–Berkeley. He is the author of the novels *Hex* (2007) and *Traitor to the Race* (1995) and the editor of *Best Black Gay Erotica* (2004).